101 QUICK FIXES

In and Around Your Home

First published in 2001 by
Thunder Bay Press
5880 Oberlin Drive, San Diego, CA 92121-4794
www.advantagebooksonline.com

St. Remy Media Inc.
President: Pierre Léveillé
Vice President, Finance and Operations: Natalie Watanabe
Managing Editor: Carolyn Jackson
Managing Art Director: Diane Denoncourt
Systems Director: Edward Renaud
Director, Business Development: Christopher Jackson

Staff for *101 Quick Fixes In and Around Your Home*
Senior Editor: Marc Cassini
Senior Editor, Production: Brian Parsons
Art Director: Robert Paquet
Designer: Roxanne Tremblay
Illustrators: Gilles Beauchemin, François Daxhelet,
   Vincent Gagnon, Jacques Perrault
Production Coordinator: Dominique Gagné
Prepress Technician: Jean Angrignon Sirois
Scanner Operator: Martin Francoeur

The following persons also assisted in the preparation
of this book:
Danny-Pierre Auger, Lorraine Doré, Sophie Doyon,
Joey Fraser, Pierre Home-Douglas, Pascale Hueber,
Monique Riedel.

ISBN 1-57145-599-X
Library of Congress Cataloging-in-Publication Data
available upon request.

Note to the Reader: Due to differing conditions, tools, and individual skills, Thunder Bay Press and St. Remy Media Inc. assume no responsibility for any damages, injuries suffered, or losses incurred as a result of following the information published in this book. Before beginning any project, review the plans and instructions carefully, and if any doubts or questions remain, consult local experts or authorities. Because local codes and regulations vary greatly, you should always check with local authorities to ensure that your project complies with all applicable local codes and regulations. Always read and observe all of the safety precautions provided by any tool or equipment manufacturer and follow all accepted safety procedures.

101 QUICK FIXES
In and Around Your Home

THUNDER BAY
P·R·E·S·S

TABLE OF CONTENTS

Chapter 1
PLUMBING

With just a little time and effort, you can solve many plumbing problems in your home yourself. The repairs in this chapter for correcting leaky faucets, clearing clogged drains, and servicing balky spray attachments are all quick fixes, requiring only basic tools and virtually no plumbing experience. Keeping plumbing fixtures in good working order will make your kitchen and bathroom more efficient—and help minor problems from becoming major ones.

The widespread use of copper and plastic pipe has made it easy for the average homeowner to take on more extensive plumbing repairs, such as replacing a section of damaged pipe, without having to call in a plumber.

Of course, not all plumbing projects are intended to resolve immediate problems. You can make a kitchen or bathroom more comfortable and noticeably update its style by removing an old fixture and installing a new one. These more chal-

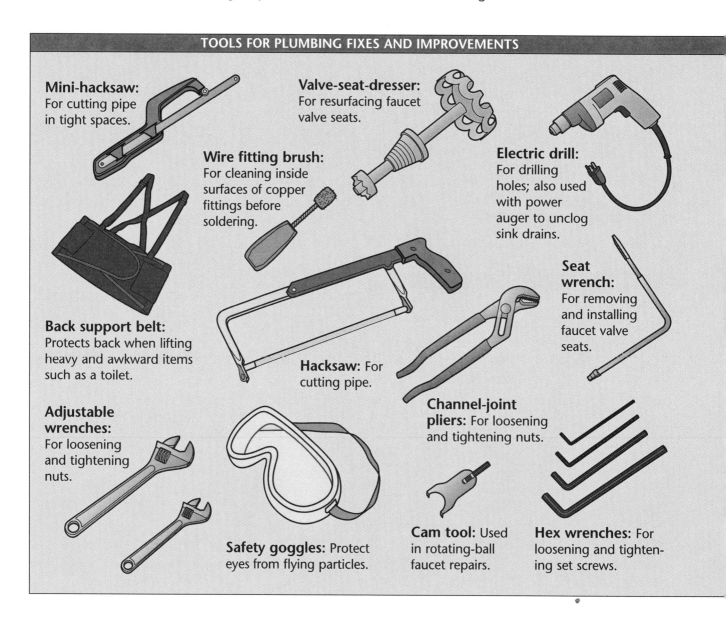

TOOLS FOR PLUMBING FIXES AND IMPROVEMENTS

Mini-hacksaw: For cutting pipe in tight spaces.

Wire fitting brush: For cleaning inside surfaces of copper fittings before soldering.

Valve-seat-dresser: For resurfacing faucet valve seats.

Electric drill: For drilling holes; also used with power auger to unclog sink drains.

Back support belt: Protects back when lifting heavy and awkward items such as a toilet.

Hacksaw: For cutting pipe.

Seat wrench: For removing and installing faucet valve seats.

Adjustable wrenches: For loosening and tightening nuts.

Channel-joint pliers: For loosening and tightening nuts.

Safety goggles: Protect eyes from flying particles.

Cam tool: Used in rotating-ball faucet repairs.

Hex wrenches: For loosening and tightening set screws.

lenging projects may sometimes call for specialized tools and more than basic skills. But whether you wish to replace a toilet or bathtub or install a sink, garbage disposal unit, or under-counter water treatment system, you will discover that none of the plumbing improvements in this chapter are beyond your capability.

Backyard plumbing projects such as installing a hose bibb or drip-irrigation system are not substantially different from indoor work. However, the results can make gardening and other outdoor tasks more convenient and enjoyable.

The step-by-step projects that follow conform to national plumbing codes, but many states and municipalities apply their own standards to plumbing work. Check with your local building department for information about codes and permits before you undertake a renovation project that involves adding a fixture or extending a plumbing line.

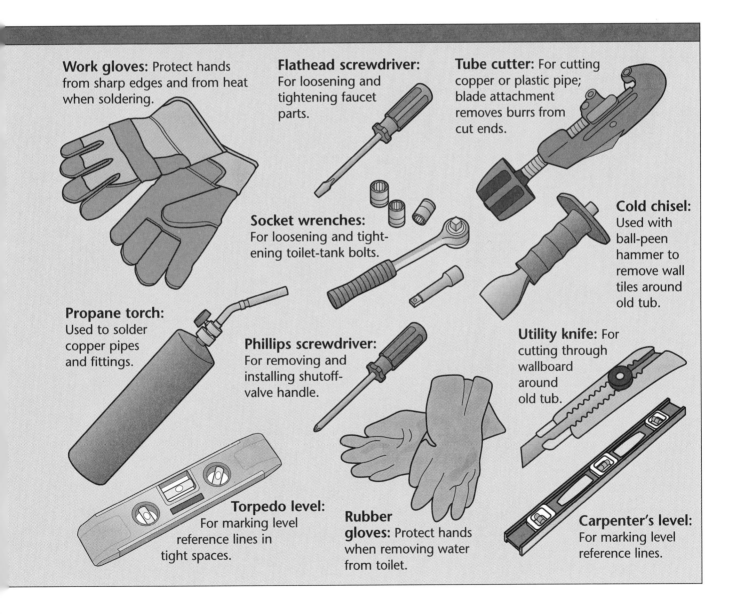

Work gloves: Protect hands from sharp edges and from heat when soldering.

Flathead screwdriver: For loosening and tightening faucet parts.

Tube cutter: For cutting copper or plastic pipe; blade attachment removes burrs from cut ends.

Socket wrenches: For loosening and tightening toilet-tank bolts.

Cold chisel: Used with ball-peen hammer to remove wall tiles around old tub.

Propane torch: Used to solder copper pipes and fittings.

Phillips screwdriver: For removing and installing shutoff-valve handle.

Utility knife: For cutting through wallboard around old tub.

Torpedo level: For marking level reference lines in tight spaces.

Rubber gloves: Protect hands when removing water from toilet.

Carpenter's level: For marking level reference lines.

FIXES FOR SINK FAUCETS

PLUMBING

Sink faucets can be divided into four main types according to their working mechanism: compression, rotating ball, ceramic disk, and cartridge. A compression faucet usually has two handles controlling the water supply valves; it's identifiable by the pressure required to close it. The other faucet types have a distinct closed position. The rotating-ball type is controlled by the circular movement of a single handle. Disk and cartridge faucets are generally controlled by a single handle that moves forward and back and side to side. Double-handle cartridge faucets also exist.

The type of faucet you are working on will determine the parts needed. Kits are available for each type and often include simple installation tools.

Before beginning work, close the shutoff valves under the sink basin, then open the faucet all the way to drain water out of it.

HOW LONG WILL IT TAKE?
Two to four hours

TOOLS
• Flat-head screwdriver • Phillips screwdriver • Channel-joint pliers • Adjustable wrench • Hex wrench • Seat wrench • Seat-dressing tool

MATERIALS
• Stem washers • O-rings • Valve seats • Cam and cam washer • Rotating ball repair kit (including ball, seals, springs, cam, cam washer, and cam tool) • Ceramic disk cartridge • Dish soap • Tape

COMPRESSION

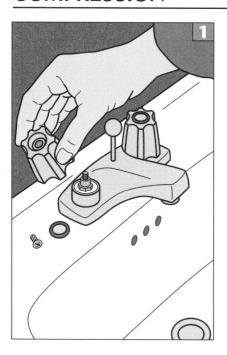

1. Removing the handle

A dripping compression faucet generally needs a new seat or seat washer. Leaks around the handle are caused by wear to the O-rings around the stem. All replaceable parts are located under each faucet handle.

● With a small, flat-head screwdriver, pry the index cap off the top of the handle, exposing the handle screw.

● Remove the handle screw and lift off the handle (#1).

2. Removing the stem assembly

To inspect and replace the washers and O-rings, the faucet stem assembly must be removed.

● With an 8-inch adjustable wrench, loosen the hexagonal retaining nut (#2).

● Pull the stem assembly out of the valve seat.

Note: *If the retaining nut is round, use channel-joint pliers.*

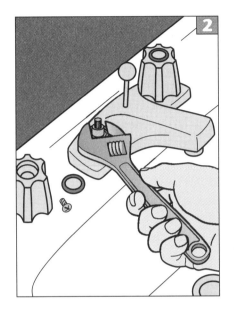

4. Replacing the O-ring

The O-ring is a rubber gasket located near the center of the stem assembly. It prevents leaks around the faucet handles.

● Unscrew the threaded spindle (the central section of the stem assembly) from the retaining nut (#4).

● Fit the end of a small flat-head screwdriver between the O-ring and the spindle. Lift it out of position and slide it off of the spindle.

● Replace the O-ring with a new one of the same size—lubricate the new ring first with a couple of drops of dish soap.

5. Replacing the valve seat

The valve seat sits against the stem washer to close the valve. Trapped pieces of dirt and rust can wear the surface, causing dripping.

● Insert the end of a seat wrench into the valve seat and turn in a counterclockwise direction to remove it (#5).

● With the seat wrench, replace the valve seat with a new one of the same size.

● Reassemble the other faucet components.

Note: *If the valve seat cannot be removed, it can be resurfaced with a seat-dressing tool, which grinds and smooths away surface defects.*

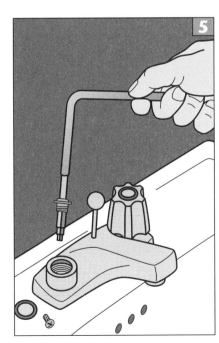

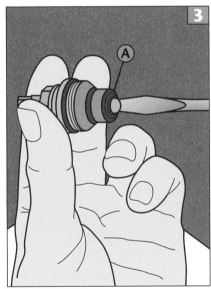

3. Replacing the stem washer

● Undo and remove the washer screw at the bottom of the stem assembly (#3).

● Remove and examine the stem washer (A). If it appears worn, replace it with a new one of the same size.

PLUMBING

CERAMIC DISK

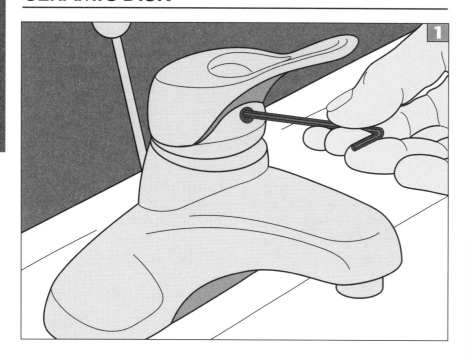

1. Removing the handle

A dripping or leaking disk faucet can only be repaired by replacing the entire disk cartridge.

● Lift the faucet handle as far as it can go. Locate the set-screw hole, usually covered by a small plastic cap.

● Insert a hex wrench into the set screw (#1). Unscrew the set screw and remove the handle.

2. Disassembling the faucet

● With channel-joint pliers, unscrew the escutcheon cap (A) under the handle—tape the jaws of the pliers first to avoid scratching the cap.

● With a 10-inch adjustable wrench, unscrew the retaining nut (B) holding the ceramic disk cartridge in place.

● Lift out the disk cartridge (#2) and replace it.

● Reassemble the handle.

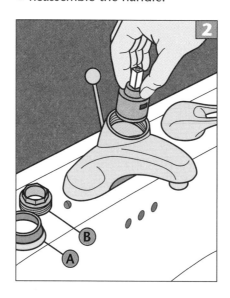

ROTATING BALL

1. Removing the handle

A leaking handle on a rotating-ball faucet can be remedied by tightening the adjusting ring under the handle. A dripping faucet can be repaired by replacing the ball itself or the gaskets and springs under it.

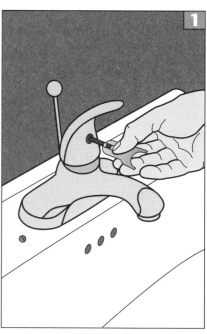

● Lift the handle and remove the plastic cap covering the set screw.

● Use the hex-wrench side of the cam tool provided in the rotating ball repair kit to unscrew the set screw (#1). Lift off the handle.

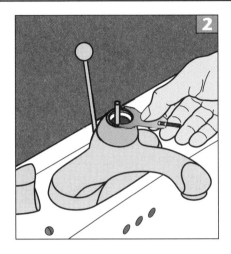

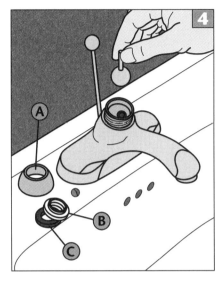

the cam (B) controls the directional movement of the ball. Lift it and the washer (C) under it out of the seat assembly.

● Lift out the ball (#4).

5. Replacing the seals and springs

● Insert a flat-head screwdriver into each valve seal, removing the seal and spring at the same time.

● Lubricate the edges of new seals with a small amount of dish soap before inserting them into the valves (#5).

● Reinstall the ball—if it appears worn, replace it with a new one.

● Install a new cam and cam washer.

● Reassemble the faucet handle.

2. Loosening the adjusting ring

To remedy leaking around the handle, tighten the adjusting ring with the cam tool. To disassemble the faucet further, loosen the adjusting ring instead (#2).

4. Accessing the ball

A dripping faucet may be caused by a damaged ball or worn seals and springs.

● Located under the faucet cap (A),

3. Disassembling the faucet

After loosening the adjusting ring, remove the faucet cap with taped channel-joint pliers (#3).

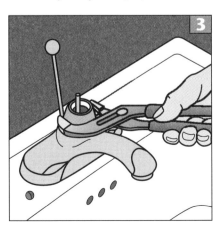

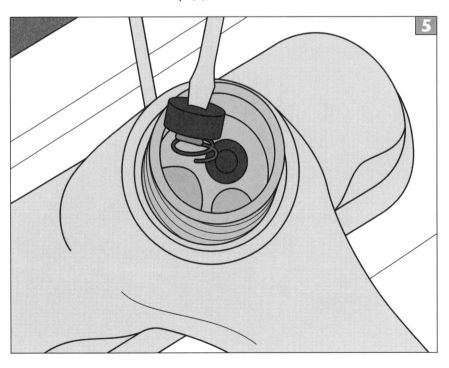

CLEARING DRAINS

PLUMBING

Like many conveniences, sinks are easy to take for granted—until they clog. Clogs in bathrooms are usually caused by a buildup of hair and soap; in the kitchen, by an accumulation of grease. While it may be tempting to reach for a chemical drain cleaner to solve the problem, these products are caustic and can damage your plumbing if used too often. And sometimes they just don't work.

In most cases, it's possible to dislodge a clog by working above the sink with a plunger or an auger. However, if this doesn't work, the next step is to work below the sink, which may involve taking apart the drain trap.

If your kitchen sink has a garbage disposal unit, don't attempt to use an auger. Try a plunger first. If that doesn't work, you'll have to remove and service the drain trap.

HOW LONG WILL IT TAKE?
Less than two hours

TOOLS
• Plunger • Manual drain auger • Power drain auger • Channel-joint pliers • Bucket (or pan) • Putty knife • Screwdriver • Cordless drill • Toothbrush

MATERIALS
• Abrasive cleaner • Cloth • Petroleum jelly • Coat hanger • Tape • Plumber's putty (or silicone-rubber sealant)

1. Removing the stopper

The first step to clearing a drain is to remove the stopper.

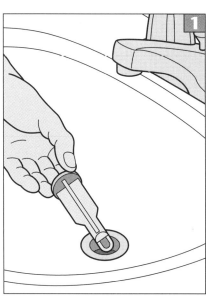

● Raise the stopper and remove it from the drain opening (#1). If you can't pull out the stopper directly, turn it counterclockwise to free it from the pivot rod. Some models are hooked on the end of a pivot rod and must be removed by unscrewing a retaining nut under the sink. In this case, have a bucket or pan on hand under the sink to catch any backed up water.

2. Cleaning the stopper

● Pry off the O-ring (A) if the stopper has one (#2).
● Wash the underside of the stopper with abrasive cleanser and a wet toothbrush, then rinse it thoroughly.

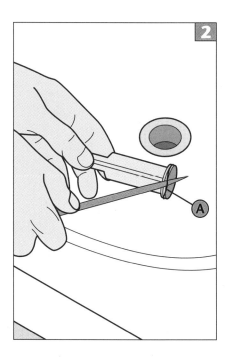

● If the O-ring shows signs of wear, replace it with a matching duplicate.

3. Using a plunger

• Stuff the bowl's overflow opening with a wet cloth.
• Coat the rim of the cup on a plunger with petroleum jelly.

• Fill the sink with enough water to cover the plunger cup.
• Lower the plunger over the drain and push the cup against the sink to expel air and create a seal (#3).
• Pump the plunger up and down quickly several times, without breaking the seal, and pull it away from the sink. Repeat the procedure, if necessary. If the drain remains clogged, move on to the next step.

4. Using a manual drain auger

• Push a trap-and-drain auger into the drain until you feel it come up against the obstruction (#4).

• Slide the handle to within a few inches of the drain opening and tighten the thumbscrew (A).
• Turn the handle clockwise with both hands and push the auger deeper into the drain. Reposition the handle as needed. Continue turning and pushing until the coil breaks through the clog or the auger can move no further.
• Withdraw the auger gently, turning it clockwise as you pull, removing the debris along with it.
• If the sink remains clogged, move on to the next step.

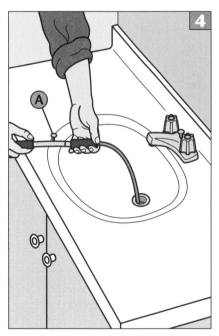

5. Servicing the trap

Some traps have a cleanout plug that allows you to clean the trap without removing it. Place a pan or bucket under the trap before you remove the cleanout plug. If you have already used a chemical drain cleaner, wear rubber gloves and eye protection for this procedure. If your trap doesn't have a cleanout plug, move on to the next step.

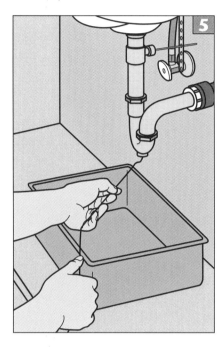

• Loosen the cleanout plug with channel-joint pliers and remove it by hand.
• Slide a bent coat hanger into the opening (#5) and probe both sides of the trap to snag and remove any debris.
• Reinstall the cleanout plug. If the drain remains blocked, move on to the next step.

Note: *To protect the nut on the cleanout plug from scratches, wrap the jaws of the pliers with tape.*

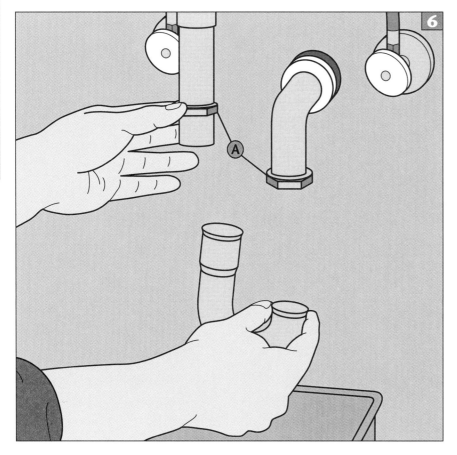

- If there is an escutcheon against the wall, pull it away with a putty knife or a screwdriver.
- With taped channel-joint pliers, loosen the slip nut connecting the trap arm to the drainpipe adapter (#7). Pull the trap arm free.
- Clean out the trap arm as you did the trap bend.

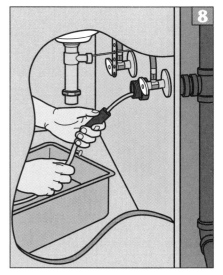

6. Removing the trap bend

- Bail as much water as possible out of the sink and place a pan or bucket under the trap.
- Loosen the slip nuts (A) on the trap bend with channel-joint pliers, then pull the trap free (#6).
- Hold the trap over a bucket or pan and pass an auger through it to clear debris. Flush the trap with water at another sink.

Note: *If the slip nuts are corroded in place, cut them with a hacksaw. Replace the trap with a new one.*

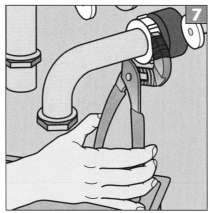

7. Removing the trap arm

Remove the trap arm to clean it out and to provide easier access to the drainpipe behind the wall.

8. Using a manual drain auger

- Push a trap-and-drain auger into the drainpipe until you make contact with the clog.
- Slide the handle to within a few inches of the drainpipe opening and tighten the thumbscrew.
- Turn the handle clockwise with both hands (#8) to break up the clog.
- Slowly pull the auger out of the drainpipe, retrieving the debris.
- Continue pushing the auger ahead, repositioning the handle as needed, to probe for more debris.

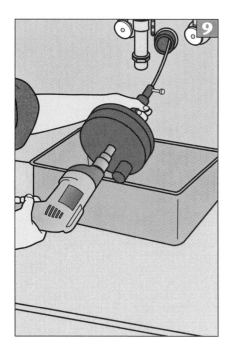

9. Using a power drain auger

A power drain auger is connected to a power drill. Because of the danger in using electrical tools around water, work with a drill that is battery-powered.

● Before connecting the auger to the drill, feed the auger into the drainpipe until it comes in contact with the clog.

● Connect the auger to the drill.

● Hold the drill in one hand and the nozzle of the auger in the other and turn on the drill.

● To help loosen the clog, move the auger ahead and back (#9).

● Once the debris is loosened, stop the drill, detach the auger, and slowly pull out the auger along with the debris.

10. Reconnecting the trap arm

● Before reattaching the trap arm, wipe away any debris from the drainpipe opening.

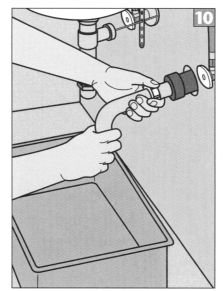

● Slide the end of the trap arm about 1½ inches into the drain-pipe opening (#10) and hand-tighten the slip nut.

11. Reinstalling the trap bend

● Coat the inside face of the slip nuts on the tailpiece and trap arm with plumber's putty or silicone-rubber sealant to prevent leaks. Slide the slip nuts into position.

● Slide the long end of the trap bend up into the tailpiece until the other end aligns with the trap arm—you may need to reposition the trap arm in the drain opening.

● With taped channel-joint pliers, tighten the slip nuts (#11)—don't overtighten; the sealant will prevent leaks.

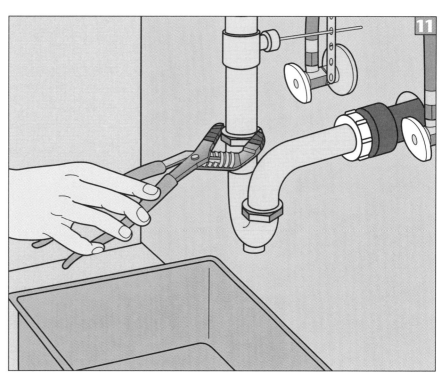

SERVICING AERATORS AND SPRAY ATTACHMENTS

Built-in aerators and spray attachments in kitchen faucets mix air into a steady stream of water to improve cleaning power and reduce water consumption. From time to time, the screens and perforated disks inside these devices become blocked by mineral deposits and must be taken out and cleaned. Other components, such as washers and hoses, may wear out or become damaged and cause leaks. All of these parts are easy to remove and replace. Take the old parts along with you when shopping for replacements. If an aerator or a spray attachment continues to leak after parts have been replaced, replace the entire unit.

HOW LONG WILL IT TAKE?	TOOLS	MATERIALS
Less than two hours	• Screwdriver • Long-nose pliers • Channel-joint pliers • Basin wrench • Toothbrush	• Tape • White vinegar

SERVICING AN AERATOR

1. Removing the aerator

• Wrap tape around the jaws of channel-joint pliers.
• Loosen the aerator by turning it counterclockwise with the pliers (#1) and remove it by hand.

2. Cleaning the screen

The components inside an aerator include a perforated plastic disk and/or one or two metal screens.
• Disassemble the aerator, noting how the parts fit together.
• Inspect the parts and replace any that are worn or broken.
• Soak the screen in white vinegar for about 5 minutes, then scrub it with a toothbrush to remove deposits (#2). Rinse the screen thoroughly with water.
• Reassemble the aerator and screw it back into place, tightening it with channel-joint pliers.

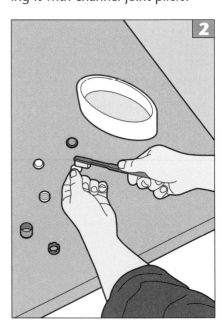

SERVICING A SPRAY ATTACHMENT

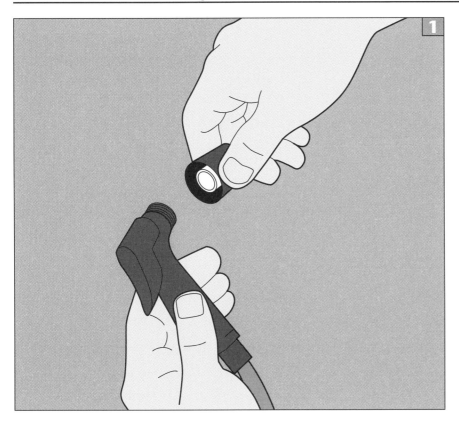

- Remove the parts inside the spray sleeve, keeping track of how they fit together.
- Inspect the parts and replace any that are damaged or worn.
- Soak the perforated disk in white vinegar for about 5 minutes, then scrub it with a toothbrush (#2) and rinse it with water.
- Reassemble the nozzle.

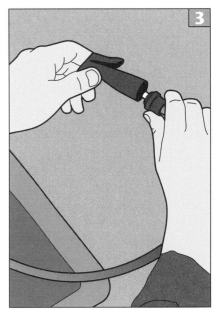

1. Removing the spray sleeve

Spray attachment designs vary. Remove the spray sleeve from the head accordingly.
- Unscrew the spray sleeve by hand (#1) or remove the retaining screw at the end of the nozzle with a screwdriver. If the screw is hidden by a cover, pry it off gently with a screwdriver.

2. Cleaning the nozzle

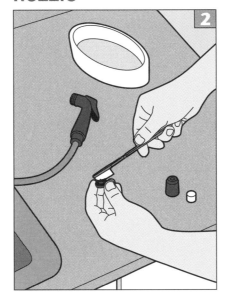

3. Fixing a blocked spray head

- Unscrew the spray head from the coupling (#3).
- If the washer in the spray head is worn or damaged, replace it.
- Soak the spray head in white vinegar for about 5 minutes and rinse it with water.

SERVICING A SPRAY ATTACHMENT (CONTINUED)

4. Removing the coupling

• Pry off the retaining clip and pull the coupling off the hose (#4). Replace any worn washer.

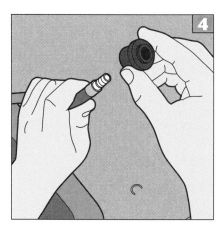

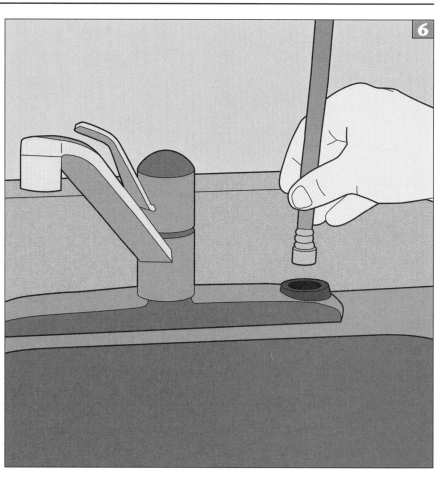

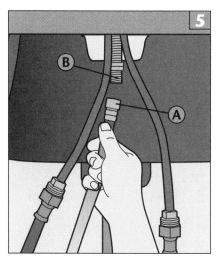

5. Replacing the hose

• Loosen the coupling nut (A) from the spout shank (B) with a basin wrench. Remove the hose by hand (#5).

6. Inserting the replacement hose

• Feed the new hose, coupling nut first, into the base of the faucet (#6).
• Reattach the coupling, the retaining clip, and the spray head.

7. Attaching the hose

• Connect the hose by screwing the coupling nut onto the spout shank with a basin wrench (#7).

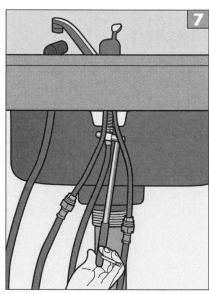

REPLACING COPPER PIPE

Replacing a short section of copper pipe involves cutting out the damaged pipe and soldering in a replacement section with fittings. Although the procedure is fairly straightforward, the do-it-yourself beginner is advised to practice the soldering technique on scrap pieces before undertaking a household repair.

Before you start the project, shut off the water supply to the pipe; if there isn't a nearby shutoff valve for the line, close the main shutoff valve for the house. Drain as much water as possible from the pipe by opening the faucets on the line. Have a bucket or pan on hand when cutting the pipe to catch remaining water.

Note: *Buy replacement pipe a few inches longer than needed and cut it to size on site.*

HOW LONG WILL IT TAKE?
Less than two hours

TOOLS
• Tube cutter • Bucket (or pan) • Tape measure • Wire fitting brush • Propane torch (and striker) • Work gloves • Safety goggles

MATERIALS
• Copper pipe and fittings • Plumber's abrasive sandcloth • Soldering flux • Wire solder • Heat-resistant pad

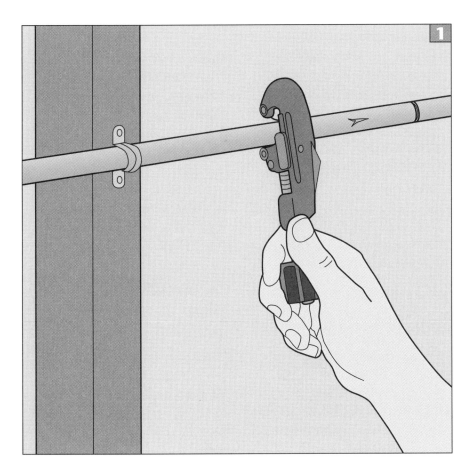

1. Cutting out the damaged pipe

Remove a section of pipe at least 3 inches in length so there is enough room for a fitting at each end of the new section of pipe.

• Position a tube cutter on the pipe and turn the adjustment knob until the cutting wheel begins to cut into the pipe.

• Rotate the cutter around the pipe and tighten the cutting wheel again. Repeat until the cutter cuts through the pipe.

• Make a second cut (#1) and remove the damaged section.

• Measure the distance between the ends of the standing pipe and cut the new section to length.

Note: *If space is too tight to use a tube cutter, cut out the damaged section of pipe with a mini-hacksaw and smooth the outside edges of the cut ends with a file.*

2. Reaming the cuts

With the pop-out reaming point on the tube cutter, smooth the inside surfaces at the ends of the standing pipe and the replacement piece.
● Press the reaming point into the end of the cut pipe and rotate the tube cutter a few times (#2).
● Repeat the procedure at the other three cut ends.

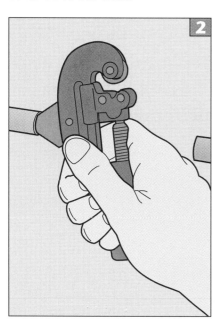

3. Preparing the cut ends

Prepare the cut ends of the standing pipe and the new piece with plumber's abrasive sandcloth.

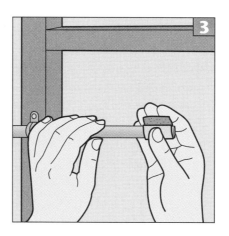

● Rub sandcloth on each cut end of the standing pipe (#3) until the surface shines.
● Prepare the ends of the replacement piece the same way.

Note: *Prepare surfaces of pipe slightly longer than the width of the fittings that will cover them.*

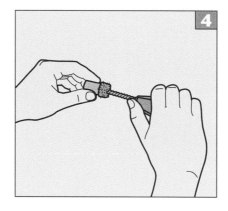

4. Cleaning the fittings

Make sure the wire fitting brush you use to clean the fittings is the right size for the pipe.
● Scour the inside surfaces of both fittings thoroughly with the wire fitting brush (#4).

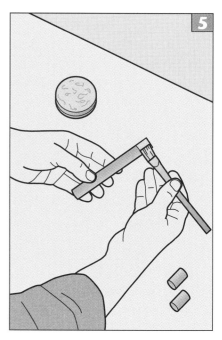

5. Applying flux

Flux is a lead-free soldering paste that cleans and etches copper surfaces to help solder seep into the joints. It is usually sold with a small applicator brush.
● Spread a thin layer of flux on the outer surfaces at the cut ends of the standing pipe and the ends of the replacement pipe (#5).
● Coat the inside surfaces of the fittings with a thin layer of flux.

6. Assembling the pipe and fitting

● Slide one end of the replacement pipe into one fitting up to the halfway point (#6) (most fittings have reference marks). Slide the other end of the replacement pipe into the other fitting the same way.

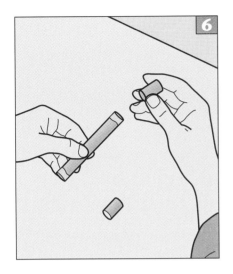

• Slide one end of the fitted pipe onto one end of the standing pipe.
• Connect the other end of the pipe, pushing the standing pipe back slightly in its brackets to allow enough room.

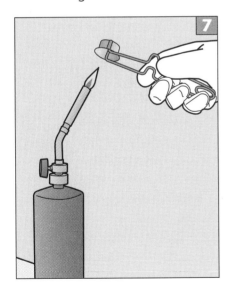

7. Lighting the propane torch

Working with a propane torch can be dangerous, so take precautions. Place a heat-resistant pad behind the work area. Keep a fire extinguisher on hand and always turn off the torch before putting it down. Pipes get very hot when soldered, so wear work gloves to protect your hands. Finally, wearing safety goggles is essential if you are soldering overhead.
• Unwind about 8 inches of wire solder and bend the leading 2 inches at a right angle.
• Light the propane torch with a striker (#7).
• Adjust the flame so it is about 1½ inches long.

8. Melting the solder

• Heat the fitting until the flux begins to sizzle, keeping the tip of the flame against the fitting.
• Touch the solder to a joint at several places so it melts on contact (#8).

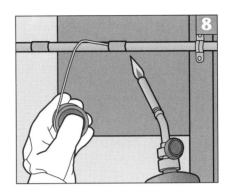

9. Soldering the joints

• Remove the flame as soon as the solder begins to melt—too much heat will burn off the flux and solder won't flow properly.
• Hold the solder in place so it is drawn into the joint (#9) and a thin bead of solder forms around the fitting.
• Solder the joint on the other side of the fitting using the same procedure, then solder each joint of the other fitting.

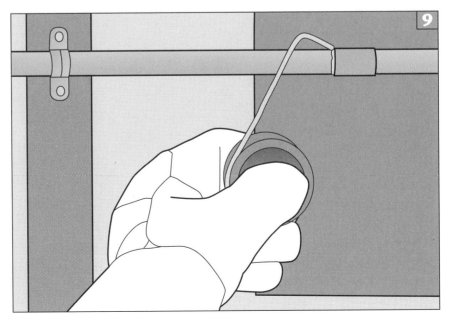

REPLACING PLASTIC PIPE

PLUMBING

Plastic pipe is a popular home plumbing choice. Less expensive than copper pipe, it is durable and easy to install. Although it is prone to cracking, repairs are simple to undertake. Among the sizes and types of plastic pipe available, ½-inch PVC (polyvinyl chloride) and CPVC (chlorinated polyvinyl chloride) products are the most common options for supply lines. The primer and solvent cement you use must be compatible with the pipe material.

The techniques for replacing an elbow, shown here, also apply to replacing a straight length of pipe or adding a T-fitting. When measuring for replacement pipe, allow for about ½ inch extra at each end to extend into a fitting and for the gap between adjacent lengths of pipe created by a fitting.

Before you start the project, shut off the water supply to the pipe; if there isn't a nearby shutoff valve for the line, close the main shutoff valve for the house. Drain as much water as possible from the pipe by opening the faucets on the line. Have a bucket or pan on hand when cutting the pipe to catch remaining water.

Note: *Buy replacement pipe a few inches longer than needed and cut it to size on site.*

HOW LONG WILL IT TAKE?
Less than two hours

TOOLS
• Mini-hacksaw (or tube cutter or plastic-pipe cutter) • Bucket or pan • Tape measure • Miter box and hacksaw (or fine-toothed backsaw)

MATERIALS
• Plastic pipe and fittings • Sandpaper • Primer • Solvent cement

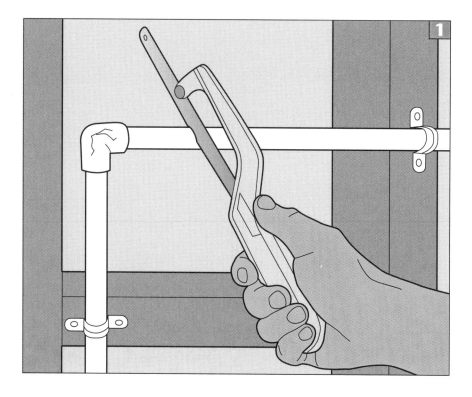

1. Cutting out the damaged pipe

A number of tools can be used to cut plastic pipe, including a mini-hacksaw, as shown here, a tube cutter fitted with the right blade, or a special plastic-pipe cutter that functions much like scissors.
● Cut out the damaged pipe, making the cuts about 3 inches beyond each end of the damaged section (#1).

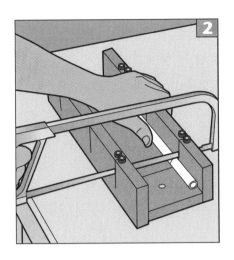

2. Cutting the replacement pipe

Cut replacement sections of pipe to length, allowing for an extra ½ inch at each end to extend into a fitting.

● Mark the pipe to length.

● Cut the pipe in a miter box with a hacksaw (#2) or a fine-toothed backsaw.

● Smooth the cut edges of the pipe with sandpaper.

3. Test-fitting the pipe

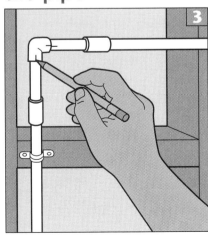

● Test-fit the pipe and fittings. If the replacement pipe is too long, trim it accordingly, smooth its edges with sandpaper, and test-fit it again.

● Draw a line across the joints between the elbow and the pipe (#3) to use as a reference when reassembling the pieces for gluing (reference lines are not needed on fittings for straight runs).

● Take apart the assembly.

4. Priming the pipes and fittings

Primer cleans and etches plastic surfaces so that solvent cement adheres properly. Follow the manufacturer's instructions.

● Brush primer evenly onto the outside ends of the replacement pipe and the standing pipe and onto the inside of the couplings and the elbow (#4).

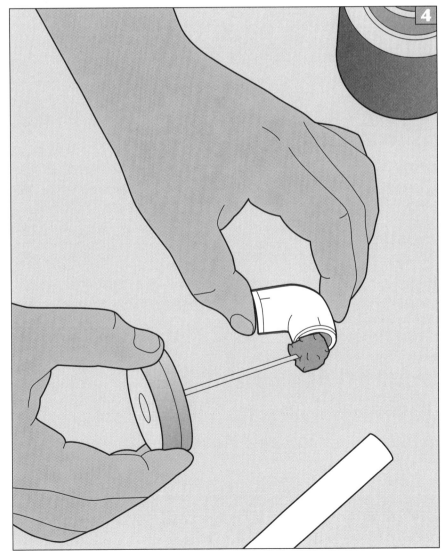

PLUMBING

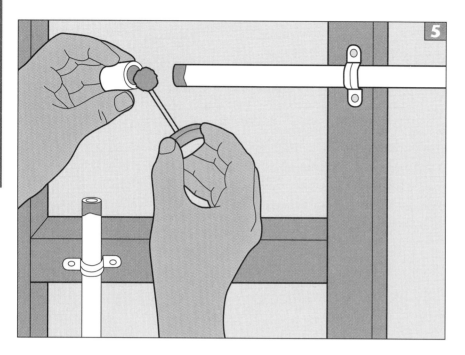

7. Installing the new section

● Fit the new section into place in the couplings (#7). Twist the couplings back and forth a few times to spread the solvent cement uniformly.

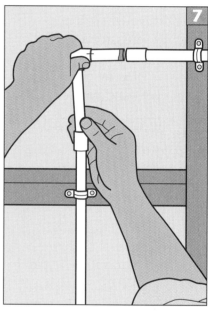

5. Applying solvent cement

Because solvent cement emits toxic fumes and is flammable, ventilate the site and don't smoke or light matches. Work quickly: Solvent cement sets in less than a minute.

● Apply solvent cement evenly to the primed ends of the standing pipe and inside surfaces of the couplings (#5).

● Slide the couplings onto the ends of the standing pipe, twisting them back and forth a few times to spread the cement uniformly.

6. Gluing the pipe to the elbow

● Apply solvent cement to the ends of the replacement pipe and to the inside of the elbow. Insert the pipe into the elbow and twist it a few times to spread the solvent cement.

● Line up the marks on the pipe with the marks on the elbow (#6).

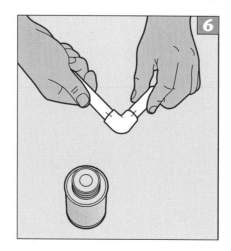

● Hold the assembly together for 15 to 20 seconds until the solvent cement sets.

● Allow the solvent cement to dry according to the manufacturer's instructions before running water through the pipes.

MATING PLASTIC PIPE TO COPPER PIPE

Substituting plastic pipe for copper pipe is a handy plumbing option, especially when tapping into and extending a supply line—simply install a plastic T-fitting following the steps shown here. Some localities prohibit joining plastic pipe and copper pipe, though, so consult your building codes.

A plastic-to-copper adapter usually has four parts: a copper fitting (soldered to the standing copper pipe); a plastic fitting (glued to the new plastic pipe); a washer (placed between the fittings); and a connecting ring.

Before you start the project, shut off the water supply to the pipe; if there isn't a nearby shutoff valve for the line, close the main shutoff valve for the house. Drain as much water as possible from the pipe by opening the faucets on the line. Have a bucket or pan on hand when cutting the pipe to catch remaining water.

Note: *Buy replacement pipe a few inches longer than needed and cut it to size on site.*

HOW LONG WILL IT TAKE?

Less than two hours

TOOLS

• Tube cutter • Bucket (or pan) • Tape measure • Wire fitting brush • Propane torch (and striker) • Work gloves • Safety goggles • Miter box and hacksaw (or fine-toothed backsaw) • Adjustable wrench • Channel-joint pliers

MATERIALS

• Plastic pipe • Plastic-to-copper adapters • Plumber's abrasive sandcloth • Heat-resistant pad • Soldering flux • Sandpaper • Primer • Solvent cement

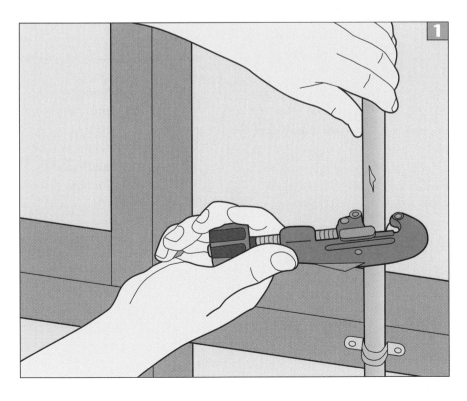

1. Removing the damaged pipe

The section of pipe you cut out should be at least 3 inches long so you have enough room for an adapter at each end.

● Position a tube cutter on the pipe and turn the adjustment knob until the cutting wheel cuts into the pipe (#1).

● Rotate the cutter around the pipe and tighten the cutting wheel again. Repeat until you cut through the pipe.

● Make another cut the same way on the other side of the damaged area and remove the section of pipe.

PLUMBING

Note: *If space is too tight to use a tube cutter, make the cuts with a mini-hacksaw, then file the cut ends of the standing pipe to smooth them.*

2. Reaming the pipe ends

With the pop-out reaming point on the tube cutter, smooth the inside surfaces at the ends of the standing pipe.

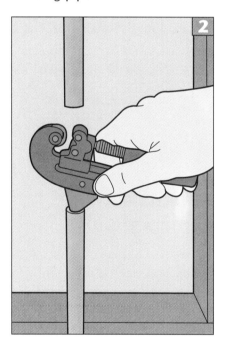

• Press the reaming point into the end of the cut pipe and rotate the tube cutter a few times (#2).
• Repeat the procedure at the end of the other cut pipe.

3. Soldering the copper fitting

Preparing surfaces for soldering involves rubbing them with plumber's abrasive sandcloth and treating them with flux—a paste that cleans surfaces and helps draw solder into the joint.

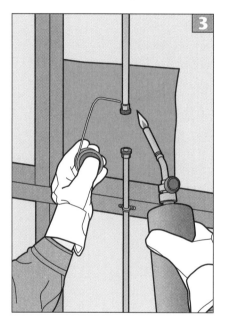

Working with a propane torch can be dangerous, so take precautions. Put a heat-resistant pad behind the work area. Keep a fire extinguisher on hand and always turn off the torch before putting it down. Wear work gloves; also safety goggles if soldering overhead.
• Rub the outside ends of the standing pipe and the inside of the copper fittings with plumber's abrasive sandcloth until shiny.
• Brush soldering flux evenly onto the shined surfaces, then slip the fittings into place.

• Light the torch and adjust the flame until about 1½ inches long.
• Place the tip of the flame at the joint between the adapter and the pipe, heating the entire joint as evenly as possible.
• Touch the tip of an 8-inch length of wire solder to the joint so it melts (#3).
• Feed solder into the joint until a thin bead forms around the edge. Allow the joint to cool.

4. Marking the new pipe

• Insert the plastic fittings and the washers in the copper fittings, then screw on the connecting rings.
• Position a piece of plastic pipe against the adapters and mark cutting lines (#4), allowing for an extra ½ inch to extend into each plastic fitting.
• Unscrew the connecting rings from the copper fittings and remove the plastic fittings.

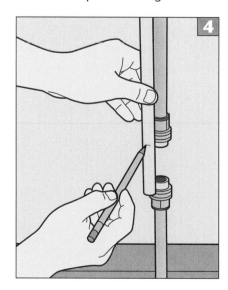

5. Smoothing the pipe ends

- Cut the new pipe to size with a hacksaw and a miter box.
- Smooth the cut ends of the pipe with sandpaper (#5).

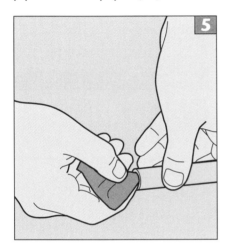

6. Priming and cementing

Primer cleans and etches plastic surfaces so that solvent cement adheres properly. Because solvent cement emits toxic fumes and is flammable, ventilate the site and don't smoke or light matches. Work quickly: Solvent cement sets in less than a minute.

- Brush primer onto one end of the replacement pipe and to the inside of one fitting, then let the primer dry.
- Apply solvent cement to the same surfaces, then fit the replacement pipe into the plastic fitting.
- Join another fitting onto the other end of the replacement pipe the same way (#6).

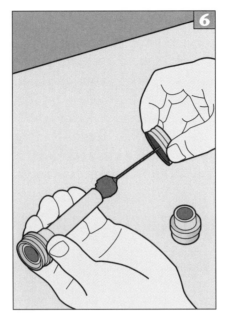

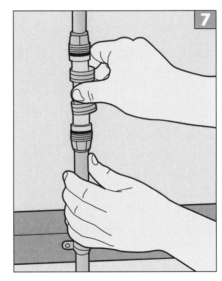

7. Installing the replacement pipe

- Slide the connecting rings into position on the replacement pipe, then fit the pipe into place so the washers are seated snugly against the copper fittings (#7).
- Hand-tighten the connecting rings onto the copper fittings.

8. Tightening the connecting rings

- Holding one copper fitting steady with an adjustable wrench, tighten the connecting ring a half turn with channel-joint pliers (#8). Don't overtighten.
- Tighten the other connecting ring the same way.
- Wait for the time specified by the solvent-cement manufacturer before turning the water back on.

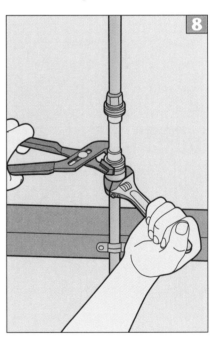

REPLACING A TOILET

Replacing a faulty toilet or changing a toilet for a new look isn't as difficult a job as you might think. However, call a professional if the toilet has been slowly leaking over a long period of time—the flooring may be rotted.

Before you go shopping for a toilet, measure the distance from the wall (not the baseboard) to the center of the bolts holding the bowl to the floor, referred to as the "footprint." The standard footprint is 12 inches, but it can vary depending on the age and style of the toilet. Make sure your new toilet will fit. Also check your local codes to determine whether low-flush toilets are required in your area.

Once you've bought a new toilet, remove all the packaging and inspect the toilet carefully for cracks or blemishes in the glazing that may have occurred during shipping.

HOW LONG WILL IT TAKE?	TOOLS	MATERIALS
Two to four hours	• Adjustable wrenches • Socket wrench • Putty knife • Phillips screwdriver • Flat-head screwdriver • Rubber gloves • Sponge • Bucket • Back support belt	• Toilet • Wax ring • Flange bolts • Rag

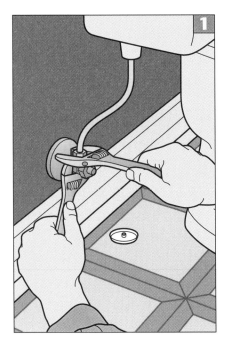

1. Disconnecting the water supply

• Turn off water supply to the toilet at the shutoff valve. If there is no shutoff valve, close the main water shutoff valve.
• Flush the toilet to drain as much water as possible out of the tank.
• Wearing rubber gloves, sponge out the remaining water from the tank. Plunge and bail as much water as possible out of the bowl.
• Unscrew the handle from the shutoff valve. With two adjustable wrenches, disconnect the water supply line from the shutoff valve (#1) and from the toilet tank.

2. Removing the old tank

• With a socket wrench, unscrew the nuts from the bolts securing the tank to the bowl (#2)—hold the bolts inside the tank with a screwdriver to keep them from turning, if necessary.
• Lift the tank off the bowl and remove it from the work area.

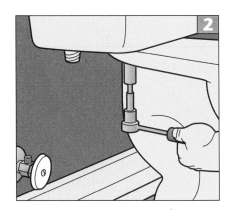

The tank and bowl are heavy so wear a back support belt and lift using the leg muscles. If possible, work with a helper.

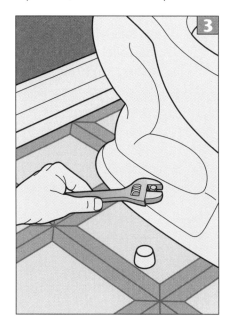

3. Freeing the old bowl

● Use a screwdriver to pry the caps off the bolts on each side of the toilet bowl.
● Remove the nuts from the floor bolts with an adjustable wrench (#3).

Note: *If the nuts securing the toilet to the floor won't turn, cut through the bolts with a mini-hacksaw.*

4. Removing the old bowl

● Rock the bowl back and forth to break the seal between the toilet and the flange. Lift the bowl off the bolts. With a helper, remove the bowl from the work area. The bottom of the bowl will have some wax on the bottom so set it down on cardboard or newspaper.
● Plug the drain opening with a rag to prevent sewer odors from escaping and to keep tools from being dropped into the drain. If you're not installing the new toilet right away, cover the drain opening with cardboard and a concrete block to avoid any risk of a rodent invading from the sewer.
● Scrape the wax off the flange with a putty knife (#4). Remove the flange bolts and wipe the flange clean with a rag.
● Inspect the flange carefully. If it is cracked, bent, or otherwise damaged, call a plumber to replace it.

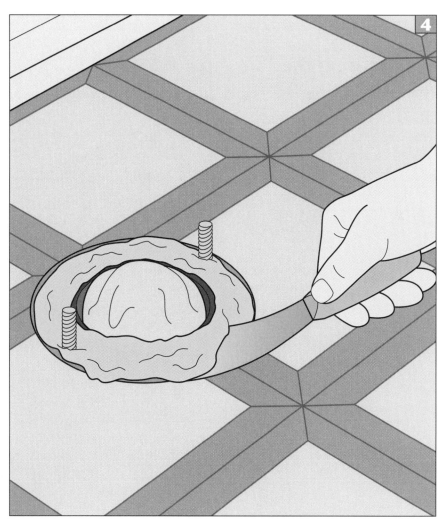

PLUMBING

5. Preparing the new bowl

The toilet is sealed to the drain with a wax ring placed over the horn of the toilet. Inspect the drain. If the pipe sealed to the flange is rigid plastic, use a wax ring fitted with a plastic sleeve. For lead pipe, a wax ring without a sleeve is required.

● Turn the new bowl upside down and position a new wax ring over the horn (#5). If you are using a wax ring with a sleeve, position the sleeve away from the bowl.

● Remove the protective plastic from the wax ring.

6. Installing the bowl

● Insert new flange bolts into the bolt slots in the flange, positioning them an equal distance from the wall—usually 12 inches.

● Remove the rag from drain.

● Turn the bowl over and lower it on the bolts (#6).

● Straddle the bowl and rock and twist it to compress and spread the wax.

● If the toilet doesn't sit flat on the floor, shim the low spot with a copper or brass washer.

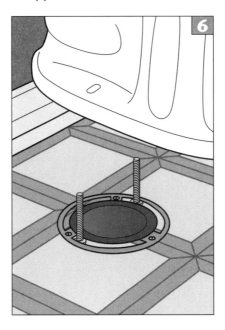

● Slide a plastic cap base onto each bolt, then a washer and the nut. With an adjustable wrench tighten the nuts down evenly on each side. Don't overtighten or force the nuts—you could crack the bowl. Leave the bolt caps for later in case the nuts need to be tightened further.

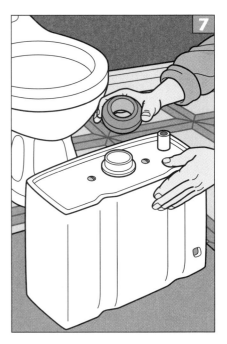

7. Preparing the tank

● If they aren't already installed, follow the manufacturer's instructions to install the ballcock and flush valve assembly. Leave the handle assembly and float ball for later so that it won't interfere with the fastening of the tank bolts.

● Turn the tank upside down and slip the spud washer over the end of the flush valve (#7).

8. Installing the tank

● Lift the tank onto the bowl, lowering the spud washer into the water inlet opening (#8).

● Shift the tank slightly until the bolt holes inside the tank line up with those on the bowl.

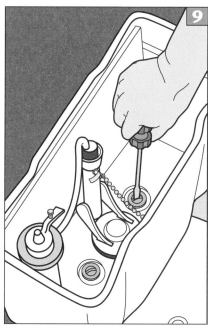

9. Fastening the tank

● Place a rubber washer onto each bolt and slide them through the tank holes from inside the tank.

● Under the back rim of the bowl, place a rubber washer and a nut over each bolt. Holding the bolts with a screwdriver from inside the tank (#9), tighten the nuts with an adjustable wrench—be careful not to overtighten them.

● Install the handle assembly and float ball according to the manufacturer's instructions.

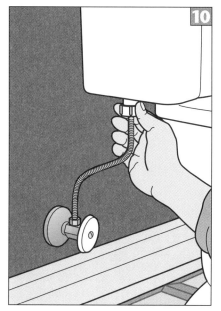

10. Connecting the water supply

The original copper or chrome supply pipe may not be shaped to fit the new installation and it can be difficult to bend without kinking. It's best to replace it with braided flexible supply tubing. Be sure to buy a piece of tubing long enough to reach from the tank to the valve.

● Attach the new supply tube to the shutoff valve and tighten with

an adjustable wrench. Reinstall the valve handle. Hand-tighten the supply tube to the base of the ballcock under the tank (#10).

● Turn on the water supply. After the tanks fills, flush the toilet and carefully inspect all joints and seals for leaks. Tighten the tank or bowl bolts as necessary.

● Snap the plastic caps onto the bowl bolts—trim the bolts with a mini-hacksaw, if necessary.

11. Installing the toilet seat

Slip the seat bolts through the mounting holes in the seat and the bowl. Holding each bolt steady with a screwdriver, thread a nut onto it (#11). Tighten the bolts with the screwdriver.

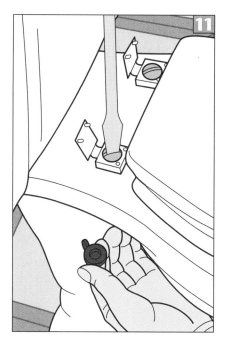

PLUMBING

REPLACING A BATHTUB

Removing an old tub, especially a heavy cast-iron model, can be the most difficult part of replacing a bathtub. Most new tubs are made of acrylic plastic, fiberglass, or steel and can be moved quite easily with a helper.

You'll need access to the plumbing behind the wall at the faucet end of the tub. If you don't have an access panel to these pipes, cut one before starting the job. You'll also need to reach the pipes under the tub from the floor below. The plumbing work involves replacing the drain assembly—C to I in the anatomy shown below. These pieces are sold together in waste-and-overflow kits and are available in metal or plastic (ABS). Although you will not be working on the supply pipes except to remove the faucet handles and the spout, it's a good idea to shut off the water to the tub before beginning work.

HOW LONG WILL IT TAKE?
More than four hours

TOOLS
· Tape measure · Flat-head screwdriver · Long-nose pliers · Channel-joint pliers · Pry bar · Carpenter's level · Utility knife · Cold chisel · Ball-peen hammer · Hammer · Saw · Cordless drill · Rectangular trowel · Work gloves · Safety goggles

MATERIALS
· Bathtub · Waste-and-overflow kit · Flange clips (and screws) · Plumber's putty · Plumber's tape · Premixed mortar · 1x4s · 2x4 · Cedar shims · Wood screws

Anatomy of a bath

A cast-iron or steel bathtub has a flange (A) along its inside edge that is attached to a wood ledger (M) fastened to wall studs. The overflow and drain assembly (C to I) are attached to drain piping (J to K). The water supply pipes and the spout (B) are not directly attached to the tub, but the spout and faucets must be disconnected before the old tub is removed.

A	Tub flange
B	Spout
C	Spud (drain flange)
D	Shoe fitting
E	Waste pipe
F	Overflow drain
G	Overflow pipe
H	T-fitting
I	Tailpiece
J	P-trap
K	Branch drain
L	Supply pipe
M	Ledger

1. Removing the faucet handles, spout, spud, and overflow plate

- With a flat-head screwdriver, pop the covers off the faucet handles, then undo the screws and remove the handles.

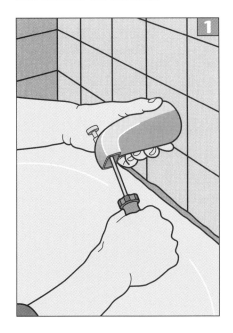

- To remove the spout, fit a screwdriver into its opening. Unscrew the spout from its threaded pipe (#1).
- Loosen the screws holding the overflow plate to the overflow drain. Remove the plate along with the lift rod attached to it (see #12).
- Lift the pop-up stopper out of the drain.
- To remove the spud—also known as the drain flange—unscrew it from the shoe fitting

(see #11): Insert long-nose pliers into the drain and turn counterclockwise.

2. Removing the drain assembly

- From under the tub, disconnect the tailpiece (A) from the T-fitting (B). For threaded steel pipes, use channel-joint pliers to loosen the metal collar (#2). If the tailpiece and T-fitting are made of plastic, cut through the tailpiece with a hacksaw. Make sure the cut is straight; otherwise, you'll have to cut the pipe again later when installing the new drain assembly.

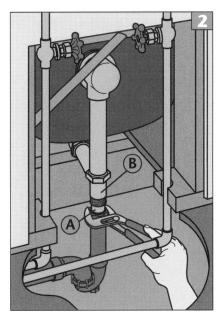

- Remove the drain assembly from the tub.
- If you are removing an acrylic or fiberglass tub, skip to Step 4. For a cast-iron or steel model, continue on to Step 3.

3. Uncovering the tub flange

For a steel tub, you need to expose the flange fastened to the wall studs along the inside of the tub. You will have to remove the first 8 inches of tiles and wallboard above the tub.

- Wearing safety goggles, knock away the tiles above the tub with a cold chisel and ball-peen hammer.
- Use a carpenter's level to mark a line 6 inches above the tub on the exposed wallboard.
- With a utility knife, cut through the wallboard along the marked line (#3), then pull out the pieces of wallboard.

4. Removing the old tub

- If you're removing a steel tub, take out the screws holding the two flange clips to the studs. For an acrylic or fiberglass tub, simply cut away the caulk and any grout along the wall. An acrylic or fiberglass tub may be embedded in mortar on the floor—if so, you will have to break it into pieces with a reciprocating saw or sledgehammer to remove it; you will also have to remove the mortar.
- With a pry bar, lift the front edge of the tub and slide two soaped 1x4s under it. The boards will serve as runners for sliding the tub out of the way.
- Wearing work gloves, pull the tub out from the wall (#4); if necessary, work with a helper.

- If you're installing an acrylic or fiberglass tub, the next step is to prepare a mortar bed (Step 7). For a steel tub, position and install a ledger (Step 5 to Step 6).

5. Positioning a ledger

The ledger is a 2x4 support for the back edge of a steel tub. If an existing ledger is at the correct height, it can be used as support for the new tub.
- Measure the height of the tub from its bottom edge to just under the flange.
- Transfer the distance to one of the studs on the back wall, measuring up from the floor. Transfer the mark to the other studs with a carpenter's level (#5).

6. Installing the ledger

- Cut a 2x4 ledger to the length of the bath—typically 5 feet.
- Aligning the top edge of the ledger with the marks on the studs, fasten the ledger in place with two $2\frac{1}{2}$-inch wood screws at every stud (#6). A steel tub does not require a mortar bed (Step 7), so you can proceed directly to installing it (Step 8).

7. Laying a bed of mortar

Acrylic and fiberglass tubs aren't as rigid as steel models so they need a rigid base. This base is provided by a bed of mortar.
- Prepare a batch of premixed mortar, adding a little more water than recommended by the product manufacturer.

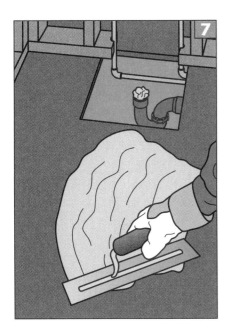

● With a rectangular trowel, spread a 2-inch bed of mortar on the floor area that will be under the tub (#7). Install the tub (Step 8), then sit in it for a couple of minutes to embed it in the mortar before the mortar hardens.

8. Installing the tub

● Put two soaped 1x4 runners on the floor. Working with a helper, set the new tub on the runners and slide it into place. For a steel model, lift the leading edge of the tub and rest it on the ledger.
● Hold a carpenter's level on the rim of the tub to check if the tub is level. If the tub isn't level, place a cedar shim under the low end and tap the shim until the tub is level (#8).
● With a utility knife, trim all shims flush with the edge of the tub.
● If you are installing an acrylic or

fiberglass tub, you can now install the drain assembly (Step 10). For a steel tub, first fasten the flange to the studs (Step 9).

9. Fastening the tub to the studs

Steel tubs are fastened to two studs with flange clips. The clips should be evenly spaced—on a standard 5-foot tub, attach them to the second and third studs from the faucet end of the tub.

● With a clip in position on the flanged edge of the tub, fasten it to the stud with the screw provided (#9).

10. Installing the drain assembly

● Connect the overflow pipe (A) to the waste pipe (B) with the T-fitting (C). Tighten the collar (D) with channel-joint pliers.
● Press the rubber gaskets provided with the kit into place on the shoe fitting (E) and the overflow drain (F).

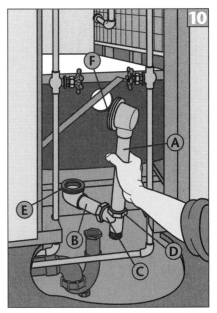

● Position the drain assembly (#10), pressing the gaskets against the rims of the overflow and drain holes in the tub. You will need to hold the drain assembly in place while a helper attaches the drain flange and lift-rod overflow plate (Step 11 to Step 12).

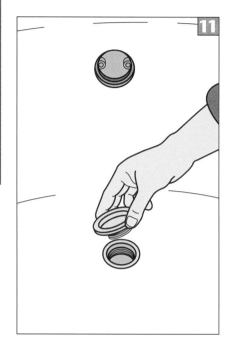

11. Attaching the spud

The bottom end of the drain assembly is secured to the tub by the spud, or drain flange.
● Apply a bead of plumber's putty around the underside of the spud.
● Screw the spud into the shoe fitting (#11), then wipe away any excess putty.

12. Adding the lift rod

The lift rod is attached to the overflow plate; together, they mechanically open and close the pop-up stopper, and secure the top end of the drain assembly to the tub.
● Set the pop-up stopper into the spud.
● Insert the lift rod into the over-

flow pipe (#12). Then, holding the overflow plate in position over the opening, test the drain mechanism with the trip lever on the overflow plate. The pop-up stopper should open and close fully. If necessary, remove the lift rod and adjust the mechanism by changing the position of the threaded fitting on the bottom of the rod.

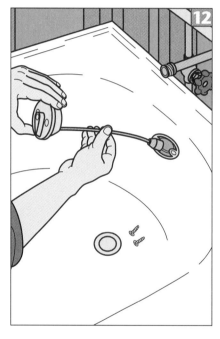

● Once the drain mechanism is properly adjusted, screw the overflow plate to the overflow drain.

13. Plumbing the P-trap

To connect the drain assembly to the P-trap, you will have to work from below the tub.
● For a tight-fitting connection between the T-fitting (A) and the tailpiece (B), first wrap teflon

plumber's tape snugly around the threads of the tailpiece.
● Insert the untaped end of the tailpiece into the adapter above the P-trap, then insert the taped end into the T-fitting and tighten the connections (#13).

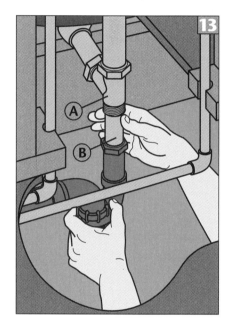

● With channel-joint pliers, tighten the collar between the P-trap and the T-fitting.
● Replace any wallboard and tiles you removed. Install the spout and faucet handles, then turn on the water to the tub. Fill the tub with water and apply caulk between the edges of the tub and the wall.

INSTALLING A GARBAGE DISPOSAL UNIT

The principal challenge in installing a garbage disposal unit is hooking it up to your kitchen drain system. Most disposal units are sold with a discharge elbow; the other fittings you need depend on whether you have a single or double sink. For a single sink, the discharge elbow is connected to the drain trap with an adapter. For a double sink—as shown here—a waste-T is required. If your dishwasher is located near the sink, it can be drained through the disposal unit. Simply remove the knockout from the nipple on the disposal unit just above the discharge elbow and connect the drain hose to the nipple with hose clamps.

Power for the disposal unit is supplied by NM (nonmetallic) cable connected to a separate circuit. You may need to install an electrical box and wire it to the disposal unit and to the service panel. Other models are wired directly to the service panel. Have an electrician hook up the cable to your service panel—do your work on unconnected wires.

HOW LONG WILL IT TAKE?

More than four hours

TOOLS

• Wire cutters • Multipurpose tool • Screwdriver • Wrench • Channel-joint pliers

MATERIALS

• Garbage disposal unit and fittings • Drain and strainer assembly • Plumber's putty • Solvent cement • NM cable • Electrical box • Combination switch/outlet • Wire caps

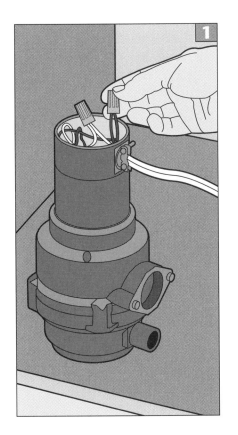

1. Attaching cable to the unit

• Cut a length of NM cable long enough to run from the disposal unit to where you intend to install the electrical box or to the service panel, depending on the model.
• Run a multipurpose tool over the last 4 inches of the cable to split the sheathing. Pull back the sheathing to expose the black and white wires and the bare copper ground wire.
• Strip ¾ inch of insulation off the black wire and the white wire.
• Unscrew and remove the bottom panel of the disposal unit.
• Pull the wires through the cable entry hole along with ½ inch of unstripped cable. Tighten the clamp at the entry hole against the cable.
• Attach the cable's ground wire to the grounding screw on the body of the disposal unit.
• Twist the cable's white wire together with the disposal unit's white wire and cap them, then do the same with the cable's black wire and the disposal unit's black wire (#1).

2. Removing the sink drain assembly

A garbage disposal unit requires a special drain-and-strainer assembly. Use channel-joint pliers to loosen the slip nuts on the drain-pipe and to unscrew the lock nuts on the tailpiece and strainer.

PLUMBING

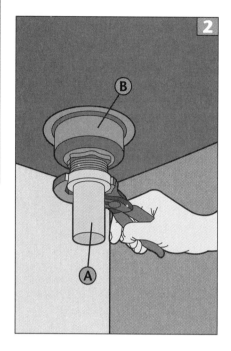

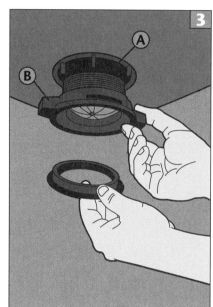

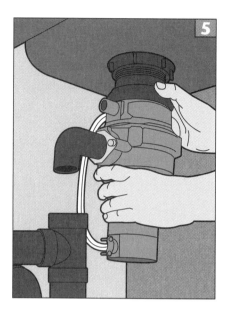

● Slide the support ring (B) onto the tailpiece and secure it in place with the rubber gasket (#3).

● Loosen the slip nuts on the drainpipe and remove it.
● Remove the tailpiece (A) by unscrewing the lock nut securing it to the strainer (#2).
● Unscrew the lock nut below the sleeve (B) and lift out the strainer and sleeve from above the sink.

3. Installing the new drain assembly

Installation varies according to the design of the disposer; check the manufacturer's instructions.
● Apply plumber's putty to the underside of the flange on the strainer. From above the sink, push the strainer into the drain hole, pressing down firmly to form a solid bond.
● From under the sink, slide the fiber gasket onto the tailpiece and screw the lock nut (A) into place.

4. Preparing the unit

● Slide the rubber gasket onto the end of the discharge elbow and attach the elbow with the fasteners provided by the manufacturer, tightening them accordingly with a wrench (#4) or a screwdriver.

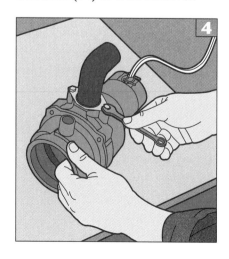

5. Mounting the unit

● Slide the projections on the top edge of the disposal unit into the corresponding slots in the mounting ring. Position the unit so the discharge elbow is aligned above the main drain assembly (#5).
● Turn the mounting ring in a clockwise direction to lock the disposal unit in place.

6. Hooking up the unit to the drain

Two attachments are required to connect the discharge elbow to the drain: a waste-T (A) and a connecting adapter with a built-in gasket (B). Dry-fit the pieces, then glue them with solvent cement and tighten the slip nuts.
● Connect the waste-T to the drainpipe leading from the second sink and to the pipe leading to the trap bend.

• Connect the waste-T and the discharge elbow with an adapter, installing the adapter gasket-side up. Tighten the slip nut at the end of the discharge elbow to secure it to the adapter (#6).

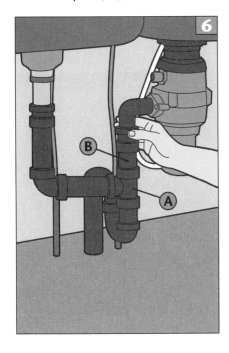

• When the assembly is complete, run hot water through the unit into the drain for about 2 minutes to test for leaks.

7. Wiring the unit

Where local codes permit, a combination switch/outlet is a useful option for a disposal unit.
• Install an electrical box at a convenient location near the disposal unit's power cable.
• Strip 6 inches of sheathing off the cable running from the service panel and off the cable running from the disposal unit.

• Strip ¾ inch of insulation off the end of both cables' black and white wires.
• Pass the cables into the box through their access holes and tighten the clamps to hold the cables in place.
• Connect the black wire from the disposal unit's cable to the brass screw closest to the switch and the black wire from the other cable to the brass screw closest to the outlet.

• Twist together the two white wires and an additional short length of white wire. Cap the wires, then connect the end of the added white wire to the silver screw nearest to the outlet.
• Connect a green jumper wire to the grounding screw on the box and another jumper to the grounding screw on the switch/ outlet. Twist together the cables' ground wires and the jumpers, then cap the four wires (#7).

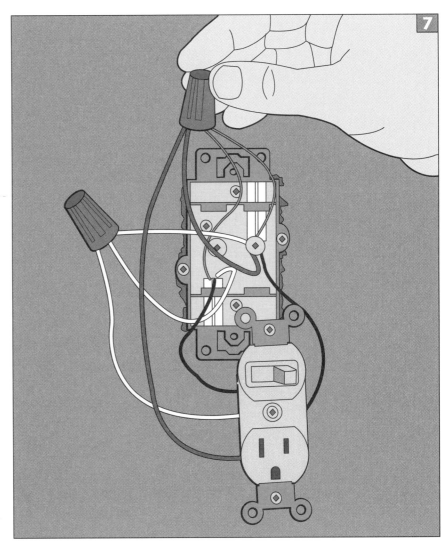

PUTTING IN A SELF-RIMMING DOUBLE SINK

PLUMBING

Are you tired of dishes piling up on the countertop because there is no room in the sink? Why not install a double sink? Whatever your reasons for putting in a new sink, the self-rimming type—double or single—is a good choice for the do-it-yourselfer. Simply cut a hole in the countertop, drop the sink into place, do some basic plumbing, and you're done.

PVC (polyvinyl chloride) plastic is the drainpipe material of choice because it is inexpensive, light in weight, and easy to work with. If you are connecting the drainpipe to a stub-out made of a different material, you'll need an adapter. If possible with your model of sink, connect the faucets before installing the sink—making the connections from below can be awkward.

HOW LONG WILL IT TAKE?
More than four hours

TOOLS
• Screwdriver • Electric drill • Saber saw • Hole saw • Caulking gun • Adjustable wrenches • Work gloves

MATERIALS
• Self-rimming sink (and cutting template) • Masking tape • 1x2 • Wood screw • Silicone caulk • Plumber's putty • Drainpipe • Tailpiece • T-fitting • Elbows • S-trap (or P-trap) • Primer • Solvent cement

1. Marking the sink opening

Drop-in sinks are sold with cardboard templates to help you draw cutting lines.

• Place the template on the countertop above the stub-out for the drain.

• Mark cutting lines for the sink and faucets.

• Affix masking tape along the cutting lines and draw the lines again (#1). The masking tape will prevent splintered edges when you cut the opening.

• Remove the template.

2. Cutting the sink opening

• Place a scrap 1x2 longer than the width of the outline across the countertop and screw it to the center of the outline. This will keep the waste piece from falling

through before you finish cutting the opening.

• Drill an entry hole for the blade of a saber saw inside one corner of the outline.

• Fit a saber saw with a blade suitable for the countertop material, then cut from the drilled hole to the cutting line and along it (#2). Turn the 1x2 a little to let the saw get by, then turn it back.
• Drill the holes for the faucets with a hole saw.

3. Caulking the sink

Not all sinks need to be caulked. Some models come with adhesive-backed foam pads that must be stuck in place; others have pads in place already; and still others come with plumber's putty that must be applied by hand.
• Install the faucets on the sink following the manufacturer's instructions.
• Place the sink upside down on the countertop and, according to the manufacturer's instructions, apply a bead of silicone caulk to the sink flange with a caulking gun (#3), position the adhesive pads into place, or apply the plumber's putty.

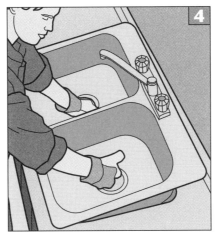

4. Dropping in the sink

• Wearing work gloves to protect your hands from sharp edges, hold the sink by the drain openings and lower it into the cutout, fitting the faucet shanks into their holes (#4).
• Push down firmly on the sink to seat it securely.

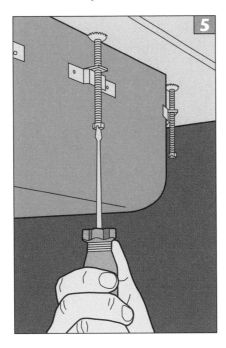

5. Installing hold-down bolts

• Screw in hold-down bolts along the sides of the sink from below, making sure they press firmly against the underside of the countertop (#5).
• Clean off any excess caulk or putty around the sink.

6. Connecting the supply pipes

• Connect the supply pipes to the faucet shanks and to the shutoff valves, hand-tightening the nuts.
• Complete the tightening of the nuts with two adjustable wrenches, holding the faucet shanks and the shutoff valve in turn with one wrench and tightening each nut one-quarter to one-half turn with the other (#6).

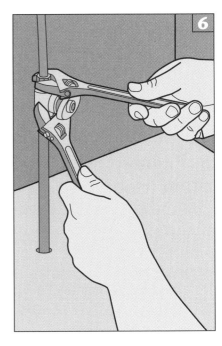

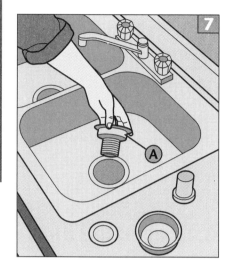

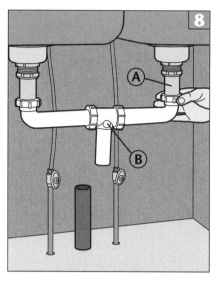

7. Preparing the drain assembly

• Apply plumber's putty to the underside the strainer flange (A). Push the strainer into the drain opening (#7), pressing the flange firmly against the sink.
• Working under the sink, slip a gasket and a strainer sleeve onto the strainer and secure them by tightening the lock nut with channel-joint pliers.
• Repeat the procedure for the other drain opening.
• Clean away any excess putty in the sink.

8. Plumbing the drain assembly

• Add a tailpiece (A) to each drain and tighten the lock nuts.
• Connect a T-fitting (B) to a pair of elbows and connect them to the tailpieces (#8). Tighten the slip nuts one-quarter to one-half turn with channel-joint pliers.

9. Installing the trap

Where local codes permit, install an S-trap if the stub-out comes out of the floor; if the stub-out comes out of the wall, install a P-trap. Make sure the primer and solvent cement you use are compatible with the plastic pipes.
• Connect a trap to the T-fitting and run a drainpipe to the stub-out, gluing the pieces together and tightening the slip nuts on the S-trap (#9).

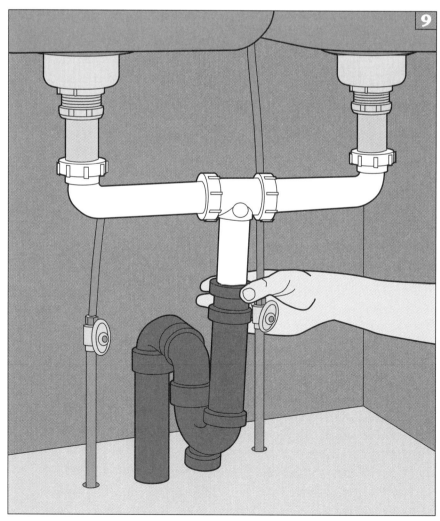

INSTALLING AN UNDER-COUNTER WATER TREATMENT SYSTEM

A water treatment system will both improve the taste of your drinking water and allay concerns about possible impurities. A number of filter systems are available—ranging from small faucet-mounted types, which are easiest to install, to large under-counter models, which filter more water in a shorter period of time. Under-counter models are available with activated-carbon filters—the most common type on the market—or top-of-the-line reverse-osmosis filters.

Installing an under-counter water treatment system involves mounting the unit on the back wall of the cabinet under the sink, then cutting into the cold-water supply pipe and connecting the unit to it with fittings and tubes.

HOW LONG WILL IT TAKE?	TOOLS	MATERIALS
Less than two hours	• Torpedo level • Electric drill • Screwdriver • Tube cutter • Utility knife • Adjustable wrench	• Under-counter water treatment system • Wood screws • Dual compression fittings • Cloth

1. Mounting the unit

Install the unit under the sink near the cold-water supply pipe. Allow for enough room under the unit

to change cartridges—3 to 4 inches is usually sufficient.
● With a level, mark a line on the cabinet at the desired height for the unit—the torpedo level shown is handy for use in tight spaces.
● Hold the unit at the line and mark the location of the screw holes in the mounting bracket.
● Drill pilot holes at the marks and drive in screws partway. Hang the unit on the screws, then tighten them (#1).
● Close the cold-water shutoff valve and open the faucet to drain as much water as possible from the supply pipe.

2. Cutting the supply pipe

Use a tube cutter to remove a 5-inch length of supply pipe

3 inches above the shutoff valve. Have a cloth on hand to wipe up water trapped in the pipe.

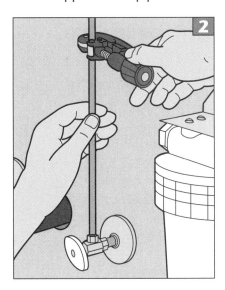

● Position the tube cutter on the supply pipe and turn the adjustment knob until the cutting wheel cuts into the pipe (#2).

- Rotate the cutter around the pipe, then tighten the cutting wheel again. Repeat until the cutter cuts through the pipe.
- Make a second cut 5 inches higher the same way and remove the length of pipe.

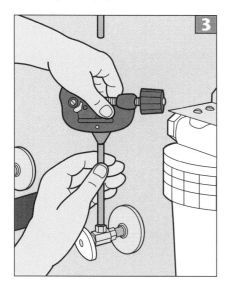

3. Reaming the pipe ends

Cutting metal pipe creates jagged edges, or burrs, that can catch debris and block water flow if not smoothed away.

- Remove burrs by reaming the cut ends of the standing pipe with the pop-out point on the tube cutter, rotating the tool several times (#3).

4. Attaching the fittings

- Push a dual compression fitting onto each end of the standing pipe (#4) and hand-tighten it.

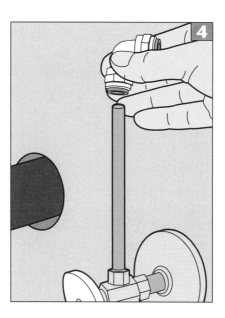

- Tighten the fittings a quarter-turn with an adjustable wrench to create a seal.

5. Hooking up the unit

Two plastic tubes are supplied with the unit. Trim them, if necessary, with a utility knife—but not so short that they bend sharply.

- Fit one end of one tube into the upper compression fitting and the other end into the unit's "out" port (A).
- Fit one end of the other tube into the lower compression fitting and the other end into the unit's "in" port (B) (#5).
- Open the cold-water shutoff valve, then turn on the faucet and allow the water to run for about 5 minutes to flush the cartridge.

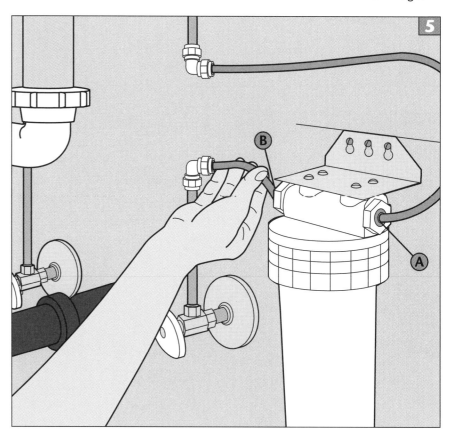

INSTALLING A HOSE BIBB

Extending your water supply outside to a hose bibb involves drilling a hole through the wall and tapping into a cold-water supply pipe. Placement of the hose bibb depends on the desired location for an outdoor hose and the location of the indoor supply lines. In most cases, supply lines are attached to the bottom of the joists below the floor, putting them close to foundation level. A hose bibb requires $\frac{1}{2}$-inch-diameter supply pipe; add a stop-and-drain valve if you live in a cold climate so water can be drained before the temperature drops below freezing. (Water that freezes will damage the pipe and the hose bibb.)

Prepare surfaces to be soldered with plumber's abrasive sand-cloth or a wire fitting brush and apply flux—a soldering paste that cleans and etches to help solder seep into the joints.

Working with a propane torch can be dangerous, so take precautions. Place a heat-resistant pad behind the work area. Keep a fire extinguisher handy and always turn off the torch before putting it down. Pipes get very hot when soldered, so wear work gloves to protect your hands. Finally, wearing safety goggles is essential when soldering overhead.

HOW LONG WILL IT TAKE?

More than four hours

TOOLS

- Tape measure • Screwdriver
- Electric drill (and twist bit)
- Spade bit • Tube cutter • Wire fitting brush • Bucket • Propane torch (and striker) • Work gloves
- Safety goggles

MATERIALS

- Hose bibb • Copper pipe
- T-fitting • Stop-and-drain valve
- Plumber's abrasive sandcloth
- Soldering flux • Wire solder
- Silicone caulk • Heat-resistant pad

Anatomy of a hose-bibb assembly

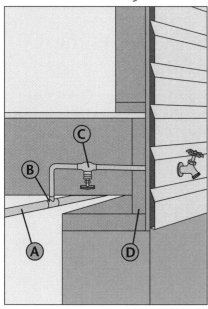

Tap into a cold-water supply pipe (A) with a T-fitting (B). If you live in an area where temperatures fall below freezing, install a stop-and-drain valve (C) on the run of pipe after the T-fitting. Drill a hole for the supply pipe to the hose bibb through the rim joist (D).

1. Drilling a hole through the wall

- Working indoors, drill a pilot hole in the center of the rim joist with a $\frac{1}{4}$-inch twist bit.
- Working outdoors, fit the drill with a spade bit that matches the diameter of the adapter on the

hose bibb; if the hose bibb does not have an adapter, use a $\frac{3}{4}$-inch spade bit.

- Place the tip of the spade bit in the pilot hole and drill the larger hole (#1).

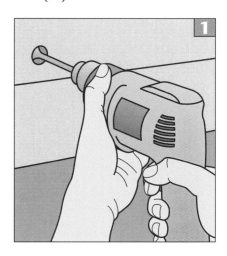

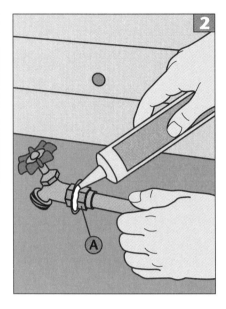

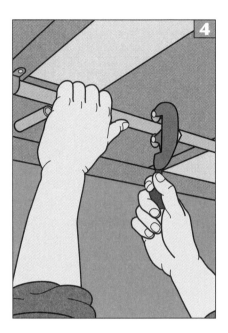

• Apply a bead of silicone caulk along the inside rim of the hose-bibb flange (#2).

3. Attaching the hose bibb to the wall

• Slide the end of the pipe into the hole in the wall.
• Press the flange of the hose bibb firmly against the wall and secure it with screws (#3).

4. Tapping into a supply pipe

Before cutting into the supply pipe, shut off the water at the main shutoff valve and open faucets to drain the pipe. Have a bucket on hand to catch drips. Cut a gap big enough for a T-fitting in the pipe directly opposite the center of the hose-bibb pipe.

2. Assembling the bibb

• Cut a length of copper pipe 6 inches longer than the thickness of the wall with a tube cutter.
• With the pop-out reaming point on the back of the tube cutter, ream the jagged edges of the newly-cut ends of the pipe, sticking the point as far as it will go into the pipe and rotating it several times.
• Rub plumber's abrasive sand-cloth on one end of the pipe until the surface shines.
• Scour the inside of the adapter (A) thoroughly with a wire fitting brush.
• Spread a thin 1-inch-wide layer of flux on the end of the pipe and on the inside of the adapter.
• Solder the adapter (A) to the end of the pipe, heating the joint and touching solder to it until a bead forms around it.

• Slide a tube cutter onto the pipe and turn the adjustment knob until the cutting wheel begins to cut into the pipe (#4).
• Rotate the cutter once around the pipe and tighten the cutting wheel again. Continue until the cutter cuts through the pipe.
• Repeat to make the other cut.

5. Soldering the T-fitting

Make sure the pipes are dry before installing the T-fitting; wet pipes don't get hot enough for soldering. Place a heat-resistant pad (A) against nearby wooden surfaces.
• Prepare surfaces for soldering: Ream the ends of the pipe and rub them with plumber's abrasive sandcloth, scour the ends of the T-fitting with a wire fitting brush, and apply flux.

• Slip the T-fitting into place and heat it with a propane torch until the flux begins to sizzle, then touch solder to a joint so it melts on contact (#5).

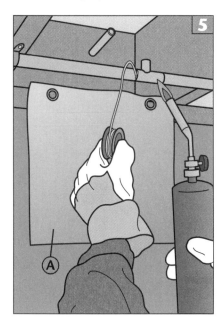

• As solder is drawn under the fitting, add more until a bead forms around the joint.
• Solder the other joint the same way.

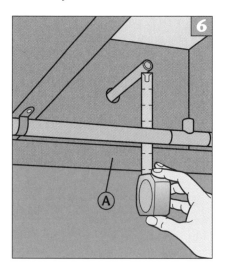

6. Measuring for the connecting pipe

• Measure the distance between the top of the sill plate (A) and the bottom of the hose-bibb pipe (#6), then cut a pipe to this length.
• Insert one end of the newly-cut pipe into the T-fitting.

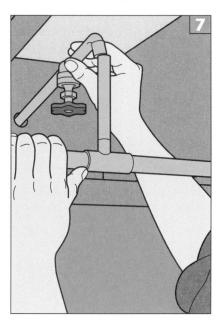

7. Adding the stop-and-drain valve

When measuring and cutting lengths of pipe, take into account the 1/2 inch needed at each end to fit into the stop-and-drain valve, the T-fitting, and an elbow. Test-assemble components before beginning to solder to be sure that pipes are cut to the right length.
• Place the stop-and-drain valve on the end of the pipe connected to the hose-bibb. Orient the

handle so it will be easy to reach in the future.
• Measure the distance between the stop-and-drain valve and the vertical standing pipe, then cut a pipe to this length.
• Insert the pipe into the stop-and-drain valve and complete the connection with an elbow (#7).

8. Soldering the connections

• After test-fitting components, disassemble them and prepare the surfaces for soldering.
• Solder each joint in turn (#8).
• Turn on the water supply to test for leaks.

INSTALLING A DRIP-IRRIGATION SYSTEM

A drip-irrigation system is a convenient garden-watering option that consists of a grid of hose lines hooked up to a hose bibb. Small holes punctured in the hoses are fitted with feeder lines and emitters that provide plants with water. By creating a steady directed drip of water at ground level instead of an intermittent broad spray, these systems lose little water to evaporation; and since the foliage stays dry, plants are protected from mildew.

Drip-irrigation systems are available as kits that include various clamps, fittings, and connectors. Sections of hose—the main line, the branch lines, and the feeder lines—are cut to length on site. Most kits include a backflow preventer, a device that attaches to the hose bibb and stops water in the hoses from being pulled back into the water supply.

Plan out your system on a piece of paper to determine how much hose you need. Measure the length of each hose section carefully. Consider the type of soil when spacing emitters: Install one every 12 inches in sandy soil, every 18 inches in loamy soil, and every 24 inches in clay-rich soil.

HOW LONG WILL IT TAKE?
Two to four hours

TOOLS
• Plastic-pipe cutter (or utility knife) • Screwdriver

MATERIALS
• Drip-irrigation system
• Backflow preventer • Hose adapter • Hose clamps

Anatomy of a drip-irrigation system

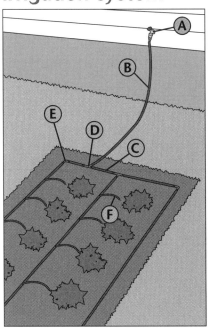

In the typical drip-irrigation system shown here, a hose bibb (A) fitted with a backflow preventer and a hose adapter is connected to the main line (B). A branch line (C) is added with a T-fitting (D) or an elbow (E); the end of the line is plugged with a cap. Each hose connection is secured with a hose clamp. A feeder tube (F) is connected to a hole in a branch line and fitted with an emitter.

1. Laying out the system

• Cut sections of hose to length with a plastic-pipe cutter (#1) or a utility knife and lay them loosely in place.

• Screw a backflow preventer onto the hose bibb, then screw a hose adapter onto the preventer.
• Slide a hose clamp onto the end of the main line, then fit the line onto the hose adapter and tighten the clamp with a screwdriver.

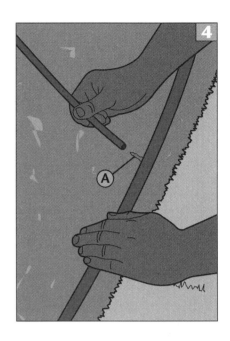

3. Punching holes for feeder lines

A drip-irrigation system usually includes a special feeder line hole-punching tool.
- Punch a hole in the hose at each desired location for a feeder line (#3).

4. Installing feeder lines

- Insert a feeder-line connector (A) into each punched hole and slide a feeder line onto the protruding end of it (#4).
- Install an emitter at the open end of each feeder line.
- Position each feeder line so the emitter lies just a few inches from the stalks of plants.

Note: *Soak the feeder lines in hot water to make them easier to fit onto the connectors.*

2. Connecting lines

- Connect the main line to a perpendicular branch line with a T-fitting and three hose clamps.
- Connect other lines to the branch line with a T-fitting or an elbow and hose clamps (#2).

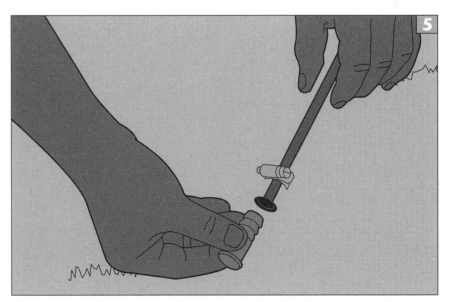

5. Capping the lines

- Flush the system by turning on the water for a few minutes.
- Turn off the water, then plug the end of each line with a cap (#5) and secure the cap with a hose clamp.

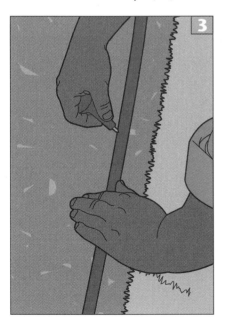

Chapter 2
ELECTRICAL & HEATING

Many homeowners consider their electrical and heating systems to be complicated and hazardous to work on. But in fact, household wiring relies on standard practices and equipment that make most electrical jobs straightforward, simple, and safe.

Whether you're replacing a light fixture, wiring a new switch, or installing a programmable thermostat, many electrical fixes involve little more than shutting off the power, disconnecting the old fixture or device, and attaching a replacement to the same wires.

Some projects in this chapter—from putting in an exhaust fan to adding an outdoor low-voltage lighting system—entail bringing electricity to a new part of your house or yard. Extending your electrical system in this way is not difficult. The job is rarely more complex than running new

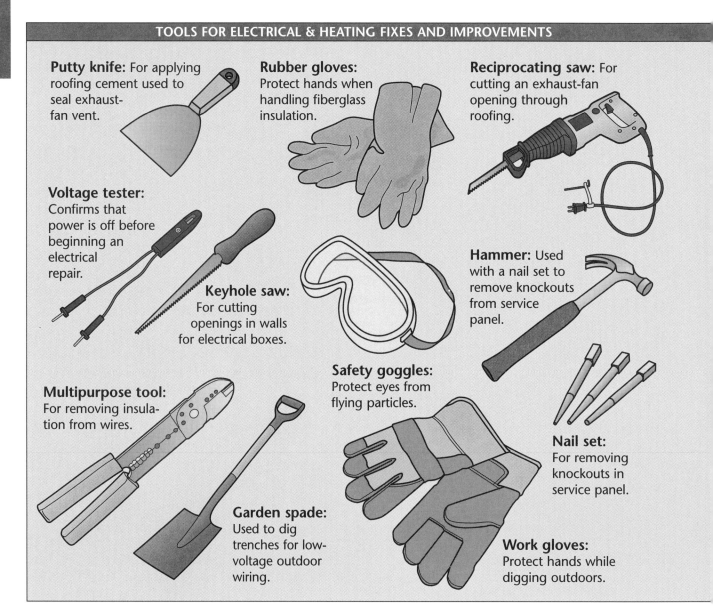

TOOLS FOR ELECTRICAL & HEATING FIXES AND IMPROVEMENTS

Putty knife: For applying roofing cement used to seal exhaust-fan vent.

Voltage tester: Confirms that power is off before beginning an electrical repair.

Multipurpose tool: For removing insulation from wires.

Rubber gloves: Protect hands when handling fiberglass insulation.

Keyhole saw: For cutting openings in walls for electrical boxes.

Garden spade: Used to dig trenches for low-voltage outdoor wiring.

Safety goggles: Protect eyes from flying particles.

Reciprocating saw: For cutting an exhaust-fan opening through roofing.

Hammer: Used with a nail set to remove knockouts from service panel.

Nail set: For removing knockouts in service panel.

Work gloves: Protect hands while digging outdoors.

cable, doing some basic carpentry work, and making simple electrical connections.

You can eliminate the danger from any electrical job by following a few simple precautions. Always shut off the power to the circuit you are working on. Then, use a voltage tester to confirm that the power is off. Leave a sign on your service panel so that no one accidentally turns the power back on while you are working. Never restore electricity to the circuit until you are finished working. Electrical installations are tightly controlled by both national and local codes. Be sure to check them before beginning an electrical job.

Two of the most effective "fixes" you can make to your heating system are to keep the heat in and block out the cold. Insulating an attic and sealing air leaks are easy projects and both will help lower your energy bills.

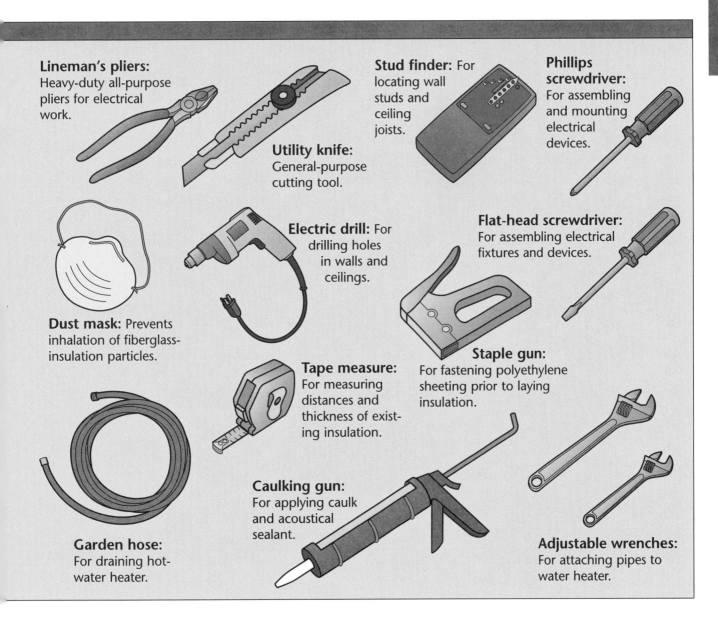

Lineman's pliers: Heavy-duty all-purpose pliers for electrical work.

Utility knife: General-purpose cutting tool.

Stud finder: For locating wall studs and ceiling joists.

Phillips screwdriver: For assembling and mounting electrical devices.

Dust mask: Prevents inhalation of fiberglass-insulation particles.

Electric drill: For drilling holes in walls and ceilings.

Flat-head screwdriver: For assembling electrical fixtures and devices.

Tape measure: For measuring distances and thickness of existing insulation.

Staple gun: For fastening polyethylene sheeting prior to laying insulation.

Garden hose: For draining hot-water heater.

Caulking gun: For applying caulk and acoustical sealant.

Adjustable wrenches: For attaching pipes to water heater.

HANGING A FLUORESCENT LIGHT FIXTURE

Fluorescent lighting has a lot going for it. It is energy-efficient and provides more uniform lighting than standard incandescent bulbs. And improvements to fluorescent tubes have gone a long way to changing the reputation of this lighting as cold and harsh.

Hanging a fluorescent fixture on an electrical box on an existing circuit isn't very complicated. You will need to drilling two mounting holes in the ceiling, add a crossbar to the box, and connect the fixture wires. Because the fixture can be quite heavy, the hardest part of the job is often lifting it into place. Have at least one helper on hand to help with the lifting; you may also want another set of eyes to help you position the fixture at the right angle.

Always use extreme caution when doing electrical work. Before you begin, shut off the breaker for the circuit you'll be working on and put a sign on the service panel warning others not to switch the breaker back on. To be doubly sure that the circuit is not live, test the wires at the box with a voltage tester.

SAFETY TIP *Never work on a live electrical circuit. Shut off power to the circuit at the service panel.*

HOW LONG WILL IT TAKE?

Less than two hours

TOOLS

• Screwdriver • Voltage tester
• Long-nose pliers • Electric drill
• Safety goggles

MATERIALS

• Fluorescent light fixture (and tubes) • Jumper wires • Wire caps • Crossbar • Threaded nipple

1. Shutting off the power

• At your home's service panel, turn off the breaker for the circuit to the light fixture (#1).

• Hang a sign on the service panel warning others not to turn the electricity back on.

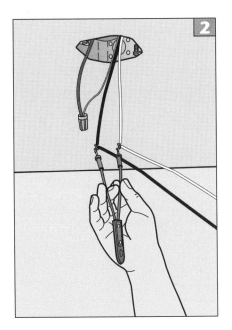

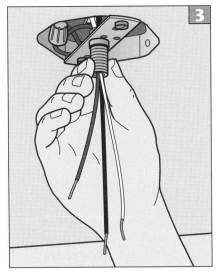

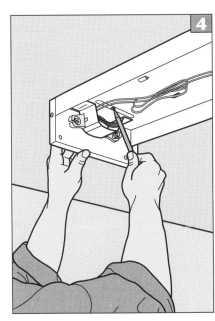

2. Testing for voltage

● Unscrew the existing fixture. Without touching any bare wires, remove the wire caps.

● Check that the power is off with a voltage tester. Touch one probe to the ends of the black wires and touch the other probe in turn to the ends of the white wires (#2) and to the electrical box. The tester light should not glow.

● Once you confirm the power is shut off, remove the fixture.

3. Adding jumpers and a crossbar

To ground the new fixture, you'll need three 6-inch green jumper wires, each with ¾ inch of insulation stripped from each end. Two jumpers are attached at this stage; keep the third on hand for later.

● Twist one end of two jumpers clockwise to the end of the cable's ground wire with long-nose pliers, then cap the wires. Connect one jumper to the grounding screw on the electrical box.

● Slide a crossbar over the black and white wires and the other jumper, then screw the crossbar to the electrical box.

● Slide a threaded nipple over the wires and screw it into the crossbar (#3).

4. Positioning the fixture

● Remove the center knockout on the back of the fixture with a screwdriver.

● Working with a helper, position the fixture on the ceiling, sliding the knockout over the nipple and pulling the wires through. Mark the fixture's mounting-hole locations with a pencil (#4), then take down the fixture.

5. Drilling the mounting holes

● Wearing safety goggles, drill mounting holes at the marks on the ceiling large enough for the toggle bolts supplied with the fixture (#5).

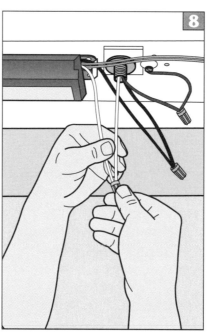

6. Preparing the toggle bolts

• Thread a washer onto each toggle bolt and push the bolts through the mounting holes from inside the fixture.

• From the back of the fixture, screw the toggles onto the bolts with just a few turns (#6).

7. Mounting the fixture

• Working with a helper, put the fixture back into place.

• Push the toggle bolts into the mounting holes, pinching the wings closed to fit them through the holes.

• Slide a washer over the nipple and secure the fixture to the electrical box with the lock nut supplied. Tighten the lock nut with an adjustable wrench.

• Tighten the toggle bolts with a screwdriver (#7).

8. Wiring the fixture

• Twist one end of the third jumper to the incoming ground wire and cap the wires. Connect the other end of the jumper to the grounding screw on the fixture.

• Twist together the incoming black wire and the fixture's black wire and cap the connection. Join the incoming white wire and the fixture's white wire in the same way (#8).

9. Finishing the job

• Attach the cover panel to the fixture.

• To install each fluorescent tube, line up the pins at the ends with the slots in the fixture's sockets, then slide the pins into place (#9). Twist the tube a quarter turn, locking it in place.

• Attach the diffuser cover to the fixture.

• Turn the power to the circuit back on at the service panel.

INSTALLING AN OUTDOOR LOW-VOLTAGE LIGHTING SYSTEM

A low-voltage lighting system can provide attractive outdoor lighting for much less effort and expense than extending a standard 120-volt circuit outside. Rather than being buried in a deep trench, for example, low-voltage cable can be laid just inches below ground. The cable is connected to a transformer, which is attached to a wall and plugged into an outdoor ground-fault circuit interrupter (GFCI) outlet. The transformer steps down household current from 120 volts to 12 volts.

Low-voltage lighting systems are available in kits, which typically include the transformer, low-voltage cable, a set of lights, and other features—such as a photoelectric cell that automatically turns the system on at dusk and off at daylight. If you are buying the components separately, make sure the transformer is rated rain-tight. Also check its rating in watts—usually between 100 and 300 watts. Your dealer will help you buy the appropriate transformer for the number of light fixtures you plan to install.

SAFETY TIP *When selecting the outlet that will power the system, bear in mind that the transformer should be at least 10 feet away from the edge of a pond, pool, or other water source.*

HOW LONG WILL IT TAKE?

More than four hours

TOOLS

• Tape measure • Garden edger (or spade) • Pick (or mattock) • Flat-head screwdriver • Wire cutters • Work gloves

MATERIALS

• Low-voltage lighting system • Electrical tape • Wood screw (or masonry screw and anchor shield) • Coax-cable clips • GFCI cover (with opening for power cord) • Padlock

1. Laying out the light fixtures

There are no hard and fast rules for laying out the light fixtures of an outdoor system. However, keep in mind that even spacing of the fixtures will provide the most uniform lighting.
● Assemble the fixtures following the manufacturer's instructions, then lay them on their side at the desired locations.
● Unroll the low-voltage cable, laying the end with the connectors close to the GFCI outlet. Leave enough slack at this end for connection of the cable to the transformer.
● Snake the cable along the ground from fixture to fixture, starting at the one closest to the outlet. Leave a loop of cable 2 feet long at each fixture to allow for connection (#1).

2. Digging the trench

The trench for a low-voltage cable can be as shallow as 6 inches.
● Wearing work gloves, dig a trench with a garden edger or spade, following the path of the

cable (#2). If you plan to reuse the sod, carefully cut and peel it up in strips, and set it aside.

• Lay the cable in the trench, but don't backfill yet. You need to wire and plant the fixtures first (Step 3 to Step 4).

3. Wiring the fixtures

Connect the low-voltage cable to the light fixtures following the manufacturer's instructions.

• For the model shown, fold the cable into a loop at each fixture and slide the fixture's pole (A) over the loop.

• Insert the looped end of the cable into the fixture's base as far as it will go (#3). This will press the cable up against the spiked terminals inside the fixture.

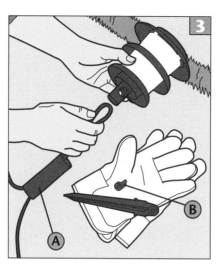

• Insert the fixture's cam (B) into the base so the triangle on the cam points downward. With a flat-head screwdriver, turn the cam until the arrow on it points down-ward. This will force the cable against the terminals, which will pierce the insulation and make the electrical connection between the cable and the fixture.

• Slide the pole into position over the fixture's base.

• Cut off excess cable at the end of the run. Wrap each wire with electrical tape and slip the end of the cable into the last fixture.

4. Planting the fixtures

• At the first fixture, gently tug on the cable at the bottom of the pole, removing any slack.

• Slip the fixture's stake into the pole between the lengths of looped cable. This will anchor the stake to the fixture and lock the cable in place.

• Holding the fixture upright at its desired location with one hand, use your other hand to push the stake straight into the ground up to the bottom of the pole (#4). Don't push down on the lamp; you may damage it.

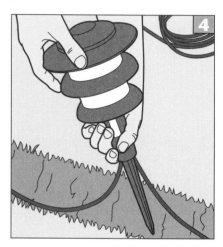

• If the ground is too hard to drive in the stake or the stake hits an obstruction, use a pick or mat-tock to dig an 8-inch-deep hole at the desired location. Place the stake in the hole and repack soil around it so it stands upright.

• Plant the remaining fixtures the same way.

5. Burying the cable

• Once all the fixtures are planted in place, backfill the trench with the soil removed (#5) and cover the soil with the sod set aside.

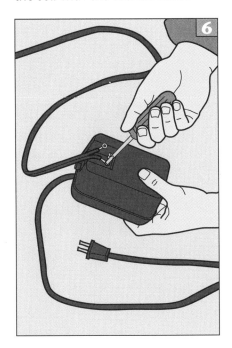

6. Wiring the transformer

Most transformers for outdoor lighting systems come with two screw terminals for connection to the cable.

• Remove the terminal screws with a flat-head screwdriver.

• Align one of the ring connectors at the end of the cable with a terminal screw hole, then tighten the screw back into place.

• Fasten the second connector the same way (#6).

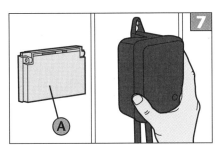

7. Mounting the transformer

Choose a location for the transformer that is close to an outdoor GFCI outlet (A). If your transformer has a photoelectric cell, pick a spot that is exposed to natural light so that the fixtures will go off automatically in daylight.

• Drive a screw partway into the wall at the transformer location. In wood siding, use a wood screw; in masonry, use a masonry screw and an anchor shield.

• Hook the transformer onto the screw (#7), then tighten the screw all the way.

• Attach the cable below the transformer to the wall with coax-cable clips.

8. Attaching a GFCI cover

Because the transformer will be plugged into the GFCI outlet on an ongoing basis, the plug needs to be protected from the weather. You can replace the standard trap-door cover on the outlet with a special plastic cover that has an opening for the power cord. The model shown can be padlocked

to prevent tampering.

• Undo the retaining screws that secure the standard cover to the GFCI outlet.

• Remove the cover and screw on the new one (#8).

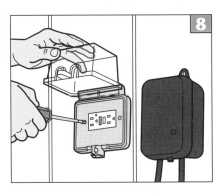

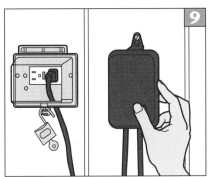

9. Testing the system

A transformer with a photoelectric cell can be tested during daylight.

• Plug the transformer into the GFCI outlet and close the cover.

• Cover the photoelectric cell with a finger for 10 to 15 seconds (#9). The lights should come on. If not, unplug the transformer and check the cable connections. Test the cell again.

• Once the system is working properly, padlock the outlet cover.

INSTALLING AN OUTDOOR SECURITY FLOODLIGHT

Outdoor floodlights are a boon to both safety and security. They illuminate doorways and walkways at night, and ward off would-be intruders. Most systems have a motion detector that activates the lights when motion is detected up to 50 feet away. Many also have photoelectric cells that automatically switch the lights on at dusk and off at dawn. Models with adjustable fixtures allow you to aim the lights in a specific direction. Bulbs, however, are usually not included. Ask your dealer to recommend bulbs that are compatible with the system you buy.

The following steps show how to extend an electrical circuit from an indoor outlet outdoors to the light fixture. It's most convenient to tap into an outlet on the interior of the same wall on which you plan to mount the fixture. Hooking up the fixture to an existing outdoor circuit is even simpler. Either way, add up all the electrical loads on the circuit to make sure it has enough capacity for the fixture. If there is no available circuit, have an electrician run a new circuit from your service panel to the fixture location.

SAFETY TIP *Never work on a live electrical circuit. Shut off power to the circuit at the service panel.*

HOW LONG WILL IT TAKE?

More than four hours

TOOLS

• Voltage tester • Flat-head screwdriver • Utility knife • Wire strippers (or multipurpose tool • Fish tape • Long-nose pliers • Keyhole saw • Electric drill

MATERIALS

• Floodlight (and bulbs) • NM cable • Electrical box • Electrical tape • Jumper wire • Wire caps • Wood screws

1. Shutting off power to the feed outlet

• Shut off the electricity to the circuit for the feed outlet at the service panel.
• To check that the power is off, insert the probes of a voltage tester into each pair of slots in the feed outlet (#1). If the tester lights up during either test, the circuit is live. Go back to the service panel, turn off power to the correct circuit, and test again.
• Remove the cover plate, then unscrew the outlet and pull it out of the electrical box. Confirm that the power is off by touching the tester probes to the terminal screws on each side of the outlet, then to any metal part of the box and each terminal screw in turn.

Note: *You can also perform these tests with a voltage sensor. Simply pass the tool over each wire connected to the outlet. The sensor will light up or beep if the circuit is live.*

2. Removing the electrical box

To make room for the electrical cable that will supply power to the new fixture, the electrical box housing the feed outlet must be temporarily removed. It's best to tap into an end-of the-run outlet—one that contains only one cable. In most cases, you will be able to extend the circuit from the existing box. If the outlet is middle-of-the-run (containing two or more cables), you will most likely have to replace the box with a deeper one to accommodate the new cable.

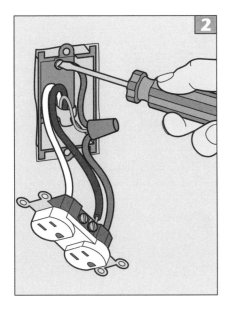

• Loosen the screws that secure the electrical box to the stud with a screwdriver (#2). Depending on the angle at which the screws were driven, you may need to use an offset screwdriver.
• Leaving the existing cable clamped to the box, pull the box out of its opening in the wall.

3. Cutting the fixture opening

For a fixture that will be recessed in a wall, as shown here, an octagonal electrical box is your best choice because it is easy to anchor in place. Boxes are usually fastened to a stud, but a flanged type can be attached directly to the wall sheathing. For a surface-mount, you can use a circular box.
• Hold the box at the desired fixture location and mark its outline on the wall.

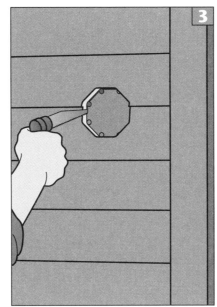

• For vinyl siding, as shown here, start the opening by cutting around the outline with a utility knife and removing the section of siding. Cut out the sheathing under the siding with a keyhole saw (#3). You may be able to begin the cut by plunging the tip of the blade through the sheathing. If not, drill a starter hole large enough to fit the blade.

4. Passing fish tape to the feed outlet

Getting electrical cable from the feed outlet to the new fixture may seem insurmountable, but a fish tape makes the job relatively easy.

It is flexible enough to snake through the tight spaces between walls and rigid enough to be fed upward or downward. Fishing cable is a two-step operation. Start by feeding the fish tape from the fixture opening to the feed outlet. Then, attach the new cable to the fish tape and pull it to the fixture opening (Step 5).
• Unreel the fish tape and pass it into the fixture opening (#4). Feed the end of the tape along the stud to which the feed-outlet box was fastened. Have a helper at the indoor outlet look for the tape and pull the end through the opening.

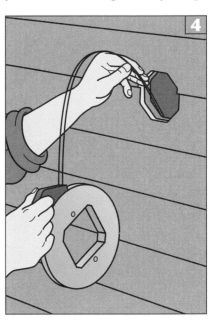

• If the fish tape encounters an obstruction between studs, such as a firestop or a brace, you will have to cut an opening in the interior wall at the obstruction and cut a notch in it to allow the cable to pass.

5. Fishing electrical cable to the fixture location

- Use a utility knife to strip off about 8 inches of sheathing from the end of the new cable.
- Cut the black and white wires back to the sheathing, leaving only the ground wire protruding from the sheathing.

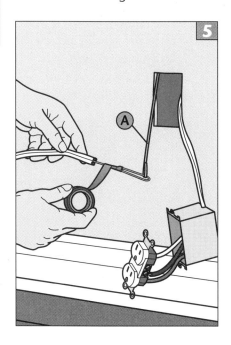

- Loop the end of the ground wire around the hook at the end of the fish tape (A).
- Secure the ground wire and the fish tape together with electrical tape (#5).
- At the fixture opening, reel the fish tape back in, pulling the new cable to the opening. Detach the cable ground wire from the fish tape and cut the wire flush with the cable sheathing.

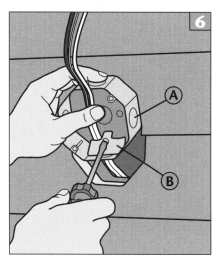

6. Securing the cable to the box

- Strip off another 8 inches of sheathing from the cable.
- With a screwdriver, pry out one of the removable knockouts (A) in the side of the electrical box.
- Loosen one of the internal clamps (B) in the box, then feed the cable through the knockout hole and behind the clamp until about 1 inch of the sheathed section is inside the box.
- With the clamp covering the sheathed section of cable, tighten the clamp with a screwdriver to secure the cable in place (#6).
- With wire strippers, strip about ¾ inch of insulation off the end of the cable's black and white wires.

7. Anchoring the fixture box

- Fit the fixture box into its opening in the wall so its front edge is flush with the siding.

- Fasten the box to a stud by driving two screws through holes in the side into the stud (#7). If the box is not at a stud, you can attach it to the wall sheathing by driving screws through flanges on the sides of the box.

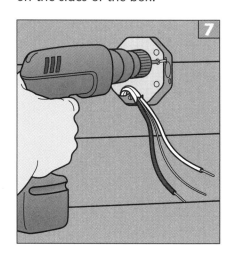

8. Wiring the fixture

- Twist together the end of the cable's white wire with the fixture's two white wires. Screw a wire cap onto the connection.

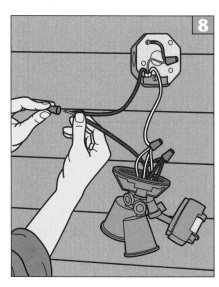

- Join the black wires of the fixture lights with the fixture sensor's red wire the same way.
- Fasten a short length of green jumper wire to the ground screw at the back of the fixture box and join the other end of the wire to the cable's ground wire with a wire cap.
- Finally, connect the cable's black wire to the fixture sensor's black wire (#8).

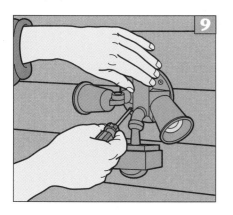

9. Mounting the fixture

- Carefully fold the wires into the fixture box, then position the fixture's mounting plate on the wall, lining up its screw holes with those on the box.
- Secure the fixture to the box with the screws supplied (#9).

10. Wiring the feed outlet

- Measure the depth of the feed-outlet electrical box. A standard 2½-inch-deep box may be too shallow to accept the new cable.

According to code, a standard box can have up to three cables entering it. If the new cable would put the box over the limit, replace the box with a deeper one: 3½ inches. If you are unsure, have an electrician check your connection.

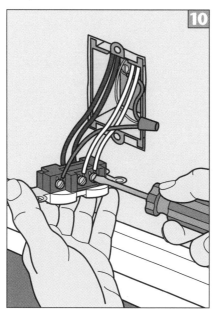

- Cut the new cable at the feed-outlet box so there is about 8 inches of slack, then secure the cable to the box and strip the wires as you did in Step 6. Gently push the box into the wall and screw it in place.
- With long-nose pliers, bend the end of the cable's black wire and white wire clockwise into a semi-circular hook.
- Loosen the unused screw terminals on the outlet. Loop the white wire clockwise around the silver terminal and the black wire clockwise around the brass terminal. Tighten the terminals (#10).

- Undo the wire cap joining the ground wires. Twist the ground wire from the new cable with the other ground wires and secure the connection with a wire cap.
- Fasten the outlet to the box and screw on the cover plate.

11. Adjusting the light fixture

- Screw a bulb into each fixture socket (#11).
- Restore power to the circuit at the service panel.
- If the fixtures are adjustable, loosen the screws that hold the fixtures in a fixed position, swivel the fixtures to direct the lights in the desired direction, then tighten the screws.

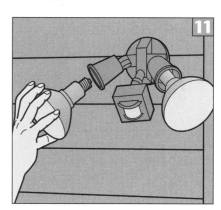

- Adjust the position of the motion detector.
- If your fixture has a photoelectric cell, test it by covering it with a finger. The lights should come on within about 10 seconds.
- If your fixture has a timer, set it following the manufacturer's directions.

WIRING 240-VOLT OUTLETS AND PLUGS

ELECTRICAL & HEATING

A 240-volt circuit is needed by most major appliances. Two basic types of outlets have 240-volt capacity: the dedicated 240-volt outlet, shown here, and the combination 120/240-volt outlet. The outlets require matching plugs—a plug with a different voltage and amperage rating will not fit the outlet. Always replace a 240-volt outlet or plug with a matching duplicate. Both the outlet and its electrical box must be properly grounded to protect against shock in the event of a short circuit.

A dedicated 240-volt outlet serves appliances with heavy-duty power requirements, such as a water heater or an air conditioner. A 120/240 30-amp outlet can service a clothes dryer with a heating element that operates on 240 volts and a motor and a timer that run on 120 volts. An electric range uses a 120/240 50-amp outlet: 240 volts for the burners and the oven, 120 volts for the clock, the lights, the timer, and other features.

SAFETY TIP *Never work on a live electrical circuit. Shut off power to the circuit at the service panel. Post a sign on the panel warning others not to turn the power back on.*

HOW LONG WILL IT TAKE?
Less than two hours

TOOLS
• Voltage tester • Screwdriver

MATERIALS
• 240-volt 30-amp outlet and plug • Electrical tape • Jumper wires • Wire caps

REMOVING A 240-VOLT OUTLET

1. Testing for voltage

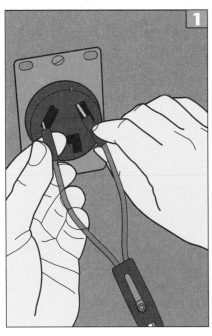

Confirm that power to the circuit is shut off with a voltage tester rated for at least 240 volts.
• Touching only the insulated handles, insert the probes of the voltage tester into two slots of the outlet (#1) so they contact metal parts inside. The tester light should not glow.
• Test for voltage the same way at each pair of slots in the outlet.

2. Disconnecting the outlet

Once you are certain that the power to the circuit is shut off, remove the outlet from the wall.
• Unscrew the mounting plate

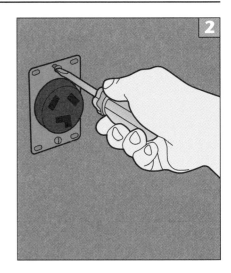

(#2), then carefully pull the outlet out of the electrical box.
• Disconnect the wires from the outlet. (Take the outlet with you to purchase a replacement.)

WIRING A 240-VOLT 30-AMP CIRCUIT

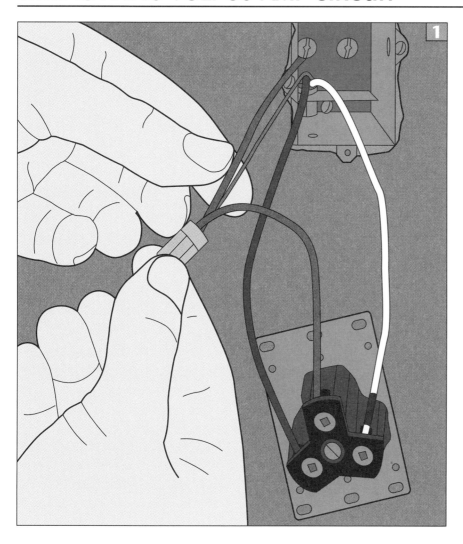

- Tuck the wires into the electrical box and screw the outlet's mounting plate in place.

2. Wiring the plug

Two-conductor cable is used to wire a 240-volt 30-amp plug. The hot wires are black and red (or white); the ground wire is green.
- Take the cover off the plug and loosen the terminal screws.
- Wrap the green ground wire clockwise around the ground terminal and tighten the screw.
- Connect the black and the red (or white) wires to the two other terminals and tighten the screws.
- Fit the cover back on the plug (#2) and tighten the screws.

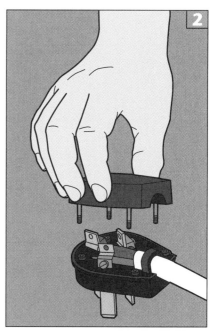

1. Connecting the receptacle

A dedicated 240-volt 30-amp outlet is usually wired with two-conductor cable. In this set-up, the white wire is not neutral and it should be labeled black (hot) with electrical tape.
- Fit the cable's black and white wires into the outlet's brass terminal slots and tighten the screws.

- Twist together the cable's ground wire and two green jumper wires, then screw a wire cap onto the connection.
- Connect one jumper to the grounding screw on the electrical box and the other jumper to the grounding terminal (marked "GR") on the outlet.
- Gently tug each ground wire to make sure the grounding connections are secure (#1).

WIRING A NEW CIRCUIT

ELECTRICAL & HEATING

Wiring a new circuit at your home's service panel is not a complicated job. It basically involves running an electrical cable from the end of the circuit to the service panel and connecting it to a new circuit breaker. The type of cable and breaker you will need depends on the electrical load of the new circuit. For example, a typical indoor light fixture or standard duplex outlet requires 14/2 (14-gauge two-conductor) NM (non-metallic) cable and a 15-amp single breaker. This type of cable contains a black (hot) wire, a white (neutral) wire, and a bare copper ground wire. Building codes require a circuit outdoors or indoors within 6 feet of a sink, a tub, or other plumbing fixture to be protected by a ground-fault circuit interrupter (GFCI).

Any electrical work you do should be approached with caution. Working at the service panel can be particularly dangerous, especially if you are unfamiliar with the way your electrical system works—if this is the case, have an electrician make the final connections. After shutting off the power at the service panel, verify that it is indeed shut off using a voltage tester.

HOW LONG WILL IT TAKE?

More than four hours

TOOLS

• Electric drill • Screwdriver
• Voltage tester • Nail set
• Hammer • Cable stripper
• Multipurpose tool

MATERIALS

• NM cable • Cable staples
• Box connector • Circuit breaker

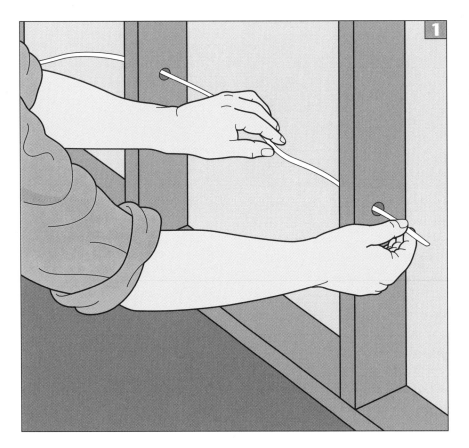

1. Running the cable

● Run electrical cable from the end of the new circuit to your home's service panel.
● Drill holes through the center of wall studs or ceiling joists and feed the cable through them (#1).
● When running the cable up or down studs or along joists, secure it with cable staples at 12-inch intervals.
● Complete the wiring at the end of the circuit before connecting the cable to the service panel.

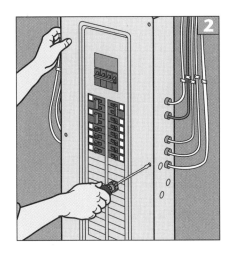

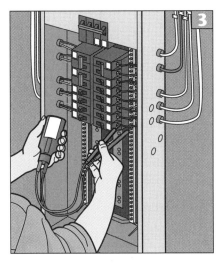

2. Removing the panel cover

● Shut off the power to each circuit at the service panel to avoid a surge when it is restored. Shut off the main disconnect breaker.

● With a long, rubber-handled screwdriver, remove the mounting screws from the cover of the service panel (#2), then lift off the cover. Don't touch anything inside the service panel until you verify that the electricity is shut off.

3. Checking for voltage

Use a voltage tester to confirm that the power is shut off.

● Holding both probes of the tester in one hand, touch one probe to the terminal screw on the lowest circuit breaker and the other probe to the closest ground/neutral bus bar (#3)— the vertical bar on the back of the panel to which the white (neutral) wire and the ground

wire of the circuit's cable are secured with clamping screws.

● Test the other circuit breakers in turn the same way. If the tester registers any indication of voltage, put the cover back on the panel and consult an electrician.

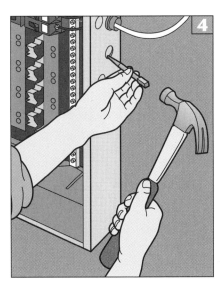

4. Removing a panel knockout

Remove one knockout from the side of the service panel to create

an opening for the new circuit's cable and remove another one from the panel cover to make room for the new circuit's breaker.

● Place the tip of a nail set on the edge of a knockout close to the available breaker slot and tap it inward with a hammer (#4). From inside the service panel, work the knockout free with pliers.

● Remove the appropriate knockout from the cover of the service panel the same way.

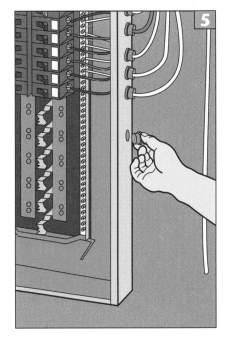

5. Installing a box connector

A box connector helps anchor the cable for the new circuit to the service panel.

● Snap the box connector into place at the knockout (#5).

ELECTRICAL & HEATING

6. Preparing the cable wires

- Slide the cable into the panel and pull through a long enough section to easily reach the breaker.
- Split the cable's sheathing with a cable stripper and trim 8 to 10 inches off the end.
- Strip about ¾ inch of insulation off the end of each wire with a multipurpose tool (#6).

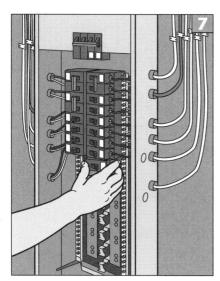

7. Inserting the breaker

- With the new breaker flipped to the OFF position, snap it into place in the service panel (#7).

8. Wiring the ground/neutral bus bar

- Loosen two terminal screws on the ground/neutral bus bar next to the new breaker.
- Insert the end of the cable's ground wire into one terminal and the end of the cable's white (neutral) wire into the other terminal, then tighten the screws (#8).
- Tug on each wire to make sure the connection is secure.

Note: *If your service panel has separate ground and neutral bus bars, follow the example of the other circuits to connect the ground wire to the ground bus bar and the white wire to the neutral bus bar.*

9. Wiring the breaker

- Loosen the terminal screw on the breaker with a screwdriver.
- Insert the end of the cable's black wire into the terminal and tighten the screw (#9). Tug on the wire to make sure the connection is secure.

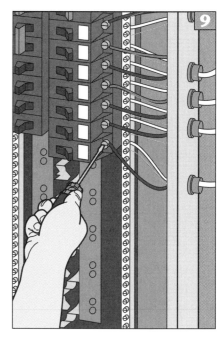

- Put the cover back on the service panel and screw it in place.
- Turn on the main disconnect breaker, then restore the power to all the circuits.

INSTALLING AN ELECTRICAL BOX

Installing an electrical box isn't complicated—there's not much more to it than cutting a hole in a wall or ceiling and running cable into it. Boxes are available in metal or plastic in a number of sizes and shapes. Boxes installed in walls for outlets and switches are usually rectangular, while light-fixture boxes are usually round. Be sure to install a box large enough for the number of cables that will run into the box. (If you're not sure which box is right for your project, consult the National Electrical Code.) Some boxes are designed to be attached to the side of a stud or joist, requiring you to find one with a stud finder. Others, like the one shown here, can be installed where there is no stud or joist.

Always use extreme caution when doing electrical work. Run cable from the end of the new circuit to the power source, then complete the wiring at the new box before connecting the circuit to the power source.

SAFETY TIP *Never work on a live electrical circuit. Shut off power to the circuit at the service panel. Post a sign on the panel warning others not to turn the power back on.*

HOW LONG WILL IT TAKE?

Less than two hours

TOOLS

- Keyhole saw · Cable stripper
- Utility knife · Screwdriver
- Multipurpose tool

MATERIALS

- Electrical box · NM cable

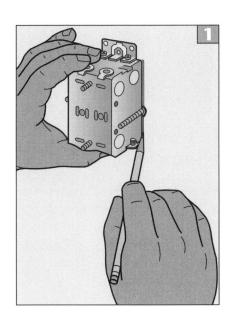

1. Outlining the box

- Hold the electrical box against the wall and draw an outline around it with a pencil (#1).

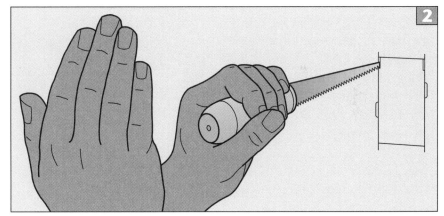

2. Starting the cut

Cut an opening in wallboard or plaster for the electrical box with a keyhole saw.
- Place the tip of the saw blade at a corner of the outline.
- Strike the handle of the saw several times with the heel of your hand to drive the blade through the wall (#2).

Note: *If you have trouble pushing the blade into the wall, drill holes with a spade bit inside the corners of the outline and use the saw to cut from hole to hole.*

ELECTRICAL & HEATING

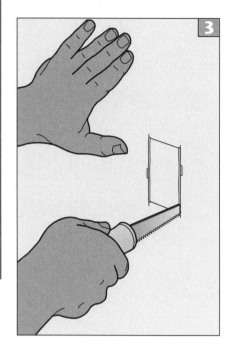

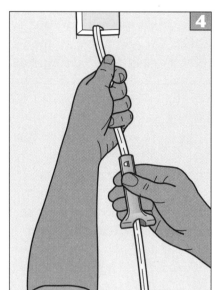

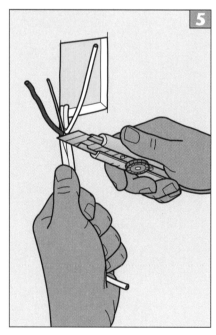

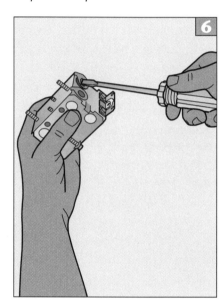

3. Cutting the opening

• Cut along the outline with the saw, bracing the wall with your free hand (#3).
• Remove the waste piece.
• Run NM (non-metallic) cable from the opening for the box to the power source.

Note: *To avoid breaking the edges of the opening, apply pressure to the saw only on the pull stroke.*

4. Stripping the cable

• Cut off the cable at the opening for the box, leaving about 12 inches of surplus for connections.
• Pass a cable stripper over the last 8 to 10 inches of the cable to split the sheathing (#4).

5. Exposing the wires

The wires inside the cable are color-coded. Typically, the hot wire is black, the neutral wire is white, and the ground wire is bare copper.

• Peel back the cable sheathing to expose the wires.
• Trim off the excess sheathing with a utility knife (#5).

SAFETY TIP *If you accidentally cut into a wire inside the cable, cut off the exposed wires and repeat Step 4 to Step 5.*

6. Removing a knockout

The walls of electrical boxes have removable pieces called knockouts that are punched out or bent back to provide access holes for cables. Open one knockout in the box for each cable it will hold.

• Push the tip of a screwdriver under the knockout and bend it back until it snaps off (#6).

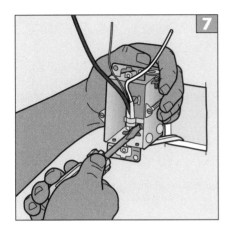

7. Clamping the cable

The type of clamp used to hold the cable to the box depends on the design of the box. Some boxes have no clamp but make use of cable connectors.

● Pull the wires through the knockout into the box along with $\frac{1}{2}$ inch of unstripped cable.

● For a box with a built-in clamp, tighten the clamp with a screwdriver so it holds the cable without cutting into the sheathing (#7).

● For a box with a cable connector, tighten the locknut onto the threaded connector.

8. Installing the box

Install a surface-mounted box, such as the one shown here, following the manufacturer's instructions.

● Slide the box into the opening until the mounting tabs are against the wall. If the opening is too small for the box, trim the edges with a utility knife.

● Screw the box to the wall (#8).

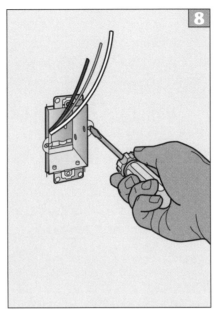

9. Stripping the wires

Use a multipurpose tool to strip about $\frac{1}{2}$ inch of insulation from the end of the black wire and the white wire. If you accidentally nick one wire, cut them both back and start again.

● Fit each wire into the slot on the tool that matches its gauge, then squeeze and turn the tool to cut through the insulation (#9).

● Keep the jaws of the tool closed and pull the insulation free off the end of the wire.

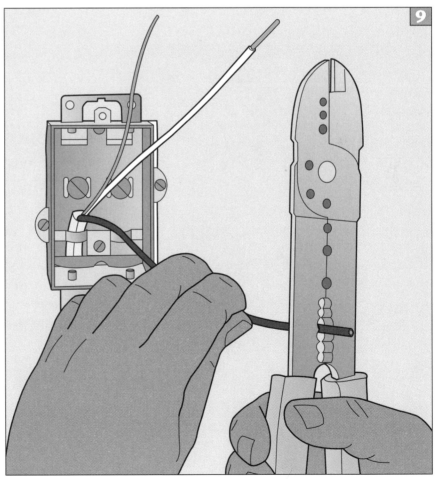

REPLACING A THREE-WAY SWITCH

Three-way switches, always installed in pairs, control one or more lights from two locations. Three-way switches differ from standard single-pole switches because they feature no On/Off markings and have three terminal screws: two "travelers" and a darker-colored "common."

Rewiring a three-way switch circuit is a specialized job best left to an electrician. Replacing a three-way switch, though, is easy. First, eliminate other possible causes for the problem—a faulty light bulb or a loose wire connection, for example.

The position of terminal screws on three-way switches can vary from manufacturer to manufacturer; some switches have an extra grounding screw. Take along the old switch with you when buying a new one.

SAFETY TIP *Never work on a live electrical circuit. Shut off power to the circuit at the service panel. Post a sign on the panel warning others not to turn the power back on.*

HOW LONG WILL IT TAKE?
Less than two hours

TOOLS
• Screwdriver • Voltage tester   • Wire cutters • Long-nose pliers

MATERIALS
• Three-way switch • Masking tape • Wire caps

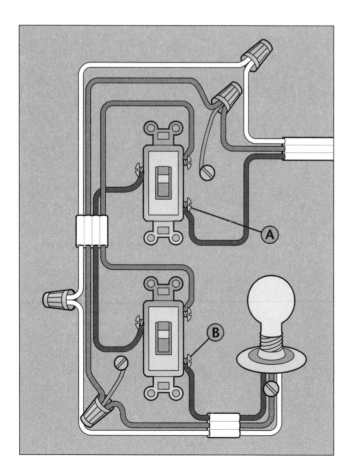

Anatomy of a three-way series

In this schematic of a basic three-way series, a light fixture is at the end of the circuit. A black wire feeding in from the power source is connected to the common terminal of the first switch (A). A black wire leading out to the light fixture is connected to the common terminal of the second switch (B). Black and red wires are connected to the traveler terminals of both switches. At each electrical box, the white (neutral) wires are capped together. The ground wires are capped together with a jumper that is connected to the grounding screw on the box.

Note: *Other wire configurations are possible. Tag the wires to identify them before removing the old switch so you can be sure to connect them to the correct terminals on the new switch.*

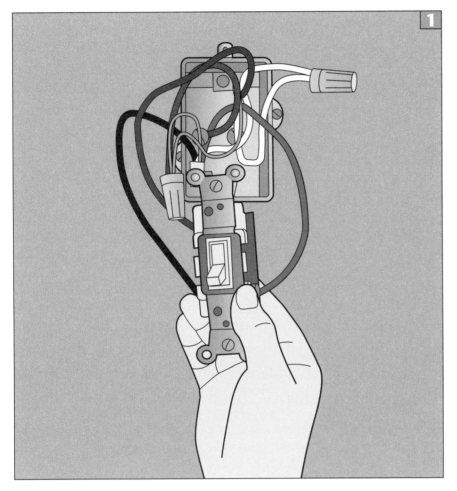

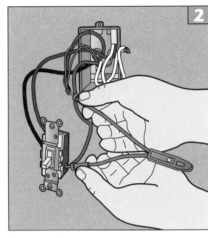

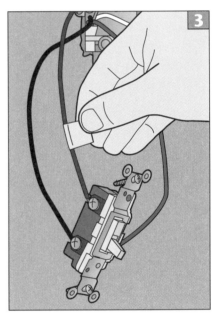

1. Freeing the switch from the box

● Shut off the power to the circuit at the service panel.
● Unscrew the cover plate and remove it from the switch.
● Remove the screws securing the switch to the electrical box.
● Without touching any bare wires, carefully pull the switch out of the box (#1) and unscrew the wire caps.

2. Testing for voltage

Use a voltage tester to verify that the circuit is dead.
● Holding the voltage tester in one hand, touch one probe to a terminal screw on the switch and touch the other probe in turn to the end of the ground wires (#2) and the white wires. Repeat the test with each other terminal screw on the switch. If the tester doesn't glow, the power is off and it is safe to continue.

3. Labeling the wires

Three wires connect the switch to the electrical box.
● Tag the black wire connected to the switch's darker-colored common terminal screw with masking tape for reference when you reconnect the wires (#3). (The two other wires connected to the switch are interchangeable.)

ELECTRICAL & HEATING

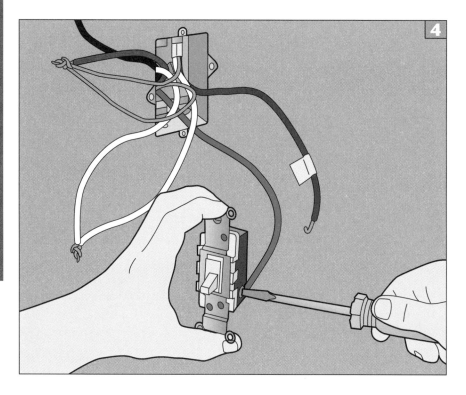

4. Removing the old switch

● Loosen the terminal screws on the switch (#4), then unhook the wires and remove the switch.

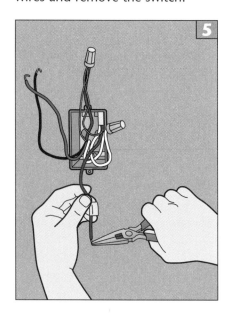

5. Checking wire connections

Check for loose or damaged wires.
● Check the white wires and the ground wires, then screw a wire cap onto each connection.
● Cut back a damaged wire, then strip off $\frac{1}{2}$ inch of insulation and form the end of the wire into a loop (#5).

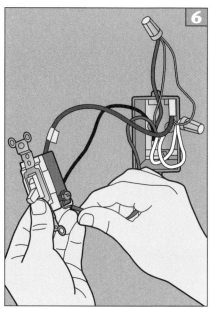

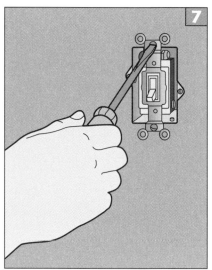

6. Connecting the new switch

● Hook the wire labeled with tape clockwise around the common terminal on the new switch and tighten the screw.
● Connect the other two wires to the traveler terminals on the switch (#6).

7. Screwing the switch to the box

● Gently fold the wires into the electrical box and screw in the switch (#7).
● Install the cover plate on the switch.
● Restore the power to the circuit at the service panel.

REPLACING A FOUR-WAY SWITCH

A four-way switch is installed between a pair of three-way switches to control a light fixture from three locations. This can be useful in large rooms or long hallways. Four- and three-way switches differ from a single-pole switch because they have no On/Off markings. A four-way switch has four terminal screws: two pairs of "traveler." Three-way switches have three terminal screws: two "traveler" and one darker-colored "common." Both four- and three-way switches may have a grounding screw.

Wiring a four-way switch circuit is job for an electrician, but replacing a four-way switch is a relatively simple procedure. However, before you do, eliminate other possibilities for the problem—a faulty light bulb or a loose wire connection, for example. Check all the switches in the series for loose or damaged wires.

SAFETY TIP *Never work on a live electrical circuit. Shut off power to the circuit at the service panel. Post a sign on the panel warning others not to turn the power back on.*

HOW LONG WILL IT TAKE?
Less than two hours

TOOLS
• Screwdriver • Voltage tester

MATERIALS
• Four-way switch • Masking tape • Jumper wire • Wire caps

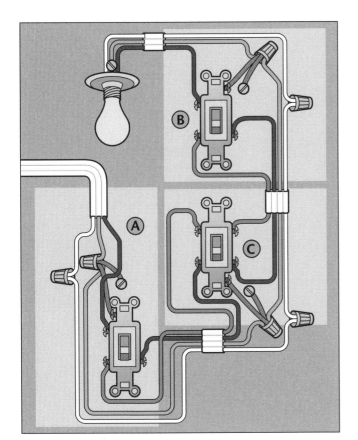

Anatomy of a four-way series

In this schematic of a four-way series, a light fixture is at the end of the circuit. The common terminal of the first three-way switch (A) is connected to a black wire that feeds in from the power source. The common terminal of the second three-way switch (B) is connected to a black wire that leads to the fixture. The traveler terminals on both three-way switches are connected to black and red wires. With the four-way switch (C), two black wires and two red wires are connected to paired traveler terminals. At each electrical box, the white (neutral) wires are capped together. The ground wires are capped together with a jumper and connected to the grounding screw on the box; if the switch has a grounding screw—as shown here—another jumper is connected to it.

Note: *Other wire configurations and color-codings are possible. Tag the wires to identify them before removing the old switch so you can be sure to connect them to the correct terminals on the new switch.*

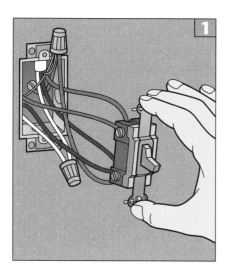

1. Freeing the switch from the box

• Shut off the power to the circuit at the service panel.
• Unscrew the cover plate from the switch.
• Remove the screws securing the switch to the electrical box.
• Without touching any bare wires, carefully pull the switch out of the box (#1).

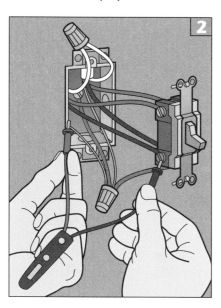

2. Testing for voltage

Use a voltage tester to verify that the circuit is dead.
• Touch one probe to a terminal screw on the switch and touch the other probe to the electrical box (#2)—if the box is plastic, touch the other probe to the bare-copper ground wire. Repeat the test with each terminal screw on the switch. If the light on the tester doesn't glow, the power is off and it is safe to continue.

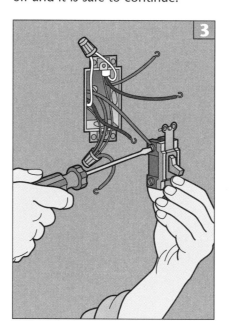

3. Removing the old switch

• Loosen the screws on the switch (#3), then unhook the wires and remove the switch.

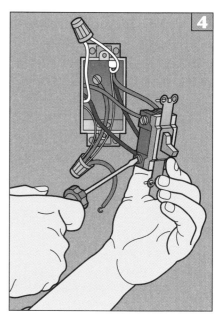

4. Connecting the new switch

• Hook the cables' red wires clockwise around one pair of traveler terminals on the switch and tighten the screws.
• Connect the cables' black wires to the switch's other pair of traveler terminals (#4) and the green ground wire to the grounding screw the same way—if the old switch did not have a ground screw, you will need to add a green jumper wire to the capped ground wires.
• Tuck the wires into the electrical box and screw the switch in place.
• Screw the cover plate onto the switch.
• Restore the power to the electrical circuit.

INSTALLING AN EXHAUST FAN

Without proper ventilation, steam from a bathtub or shower takes its toll: wallpaper and paint peels, wood and drywall decay, and tiles loosen. An exhaust fan eliminates these problems and helps rid the bathroom of odors.

Fans are rated according to the number of cubic feet of air per minute (CFM) they can remove and according to the number of sones, a measure of loudness. Choose a fan with a CFM rating slightly higher than the bathroom's square footage with a sone rating no higher than three.

In a typical bathroom set up, the exhaust fan is installed in the ceiling and connected to a vent in the roof or exterior wall with a flexible duct hose. Before working in the attic, lay plywood across the joists to support you and your tools. If the pitch of your roof is more than 4-in-12—a vertical rise of 4 inches over a horizontal distance of 12 inches—have a professional install the vent.

SAFETY TIP *Never work on a live electrical circuit. Shut off power to the circuit at the service panel. Post a sign on the panel warning others not to turn the power back on.*

HOW LONG WILL IT TAKE?

More than four hours

TOOLS

- Stud finder • Electric drill
- Keyhole saw • Screwdriver
- Reciprocating saw • Utility knife • Putty knife • Voltage tester • Wire strippers • Work gloves • Safety goggles

MATERIALS

- Exhaust fan and vent • Vent tailpiece extension • Wire
- Plywood • Wood blocking
- Sheet-metal screws • Duct tape • Roofing cement • Roofing nails • Duct hose • Hose clamps
- Electrical cable • Jumper wire

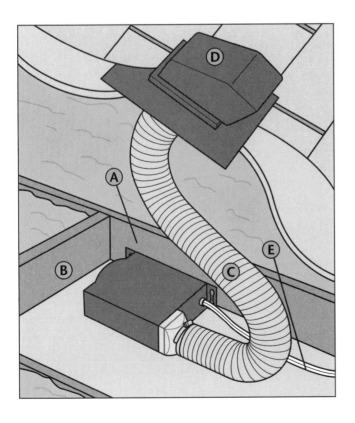

Anatomy of a fan installation

In the setup shown at left, a ceiling-mounted exhaust fan is screwed to a joist (A) in an opening in the ceiling. Blocking (B) of the same dimensions as the joists is added between the joists on each side of the fan to hold back insulation. Air drawn out of the bathroom passes through a flexible duct hose (C) and is expelled through a roof vent (D). A two-conductor electrical cable (E) connects the fan to a switch in the bathroom that is wired to a junction box on the same circuit as the bathroom light.

1. Positioning the fan

- In the bathroom, find a ceiling joist at the desired location for the fan with a stud finder.
- Drill a hole in the ceiling next to the joist, then push a length of wire up through the hole to mark the spot.

- In the attic, lay plywood over the joists to support you and your tools, then find the wire.
- Push away any insulation you find and install blocking between the joists on each side of the fan location to hold insulation back from the fan.
- Position the fan on the drilled hole with its support flange against the joist (#1) and draw its outline on the ceiling.

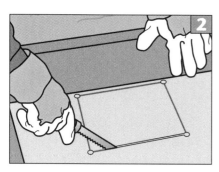

2. Cutting a hole in the ceiling

As you cut out the hole in the ceiling for the fan, have a helper in the bathroom support and catch the cutout.
- Drill a ¾-inch access hole at each corner of the outline.
- Cut along the outline with a keyhole saw (#2).

3. Mounting the unit

- Position the fan in the opening in the ceiling as suggested by the manufacturer (#3).
- Screw the fan to the ceiling joist.

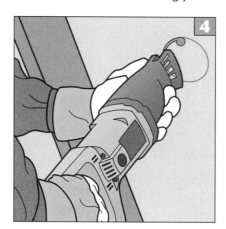

4. Cutting a hole for the roof vent

- Find a location for the roof vent between two rafters and trace around the duct hose to mark its outline at the spot.
- Drill a ¾-inch access hole just inside the outline.
- Cut along the outline with a reciprocating saw (#4).

5. Assembling the roof vent

If the tailpiece of the vent is too short to extend through the roof, attach an extension (A) to it.
- Fit the extension over the tailpiece of the vent and secure it with two sheet metal screws (#5).
- Wrap duct tape around the joint between the tailpiece and the extension .

Note: *Some vents are sold with screwless locking connectors that serve the same function as a tailpiece extension.*

6. Cutting the shingles

To provide a continuous weatherproof seal, the top and sides of the vent flange are overlapped by shingles; the bottom is seated on top of shingles.

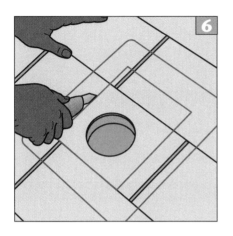

- Working on the roof, fit the tailpiece into the hole and outline the vent flange on the shingles.
- Remove the vent, then outline the inner edges of the vent flange, drawing a smaller square inside the first at a distance equal to the width of the flange.
- With a utility knife, cut along the top and sides of the inner outline (#6)—cut only exposed shingles, not shingles under them.
- Remove the cutoff pieces.

7. Mounting the vent

- Apply a layer of roofing cement to the underside of the vent flange with a putty knife.

- Peel back the tabs of shingles at the top and sides of the opening, then slide the vent into place (#7).
- Secure the vent flange to the roof with roofing nails and cover the heads with roofing cement.
- Apply roofing cement to the underside of the tabs at the top and sides of the vent and press them back into place.

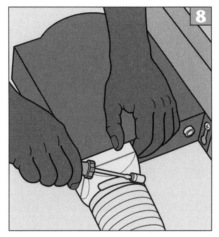

8. Connecting the duct hose

- In the attic, fit a flexible duct hose onto the fan outlet and secure it with a hose clamp (#8).
- Secure the other end of the duct hose to the roof vent's tailpiece or extension the same way.

9. Wiring the fan

The fan is usually wired to the circuit for the light fixture. Run electrical cable from the fan unit to a fan switch and from the fan switch to the power source—a junction box on the circuit.

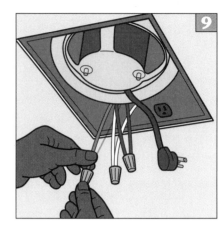

- At your home's service panel, turn off the power to the appropriate circuit. Hang a sign at the panel warning others not to turn the power back on.
- Take the cover off the junction box. Without touching any bare wire with your hands, double-check that the power is off with a voltage tester.
- Once you confirm the power is off, wire cable from the junction box to the switch and from it to the fan unit.
- In the attic, strip about 8 inches of sheathing off the cable and about $\frac{1}{2}$ inch of insulation off the black wire and the white wire. Feed the cable into the fan unit through the cable clamp and tighten the clamp.
- From below, twist together and cap the black wires, then the white wires. Connect a green jumper to the grounding screw on the fan unit, then twist it together with the bare-copper ground wire and cap the connection (#9).
- Tuck in the wires, plug in the fan, and install the grill.

INSTALLING A PROGRAMMABLE THERMOSTAT

A programmable thermostat allows you to preschedule heating and/or cooling cycles in your home, thereby reducing energy costs. The thermostat that you buy must be compatible with your system. The model shown here is designed for electrical baseboard heaters and operates on a 240-volt circuit. Other configurations and color-coding of wires are possible, so tag the wires to identify them before disconnecting the old thermostat so you can be sure to connect them to the right terminals on the new thermostat.

SAFETY TIP *Never work on a live electrical circuit. Shut off power to the circuit at the service panel. Post a sign on the panel warning others not to turn the power back on.*

HOW LONG WILL IT TAKE?
Less than two hours

TOOLS
• Screwdriver • Voltage tester
• Lineman's pliers

MATERIALS
• Programmable thermostat
• Wire caps

1. Taking off the cover plate

• Shut off the power to the circuit at the service panel.
• Take the cover plate off the thermostat (#1); if necessary, gently pry it off with a screwdriver.

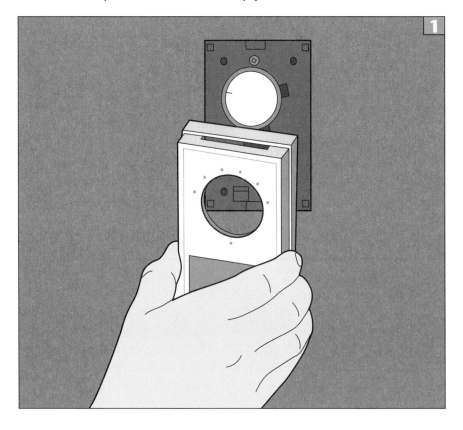

2. Removing the thermostat body

• Unscrew the body of the thermostat (#2) and pull it away from the wall.
• Unfold the wires and pull them out of the electrical box.

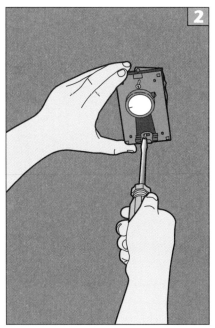

3. Disconnecting the wires

• Without touching any bare wires, remove the wire caps from the thermostat's lead wires (#3).

• Test for voltage by touching the probes of a voltage tester to the ends of the thermostat's lead wires. If the tester's light doesn't glow, the power is off and it is safe to continue.

• Disconnect the lead wires and remove the thermostat.

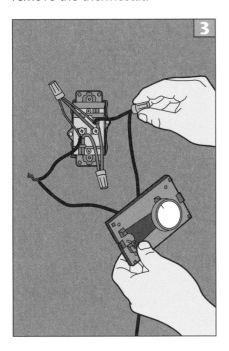

4. Connecting the new thermostat

• With lineman's pliers, twist the wire leads of the new thermostat together clockwise with the wires from the cables in the electrical box (#4).

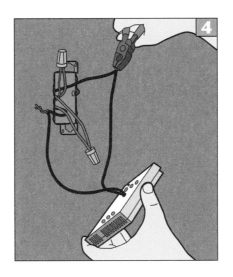

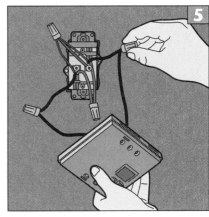

the wires together again and screw the cap back on.

5. Capping the wire connections

• Screw a wire cap snugly onto each wire connection (#5).

• Check that each connection is secure by gently tugging on the wires. If a connection is loose, remove the wire cap, then twist

6. Mounting the new thermostat

• Gently tuck the wires into the electrical box and screw the thermostat in place (#6).

• Install the cover plate on the thermostat.

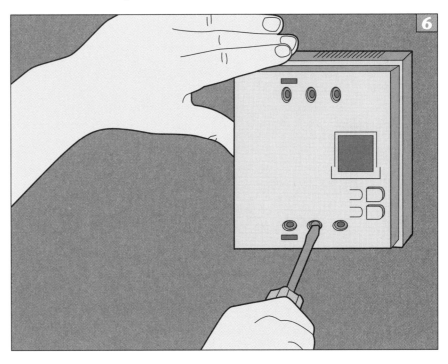

SERVICING AN ELECTRIC HOT-WATER HEATER

A ready supply of hot water is a convenience homeowners take for granted. That is, until there's a problem, such as no hot water, not enough hot water, water that isn't hot enough—or even water that is too hot.

Most hot-water tanks have upper and lower elements that heat the water. Each element is controlled by a thermostat and the upper element also has a high-limit temperature cutoff that prevents the water from becoming too hot.

The steps that follow show how to test and replace the cutoff and thermostats in an electric water heater. These repairs will solve many problems with the hot-water supply. Of course, in the event of a failure, the first thing to check for is a tripped circuit breaker or a blown fuse at the service panel or the unit disconnect switch.

HOW LONG WILL IT TAKE?
Two to four hours

TOOLS
• Rubber gloves • Screwdriver • Utility knife • Multitester

MATERIALS
• Masking tape • Thermostat • High-limit cutoff

SAFETY TIP *Never work on a water heater unless the power to the circuit has been shut off. Wear rubber gloves to protect your hands from fiberglass insulation.*

1. Removing the access panels

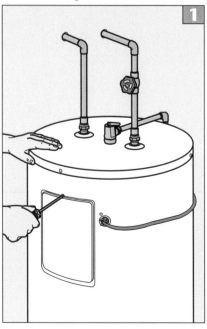

Remove the upper and lower access panels to reach the high-limit cutoff and the thermostats.
● Shut off the power to the water heater at the unit disconnect switch and the service panel.
● Loosen the screw at the top of each panel (#1), then slide the panel up and off the heater.

Note: *Some heaters have two screws securing each panel.*

2. Accessing the internal parts

Most water heaters have fiberglass insulation behind the access panels. You will need to move the insulation aside to access the high-limit cutoff and the thermostats.

● Wearing rubber gloves, peel back the insulation to expose the heating controls (#2). If the insulation has not been precut, use a utility knife to slice through it vertically. Take care not to nick the wiring behind the insulation.

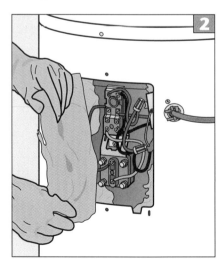

3. Verifying that power is shutoff

Before proceeding, check to make sure that power to the heater is in fact off. Use a multitester, an electrical diagnostic tool, to make this check at the high-limit temperature cutoff (A), which is where power enters the heater.

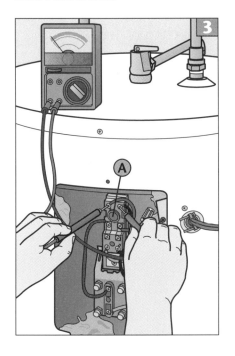

- Set the multitester to 250 volts AC. Insert the tester's black wire in the negative AC port of the tool and the red wire in the positive AC port. Touch a probe to each of the two screw terminals at the top of the cutoff (#3). The multitester should read 0 volts.
- Touch the metal interior tank wall with one probe and touch one of the screw terminals with the other. Repeat for the other screw terminal. Again, the tester

should read 0 volts during both tests. If the tester does not read 0 volts during any test, stop working and call an electrician.

4. Testing the cutoff

- If the cutoff's reset button (A) has popped out, push it in until it clicks. Restore power to the heater and wait four hours. If the lower and upper parts of the tank both feel warm, your problem may be solved. Turn off the power, repack the insulation, and screw on the access panels. Then, restore power again. If there is no change in the tank temperature, continue testing the cutoff.

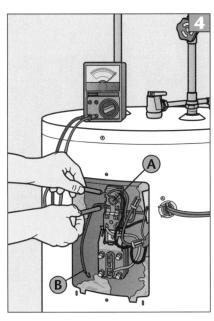

- Disconnect the lower end of one of the wires leading from the cutoff to the upper heating element by unscrewing the upper terminal screw at the element (B).

- Set a multitester to RX1 and touch the probes to the cutoff's two left terminals (#4). The needle should go to 0. Repeat for the two right terminals. Again, the needle should go to 0. If the tester does not go to 0 during either test, the cutoff is faulty—replace it (Step 8 and Step 11). If both readings are 0, the cutoff is okay—test the thermostats (Step 5 to Step 7).

5. Setting the upper thermostat dial

Start troubleshooting the thermostats by adjusting the temperature dial just below the upper thermostat.

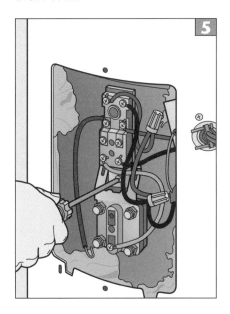

- Insert a screwdriver into the slot of the thermostat dial and turn it counterclockwise until you hear a click (#5). This will set the dial at its lowest temperature setting.
- If there is no click, the water

ELECTRICAL & HEATING

may be too hot. Turn the dial completely clockwise, then open a hot-water faucet and let the water run until it is only warm. Now, turn the dial counterclockwise to the lowest setting and you should hear a click.

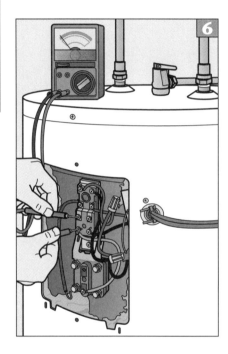

6. Testing the upper thermostat

• With the wire to the heating element still disconnected, set the multitester at RX1 and touch the probes to the two left terminals of the thermostat. The needle should not move. Then touch the two right terminals with the probes. The needle should go all the way to 0.
• With a screwdriver, turn the temperature dial clockwise to the highest setting until you hear a

click. Test the terminals again. This time the results should be reversed: The left terminals should register 0 (#6) and the needle remain still when you test the right terminals. If the thermostat fails any of the tests, it is faulty. Test the lower thermostat (Step 7) and replace the faulty thermostat (Step 9 to Step 10).

7. Testing the lower thermostat

• Disconnect the lower end of one wire leading from the lower thermostat to the lower heating element (A) by unscrewing the terminal screw at the element.

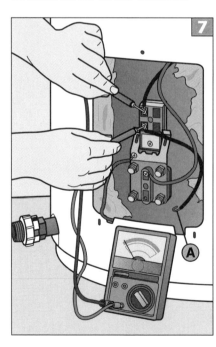

• Turn the dial of the lower thermostat to its lowest setting. Also adjust the upper thermostat dial to its lowest setting.

• Touch the multitester probes to the two terminals of the lower thermostat (#7). The needle should not move.
• Turn the lower thermostat dial to its highest setting and test with the probes again. The needle should go to 0. If the thermostat fails either test, it is faulty. Replace it (Step 9 to Step 10).

8. Removing the cutoff

You need to remove the cutoff to install a new one or to replace the upper thermostat.

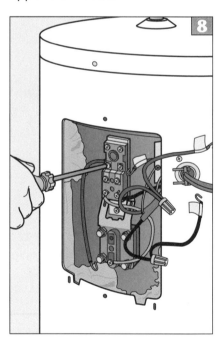

• Before removing the wires from the cutoff, identify each one with a strip of masking tape. This will help you reconnect the wires in the correct order.
• Loosen the terminal screws

with a screwdriver and carefully unhook the wires (#8).

● Depending on the model, you may need to remove metal straps securing the cutoff. Then, carefully pry back any tabs or spring clips holding the cutoff in place and gently pull it out.

9. Removing a thermostat

The thermostats are held in place by a slotted bracket.

● Identify and disconnect any remaining wires from the thermostat terminal screws.

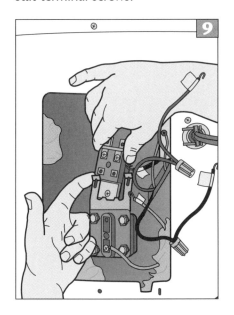

● Pull back one prong of the bracket with a finger and slide the thermostat up as far as it will go (#9). Pull back the other prong and slide the thermostat completely up and out of the bracket. If the bracket prong is too rigid, use a screwdriver to pry it back.

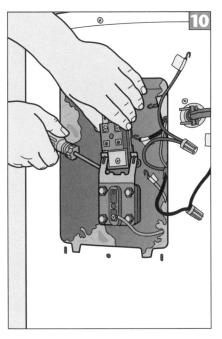

10. Installing a new thermostat

● Buy a new thermostat of the same make and model as the faulty one. Slide the thermostat down into its bracket, using a screwdriver as a lever if necessary (#10). Try not to bend the bracket prongs, but if you do, bend them back again so the thermostat sits snugly against the heater wall.

● Turn both thermostat dials to the desired temperature.

11. Reinstalling the cutoff

● If you are replacing the cutoff, buy a new one of the same make and model.

● With the reset button depressed, slide the cutoff into place above the upper thermostat

(#11). If necessary, replace the connecting metal straps.

● Reattach the wires to their terminal screws on the cutoff and the thermostats. Tighten them with a screwdriver.

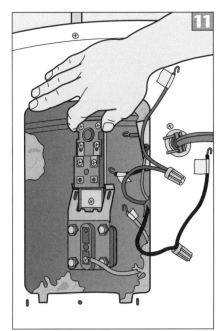

● Restore the power. The tank should feel warm near the upper and lower elements after four hours. Shut off the power to the heater, repack the insulation, put the access panels back on the heater, and restore the power.

REPLACING AN ELECTRIC HOT-WATER HEATER

ELECTRICAL & HEATING

Rust, corrosion, and routine wear and tear will eventually take their toll on your water heater. Along with some heavy lifting, replacing the water heater involves a few basic wiring and plumbing procedures.

Always use extreme caution when doing electrical work. Before you begin, shut off the breaker for the circuit you'll be working on and put a sign on the service panel warning others not to switch the breaker back on. To be doubly sure the circuit is not live, test the wires with a voltage tester.

Soldering plumbing fittings with a propane torch also requires precautions. Place a heat-resistant pad behind the work area. Keep a fire extinguisher handy and always turn off the torch before putting it down. Pipes get very hot when soldered, so wear work gloves to protect your hands. Finally, wearing safety goggles is essential when soldering above eye level.

SAFETY TIP *Never work on a water heater unless the power to the circuit has been shut off.*

HOW LONG WILL IT TAKE?

More than four hours

TOOLS

- Voltage tester • Screwdriver
- Garden hose • Bucket • Tape measure • Adjustable wrench
- Tube cutter • Wire fitting brush
- Propane torch (and striker)
- Work gloves • Safety goggles

MATERIALS

- Electric hot-water heater
- Copper pipe (and fittings)
- Plumber's abrasive sandcloth
- Heat-resistant pad • Soldering flux • Wire solder • Plumber's sealant tape

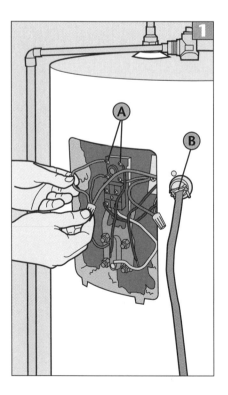

1. Disconnecting the wiring

- Shut off the power to the water heater at the unit disconnect switch and the service panel.
- Remove the cover of the water heater's junction box and push the insulation aside.
- Double check that the electrical circuit is dead by touching the probes of a voltage tester to the top pair of terminal screws (A).
- Uncap and disconnect the incoming cable's black, red, and ground wires (#1).
- Loosen the cable clamp (B) and pull the cable free.

2. Shutting off the water supply

- Turn the water heater's shutoff valve clockwise to close it (#2). If your water heater has no shutoff valve, turn off your home's main water shutoff valve.

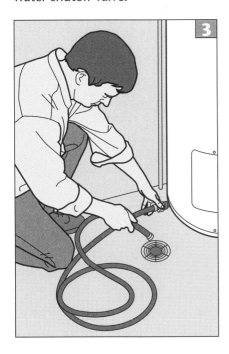

3. Draining the tank

Drain the tank into a nearby floor drain or by bucket. This may take as long as an hour or more.

- Screw a hose to the drain valve at the bottom of the tank.
- Holding the end of the hose over a floor drain, open the drain valve (#3). If you are draining the tank by bucket, shut off the valve to empty the bucket as needed.

Note: *If the drain valve clogs, unscrew the hose and probe the valve with an old screwdriver or a coat hanger. Be ready to shut the valve quickly once it is unclogged.*

4. Cutting the pipes

The easiest way to free the water heater is to cut the water intake and outlet pipes at the top 6 to 8 inches from the tank—and at least 3 inches from the water shutoff valve. You will also need to disconnect the discharge pipe (A) if it is connected to a drain or if you plan to reuse it with the new water heater.

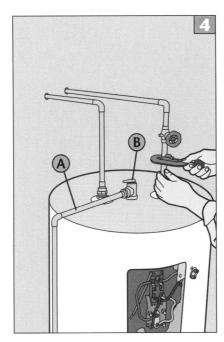

- Slide a tube cutter onto the water intake pipe and turn the adjustment knob until the cutting wheel begins to cut into the pipe (#4).
- Rotate the cutter around the pipe and tighten the cutting wheel again. Repeat until the cutter cuts through the pipe.
- Cut the water outlet pipe in the same way.

- To disconnect the discharge pipe, use a propane torch to desolder it from the adapter on the relief valve (B).

5. Removing the water heater

- Holding the water heater by the pipe stubs at the top, tilt it toward you and "walk" it out of the way by shifting its weight from side to side as you pull (#5).
- Move the new water heater into its approximate position the same way.

6. Preparing intake and outlet pipes

New intake and outlet pipe sections are each soldered to an adapter, then screwed into the new water heater.

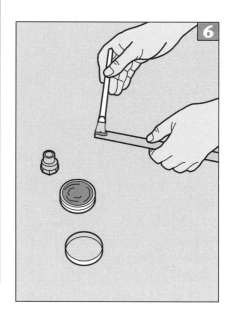

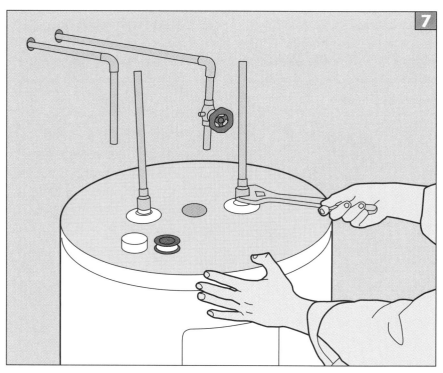

- Cut two 12-inch lengths of copper pipe with a tube cutter.
- With the pop-out reaming point on the tube cutter, ream the cut ends of the pipes, pushing the point as far in as it will go and rotating the tool several times to remove burrs.
- Rub one end of each pipe with plumber's abrasive sandcloth until it is shiny.
- Scour the inside of two adapters with a wire fitting brush.
- Brush a thin, even layer of flux onto the interior of each adapter and apply a strip of flux on the shiny end of each pipe (#6).
- Seat each pipe in turn in its adapter and heat the adapter with a propane torch until the flux begins to sizzle. Pull the flame away and touch the tip of a length of solder to the joint so it melts on contact and seeps in. Continue soldering until a bead forms around the joint.

7. Installing intake and outlet pipes

- Let the new intake and outlet pipes and adapters cool.
- Wrap the threads of the adapters with plumber's sealant tape and screw them into the intake and outlet openings at the top of the water heater.
- Tighten each adapter one-quarter to one-half turn with an adjustable wrench (#7).

8. Installing the relief valve

- Wrap the threads of the relief valve with plumber's sealant tape, then screw it into its opening at the top of the water heater by hand (#8).

- Tighten the relief valve one-quarter to one-half turn with an adjustable wrench, orienting it so installation of a discharge pipe will not be obstructed and will not block access to the water heater's junction box.

9. Trimming the pipes

● Trim the new lengths of intake and outlet pipes to about $\frac{1}{4}$ inch from the standing pipes (#9).

● Ream the end of the new and standing pipes with the pop-out reaming point on the tube cutter to remove burrs.

● Rub the end of the pipes with plumber's abrasive sandcloth until shiny and scour the interior of two fittings with a wire fitting brush.

● Apply a thin, even layer of flux to the inside of the fittings and to the end of the pipes, then shift the water heater into position to align the pipes and slide the fittings in place.

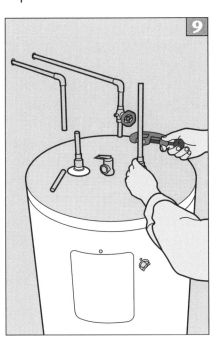

10. Soldering the fittings

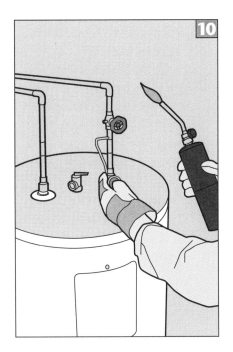

● With a propane torch, heat a fitting until the flux begins to sizzle, keeping the tip of the flame against one of the joints.

● Pull the flame away and touch solder to the joint at several places so it melts on contact (#10).

● As solder is drawn under the fitting, add more until a bead forms around the joint.

● Solder the other joints in the same way.

11. Completing the connections

Depending on the design of the water heater, the discharge pipe may be connected to the relief valve with an adapter or soldered directly to it.

● If an adapter is required, screw it onto the relief valve and tighten it with an adjustable wrench (#11).

● Prepare the adapter or relief valve and the discharge pipe for soldering, then assemble the pieces and solder them.

● Take the cover off the water heater's junction box and push aside the insulation, then feed in the electrical cable through the clamp and tighten the clamp.

● Connect the cable's black wire and the water heater's black wires and cap the connection. Join the cable's red wire and the water heater's red wires the same way.

● Attach the cable's ground wire to the grounding screw in the junction box.

● Put the cover back on the junction box, then turn on the water supply and restore the electricity.

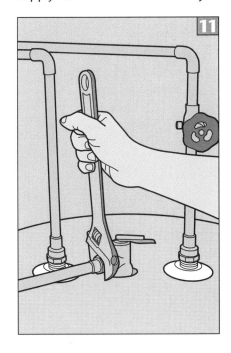

INSULATING AN ATTIC

The R-value of insulation indicates its resistance to heat flow. For cold climates, an R-value of 40 is recommended in the attic. This can be conveniently provided with a total of 12 inches of fiberglass insulation, available in batts that fit between joists.

Warm, moist air rising into the attic can lead to condensation on the roof framing and insulation. Insulation doesn't block all the flow of vapor, so in modern houses sheets of polyethylene (or aluminum) under the insulation serve as a vapor barrier. In the attic of an older house with no vapor barrier, seal openings into the attic and paint the ceiling below with vapor-retardant paint. Proper cross-ventilation in the attic will also help to reduce condensation—make sure that insulation doesn't obstruct air vents.

Fiberglass particles are harmful if inhaled and can cause skin irritation. Wear a dust mask, a long-sleeved shirt, long pants, work gloves, and safety goggles when handling it. After working, wash with soap and warm water. Wash clothes separately and rinse out the washing machine.

SAFETY TIP *Working in a cramped attic, you will inevitably bang your head on rafters or on nails protruding from the sheathing— wear a hard hat.*

HOW LONG WILL IT TAKE?

More than four hours

TOOLS

- Work light · Tape measure
- Caulking gun · Cordless drill
- Utility knife · Staple gun
- Safety goggles · Work gloves
- Dust mask · Hard hat

MATERIALS

- Plywood · Polyethylene sheeting · Fiberglass insulation · Foam baffles · Polystyrene insulation · Acoustical sealant · Duct tape · Staples · Wood screws and washers · Foam adhesive

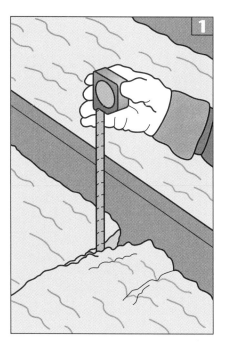

1. Checking existing insulation

Insulation is usually installed in two layers, the first filling the space between joists, the second running across the joists. Existing insulation can be left in place unless it is wet or badly matted.

● Lay plywood across the joists as a temporary work floor—never step between the joists as the ceiling below can break. Run work lights into the space.

● Measure the depth of the existing insulation (#1). Calculate the thickness of insulation required for each new layer to obtain a total insulation depth of 12 inches.

● Pull back a section of the insulation to check if there is a vapor barrier. If not, paint the ceiling below with alkyd paint or specially formulated vapor-retardant paint.

2. Sealing around plumbing stacks

Some plumbing stacks move up and down with variations in temperature. Polyethylene sheeting around the pipe must provide an airtight seal, but still allow the pipe to move.

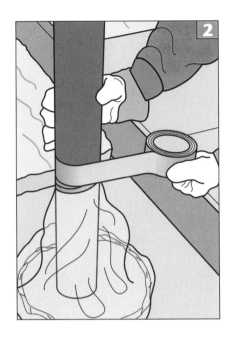

- Pull back the existing insulation around the stack.
- Cut a 2-foot-diameter circle of polyethylene sheeting and make a slit from the edge of the circle to the center.
- Apply a bead of acoustical sealant to the ceiling wallboard or vapor barrier around the pipe.
- Pull the piece of polyethylene over the pipe and press it into the sealant. Staple the polyethylene to the ceiling through the sealant.
- Seal the seam with a bead of acoustical sealant and press it closed. Then, cover the seam with duct tape.
- Tape the top of the polyethylene sleeve around the plumbing stack (#2), making sure that there is enough slack to allow the pipe to move.

3. Sealing around electrical boxes

- Pull back the existing insulation.
- Cut a piece of polyethylene large enough to cover the box.
- Lay a bead of acoustical sealant around the box and press the polyethylene into the sealant (#3).
- Staple the edges of the sheeting to the ceiling through the sealant. Be careful not to puncture the electrical wires.
- Caulk around any wires that pass through the top plate of the walls below.
- In an attic, recessed lights must be rated IC for contact with insulation and should also be airtight. Other models should be removed and the holes sealed or fitted with airtight models rated IC.

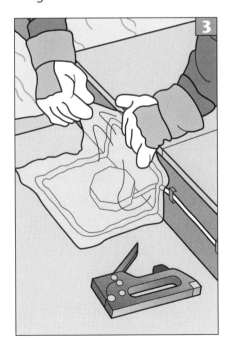

4. Fitting in foam baffles

Soffit vents located in the eaves allow outside air into the attic. When it is above freezing, the moving air helps control and remove moisture. In the winter, cold air helps prevent ice dams from developing along the eaves by keeping the snow pack frozen. Foam baffles between the rafters prevent the insulation from blocking the flow of air from these vents. They can be purchased in 15- and 23-inch widths to fit between the rafters.

- Fit the baffles between the rafters. Slide them down so the ends are about 1 inch from the vents under the eaves (#4).
- Fasten the baffles with $\frac{3}{4}$-inch wood screws fitted with washers. Don't use longer screws; they may puncture the roofing material.

5. Insulating the entrance hatch

A wallboard hatch should be weatherstripped and the gap between the casing and ceiling caulked. A latch will hold the hatch tightly against the weather-stripping. Insulate the hatch with two layers of 2-inch-thick extruded polystyrene insulation.

- With a utility knife and a straightedge, cut the insulation to fit the hatch.
- Apply a bead of foam adhesive to the surface of the hatch, keeping the adhesive 3 inches from the edges. Press the insulation into place on the hatch.
- Apply adhesive to the exposed side of the first piece of insulation and press the second piece into place (#5).

Note: *To insulate a folding stair-way, build a plywood box around it and attach fiberglass batts to the outside of the box.*

6. Laying the first layer

- Starting at one end of the attic, press the batts into place between the joists (#6). Cover the top plates of the exterior walls, but avoid blocking the soffit vents. Butt the ends of the batts together snugly so there are no gaps.
- Keep insulation away from any-thing that emits heat, such as chimneys or recessed light fixtures not rated for contact with insula-tion. Check your local building codes for the required space—about 3 inches is usually specified.

7. Cutting batts to fit

To cut batts to fit at the other end of the attic, lay them on a piece of plywood and compress the material with a straightedge, a board, or a piece of plywood. Slice through the insulation with a utility knife (#7). Leftover scraps can be used to fill in around cross-braces and other obstacles.

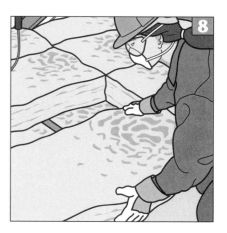

8. Installing the top layer

Placing the top layer of batts per-pendicular to the first layer helps prevent heat loss along the joists.
- Lay the batts (#8), starting in the corner farthest from the hatch and working around the attic so the area around the hatch is last to be insulated. Be sure to lay the batts tightly together.
- Cut the final batts to fit around the hatch.
- Seal any unused insulation in the original packaging material with duct tape.

SEALING AIR LEAKS

Air leaks result in drafts and higher energy bills. Structural damage can also occur as cold air enters and forces out warm, moist air. Rising warm air that escapes through the attic can lead to problems such as rotting of the roof sheathing, wet insulation and growth of mold, and deterioration of the siding.

Most air leaks are found at openings and joints between materials. Check window and door frames and electrical boxes for outlets, switches, and fixtures. The attic is another place to focus efforts: Seal around the plumbing stack. Fit the trapdoor with weatherstripping and insulation.

SAFETY TIP *Never work on a live electrical circuit. Shut off the power to the circuit at the service panel. Wear a dust mask to avoid inhaling harmful fiberglass-insulation particles.*

HOW LONG WILL IT TAKE?
More than four hours

TOOLS
• Screwdriver • Putty knife • Pry bar • Utility knife • Caulking gun • Staple gun • Stepladder • Work gloves • Dust mask

MATERIALS
• Gaskets • Weatherstripping • Spray foam insulation • Staples • Caulk • Polyethylene sheeting • Acoustical sealant • Pipe clamp • Polystyrene insulation

CHECKING FOR AIR LEAKS

Testing with smoke

To locate air leaks, wait for a very cold or windy day and use a simple draft detector.
• Light a stick of incense or a candle and hold it near the source of a potential air leak (#1). Smoke drawn toward or away from the source indicates air leakage.

Testing with plastic sheeting

A piece of thin plastic sheeting cut from a dry-cleaning bag is a good air-leak diagnostic material.
• Drape the plastic sheeting over a coat hanger and tape it in place, then pass the coat hanger near the source of a potential air leak (#2). If the plastic sheeting is drawn toward or away from the source, there is air leakage.

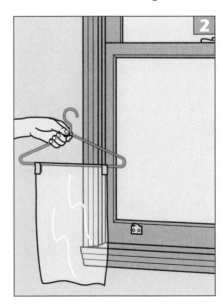

ELECTRICAL & HEATING

SEALING ELECTRICAL BOXES

Sealing outlets and switches

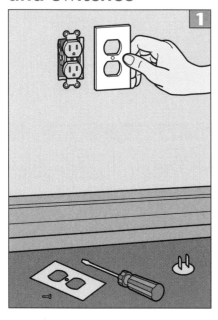

Specially-made gaskets are available to seal electrical boxes containing outlets and switches.
- Turn off power to the circuits for the room.
- Unscrew each cover plate, then install a gasket (#1).
- Screw the cover plates back into place, then restore the power.

Sealing ceiling fixtures

Seal electrical boxes for ceiling fixtures with weatherstripping.
- Turn off power to the circuit for the fixture.
- Remove the fixture's cover plate, then wedge weatherstripping into

place around the outside edge of the box (#2). Trim the weatherstripping with a utility knife.
- Reinstall the fixture's cover plate, then restore the power.

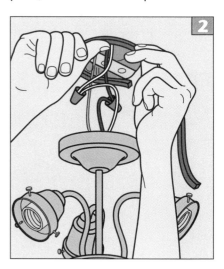

SEALING WINDOWS

1. Removing trim

Newer windows have specially designed weatherstripping that is easily replaced when it wears out.

Older windows may have gaps behind the trim that should be filled with insulation.
- Slip a putty knife behind the trim to protect the wall.
- Fit a pry bar between the blade of the putty knife and the trim, then lever the trim away from the wall (#1).
- Repeat at 18-inch intervals until the trim is free.

2. Applying insulation

- Spray foam insulation into gaps behind the trim (#2) without over-

filling them—the insulation expands considerably.
- Reinstall the trim, then seal the joint between the wall and the trim with paintable caulk. Smooth and shape the caulk by running a wet finger along it.

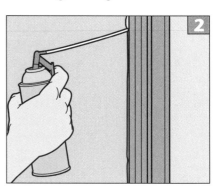

SEALING A PLUMBING STACK

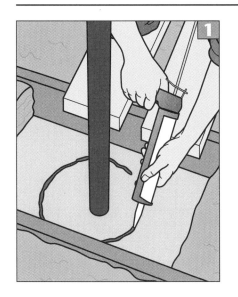

1. Applying sealant

Seal gaps around a plumbing stack where it enters the attic with polyethylene sheeting, a pipe clamp, and acoustical sealant. When working in the attic, place several boards across the joists to support your weight.

- Pull any insulation away from the plumbing stack.
- With a caulking gun, apply a circle of acoustical sealant around the plumbing stack (#1).

2. Installing sheeting

- Wrap a piece of polyethylene sheeting around the pipe, pushing the bottom edge into the sealant.
- Secure the bottom edge of the sheeting with a staple gun.
- Seal the top edge of the sheeting

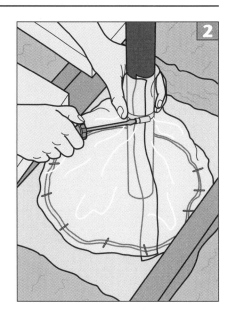

to the plumbing stack with a pipe clamp (#2).

- Put back any insulation removed.

SEALING AN ATTIC TRAPDOOR

1. Installing weatherstripping

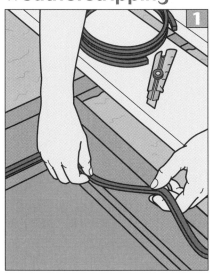

Seal an attic trapdoor with weatherstripping and insulate it with polystyrene insulation. When working in the attic, place several boards across the joists to support your weight.

- Line the upper edges of the trapdoor opening with weatherstripping (#1), trimming pieces to length with a utility knife.

2. Adding insulation

- Remove the trapdoor and cut a piece of polystyrene insulation to fit the back of it.
- With a caulking gun, apply

acoustical adhesive in a zigzag to the back of the trapdoor (#2).

- Push the insulation into place over the adhesive.
- Let the adhesive set, then reinstall the trapdoor.

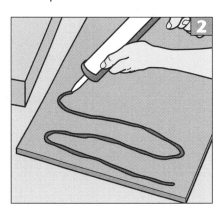

Chapter 3
FLOORS & WALLS

The emergence of user-friendly home-repair and renovation products has placed many household fixes and remodeling projects that were once the province of contractors within easy reach of the average homeowner. This chapter shows how straightforward it is to work on the flooring and walls of your home.

From hardwood floorboards to ceramic tiles, it's never been easier to lay down new flooring. Home supply centers carry a wide range of floor-

ing options. Coupled with the step-by-step instructions on the following pages, these materials will enable you install a new floor for a fraction of the cost a contractor would typically charge.

Few elements can change the character of a room as dramatically as its walls. Modern materials and techniques make it easy to transform a room, dividing it into sections by hanging wallboard panels or opening up a space by taking down a nonbearing wall. Or, you can make an

TOOLS FOR FLOORS & WALLS FIXES AND IMPROVEMENTS

Staple gun: For stapling building paper and polyethylene sheeting.

Tile cutter: For trimming ceramic tiles.

Flooring nailer: For laying wood flooring.

Pry bar: For removing trim and wedging floorboards into place.

Jamb saw: For trimming door trim flush with floor.

Circular saw: For cutting floorboards.

Hammer: For driving nails.

Carpenter's level: Used to check surfaces for level or plumb.

Electric drill: For making pilot holes and driving screws.

Chalk line: For marking straight guidelines.

Nail set: For sinking nails below surface.

ordinary room more attractive by covering one or more walls with tile or render it more useful by hanging shelves on the walls or soundproofing one of the walls.

Kitchen renovations can be one of the most costly remodeling projects a homeowner can undertake. Cabinets typically consume a huge slice of a renovation budget, but you can cut costs significantly by installing them yourself. With the steps shown in the following projects, it's simple.

You'll find below and on the pages that follow the tools professionals use to speed the work of fixing and improving floors and walls. Many of them, such as hammers, carpenter's levels, and taping knives, deserve a permanent place in your toolbox as you'll call on them again and again in your home-repair and renovation work. Other tools, such as the flooring nailer and tile cutter, which you'll use occasionally, can be rented at a tool rental agency.

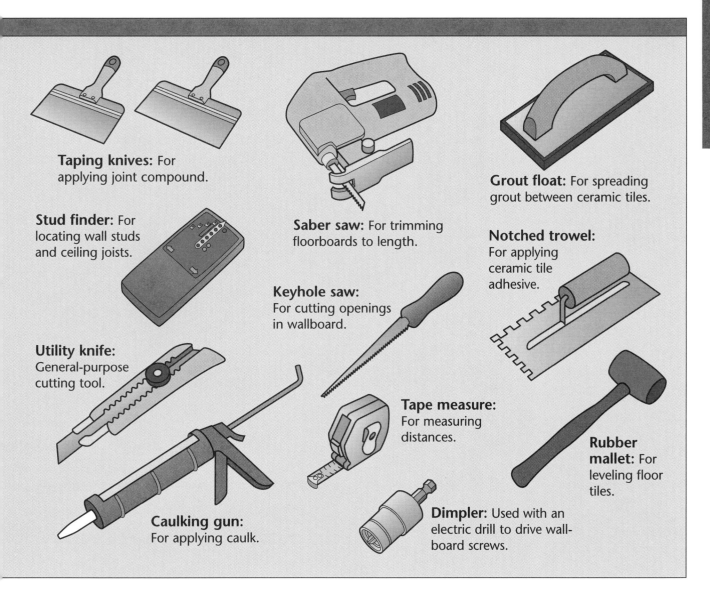

Taping knives: For applying joint compound.

Stud finder: For locating wall studs and ceiling joists.

Utility knife: General-purpose cutting tool.

Caulking gun: For applying caulk.

Saber saw: For trimming floorboards to length.

Keyhole saw: For cutting openings in wallboard.

Tape measure: For measuring distances.

Dimpler: Used with an electric drill to drive wallboard screws.

Grout float: For spreading grout between ceramic tiles.

Notched trowel: For applying ceramic tile adhesive.

Rubber mallet: For leveling floor tiles.

LAYING HARDWOOD FLOORING

Hardwood flooring is available in a number of wood species and grades. To save the work of sanding and finishing the flooring once it is in place, choose prefinished flooring.

Strip flooring is usually laid parallel to the length of the house, perpendicular to the joists. If your existing finish flooring is wood or ceramic, remove it and lay the wood flooring on the subfloor. If you discover that the subfloor is less than ¾ inch thick or is badly warped or cracked, you'll need to cover it with ⅝-inch plywood underlayment. If the existing flooring is resilient sheet or tile, it is best to install the wood flooring right over it—resilient flooring often contains asbestos and can be hazardous to remove. Wood flooring also can be laid on a concrete floor, but this requires special preparation to protect the flooring from moisture.

To estimate how much flooring to buy, calculate the total square footage of your room and add 10 percent for waste. The square footage a bundle of flooring will cover is generally indicated on the package.

HOW LONG WILL IT TAKE?

More than four hours

TOOLS

• Pry bar • Carpenter's level • Hammer • Jamb saw • Staple gun • Chalk line • Circular saw • Tape measure • Saber saw • Cordless drill • Utility knife • Nail set • Flooring nailer (with mallet) • Knee pads • Safety goggles

MATERIALS

• Strip flooring • Casing nails • Building paper • Staples • 2x4 • Reducer strip • Wood filler

1. Preparing the subfloor

• With a hammer or pry bar, remove the baseboard and shoe molding. (Protect the woodwork and wall with scrap wood.)
• Remove the existing flooring.
• Sink or remove popped nails.
• Gauge the slope of your floor by placing a level on top of a straight 6-foot-long 2x4 (#1). Check the floor in several spots. If the floor slopes more than ½ inch over a distance of 10 feet, call a professional to correct the problem.
• Check also for gaps under the 2x4. Dips or rises of ¼ inch or more should be sanded or filled with leveling compound.

2. Preparing the door casing

To allow flooring to slip under the door casing and doorstop, you will have to trim the molding to leave a gap at floor level.
• Take off the door.
• Place a strip of flooring upside down on a piece of building paper. Butt the flooring and paper flush against the doorstop and cut into it with a jamb saw.
• Reposition your guide flush against the casing, then trim it the same way (#2).
• Measure the door and the jamb. If the door is longer, it will need to be trimmed to clear the flooring.

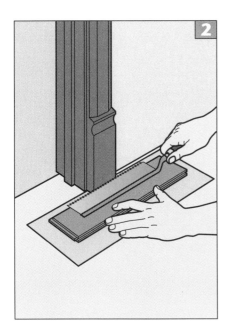

along the length of the room rather than across its width.

● Starting at a corner, unroll the first sheet. When you reach the opposite wall, trim the paper to fit with a utility knife.

● Fasten the paper to the subfloor with a staple gun, stapling at corners and every 3 feet along edges.

● Lay the remaining sheets the same way, overlapping them enough to allow you to staple through the two layers at the same time (#3).

3. Laying building paper

A layer of building paper between the subfloor and your new wood flooring makes for a snugger fit, preventing squeaks. Lay the paper

4. Marking a starter line

Start laying the flooring along the most visible wall—generally the one opposite the doorway. Since walls rarely are perfectly straight, you'll need to snap a guideline for your first row.

● At each end of your starting wall, mark the width of a flooring

strip—excluding its tongue—plus ¾ inch to allow for a gap along the wall.

● Stretch a chalk line between the marks and snap the line onto the building paper (#4).

5. Making a dry run

The grain and color of strip flooring will vary, even within the same bundle. A dry run allows you to distribute colors randomly and arrange boards so their ends will be staggered.

● Open up a couple of flooring packages and lay out the boards on the floor.

● Lay enough boards for six to eight rows, leaving gaps between the rows but butting the ends of the boards tightly (#5). Select boards to keep joints in adjacent rows offset by at least 6 inches.

FLOORS & WALLS

6. Nailing the first row

Since the grooved side of the first board doesn't butt against another board, it must be nailed through the face.

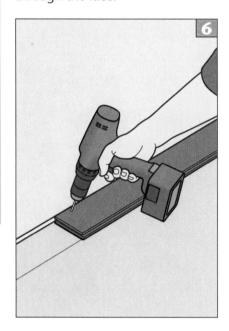

- Slide the boards out of the way of your starting place.
- Line up the edge of the first strip with the starter line and place a $\frac{1}{4}$-inch spacer between the end of the strip and the wall.
- Drill pilot holes every 8 inches along the strip $\frac{1}{4}$ inch from the grooved edge. Position the end holes $1\frac{1}{2}$ inches from the ends of the board (#6).
- Drive the nails so the heads are just above the board's surface, then sink them with a nail set.

SAFETY TIP *Wear safety goggles when drilling or nailing.*

7. Blind-nailing

To keep nails out of sight, flooring is fastened to the subfloor through the tongues. The nail heads of one board are hidden by the next board put into place.
- Drill pilot holes along the edge of the board, angling the bit at 45 degrees (#7). Align the nail holes with the nails in the board's face.
- Drive nails partway into the board, then sink them with a nail set.
- Continue the first row, fitting the groove in the end of the next board over the tongue of the one already installed.
- At the end of the row, trim the last piece to fit.

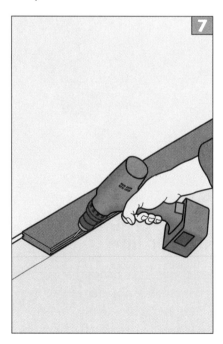

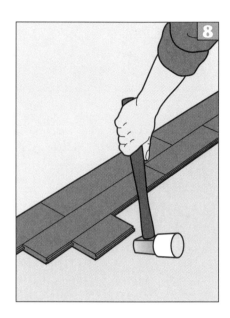

8. Installing the following rows

- To begin the second row, slide the grooved edge of a strip into place over the tongue of the first strip you laid. Place a shim between the end and the wall to maintain spacing.
- Fit a scrap piece of flooring against the edge of the strip, fitting the groove of the scrap over the tongue of the strip to be fastened. With the metal head of a mallet (provided with a power nailer), tap the scrap to snug the strip into place (#8). Drill pilot holes and blind-nail the strip as shown in Step 7.
- Continue to nail the board at 8-inch intervals, snugging it before driving each nail.

Note: *The scrap pieces cut off at the end of the last row can be used to start the next one.*

9. Power-nailing

After completing three or four rows, you'll be far enough from the wall to work with a flooring nailer. To use the nailer, position the notch over the tongue of the strip. Strike the nailer with the rubber head of the mallet provided with the nailer (#9). Drive in nails every 8 inches as with the first rows.

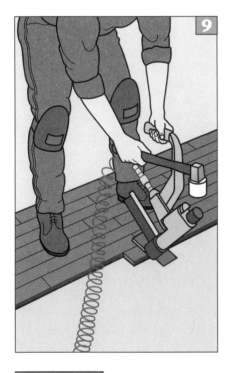

10. Installing the last row

When you reach the opposite wall, there's a good chance you'll have to trim the last board to fit.

• Select your strips for the last row. Measure along the wall at several locations to determine how much you'll need to trim off the strips—allow for a ¾-inch gap at the wall.

• Depending on the amount to be removed, trim the boards with a saber saw, a hand plane, or a belt sander.
• Before putting the strips in place, drive nails partway into the faces ¼ inch from the edges of the tongues.
• Using a pry bar with a piece of scrap wood against the wall for leverage, wedge each strip into place, making sure the groove fits tightly over the tongue of the previous strip. Holding the strip in place with the pry bar (#10), drive in the nails the rest of the way and set the heads.

11. Completing the final touches

A reducer strip is a sloped flooring strip that makes the transition in height between new flooring and flooring of the adjoining room.
• Measure a final flooring strip to fit around the door frame and into the gap cut in the molding (see Step 2). Cut the strip with a saber saw, then fit it into place and blind-nail it.
• Measure and cut the reducer strip to fit the door frame.
• Tap the reducer strip into place over the tongue of the last flooring strip. The rounded edge of the strip should lap onto the flooring of the adjoining room. Drill pilot holes and nail the strip every 6 inches through the face (#11).
• Sink the nails, then fill the holes with wood filler and touch up with varnish.
• Replace the baseboards and shoe molding.

CERAMIC FLOOR TILES

Ceramic tile is available glazed or unglazed. Some unglazed tiles must be sealed. Glazed tiles can be slippery when wet; if installing them in a kitchen or bathroom, consider a slip-resistant type. Be sure to get tiles intended for floors, not walls—floor tiles are generally thicker.

To provide a rigid base for tiles, it is best to remove old flooring and add an underlayment of ⅝-inch exterior-grade plywood to the subfloor. Some professional tilers prefer cement backerboard as underlayment because it is impervious to water. However, plywood is easier to work with and adequate for any installation except a shower floor. Make sure your adhesive is recommended for use over plywood. You can also lay tile directly on existing tiles if they're in good condition. Existing wood flooring can be left in place and covered with underlayment. It's best to simply cover resilient flooring with underlayment; if it contains asbestos, removing it can release harmful particles into the air. Tiles also can be laid directly on clean, flat concrete.

HOW LONG WILL IT TAKE?	TOOLS	MATERIALS
More than four hours	• Stud finder • Pry bar • Tape measure • Chalk line • Hammer • Notched trowel • Tile cutter • Tile nippers • Circular saw • Jamb saw • Rubber mallet • Spacer puller • Caulking gun • Grout sponge • Grout float • Artist's brush • China marker • Knee pads • Safety goggles • Rubber gloves	• Exterior-grade plywood • Ring-shank nails • Floor tiles • Plastic spacers • Threshold • Thinset adhesive • Grout • Grout sealer • Silicone caulk

1. Preparing the room

Since the new tiles may be thicker than the old flooring, you may need to trim door moldings to fit tiles underneath.

● Remove baseboards and shoe moulding with a pry bar. (Protect the walls and woodwork with wood pads).

● Remove existing flooring where necessary.

● Lay a piece of underlayment next to the door casing. Set a tile on top as a cutting guide. You can use a handsaw to trim the casing,

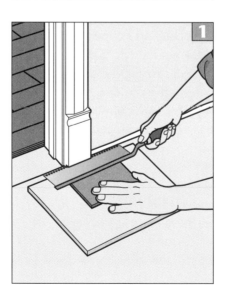

but a jamb saw (#1) makes the job easier.

2. Installing underlayment

● Use a stud finder to locate the joists under the subfloor. Mark the position of the joists on the subfloor with a chalk line.

● Measure and cut the plywood underlayment to cover the floor. Leave a ¼-inch gap along the walls and a ⅛-inch gap between sheets to allow for expansion and contraction. Stagger sheets so no joint falls directly over a seam in the subfloor. Position the edges of sheets along the chalk lines so they can be fastened to the joists.

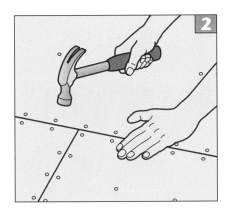

• Secure the plywood with 2¼-inch ring-shank flooring nails every 3 inches around the perimeter of each sheet and every 6 inches across it (#2). Drive the nail heads below the surface.

SAFETY TIP *Wear safety goggles when drilling or nailing.*

3. Establishing layout lines

There are two popular methods for laying out a room. One is to mark two perpendicular lines at the center of the room and work outward—the best choice for a room that is out of square, but it means cutting tiles along all four walls. If the room is square, you can start in a corner, as shown here—this way, you may need to cut tiles only along two walls.

• Lay out four tiles with plastic spacers between them along the two walls of the most conspicuous corner in the room.

• Using the tiles' outer edges as a guide, snap a chalk line along each wall. Set the tiles aside.

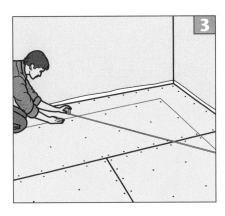

• To check that the lines are square, mark a point 3 feet from the intersection on one line and a point 4 feet from it on the other. Measure between the marks (#3). If the distance is 5 feet, the lines are square. Otherwise, adjust the lines as needed to square them.

4. Making a dry run

Once you have worked your way across the room, you're likely to need to cut tiles to fit. It's best to avoid having to cut tiles by more than half their width. Laying a dry run will allow you to make adjustments before you set the tiles.

• Starting at the layout corner, place two rows of tiles without adhesive along the walls (#4). Space the tiles with plastic spacers and place upright tiles along the walls to allow for expansion gaps.

• If you end up with room for less than half tiles at the opposite walls, shift the layout lines so that tiles will be cut equally on both sides of the room.

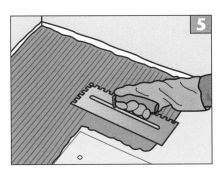

5. Applying adhesive

Tile trowels have a notched edge to allow you to "comb" the adhesive. The ridges created provide escape routes for air that can be trapped when the tiles are set.

• Mix thinset adhesive according to the manufacturer's directions.

• Starting at the corner, spread a bed of adhesive about ½-inch thick on a 3-foot area between the walls and the layout lines. Work with the smooth edge of the notched trowel, holding it at an angle of about 30 degrees. Try not to obscure the layout lines.

• Comb the adhesive with the notched side of the trowel (#5), keeping it at an angle of 45 to 75 degrees—whatever it takes to

FLOORS & WALLS

create ridges of uniform height. Comb in one direction only so the ridges are parallel. If you're having trouble forming the ridges, the adhesive may be too wet.

6. Laying the first tile

• Lay the first tile at the intersection of the layout lines (#6).
• Press lightly on the tile with a slight rocking motion to set it.
• Pick up the tile and check the back of it—adhesive should almost completely cover it. If not, the adhesive is too dry or the trowel notches are too small. If adhesive squeezes up around the tile, the trowel notches are too big. Once you've corrected the problem, reset the tile.

7. Tiling the floor

• Follow the layout lines to lay a row of tiles, inserting pairs of spacers between tiles (#7). When

you reach the opposite wall, leave a gap where a cut tile will go.
• Continue setting tiles in rows. As you work, wipe excess adhesive off the tiles with a damp sponge or cloth. Be careful not to disturb the tiles once they have been set.

Note: *If you let the tiles set overnight, you can walk on the floor to cut and set all the perimeter tiles. On a very small floor, you may have time to cut tiles for the ends of each row as you work.*

8. Bonding the tiles

Tapping the tiles after setting every three or four rows will improve the bond and settle any tile that may sit too high. Don't kneel directly on a tile.
• After laying every three or four rows, place a 2x4 across the tiles and tap lightly with a rubber mallet (#8). For the odd tile that sits too low, lift it up and spread on a little more adhesive, then reset it.

• Once the adhesive begins to set, remove the spacers with a spacer puller or an old screwdriver.

9. Marking cuts

Let the tiles set overnight before cutting the perimeter tiles.
• To mark a tile (A) for cutting, place it directly on top of the the last full tile of the row. Place another tile (B) on tile A, butting it against an upright spacer tile at the wall. Mark tile A for cutting along the edge of tile B using a china marker (#9).

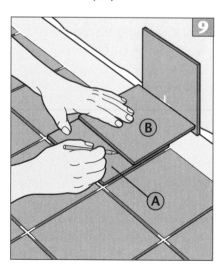

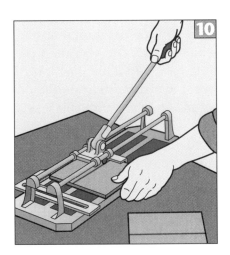

10. Making the cuts

If you have only a couple of tiles to cut, you can score them with a glass cutter and snap them by hand. For most jobs, though, you'll want a tile cutter.

• Place the tile face-up on the tile cutter. Align the marked cutting line with the scoring wheel and push or pull (depends on the tool model) the cutting wheel along the line (#10).

• Wearing safety goggles, snap the tile along the scored line by pressing down on the handle of the cutter.

11. Installing the threshold

A threshold provides the transition between the new flooring and the flooring of an adjacent room. Thresholds typically are wood or marble. A wood threshold can be cut to size; order a marble threshold to the exact size needed.

• If you're placing the threshold

in a doorway, first remove the doorstop (the vertical wood strip at the center of the door frame).

• Test-fit the threshold (#11).

• For a marble threshold, spread thinset adhesive onto the subfloor, then press the threshold firmly into place and rock it gently to set it in the adhesive. For a wood threshold, fit it in place and fasten it to the subfloor with screws.

• Trim and reinstall the doorstop.

12. Grouting

• Prepare cement-base grout according to the manufacturer's directions.

• Pour a cup of grout onto the surface of the tiles. Force the grout into the joints with a rubber grout float, holding it at an angle of 45 degrees and using a sweeping motion (#12).

• Once the joints have been packed, scrape off excess grout by dragging the float almost vertically across the tiles, working diagonally to the joints to avoid gouging them.

• Sponge grout off the surface of the tiles.

Note: *If using colored grout, mix all of the bags of dry ingredients together before adding water to be assured of a uniform color.*

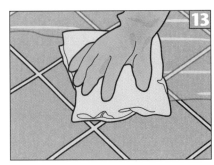

13. Finishing up

• Once the grout has dried for 15 to 30 minutes, a haze will appear on the surface of the tiles. Rub the tiles clean with a soft cloth (#13). You may have to repeat this two or three times to clean off all of the residue.

• Let the grout harden for a couple of days. If recommended by the grout manufacturer, apply grout sealer to the joints with an artist's brush.

• Reinstall the baseboards and shoe molding. Fill the gaps between the baseboards and the tiles with caulk of the same color as the tiles.

HANGING WALLBOARD

FLOORS & WALLS

Wallboard is available in 4x8, 4x10, and 4x12 sheets and the standard thickness for residential use is ½ inch. Water-resistant drywall, known as "greenboard," is recommended for humid areas such as bathrooms.

The long edges of wallboard sheets are tapered so that where they meet, compound can be applied to the joint without leaving a ridge. Where the untapered ends of sheets meet, it is very hard to achieve an invisible joint. On a long wall, it is best to choose sheets that reach to the ceiling and install them vertically to avoid any end joints. On a wall less than 12 feet long, you can install two sheets horizontally.

HOW LONG WILL IT TAKE?
More than four hours

TOOLS
• Wallboard carrier • Wallboard lifter • Chalk line • Utility knife • Cordless drill • Dimpler • Tin snips • Hammer • Keyhole saw • Edge plane • Mason's hawk • Pole sander • Sanding sponge • Wallboard T-square • Taping knives • Corner trowel • Safety goggles • Dust mask

MATERIALS
• Wallboard sheets • Colored chalk • Joint compound • Paper joint tape • Corner bead • Ring-shank nails • Wallboard screws • Painter's gap filler

1. Cutting a sheet

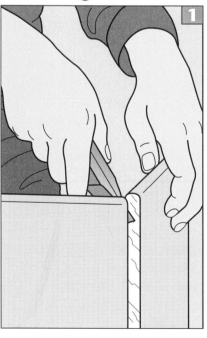

If the height or length of your wall doesn't match the length of a standard sheet, you will need to cut all your sheets to fit. You will also need to cut sheets to fit around obstacles such as windows and doors. Small adjustments can be made with an edge plane.
• With a wallboard T-square as a guide, score the front face of the wallboard with a utility knife.
• Gently snap the sheet along the scored line, bending the sheet toward you.
• With a utility knife, cut through the backing paper (#1).
• Plane the edges of the break with an edge plane if they appear rough or jagged.

2. Positioning the sheet

Wallboard sheets are designed to line up with standard joist spacings of 16 or 24 inches.

• Mark the location of the studs on the ceiling and floor.
• Position the sheet so that the edges fall at stud locations. Then snap chalk lines at the intermediate stud locations.
• Slip a wallboard lifter under the bottom of the sheet and step down on the pedal (#2) to raise the sheet snug against the ceiling. If the ceiling is uneven, slight gaps will be hidden with painter's gap filler. A gap of ¼ to ½ inch at the bottom of the wall will be hidden by the baseboard.
If you are installing sheets horizontally, install the top one first, then raise the lower one with the lifter so the two sheets fit snugly.

3. Fastening the sheet

A dimpler attachment used on an electric drill ensures that wallboard screws are set slightly below the surface without tearing the wallboard paper. Drive wallboard

screws into the studs every 12 inches (#3)—avoid angling the screws as this can damage the paper. Once you've driven four screws, you can release the lifter.

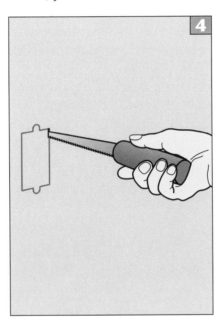

4. Fitting around electrical boxes

On walls with an electrical box, you will need to cut an opening before installing the sheet.
• Apply colored chalk to the edges of the electrical box.
• Align the sheet of wallboard with the studs and press it against the box.
• Remove the sheet, align a spare electrical box of the same size with the chalk marks, and trace a clear line with a pencil.
• With a keyhole saw, carefully cut out the hole (#4).

5. Installing corner bead

Metal corner bead protects wallboard edges at outside corners.
• If necessary, cut the corner bead to length with tin snips.
• Fasten the corner bead to the outer corner of the wallboard with ring-shank nails spaced about every 8 inches (#5).

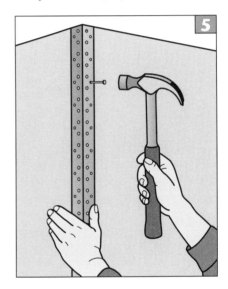

6. Covering fasteners

Screws in the middle of wallboard sheets need to be covered with joint compound; those at the edges of the sheets will be filled as the seams are taped.
• Rub off all the chalk lines.
• Drop a small amount of compound on a masonry hawk and smooth it with a taping knife.
• Apply a dab of compound to each screw head with a 4-inch taping knife. Scrape off the excess.

FLOORS & WALLS

● Apply two more coats (#6), letting each one dry overnight before applying the next.

7. Covering joints

Joints must be as smooth as possible so that no ridge is visible after you paper or paint.
● Smooth some of the compound on the masonry hawk.
● With a 4-inch taping knife spread compound over the joint (#7). Apply the compound sparingly and take your time.

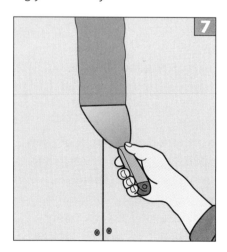

● Scrape off excess and apply joint tape (Step 8) before the compound starts to dry.

8. Taping the seams

● Press the end of a roll of joint tape into the seam with the 4-inch taping knife. Unwind the roll and continue pressing it into the joint, applying an even amount of pressure on each side of the joint (#8). Tear off the tape at the bottom of the joint.

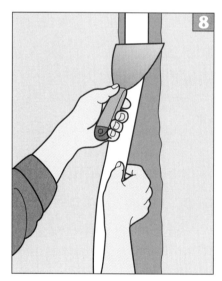

● Scrape off any compound that has squeezed out.
● Apply a sealing coat of compound to the tape and allow it to dry completely—until it is several shades lighter, which usually will take overnight.

Note: *If bubbles appear in the tape, let the compound dry, then cut out the flawed section and reapply compound and tape.*

9. Feathering the seams

Apply successive coats of compound with a wider knife, feathering the edges outward so that the seam is invisible.

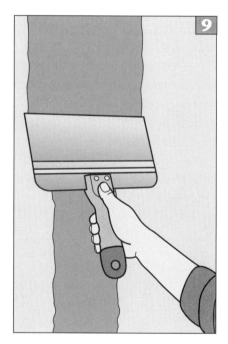

● With a 6-inch taping knife, apply a second coat of compound, scrape off the excess, and allow the coat to dry.
● Apply a third coat of compound with a 10-inch taping knife (#9), remove the excess, and allow the final coat to dry.

10. Finishing inside corners

● With a corner trowel, spread a layer of compound in the corner.
● While the compound is still damp, fold the joint tape in half

and press it into the corner (#10). Then, smooth the tape with a 4-inch taping knife.

● Scrape off any compound that has been squeezed out.

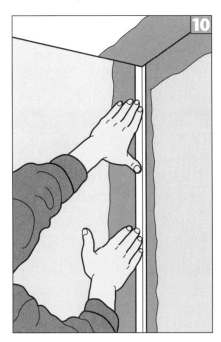

● Apply a layer of compound to each side of the corner with a 4-inch taping knife, scrape off the excess, and allow the coat to dry.
● Feather the joint using the 6- and 10-inch taping knives.

11. Finishing outside corners

● With the 4-inch taping knife, apply an even coat of compound on each side of the corner (#11).
● Allow this coat of compound to dry completely, then apply two more coats and feather with the 6- and 10-inch knives.

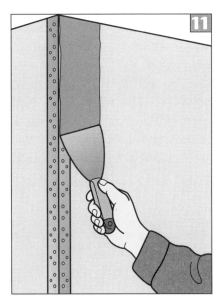

12. Sanding

Before sanding joints, make sure the compound is completely dry.
● With a sanding sponge, sand the joints lightly until they are smooth and flush with the wall.
● For areas out of reach, sand with a pole sander fitted with wallboard sandpaper (#12).

SAFETY TIP *Sanding joint compound is a messy job—wear a dust mask to avoid inhaling harmful dust and particles.*

INSTALLING KITCHEN CABINETS

FLOORS & WALLS

Modular kitchen cabinets are commonly made of plywood or particleboard and covered with plastic laminate or wood veneer. These can be combined with hardwood doors and drawer fronts. Before making your purchase, sketch a layout of your kitchen, including locations of doors, windows, plumbing, and appliances. Note all relevant dimensions and take the sketch with you to the store—your dealer can help you plan a layout. Once you have purchased the cabinets, they can be quickly assembled by driving screws through predrilled holes.

Countertops are ordered separately. Premolded laminate countertops are the simplest to install. They include a backsplash and a curved front edge, and can be cut to size by the dealer. Also provide your dealer with a template of your sink and its desired location so a hole can be cut for it.

HOW LONG WILL IT TAKE?
More than four hours

TOOLS
• Tape measure • Stud finder • Carpenter's level • Cordless drill • Spade bit • Hole saw • Utility knife • Quick-action clamps • Hammer • Nail set • Combination square • Circular saw • Compass • Belt sander • Wrench • Caulking gun • Stepladder • Safety goggles

MATERIALS
• Wall cabinets • Base cabinets • Countertop • Wood screws • Finishing nails • 1x3s or 1x4s • Shims • Filler strips • Molding • Kickplates • Silicone caulk • Wood filler

1. Marking the studs

• With a stud finder, locate and mark the position of the studs in the area where cabinets will be installed.
• With a carpenter's level, mark plumb pencil lines from ceiling to floor at each stud location.

• To position the top cabinets, measure up from the floor the height of the bottom cabinets plus 15 inches. At the mark, draw a level guideline (#1).

2. Fastening the ledgers

A ledger supports the wall cabinets during installation and helps ensure they are level.
• Cut 1x3s or 1x4s to the length of the wall cabinets.
• Holding the first length of ledger flush with the corner, align the top edge along the marked guideline. Fasten it with screws driven at the stud locations (#2).

• Fasten another ledger in the same way to the adjacent wall, butting it against the installed ledger.

SAFETY TIP *Wear safety goggles when drilling or hammering.*

3. Installing the top corner cabinet

Work with a helper to support and adjust the cabinets.

● Lift the corner cabinet into position, resting it on the ledgers and holding it flush against the walls.

● Hold a level against the front edge of the cabinet and plumb it in both directions (#3). Plumbing the cabinet may create gaps between the wall and the cabinet—fill them with shims slipped in along the stud lines.

● Measuring from the corner, mark the stud locations on the inside of the cabinet.

● Drive screws through the back of the cabinet and the hidden support rails into the shims and wall studs.

4. Adding adjacent wall cabinets

● Lift the adjacent wall cabinet into position, resting it on the ledger.

● Line up the cabinet face with that of the installed corner cabinet and clamp the cabinets together at the top and bottom with quick-action clamps.

● Plumb the other edge of the cabinet and fill any gap at the wall with shims at the stud locations.

● Fasten the cabinet to the corner cabinet with screws driven through upper and lower shelf holes in line with the hinge locations (#4).

● Fasten the cabinet to the wall studs.

● Install the remaining wall cabinets the same way. Then, remove the support ledgers.

5. Installing trim

● With a utility knife, score and snap off the shims flush with the top of the cabinets.

● Hide the joint between the back of the end cabinets and the wall with quarter-round molding.

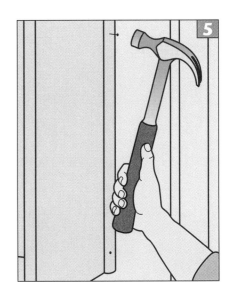

Paint the molding to match the cabinets and fasten it with finishing nails (#5). Sink the nails with a nail set, fill the nail holes with wood filler, and touch up the paint.

● Narrow gaps between the end of a row of cabinets and an end wall can be closed with filler strips ordered with the cabinets—cut the strips to size, wedge them in place, and fasten them with screws through the side of the last cabinet.

6. Leveling the corner base cabinet

The base cabinets are all leveled and fastened to each other before they are fastened to the wall.

● Position the corner cabinet and place a level along a front edge. Protect your floor with a cardboard sheet, then with a hammer and a wood block, drive a shim under the front of the side panel

FLOORS & WALLS

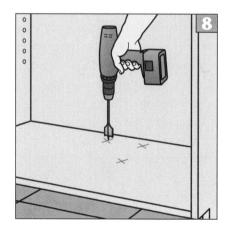

until the cabinet is level (#6). Level the cabinet in the other direction the same way.

- Plumb the cabinet as you did for the top corner cabinet, filling any gap at the wall with shims at the stud lines. If necessary, tap the shims into place with a hammer and a wood block.

7. Adding adjacent base cabinets

- Position the adjacent cabinet so its face is flush with that of the corner cabinet.
- Shim the cabinet so the top is flush with the top of the corner cabinet.
- Fill any gap at the back of the cabinet, placing shims along the stud lines.
- Secure the cabinet to the corner unit with clamps. Drive screws just above the upper and lower drawer glides at the front and back of the inside of the cabinet (#7).

8. Preparing the sink unit

Supply pipes and drainpipes for the sink usually enter the kitchen through the floor. Holes must be drilled in the base of the sink cabinet to accommodate these pipes.

- Measure the position of the pipes in relation to the wall and the adjacent cabinet. With a pencil and a combination square, transfer the measurements to the base of the sink cabinet.

- With a drill and a ¾- or 1-inch spade bit, drill the holes for the supply pipes (#8). Bore the drain-pipe hole with a 2- or 2½-inch hole saw.
- Lift the cabinet into position over the pipes.
- Align and level the cabinet, then fasten it to the adjacent cabinet.

9. Finishing the cabinet installation

- Once the cabinets are in place, fasten them to the studs through the backs and hidden rails.
- With a utility knife, trim the shims flush with the cabinet surfaces. If necessary, fasten filler strips between the cabinet ends and adjacent walls.
- Cut the kickplate to length and fasten it with finishing nails driven partway into the front edges of the cabinet sides (#9). Sink the nails, fill the holes, and touch up with plastic laminate paint of a matching color.

Note: *To ensure a clean edge when trimming laminated material, cut along a clamped guide.*

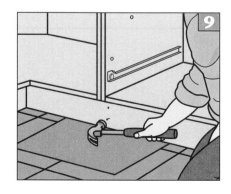

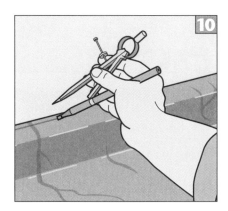

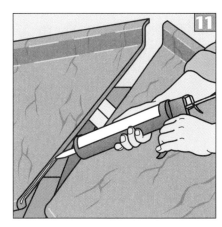

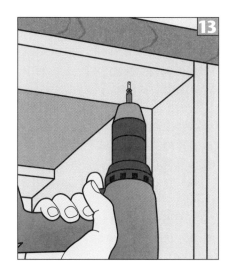

10. Fitting the countertop

Since walls are rarely even, the backsplash may need shaping to ensure a tight seal with the wall.

• Place the countertop sections in place on top of the cabinets, fitting them as tightly as possible against the wall.

• Find the widest gap between the backsplash and the wall. Fit a compass with a china marker and open the compass to this width. Run the compass along the length of the backsplash, allowing the marker to trace a line wherever it touches the surface of the backsplash (#10).

• Remove the countertop, clamp it to a work surface, and with a belt sander, sand the edge of the backsplash to the marked line.

11. Joining countertop sections

Two lengths of countertop must be joined with bolts from underneath before they are fastened to the cabinets. Short countertops

can be flipped over in place, but larger sections should be set right-side up on workhorses.

• Apply a bead of silicone caulk along the edge of one of the countertop sections (#11).

• Force the two sections together, allowing the excess caulk to squeeze out along the seam.

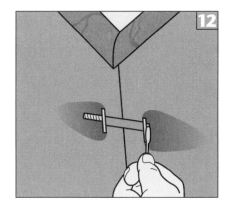

12. Bolting the sections

• Insert the bolts provided with the countertop into the recesses along both sides of the seam. Tighten the bolts with a wrench (#12).

• Let the extruded caulk dry completely, then rub off the excess.

13. Fastening the countertop

• With a helper, place the joined countertop sections back into position on the cabinets.

• Drive screws at the four corners of each cabinet through the upper support rails and into the underside of the countertop (#13).

14. Sealing the backsplash

Choose silicone caulk in a color that matches the countertop or buy a paintable type. Lay a bead of caulk along the seam between the backsplash and the wall (#14), then smooth it with a wet fingertip and wipe away any excess.

TAKING DOWN A NONBEARING WALL

Although it may seem like a major undertaking, taking down an interior wall can be accomplished with a few basic tools. Before beginning, however, make sure that the wall you wish to remove is nonbearing—a wall that is not part of the structural support of your home. Locate the ceiling joists with a stud finder. If the wall runs parallel to the joists, it is nonbearing and can be removed. If it is perpendicular to the joists, it may be either bearing or nonbearing—consult a contractor to be sure.

Determine whether any pipes or heating ducts run through the wall by checking the points at which they rise through the house from the basement. Have them rerouted by a professional. If there are outlets or switches in the wall or if you discover other wires running through it, you can remove the wallboard, but have an electrician reroute the wiring before you take down the framing.

SAFETY TIP *Never work on a live electrical circuit. Shut off power to the circuit at the service panel.*

HOW LONG WILL IT TAKE?

More than four hours

TOOLS

• Utility knife • Voltage tester • Screwdriver • Pry bar • Crow bar • Hammer • Reciprocating saw • Stud finder • Cordless drill • Dimpler • Taping knives • Dust mask • Safety goggles • Work gloves • Hard hat

MATERIALS

• Wallboard • Wallboard screws • Joint compound • Joint tape • Sandpaper • Flooring

1. Testing outlets for power

To demolish a wall safely, you must turn off power to any outlets and switches at the service panel.

Confirm that the power is off with a voltage tester.

• Insert the probes of a voltage tester into the outlets. If the tester light glows, the power is still on.

• Next, unscrew and remove the outlet cover plates. Touch the tester probes to the terminal screws at the ends of the black and white wires (#1), then the black wire and the green ground wire. If the tester light glows, there is still power to the outlet.

2. Testing switches for power

Each wall switch must be tested since it may be on a separate circuit from the outlets.

• Remove the cover plate, then unscrew the switch and gently free it from the electrical box.

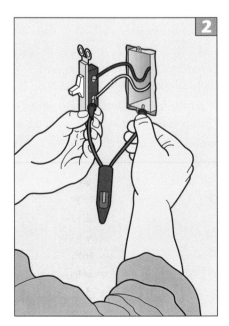

• Touch one probe of the voltage tester to the box, if it is metal, or to the green ground wire, if the box is plastic, and touch the other probe to each brass terminal on the switch (#2). If the tester light glows, the circuit supplying power to the switch is still on. Correct the problem at the service panel and test again.

3. Removing the trim

The first step in taking down the wall is removing trim, including baseboards, door and window casings, and any other decorative trim. If carefully removed, these pieces can be reused later.

• With a hammer, tap the end of a pry bar between the shoe molding and the baseboard, then pry the molding away. Repeat in several spots until the shoe molding is completely detached.

• Repeat the process to remove the baseboard, inserting a wood scrap between the pry bar and the wall for leverage (#3).

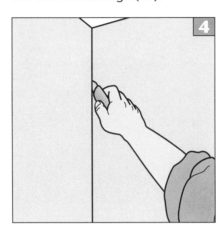

4. Cutting taped seams

Ceiling and corner seams in most wallboard construction are sealed with tape and joint compound. To prevent tearing the surface of adjacent walls and ceiling, these seams should be cut before taking down the wall. With a utility knife, slice through each corner seam, beginning at the top (#4). Repeat along the seam between the wall and the ceiling.

Note: *Before starting to demolish the wall, tape plastic sheeting over the doorway to keep dust out of the rest of the house.*

5. Taking down the wallboard

• Protect the floor with cardboard or a drop cloth.

• With a stud finder, locate the studs, then with a hammer, punch holes in the wallboard between the studs.

• Insert the hook of a crow bar into the holes and pry away the wallboard in large pieces (#5). Take care not to pull on any wires—there may be live ones that don't terminate at the the switches or outlets you checked.

SAFETY TIP *Wear safety goggles, work gloves, a dust mask, and a hard hat to protect against dust and falling debris.*

6. Removing the studs

At this point, if there is any electrical wiring running through the wall, have an electrician reroute it before you proceed. Likewise, have a plumber reroute any pipes or ducts.

• With a reciprocating saw fitted with a wood- and metal-cutting

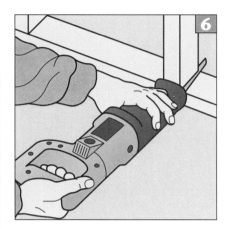

blade, cut between each stud and the sole plate (#6).
- Pull each stud and twist it to free it from the top plate.

7. Taking out the end stud

The end stud is fastened to studs in the adjoining wall and is best pried out in two sections.
- With the reciprocating saw, make a downward-angled cut through the stud.

- Tap the end of the pry bar into the cut, then pry off the lower section using the upper portion of the stud for leverage (#7).

- Pry out the remaining half of the end stud by bracing the bar against the studs behind it. Use a piece of scrap wood as leverage.

8. Removing the top plate

The top plate of a nonbearing wall is usually fastened to blocking between joists. As with the end stud, pry it out in two pieces.
- With a reciprocating saw, cut through the top plate at an angle toward the nearest wall.
- Tap the end of a pry bar into the cut and pry out the shorter section (#8).
- Use the hook of the pry bar to pull down the remaining section of the top plate.

9. Removing the sole plate

As with the top plate, the sole plate is fastened to blocking between joists below the subfloor.
- With a reciprocating saw, cut through the sole plate at an angle toward the nearest wall.

- Tap a pry bar into the cut (#9) and remove the section closest to the wall. Pry out the other section using a wood scrap for leverage.

10. Patching around the opening

The walls, floor, and ceiling will need patching.
- Cut wallboard strips to fit the spaces left by the end stud and top plate and fasten them with wallboard screws (#10). Finish the joints with joint compound and joint tape, then sand and paint.
- You can replace the flooring in half or all of the new room. Or, patch the gap in the flooring with a contrasting material—you may need to add plywood first to bring it up to the right height.
- Finally, replace the baseboards and other trim.

TILING A WALL

Ceramic tiles require a base that is clean, flat, and rigid. The best base material is backerboard, an underlayment made of thin sheets of concrete sandwiched between fiberglass mesh. But tiles can also be laid on concrete, exterior-grade plywood, or wallboard—preferably the water-resistant type, called "greenboard."

Laying out the tiles (Step 1 to Step 3) can be tedious, but the time spent is worth it. Accurate layout and marking assures you of the best finished results and helps you to avoid problems as you lay the tiles. It's much easier to shift a layout line than it is to relocate a row of adhered tiles.

Note: *Get 15 percent more tiles than you need to allow for wastage from cutting and for future repairs. Note the batch (or dye lot) number of the tiles so you can match the color if you need to buy more.*

SAFETY TIP *Wear rubber gloves to protect your hands from contact with thinset adhesive, grout, and grout sealer.*

HOW LONG WILL IT TAKE?

More than four hours

TOOLS

• Tape measure • Combination square • Carpenter's level • Notched trowel • Tile cutter • Tile nippers • Spacer puller • Grout float • Grout sponge • Foam applicator • Caulking gun • China marker • Rubber gloves • Safety goggles

MATERIALS

• Tiles • Plastic spacers • 1x2 • Thinset adhesive • Grout • Grout sealer • Silicone caulk

FLOORS & WALLS

1. Marking horizontal layout

• With a carpenter's level and a pencil, mark a horizontal layout line across the wall at your preferred location for a row of full tiles—for example, directly above a sink (#1) or half a tile or more above the floor.
• To help you lay out tiles, make a tile stick with a 1x2: Place a row of tiles separated by plastic spacers edge-to-edge on the floor, then set the 1x2 on top and mark both edges of each tile on it; draw lines between opposite marks with a combination square. If your tiles are not square, make two tile

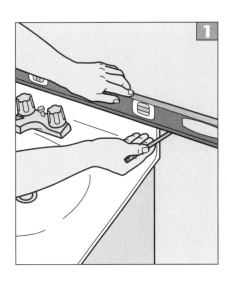

sticks: one for their height and one for their width.
• Mark the midpoint of your horizontal layout line. Starting at this point, use the tile stick to mark

edges of tiles across the wall along the layout line.
• The last tile at each end of the wall should be a half tile or more in size. If an end tile would be narrower, shift your start point to the right or left and mark edges of tiles again.

2. Marking vertical layout

• At the midpoint (or adjusted midpoint) of the horizontal layout line, mark a vertical layout line from the floor to as high up the wall as you plan to tile.
• Starting at the horizontal layout line, use the tile stick to mark

edges of tiles along the vertical layout line (#2). If not tiling up to the ceiling, make allowances for trim tiles you plan to lay (Step 8).

● Mark the outline of any fixture you plan to install—such as a vanity, a cabinet, or a sink—that will interrupt the tile layout.

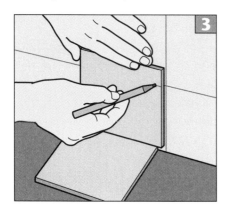

3. Marking bottom-row cuts

● At the bottom edge of the lowest full tile marked on the vertical layout line, draw a horizontal line across the wall.

● Place a tile on the floor against the wall as a spacer, then set another tile upright on it, one edge aligned with the vertical layout line.

● Transfer the horizontal line marked on the wall to the face of the tile with a china marker (#3). This will be your cutting line to fit the tile at the floor.

4. Cutting tiles

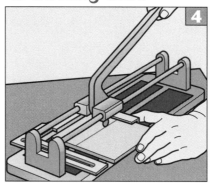

The easiest way to make straight cuts is with a tile cutter.

● Put the tile face-up on the base of the cutter, aligning the cutting line with the scoring wheel.

● Pressing down lightly on the handle of the cutter, pull or push (depends on the tool model) the cutting wheel across the tile along the cutting line (#4).

● Wearing safety goggles, press down firmly on the handle of the cutter to snap the tile in two.

5. Applying adhesive

● Mix thinset adhesive following the manufacturer's instructions.

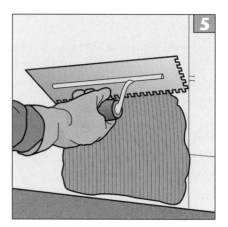

Prepare enough to cover a 3-foot-square section of wall.

● Starting at the bottom of the wall to one side of the vertical layout line, apply the adhesive with a notched trowel, holding it at a 60-degree angle (#5). (The notches ensure that adhesive is applied to the proper thickness.) Try not to obscure your layout lines.

6. Laying tiles

● Lay a row of tiles along the floor as spacers. Set your first cut tile on the spacer tiles, one edge aligned with the vertical layout line. Press the tile into the adhesive.

● Push a plastic spacer into the adhesive at the top corner of the tile. Place another spacer at the bottom corner of the tile, resting it on a spacer tile.

● Lay the next tile so its edge contacts the plastic spacers (#6). Add spacers and continue laying tiles along the bottom row.

● Work your way up the wall, laying tiles and placing spacers until the adhesive is covered.

● Continue to apply adhesive and lay tiles in a 3-foot-square section at a time.

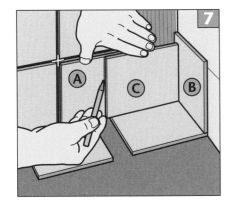

7. Trimming tiles at corners

You'll probably have to trim tiles to fit at each end of the wall.

● With a row of tiles still on the floor as spacers, position the tile to be trimmed (A) on the last full tile laid, their vertical edges aligned. Place one spacer tile (B) upright in the corner on the adjoining wall and butt a second spacer tile (C) upright against it. Using the outside edge of tile C as a guide, mark a cutting line on tile A with a china marker (#7).

● Cut the tile (Step 4), then lay it.

● Mark, cut, and lay the other tiles at each end of the wall the same way.

8. Laying trim tiles

If you are tiling only partway up the wall, a top row of trim tiles will improve the finished appearance of the job. The rounded edge of bullnose tiles provides a smooth transition border.

● Lay the trim tiles (#8), then carefully wipe any excess adhesive off the wall. (If the trim tiles do not match the size of the other tiles, the joints won't line up and you'll need to cut the top arm off the upper row of spacers.)

● Let the adhesive set for the length of time specified by the manufacturer, then pull out all the plastic spacers with a spacer puller or an old screwdriver.

9. Grouting

● Prepare enough grout to fill joints between tiles in a 3-foot-square section at a time.

● Holding a grout float at a 45-degree angle to the wall, spread grout over the tiles, forcing it into the joints (#9).

● Once all the joints are packed with grout, scrape off excess by dragging the float at almost a 90-degree angle across the tiles, working diagonally to the joints to avoid gouging them.

● Carefully sponge grout off the surface of the tiles.

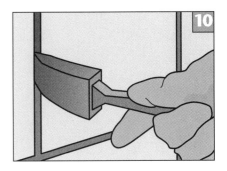

10. Sealing the joints

● Let the grout set for 15 to 30 minutes, then rub off the hazy residue with a damp soft cloth.

● After the grout hardens for a couple of days, apply grout sealer to the joints—if it is advised by the grout manufacturer—with a small foam applicator (#10).

SOUNDPROOFING A ROOM

Effective soundproofing both blocks sounds and eliminates acoustic vibrations. This is best accomplished by adding soundproofing batts and installing two layers of wallboard on resilient channels, which isolate the panels from the ceiling joists or wall studs. Leave a ⅛-inch space between panels and fill it with flexible acoustical sealant. Cover unused outlets with cover-plate gaskets.

Measure and check dimensions carefully before purchasing soundproofing materials. If you are soundproofing an entire room, do all your demolition work at the same time, then complete the ceiling before doing the walls.

HOW LONG WILL IT TAKE?
More than four hours

TOOLS
• Voltage tester • Stepladder • Screwdriver • Utility knife • Stud finder • Hammer • Crow bar • Chalk line • Cordless drill • Dimpler • Tin snips • Keyhole saw • Mason's hawk • Taping knives • Caulking gun • Work gloves • Safety goggles • Dust mask

MATERIALS
• Soundproofing batts • Box extensions • Resilient channels • 2x4s • Wallboard • Wallboard screws • Joint compound • Joint tape • Acoustical sealant

SOUNDPROOFING THE CEILING

1. Removing the wallboard

Turn off power to the circuits in the room at the service panel and check fixtures and outlets with a voltage tester to confirm that the electricity is shut off. Lay out a drop cloth to protect the floor.
● With a utility knife, cut through the joints between the ceiling and the walls.
● Locate the ceiling joists with a stud finder, then punch holes in the wallboard between joists with a hammer.
● Insert the hook of a crow bar into the holes and pry the wallboard off the joists (#1), being careful not to dislodge or damage any electrical wires.

SAFETY TIP *To protect yourself from falling debris and particles, wear safety goggles, a dust mask, a hard hat, a long-sleeved shirt, long pants, and work gloves.*

2. Putting up soundproofing batts

Each electrical box requires a box extension so it will sit flush with the finished ceiling surface— ¾-inch resilient channels and a second layer of ½-inch wallboard panels, for instance, means an added depth of 1¼ inches.
● Starting at one side of the room, push soundproofing batts snugly into place between the ceiling joists (#2).
● Continue the same way across the room and to the opposite side, trimming batts as needed to fit; if necessary, staple the edges of the batts to the joists to keep them in place.

Wear safety goggles, a dust mask, and work gloves when handling batts.

3. Marking for resilient channels

Resilient channels that support wallboard panels are installed perpendicular to the ceiling joists.

• Mark 6 inches from one end of the ceiling joists at opposite sides of the room, then snap a chalk line across the joists between the marks (#3).
• Repeat the procedure at the other end of the joists.

• Measure the distance between the two chalk lines, then snap chalk lines across the joists at equal intervals of 20 to 24 inches.

4. Installing resilient channels

Resilient channels feature a mounting flange for attaching to ceiling joists (or wall studs).
• Align resilient channels with the chalk marks on the ceiling joists, overlapping lengths by at least 2 inches at a joist; trim lengths as needed with tin snips.
• Fasten the resilient channels to the ceiling joists, driving wallboard screws through the mounting flange with a cordless drill (#4).

Wear safety goggles when cutting resilient channels and driving wallboard screws.

5. Installing wallboard panels

To help hold wallboard panels against the resilient channels

during installation, build a T-shore out of 2x4s. Measure the height of the ceiling and cut a 2x4 to this length, then screw a shorter 2x4 to the top at a 90-degree angle, forming a T.
• Starting in a corner of the room, work with a helper to hang wallboard panels, planing joints as much as possible along tapered edges—joints along untapered ends of panels are more difficult to conceal.
• With a wallboard panel held in place, mark the location of resilient channels across it with a chalk line, then screw the panel to the channels at 24-inch intervals with wallboard screws using a drill fitted with a dimpler (#5).

• Continue the same way, leaving a ⅛-inch gap around the perimeter of the ceiling and between panels. Score and snap panels to fit as needed. Make cutouts for electrical boxes and other obstacles with a keyhole saw.

SOUNDPROOFING THE CEILING (CONTINUED)

6. Sealing gaps

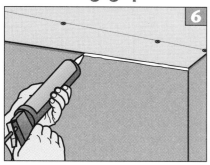

- With a caulking gun, squeeze a bead of acoustical sealant into each gap at the perimeter of the ceiling (#6) and between wallboard panels. Smooth the sealant with a wet finger.
- Mark the location of resilient channels at the top of the walls,

then hang a second layer of wallboard panels at right angles to the first layer, transferring the marks onto them. Screw each panel to the channels at 16-inch intervals.
- Caulk gaps at the perimeter of the ceiling and between wallboard panels with acoustical sealant.

7. Finishing joints

- Load joint compound onto a mason's hawk. With a 4-inch taping knife, cover the screw heads.
- Along each joint between wallboard panels, apply a layer of joint compound, then embed paper joint tape (#7). Cover the tape with a thin layer of compound.

- Let the joint compound dry overnight, then apply another layer with a 6-inch taping knife, feathering the edges outward to help disguise the seams.
- Let the joint compound dry, then repeat the entire process using a 10-inch taping knife.

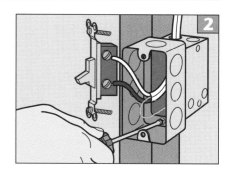

SOUNDPROOFING A WALL

1. Removing the wallboard

Turn off power to the circuits in the room at the service panel and check fixtures and outlets with a voltage tester to confirm that the electricity is shut off. Lay out a drop cloth to protect the floor.
- Cut through the joints between the wall and the ceiling.
- Locate the wall studs with a stud finder, then punch holes in the wallboard between studs with a hammer.
- Pry the wallboard off the studs with a crow bar (#1), being careful not to dislodge or damage any electrical wires.

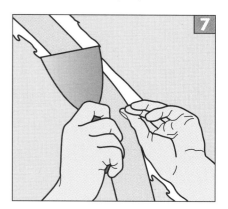

2. Installing box extensions

To accommodate the added thickness of resilient channels and a second layer of wallboard, each electrical box requires a box extension so it will be flush with

FLOORS & WALLS

the finished wall surface—$\frac{3}{4}$-inch channels and $\frac{1}{2}$-inch panels, for instance, means an added depth of $1\frac{1}{4}$ inches.

● Slide a box extension over each switch and outlet and screw it to the electrical box (#2); if necessary, loosen the cable clamp on the box to feed in more electrical cable, then retighten it.

● After the wallboard panels are hung, screw each switch and outlet to its box extension and put back the cover plate.

3. Adding soundproofing batts

● Working across the wall from top to bottom, press soundproofing batts into place between the studs (#3); trim batts to fit using a utility knife and a straightedge.

4. Installing resilient channels

Resilient channels have a mounting flange for fastening to wall studs (or ceiling joists).

● Snap a chalk line across the wall studs 6 inches from the ceiling

and 2 inches from the floor. Measure the distance between the two chalk lines, then snap chalk lines across the studs at equal intervals of 20 to 24 inches.

● Align resilient channels with the chalk marks, overlapping lengths by at least 2 inches at a stud; trim lengths as needed with tin snips.

● Fasten the resilient channels to the wall studs, driving wallboard screws through the mounting flange with a cordless drill (#4).

5. Hanging panels vertically

Hang the first layer of wallboard panels on the wall vertically.

● With a wallboard panel held in place at one end of the wall, mark the location of resilient channels across it with a chalk line, then screw the panel to the channels every 24 inches with wallboard screws using a drill fitted with a dimpler (#5).

● Continue the same way, leaving a $\frac{1}{8}$-inch gap between wallboard panels. Score and snap panels to

fit as needed. Make cutouts for electrical boxes and other obstacles with a keyhole saw.

6. Hanging panels horizontally

Install a second layer of wallboard panels horizontally.

● Mark the location of resilient channels on the adjacent walls, then hang a second layer of wallboard panels at right angles to the first layer, transferring the marks onto them. Screw each panel to the channels at intervals of 16 inches wallboard screws (#6).

● Caulk gaps between wallboard panels with acoustical sealant.

● Cover the screw heads with joint compound and tape the seams between wallboard panels.

MOUNTING GRAB BARS IN A SHOWER

A slippery shower stall or bathtub is an accident waiting to happen. That's why a grab bar on the wall of a shower stall or tub is an invaluable safety feature in any home.

Different kinds of grab bars are available, but all of them have two mounting plates, each with three screw holes. Ideally, all the screws should be driven into wall studs. On models with fixed plates, you can usually align only two screw holes per mounting plate into studs; a screw and toggle bolt are used for the third hole. The type of grab bar shown here has loose mounting plates that enable you to drive all three screws into a stud, although one of the screws may have to be driven at an angle. A detachable cover plate conceals the screw heads.

Wall studs are usually 16 inches apart, so unless the grab bar is a multiple of 16 inches long, you will have to install it at an angle in order to align the mounting plates with studs. Position the bar at a height that will be convenient and comfortable for the people who will be using it.

HOW LONG WILL IT TAKE?
Less than two hours

TOOLS
• Stud finder • Hex wrench • Electric drill (with ceramic or masonry bit) • Caulking gun • Screwdriver • Safety goggles

MATERIALS
• Grab bar • Masking tape • Silicone caulk

1. Marking the grab bar location

Depending on the length of the grab bar you are installing, you will need to adjust the height of stud marks to align the mounting plates with the studs.

● Locate studs with a stud finder and mark their position on the wall with strips of masking tape.

● Once you have chosen the height and angle of the grab bar, use the stud finder to double-check the location of the stud marks. Then, position the grab bar on the wall so each mounting plate is centered over a pair of stud marks.

● With a pencil, outline the cover plates on the masking tape (#1).

2. Marking the screw holes

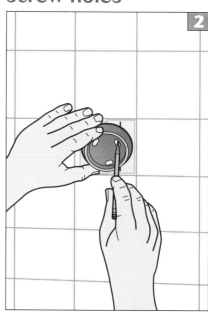

- For the model of grab bar shown here, use a hex wrench to remove the mounting plates from the grab bar.
- Position a mounting plate on one of the marked outlines so at least two of the screw holes are within stud marks and the third is as close as possible to one mark.
- Mark the screw holes with a pencil (#2).
- Repeat with the other outline.

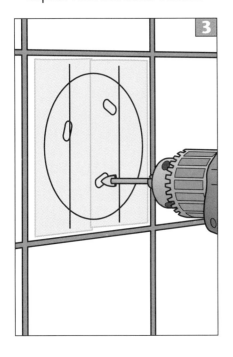

3. Drilling the screw holes

- For a tiled wall, fit an electric drill with a ceramic or masonry bit slightly larger than the diameter of the screws.
- Wearing safety goggles, drill into the wall at each mark, stopping at the stud (#3).
- Remove the masking tape.

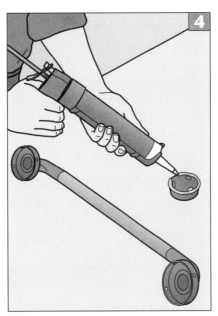

4. Preparing the grab bar

- Using a caulking gun, apply a small bead of silicone caulk around the rim of each mounting plate that will sit against the wall (#4). The caulk will prevent moisture from getting under the grab-bar cover plates and into the screw holes.

5. Attaching the mounting plates

- Position a mounting plate on the wall, aligning its screw holes with those in the wall.
- Insert the screws supplied into the screw holes and drive them into the stud. For the screw hole located just beyond the stud mark, angle the screw into the stud (#5).
- Repeat the procedure for the other mounting plate.

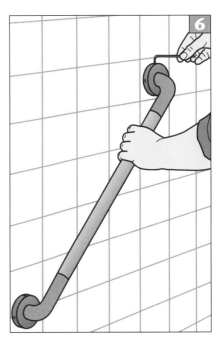

6. Mounting the grab bar

- Fit the cover plates of the grab bar over the mounting plates.
- Secure the plates together by tightening the setscrews on the cover plates with a hex wrench (#6).

INSTALLING A BATHROOM VANITY

A single-sink vanity is a popular bathroom option, especially when space is limited. Many manufacturers offer units that come with a sink. Faucets, supply tubes, drain assemblies, and drainpipe are sold separately.

Installing a vanity involves leveling it and anchoring it to the wall at studs; if the vanity has a closed back, you will need to cut holes for the shutoff valves and the drainpipe with a saber saw or an electric drill fitted with a hole saw. Connect as many of the plumbing fittings to the sink as possible before you install it in the vanity; working in the restricted room under the sink after it is installed can be awkward.

HOW LONG WILL IT TAKE?
More than four hours

TOOLS
• Stud finder • Carpenter's level • Putty knife • Pry bar • Utility knife • Hammer • Adjustable wrench • Backsaw and miter box • Caulking gun

MATERIALS
• Vanity • Sink • Faucets • Supply tubes • Drainpipe (and fittings) • Wallboard screws • Adhesive caulk • Primer • Solvent cement • Scribe molding • Finishing nails • Brads • Silicone caulk

1. Locating wall studs

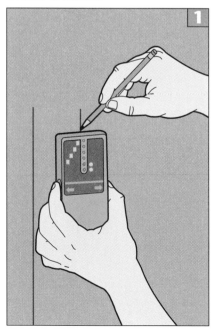

• Position the vanity against the wall, centering it on the drain stub-out and the shutoff valves. Outline the sides of the vanity on the wall with a pencil, then extend the lines to the floor and set the vanity aside.

• Locate the center of two wall studs within the marked outline using a stud finder (#1).

2. Extending the stud marks

Extend the stud-location marks so they will be visible above and below the mounting rail on the back of the vanity once the vanity is in position.

• Using a carpenter's level as a

straightedge, draw a vertical line on the wall at each stud-location mark (#2).

FLOORS & WALLS

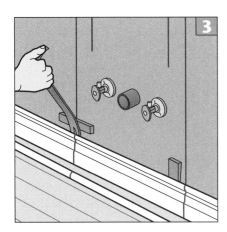

3. Removing floor trim

Remove the shoe molding and the baseboard from the wall so the vanity can sit flush against it.
- Tap the blade of a putty knife under the shoe molding, raising it far enough to fit in the tip of a pry bar. Using a wood pad under the pry bar, work along the shoe molding to free it.
- Working in the same way, lever the baseboard out from the wall far enough to fit in a wood shim. Continue along the baseboard (#3), slipping in additional shims as needed, until the baseboard comes off the wall.

Note: *Slice through any paint seal along the shoe molding and the baseboard with a utility knife.*

4. Leveling the vanity

- Put the vanity back into place against the wall.
- Level the vanity from side to side by sliding shims under it.

Checking for level with a carpenter's level, tap the shims into place with a hammer, protecting the floor with cardboard (#4).

- Level the vanity from front to back by shimming behind it.
- Trim off the shims flush with the edges of the vanity using a utility knife.

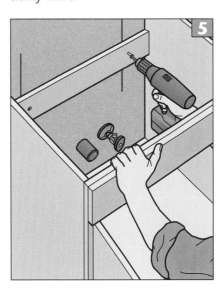

5. Anchoring the vanity

- Drive wallboard screws through the mounting rail of the vanity into the wall at the marked stud locations (#5).

6. Mounting the sink

- Equip the sink with faucets, supply tubes, a drain flange, a T-connector, a tailpiece (A), and a pop-up mechanism.

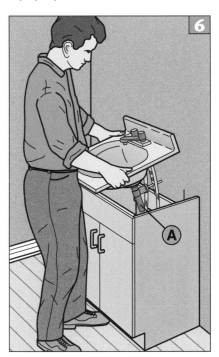

- If recommended by the sink manufacturer, apply a bead of adhesive caulk around the top edge of the vanity.
- Put the sink into position (#6), butting the backsplash tightly against the wall. Wipe away any excess caulk.

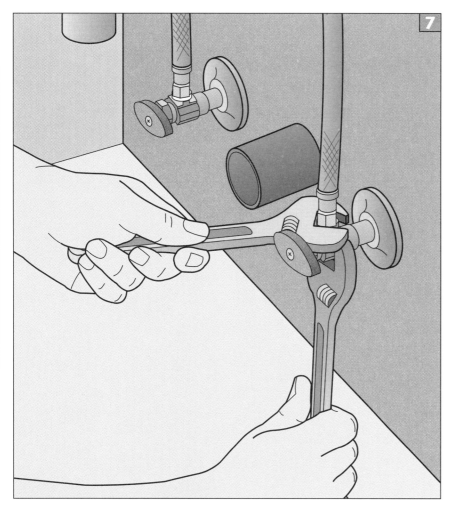

drain stub-out and hand-tighten a drain trap onto the drain extension.

● Glue a drain extension (B) to the drain trap and hand-tighten it onto the tailpiece (#8).

● Tighten each slip nut a quarter to a half turn with a wrench, then turn on the water and check for leaks.

9. Installing molding

● Cut the baseboard and the shoe molding you removed and install the pieces against the wall on each side of the vanity.

● Hide gaps between the vanity and the floor with shoe molding. Cut the pieces to length with a backsaw and a miter box, making miter cuts for corners.

● Nail the shoe molding to the floor with finishing nails (#9).

● Hide gaps between the vanity and the wall with scribe molding, nailing it to the wall with brads.

● Seal the joint between the back-splash and the wall with a bead of silicone caulk.

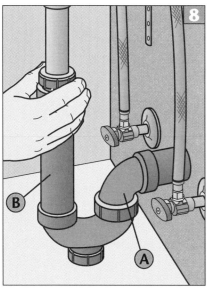

7. Connecting the supply lines

● Connect the supply tubes to the shutoff valves. Hand-tighten the coupling nuts, then tighten each one a quarter to a half turn with an adjustable wrench (#7).

8. Connecting the drainpipe

When gluing plastic pipe, be sure to use compatible primer and cement.

● Glue a drain extension (A) to the

FINISHING WALLBOARD JOINTS

Hanging wallboard may be grunt work, but finishing the joints between the sheets is more like art. It's worth taking the time to finish the joints properly so the seams appear invisible because every little imperfection will show through, whether you paint the wallboard or cover it with wallpaper.

Wallboard joints are finished with three layers of joint compound, a mudlike substance that comes premixed in a bucket. Each layer is applied with a successively wider taping knife, then sanded or sponged perfectly smooth once the compound is dry. The key to rendering the joints invisible is "feathering," the process of thinning the compound gradually with the knife as you move away from the joint until the compound is paper thin.

HOW LONG WILL IT TAKE?

More than four hours

TOOLS

- Mason's hawk • Taping knives
- Corner trowel • Tin snips
- Hammer • Sanding pole • Dust mask • Safety goggles

MATERIALS

- Joint compound • Joint tape
- Corner bead • Wallboard nails
- Sandpaper

TAPING FLAT JOINTS

1. Applying joint compound

Perform Step 1 and Step 2 on one joint at a time before moving on to the next joint.
- Scoop some joint compound onto a mason's hawk with a 4-inch taping knife. Starting at one end of the joint, pull the knife along the surface to spread the compound evenly in a thin layer (#1). Angle the handle closer and closer to the wall as you pull it along the joint.
- Once you reach the end of the joint, reverse direction to scrape away excess compound. Move on to the next step immediately—the joint compound should still be wet when you perform Step 2.

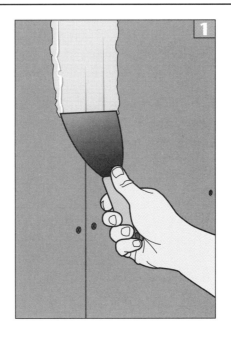

2. Embedding tape

- While the joint compound is still wet, center a strip of joint tape over the joint. Starting at one end

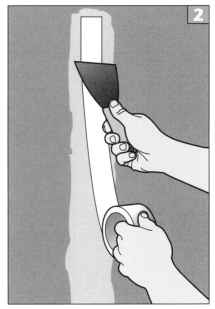

of the joint, press the tape into the compound with the taping knife (#2).
- Work your way to the other end of the joint, unrolling the tape as

TAPING FLAT JOINTS (CONTINUED)

TAPING INSIDE CORNERS

you go. Rip the tape at the end of the joint using the blade of the knife as a straightedge.

● Run the taping knife over the tape a couple of times to remove air bubbles and excess compound.

● Cover the tape with a layer of joint compound.

● Perform Step 1 and Step 2 for each joint. Allow the joint compound dry overnight.

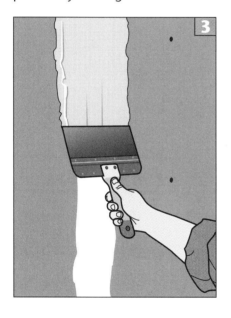

3. Adding a third coat

● Once the second coat of joint compound is dry, apply a third coat of joint compound to all the joints using an 8- or 10-inch taping knife (#3). This will "feather" the compound 2 inches beyond each edge of the first coat.

● Allow the joint compound to dry overnight.

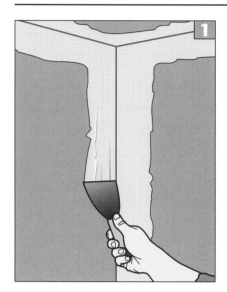

4. Smoothing the joints

Once the last coat of compound is dry, you need to smooth the joints to eliminate any remaining imperfections. You can use a wallboard sponge, but professionals always sand, as shown here.

● Fit a sanding pad with medium-grade sandpaper.

● Lightly move the pad back and forth over the joint compound until it is smooth. Don't sand the paper covering on the wallboard.

● For joints on the ceiling or other hard-to-reach areas, attach the sanding pad to a pole and smooth the compound by moving the pad in a circular motion (#4).

SAFETY TIP *Sanding joint compound is a messy job—wear a dust mask to keep from inhaling harmful dust and particles.*

1. Applying joint compound

● Apply a thin layer of joint compound along one side of the corner using a 4-inch taping knife.

● Spread a layer on the other side, pushing the compound into the corner (#1).

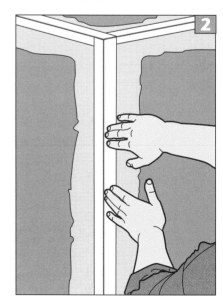

2. Embedding tape

• Tear off a piece of joint tape the length of the corner. Fold the tape down the center, along the line where it is scored.

• Beginning at the the top of the corner, embed the tape into the wet joint compound. Using your fingers, press the tape into the corner and smooth it on both sides the length of the joint (#2).

• Cover the tape with a layer of joint compound.

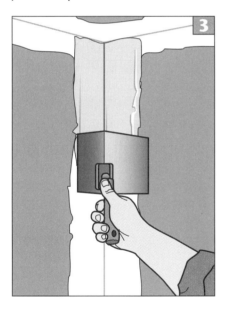

3. Squaring the corner

• Apply an additional thin layer of joint compound with a corner trowel. Run the tool smoothly along the corner from the top to the bottom (#3). Let the compound dry overnight.

Note: *A corner tool will leave the joint slightly rounded. If you'll be installing crown molding along the joint between a wall and the ceiling, this may cause problems. In such a case, square the joint with a taping knife.*

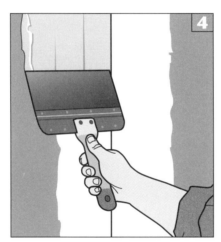

4. Feathering

• Apply a coat of joint compound along one side of the corner using a 6-inch taping knife. This will "feather" the compound in the same way as with a straight joint, blending the edge with the surrounding wall surface. Repeat for the other side of the corner and let the compound dry.

• Apply a final coat to both sides of the corner with an 8- or 10-inch taping knife (#4), feathering the compound 2 inches beyond the edge of the last coat.

• Let the compound dry, then smooth the surface with sandpaper or a wallboard sponge.

FINISHING OUTSIDE CORNERS

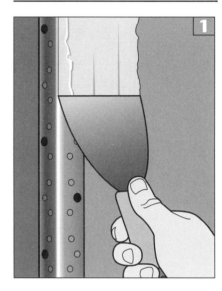

Concealing corner bead

Corner bead is a thin strip of metal shaped to fit the outside corner of a wall. It both protects and strengthens the corner joint.

• Cut a piece of corner bead to the length of the joint with tin snips, then nail it to the corner every six inches.

• With a 4-inch taping knife, apply a layer of joint compound on one side of the corner, covering the corner bead (#1).

• Apply compound to the other side of the corner the same way.

• Let the compound dry.

• Apply another layer of compound to each side of the corner, feathering 2 inches beyond the edge of the previous coat. Let the coat dry, then add a last coat.

• Sand or sponge smooth once the joint compound is dry.

GROUTING TILES

FLOORS & WALLS

Grouting tiles is not a very complicated job, but creating smooth, level joints with grout does require patience and care. After tiling a large surface, allow the adhesive to dry before grouting the joints. When repairing damaged grout, scrape and clean affected joints thoroughly before applying grout.

There are two types of grout: sanded and non-sanded. The right choice depends on the width of the joints. Sanded grout—which, as the name suggests, contains sand and is gritty in texture—is used for joints more than ⅛ inch wide. Non-sanded grout, which is mixed with a latex additive for strength and flexibility, is typically used for narrower joints.

Grout color is an important consideration. Using light colors with light-colored tiles helps hide tiling mistakes. However, avoid light-colored grout on floors at busy entryways—it will soon become discolored. A grout color that contrasts with the color of the tiles is dramatic and emphasizes tile shape.

The last step in grouting tile is applying sealer to the joints. Be sure to wipe sealer from the tile faces before it dries. Porous tiles, such as those made of slate or marble, must be sealed with a different type of sealer to protect them.

SAFETY TIP *Wet grout is mildly corrosive—wear rubber gloves to mix and apply it.*

HOW LONG WILL IT TAKE?
Two to four hours

TOOLS
• Grout saw • Broom or vacuum • Sponge • Bucket • Grout float • Caulking gun • Rubber gloves • Safety goggles • Dust mask

MATERIALS
• Grout • Grout sealer • Silicone caulk

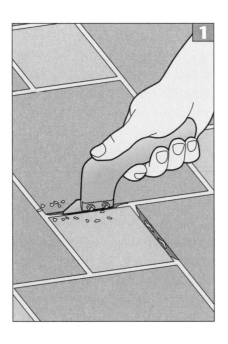

1. Removing old grout

Use a carbide-tipped grout saw to remove damaged grout from the joints between tiles. Wear safety goggles and a dust mask.
● Drag the saw blade repeatedly along the joint to remove all loose or damaged grout (#1). Work carefully to avoid damaging the edges of the tiles.
● Clean away dust and particles with a broom or a vacuum.
● Wipe the area with a clean, damp cloth.

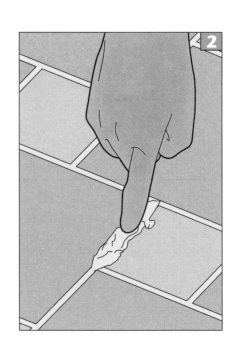

2. Grouting single joints

Prepare a small amount of grout following the manufacturer's instructions.

● Pack grout into the joint with a finger (#2).

● Wipe diagonally across the joint with a grout sponge to clean away excess grout.

3. Grouting a large area

Mix grout in a bucket following the manufacturer's instructions.

● Pour about a cup of grout onto the tiles.

● Spread the grout with a rubber float, holding it at an angle to the tiles and working diagonally across the joints (#3) to fill them completely and pack the grout.

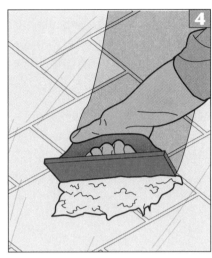

4. Removing excess grout

● Scrape excess grout off the tiles with the edge of the float, working diagonally across the joints (#4). Clean the float by scraping it against the side of the bucket.

● Continue spreading grout and removing excess until all the joints are filled.

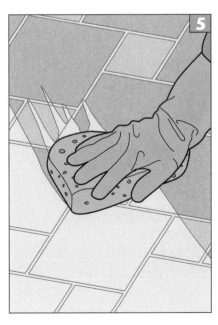

5. Cleaning the tiles

● Allow the grout to set for about 15 minutes, then wipe the tiles clean with a damp sponge, wiping diagonally across the joints (#5). Take care not to wipe grout out of the joints.

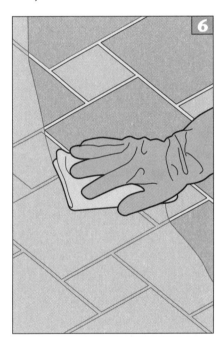

6. Removing the grout haze

Even after cleaning with a damp sponge, a thin haze of grout will remain on the tiles.

● Let the grout set overnight, then wipe the tiles with a clean, damp cloth, working diagonally to the joints (#6).

● Wait for the time specified by the grout manufacturer before applying a grout sealer.

● Apply silicone caulk at the perimeter of the tiles.

HANGING WALL-MOUNTED SHELVES

FLOORS & WALLS

Hanging simple wall-mounted shelves is a quick and easy way to increase storage space. Stationary brackets are available in a number of styles. If the arms of the brackets are a different length, secure the shorter arm to the shelf. For heavier loads, choose brackets with diagonal supports.

A shelf mounted to wallboard alone will support very little weight. Instead, mount braces to the wall studs set at 16-inch intervals behind the panels. Locate the studs with a stud finder. To prevent long shelves from sagging, mount the shelving with a bracket at every stud. Do not extend shelving past the brackets by more than 8 inches.

Never rely on the floor or the ceiling of the room as reference points when leveling a shelf since they are seldom true—even in newly constructed homes. Instead, use a carpenter's level so nothing is left to chance.

HOW LONG WILL IT TAKE?
Less than two hours

TOOLS
• Stud finder • Carpenter's level • Electric drill • Combination square • Awl • Screwdriver

MATERIALS
• Shelving • Shelf braces • Wood screws

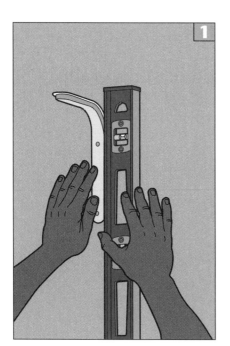

1. Locating and marking studs

• Locate the center of studs behind the wallboard with a stud finder. Mark their position.
• Along the midpoint of one stud, mark a spot at the right height for the shelf.
• At the marked spot, plumb a shelf brace with a carpenter's level (#1), centering the bubble inside the level's end vial.
• Mark the locations of the screw holes in the brace on the wall.

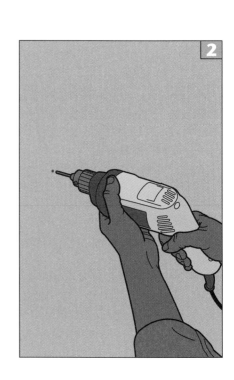

2. Drilling pilot holes in the wall

Pilot holes help prevent screws from making cracks in the wallboard or the shelf. The diameter of the drill bit should be slightly smaller than that of the screws.
● Drill holes at the marks deep enough to penetrate the stud by $\frac{1}{8}$ inch (#2).

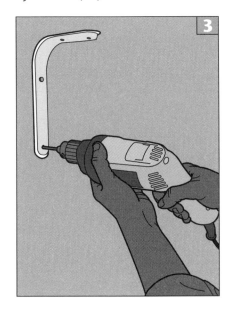

3. Fastening the first brace

● Line up the screw holes in the brace with the pilot holes and screw the brace to the wall (#3).

4. Positioning the second brace

● Measuring from each end of the shelf, make reference marks on the underside indicating where each brace will be centered. Make

sure the marks correspond to stud locations and provide for the same length of overhang at each end.
● Use a combination square and pencil to draw right-angle reference lines across the shelf at the marks (#4).

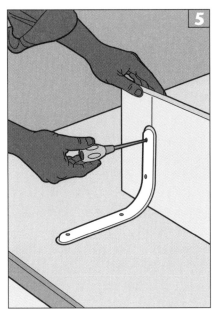

5. Marking and drilling pilot holes in the shelving

● To square the shelf bracket with the back edge of the shelf, lay the shelf on edge and slide the brace into position over the reference line.
● Mark screw hole locations with a pencil or an awl (#5) and erase the reference lines.
● Drill pilot holes at the marks and screw the brace into place.

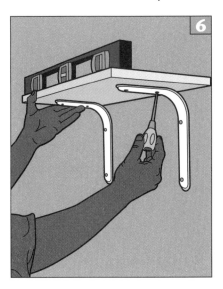

6. Leveling the shelf

● Rest the shelf on the first brace and center the reference line.
● Level the shelf and mark the screw-hole locations in the braces on the wall and the underside of the shelf (#6).
● Drill pilot holes at the marks.
● Reposition the shelf and screw it into place.

INSTALLING CABINET DOOR HINGES

FLOORS & WALLS

Many types of hinges are available for cabinet doors. Some are decorative and mounted on the exterior surfaces of the doors and cabinet frames. Others are interior-mounted, fastened to the inside edges of the doors and cabinet frames; the most common of these is the butt hinge—the focus of this project.

The butt hinge is made up of two leaves that pivot on a central pin; when the door is closed, only the loop around the pin is visible. For the door to fit snugly in the cabinet and open and close properly, the leaves need to be recessed in mortises. Cutting mortises on the inside of the cabinet is easiest to do if you turn it on its side, so cut the mortises before positioning the cabinets in place.

Locate the hinges on the doors at the same distance from the top and bottom—about 3 inches will ensure you have enough room to cut mortises inside the cabinet. To avoid splintering the wood, drill pilot holes for the hinge screws with a bit slightly smaller than them in diameter.

HOW LONG WILL IT TAKE?
Two to four hours

TOOLS
• Handscrews • Bar clamps • Combination square • Electric drill • Screwdriver • Utility knife • Wood chisel • Mallet • Safety goggles

MATERIALS
• Butt hinges • Wood screws

1. Outlining hinges on the door

● Support the door hinge-edge up on a work surface with handscrews and clamps.
● With a combination square, mark the position for the hinges on the edge of the door.
● Position each hinge and mark the location of the screw holes.
● Drill pilot holes at the marks and temporarily screw the hinges to the door.
● Score the door along the edges of each hinge leaf with a utility knife (#1), then remove the hinges and set them aside.

2. Chiseling the hinge outlines

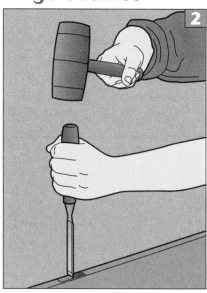

To prevent chipping of the mortise edges, deepen the scored outlines with a wood chisel and a mallet.

● Mark a cutting depth equal to the thickness of a hinge leaf on the face of the door.

● Hold the chisel upright against the outline, its beveled edge facing the waste, and tap lightly with the mallet.

● Work the same way with the chisel and mallet to score the waste wood at ⅛-inch intervals within the scored outlines (#2).

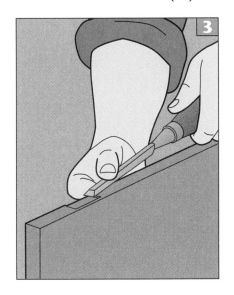

3. Clearing the hinge mortises

● Pare away chips of waste wood by holding the chisel bevel-down at a 30-degree angle and tapping with the mallet.

● Applying only hand pressure, hold the chisel bevel-up almost parallel to the surface to smooth the bottom of the mortises and square the corners (#3).

4. Fastening hinges to the door

● Set each hinge in place, pin loop facing up, and screw it to the door with the screws supplied (#4).

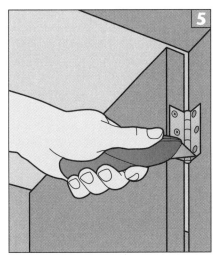

5. Outlining hinges on the cabinet

Follow the same basic steps to cut mortises inside the cabinets.

● Have a helper hold the door in position or steady it on shims. Mark screw-hole locations, drill pilot holes, and temporarily screw the hinges to the cabinet.

● Outline the hinge leaves on the cabinet with a utility knife (#5), then remove the door.

6. Fastening hinges to the cabinet

● Lay the cabinet on its side, then chisel the mortises.

● Stand the cabinet upright, then position the door and screw the hinges into the mortises (#6).

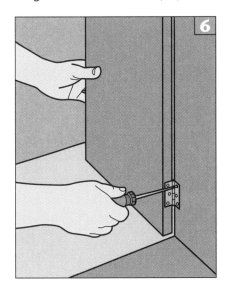

Chapter 4
DOORS & WINDOWS

The doors and windows of a home typically need frequent attention. After all, they are opened and shut several times a day, the settling of the house over the years puts a strain on their framing, and all but interior doors are exposed to the elements. This chapter presents tried-and-true—and easy—fixes for the most common door and window problems, such as binding doors and window sashes and damaged window screens.

An ailing door or window can sometimes be beyond repair. The destructive effects of the elements and constant use can make replacement of a damaged door or window your best option. The following pages offer detailed step-by-step instructions for putting in an exterior door or window and for installing a new lockset on an interior door.

Of course, there are other reasons for wanting to install new doors and windows in a home.

TOOLS FOR DOORS & WINDOWS FIXES AND IMPROVEMENTS

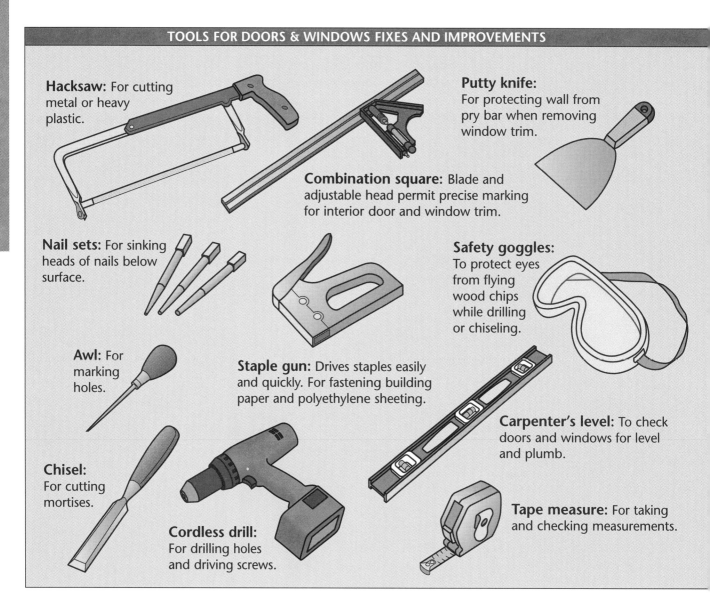

Hacksaw: For cutting metal or heavy plastic.

Putty knife: For protecting wall from pry bar when removing window trim.

Combination square: Blade and adjustable head permit precise marking for interior door and window trim.

Nail sets: For sinking heads of nails below surface.

Safety goggles: To protect eyes from flying wood chips while drilling or chiseling.

Awl: For marking holes.

Staple gun: Drives staples easily and quickly. For fastening building paper and polyethylene sheeting.

Carpenter's level: To check doors and windows for level and plumb.

Chisel: For cutting mortises.

Cordless drill: For drilling holes and driving screws.

Tape measure: For taking and checking measurements.

Doors and windows are more than just holes in the shell of a house. They bring in light, highlight exterior views, provide architectural accents, and add a sense of openness and warmth. New doors and windows aren't difficult to install, as you'll see in the following pages. We will also show you how to put in a new skylight.

Apart from contributing to the character of your home, your front door plays a major role in your household security. Deadbolt locks are the most secure type, and we'll show you how install one. Doors and windows are also your first line of defense in keeping your home cozy and warm in winter. Weatherproofing doors and windows is easy to do, and will pay big dividends by reducing heating bills and eliminating annoying drafts.

Whichever door or window project you undertake, none of the fixes or improvements in this chapter calls for any specialized tools. All you need are the basic carpentry tools shown below.

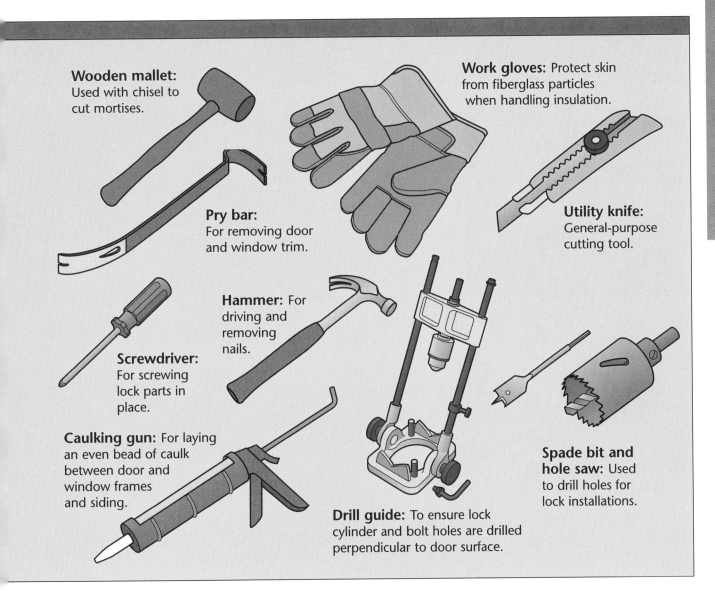

Wooden mallet: Used with chisel to cut mortises.

Work gloves: Protect skin from fiberglass particles when handling insulation.

Pry bar: For removing door and window trim.

Utility knife: General-purpose cutting tool.

Screwdriver: For screwing lock parts in place.

Hammer: For driving and removing nails.

Caulking gun: For laying an even bead of caulk between door and window frames and siding.

Drill guide: To ensure lock cylinder and bolt holes are drilled perpendicular to door surface.

Spade bit and hole saw: Used to drill holes for lock installations.

INSTALLING AN EXTERIOR DOOR

Most new exterior doors are made from strong but lightweight steel. They come prehung in wood frames that are usually covered with vinyl cladding. Measure the height and thickness of the existing jambs and choose a model of door that is suitable in size. Be sure to allow space for shims between the doorjambs and the rough framing. Also consider which way you want the door to open. Although building codes usually require residential exterior doors to open inward, you will need to decide whether you want your door to swing open to the right or to the left.

If your old door was installed with exterior casing, you will need to install new casing at least as wide to fill the gap. You can order vinyl-clad casing to match the door or make your own wood moldings. If the old door had no exterior casing, you can install the new one without and simply caulk between the doorjambs and the siding.

To remove the old door, first pry off the interior and exterior casing, then unscrew or cut away the doorjambs and the threshold from the rough framing.

HOW LONG WILL IT TAKE?
Two to four hours

TOOLS
• Tape measure • Carpenter's level • Cordless drill • Circular saw • Saber saw • Hacksaw • Hammer • Nail set • Staple gun • Utility knife • Stepladder • Safety goggles • Work gloves

MATERIALS
• Prehung exterior door • Lockset and handle • Cedar shims • Wood screws • Vinyl screw caps • Finishing nails • Drip edge • Building paper • Staples • Silicone caulk • Fiberglass insulation • Casing stock

1. Positioning the door

An exterior door can be awkward to maneuver—you may want to work with a helper.

• Move the door into position so that the front edge of the jamb is flush with the exterior sheathing or furring strips.

• On the inside, tack 1x2 retaining braces across the top corners of the door to keep it from tipping out.

• From the outside, slide shims into each corner above the doorjambs and below the threshold.

• Check the threshold for level and adjust it as necessary by lightly tapping the shims (#1).

DOORS & WINDOWS

2. Shimming the sides

- Shims are inserted in the space between the doorjambs and the rough framing.
- Put pairs of shims together, the thin end of one against the wide end of the other. Fit pairs between the jambs and the rough framing at the top and bottom corners and at the hinge and lockset positions. Add extra pairs every 12 to 16 inches.
- With a carpenter's level, check for plumb on both faces of the jamb. Make adjustments as needed by gently tapping shim pairs at different locations (#2). Be careful not to drive in the shims so far that the jambs bow.
- To keep the door in position, drive a nail partway through the jamb into the rough framing on both sides of the top of the door.
- Remove the retaining braces and check that the door opens and closes properly. If you have difficulty closing the door, the fit is too tight. Loosen some shims and check again for plumb.

3. Fastening the door

The door is fastened to the rough framing with pairs of 3-inch No. 10 wood screws driven at each shim location. On some doors, you may be able to peel back the weatherstripping and hide one screw of each pair underneath it.

- With a cordless drill, drill pilot holes, then drive and countersink the screws (#3).
- For added support, replace two of the screws on the top hinge with the longer screws used along the jambs.

- Cover the screw heads with vinyl caps that match the vinyl cladding of the jambs.
- Pull out the temporary nails driven into the top of the jambs.

SAFETY TIP *Wear safety goggles when drilling.*

4. Trimming the shims

Once the doorjambs are fastened, cut the shims flush with the jamb edges. With a utility knife, score the shims on both sides (#4), then snap them off. If a cut is not quite clean, trim off the excess with the knife.

5. Marking the siding

If your new exterior casing is wider than the old casing or if there was no casing to begin with, you'll need to trim back the siding.

- Set the casing against the outside face of one side jamb, leaving $1/8$ to $1/4$ inch of the jamb edge revealed.
- Using the casing as a guide, mark a line along the siding (#5).
- Repeat on the other side and at the top of the door.

Note: *For vinyl or aluminum siding, mark a parallel second cutting line to allow for siding trim pieces.*

6. Cutting the siding

- Set your circular saw to the depth of the siding to avoid cutting into nails in the sheathing or furring strips.
- Cut along the line, starting from as close to the bottom as possible (#6). When you reach shoulder height, stop and climb a stepladder to continue. Stop just short of the corners to avoid cutting into the siding that will remain.
- Finish the cuts at the bottom and corners with a saber saw.
- Pry away the cut siding.

7. Protecting against the elements

A drip edge, insulation, and building paper all help to keep out cold and moisture.
- Stuff strips of fiberglass insulation into the spaces between the jambs and the rough framing. (You can use expanding foam insulation, but take care not to bow the jambs.)
- Cover exposed sheathing or furring strips with building paper and staple it in place. Trim the paper

so it reaches to the middle of the edge on each jamb.
- Trim the drip edge with a hacksaw to fit snugly between the two cut edges of the siding above the door. Slide the flange up between the siding and the building paper (#7). It will stay in place without nailing.

8. Fastening the casing

You can install the exterior casing with 45-degree mitered corners or simply butt the pieces together. If you choose butt joints, the top casing should span the entire width to protect the ends of the side casings from moisture.

- Push the top casing into place under the drip edge. Nail it to both the sheathing or furring strips and the jamb face, driving pairs of 2-inch finishing nails every 10 to 12 inches $\frac{1}{2}$ inch from opposite edges (#8). Drive the nails so the heads are just above the surface of the casing, then sink them with a nail set.
- Fasten the side casings the same way, making sure they sit tightly against the cut siding.

9. Finishing touches

- Seal the seam between the casings and the siding with a bead of paintable silicone caulk (#9).
- Fill nail holes with caulk.
- Lightly sand and repaint the casings.
- Install the door lockset and handle according to the manufacturer's instructions.
- On some doors, the threshold or door sweep is adjustable to make a tight seal. Make any adjustments, being careful not to make the fit too tight to prevent excessive wear.
- Reinstall the interior casings.

DOORS & WINDOWS

A PASSAGE LATCH FOR AN INTERIOR DOOR

A passage latch is not difficult to install, but you may have trouble latching the door when you are done unless your measurements are precise. To assist with installation, most manufacturers provide a template for positioning the drill holes for the doorknobs and latch assembly. The following steps are fairly standard for latches and locksets, but it's a good idea to check the manufacturer's instructions before starting in case installation of your model is different.

This project shows how to install a passage latch on a new door. Measure the door's thickness before buying the latch; most models fit on either $1\frac{3}{8}$- or $1\frac{3}{4}$-inch-thick doors. If all you need to do is replace a malfunctioning passage latch with a new one, your work will be much easier: There are no holes to drill or mortises to chisel. But buy a replacement model compatible with the old one to make sure all the parts fit in the door and jamb.

| SAFETY TIP | *Wear safety goggles when using an electric drill.*

1. Marking the center points

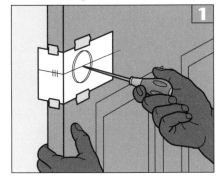

- Mark a line on the face of the door 36 inches up from the floor.
- Tape the template supplied with the passage latch to the door, aligning its center point with the marked line and folding the template around the edge of the door at its vertical reference line. Most templates have two circles for the doorknob center point: $2\frac{3}{8}$ or $2\frac{3}{4}$ inches from the edge of the door. Check the manufacturer's instructions to determine which measurement—known as the backset—is correct, then mark the doorknob center point on the face of the door with an awl (#1).
- Mark the correct center point for the latch assembly on the edge of the door, then remove the template.

2. Drilling the doorknob hole

- Fit an electric drill with a hole saw—check the manufacturer's instructions for the appropriate diameter.

- With the hole saw's pilot bit on the awl mark on the face of the door, drill into the door just until the pilot bit emerges from the other side. Hold the drill level and steady the door with your free hand (#2). Do not finish drilling all the way through the door from this side. Otherwise, the hole saw will leave marks on the surface of the door.

DOORS & WINDOWS

● Move to the other side of the door and insert the pilot bit into the hole. Continue drilling until the hole saw hole cuts completely through the door.

3. Drilling the latch assembly hole

● Fit the drill with a spade bit, once again checking the manufacturer's instructions for the correct diameter.
● Steadying the door and holding the drill level, drill into the edge of the door at the center point of the latch assembly (#3). Continue drilling until the full width of the bit cuts through to the hole for the doorknob.

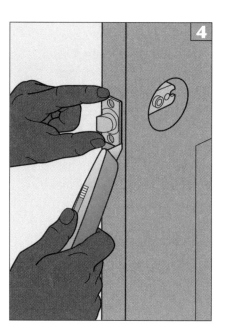

4. Marking the latch assembly faceplate

● Insert the latch assembly into its hole in the door so the rounded side of the latch bolt faces in the direction that the door will close.
● Holding the latch assembly faceplate so its edges align with the door edge, outline the plate on the door with a utility knife (#4). Remove the latch assembly.

5. Chiseling the mortise outline

Making the mortise for the latch assembly faceplate is a two-step operation. Start by deepening the scored outline with a wood chisel the same width as the faceplate, as shown here. Then use the chisel to remove the waste, as shown in Step 6.

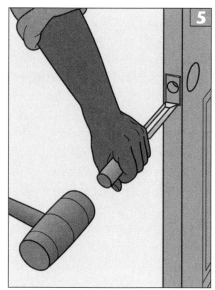

● Holding the chisel straight against the outline with the beveled side of the blade facing into the mortise, strike the handle with a wooden mallet (#5).
● Repeat until the chisel reaches as deep as the thickness of the faceplate.
● Deepen the scored lines all around the outline the same way.

6. Chiseling out the mortise

● Holding the chisel bevel-side down at an angle to the edge of the door, pare out the waste from the mortise outline (#6). Start from the bottom of the outline and work your way up.
● To help you cut to the correct depth, periodically test-fit the faceplate in the mortise. Continue paring away waste from the mortise until the faceplate is flush with the edge of the door.

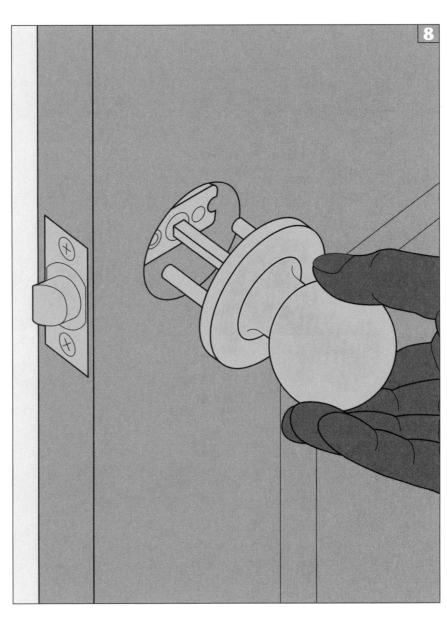

7. Attaching the bolt assembly

- Insert the latch assembly into its hole and fit the faceplate into its mortise. Mark the screw holes, then remove the latch assembly.
- Drill a pilot hole at each marked point for screws supplied.
- Put the latch assembly back in its hole and screw the faceplate to the door (#7).

8. Installing the doorknobs

The exact procedure for fitting the doorknobs into the latch assembly depends on the model of passage latch. Check the manufacturer's instructions. If one of the knobs has a lock, be sure to install it on the appropriate side of the door.

- For the model shown, fit the exterior knob's drive bar and screw posts into their respective holes in the latch assembly (#8). For some models, you need to depress the latch bolt first to align the bar and posts with their holes.
- Slide the interior knob over the drive bar and screw posts of the exterior knob.

9. Fastening the knobs together

- Insert the screws supplied into their holes on the interior knob so that they fit into the screw posts.
- Tighten the screws to fasten the knobs together (#9).

10. Outlining the latch bolt hole

On a new doorjamb, you will need to drill a hole for the latch bolt (Step 10 to Step 11) and install a strike plate (Step 12).

- Close the door so the latch bolt contacts the doorjamb. Mark the top and bottom of the latch bolt on the jamb. Open the door and extend the marks across the face of the jamb with a combination square.
- Measure the distance from the face of the door to the straight edge of the latch bolt (#10). Take a second measurement from the face of the door to the rounded edge of the latch bolt.

- Transfer your measurements to the jamb, marking vertical lines that intersect those indicating the top and bottom of the latch bolt. You will end up with a rectangular outline for the latch bolt hole mortise.

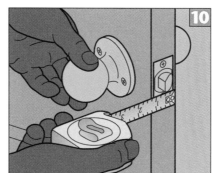

11. Drilling the latch bolt hole

- Score the latch bolt hole outline with a chisel as in Step 5.
- Fit an electric drill with a spade bit slightly smaller than the width or height of the outline. Holding the drill level, bore into the jamb within the outline (#11). Make the hole as deep as the amount by which the latch bolt extends from the edge of the door.
- Square the sides of the hole with a chisel.

12. Fastening the strike plate

- Position the strike plate on the doorjamb so its opening is centered over the latch bolt hole and its curved tongue faces the door.
- Outline the strike plate on the jamb using a utility knife.
- Deepen the strike plate outline with a wood chisel as in Step 5, then pare out the waste within the outline to the depth of the plate's thickness.
- Set the strike plate in the mortise and mark its screw holes. Remove the plate and drill a pilot hole for the screws supplied at each mark.
- Screw the strike plate to the doorjamb (#12).
- If the door rubs against the strike plate as you open and close the door, adjust the fit by bending the strike plate tongue in or out.

SHIMMING A BINDING DOOR

Correcting a binding door is seldom a complicated task. In some cases, simply tightening the hinge screws will solve the problem. If the screw holes have been stripped and the screws cannot be tightened, drill out the holes and pack them with short dowels, then drive the screws through the hinge into the dowels.

If tightening the screws doesn't solve the problem, the solution may be to shim the top or bottom hinge. This involves placing one or more cardboard shims between the doorjamb and the hinge leaf.

When all else fails, you may have to remove the door to sand or plane the edges or deepen the hinge mortises.

HOW LONG WILL IT TAKE?

Less than two hours

TOOLS

• Hammer • Screwdriver • Utility knife • Nail set • Straightedge • Awl • Putty knife

MATERIALS

• Wood shims • Cardboard

DOORS & WINDOWS

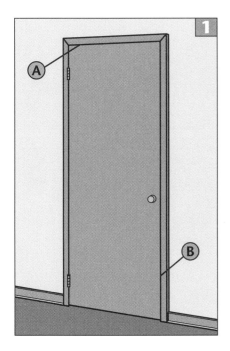

1. Diagnosing door binding

An interior door should have a gap of at least $\frac{1}{16}$ inch between it and each jamb. A binding door usually leaves a mark where it rubs against the jamb. However, if no mark is visible, run a putty knife between the door and the jamb to determine where the door is sticking.

• (A) If the door sticks here, shim the top hinge.
• (B) If the door sticks here, shim the bottom hinge.

2. Wedging the door open

Wedging the door open, without forcing it upward, allows you to remove the pin from the hinge more easily.

• Open the door wide enough to unscrew the hinges and tap wood shims under it with a hammer (#2), using a piece of cardboard to protect the floor.

3. Removing the hinge pin

Remove the pin from the hinge you plan to shim.

• Use a utility knife to slice through any paint sealing the head of the pin to the hinge.
• Place the tip of a nail set against the bottom of the hinge pin and strike it upward with a hammer.
• Once the top of the hinge pin is exposed, pull it out by hand.

DOORS & WINDOWS

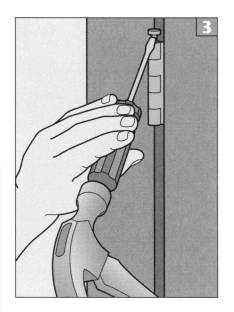

If the pin jams, place the tip of an old screwdriver under the head and strike it upward with a hammer (#3).

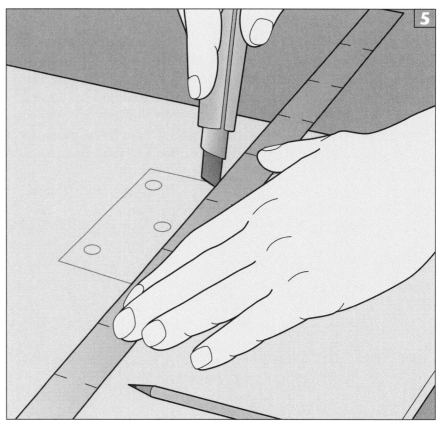

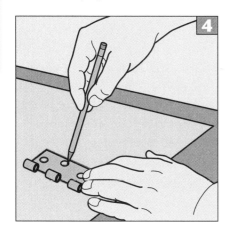

4. Tracing the hinge leaf

- Unscrew the hinge leaf from the doorjamb and pull it free.
- On a thin piece of cardboard, draw four or five outlines of the hinge leaf and its screw-hole locations (#4).

5. Making the shim

- Cut along each marked shim outline with a utility knife and a straightedge (#5).
- Punch a hole at the center of each screw-hole outline on the shims with an awl.

6. Inserting the shim

The number of cardboard shims you need depends on how badly the door sticks. However, don't shim beyond the depth of the hinge mortise.

- Join the hinge leaves and insert the pin into place.
- Place one or more shims in the

hinge mortise (#6) and screw the leaf to the jamb.

- If the door still sticks, unscrew the hinge leaf from the door and add more shims.

INSTALLING DOORSTOPS

Doorstops live up to their name. Installed on the jambs at the top and the sides of a door, their main purpose is to keep the door from closing any further once the latch bolt engages the strike plate. Doorstops also serve as decorative trim, hiding any irregularities in the gap between the door and the jambs.

If you've installed a prehung door with jambs that have stops, your work is done. However, if you are replacing old stops or you have installed a new door and jambs without stops, you will need to cut and install the stops yourself.

Doorstops are sold as strips about ¼ inch thick and 1 inch wide. For a high-quality installation, the stops should fit together at the corners like a picture frame, so you will need to make bevel cuts when sawing the stops to length. This is easy to do with a miter box. Fasten the stops after the door and the lockset are installed. This will enable the door to close properly and stay latched without rattling.

SAFETY TIP *Wear safety goggles when driving nails.*

DOORS & WINDOWS

1. Measuring for the stops

• Close the door, then measure along the hinge-side jamb from the floor to the head (top) jamb (#1).
• Transfer your measurement to a strip of doorstop, then repeat the procedure to measure and mark strips for the latch-side jamb and the head jamb.

2. Beveling the stops

You need to bevel both ends of the head-jamb stop and the top end of the side-jamb stops.
• Lay a strip of doorstop face down in a miter box, setting one edge against the fence so your cutting mark is aligned with the 45-degree bevel slots.

• Slip a backsaw into the bevel slots and, holding the strip flush against the fence, make the cut (#2).

5. Attaching the hinge-side stop

- Fit the hinge-side stop against the jamb so its top end is snug against the beveled end of the head-jamb stop.
- With the spacer between the strip and the door, nail the stop in place (#5).
- Open the door and try closing it again. If the door fails to latch, reposition the stops as necessary.

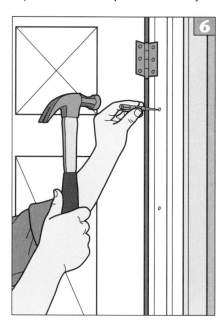

4. Adding the head-jamb stop

- Position the head-jamb stop so one end is tight against the beveled end of the latch-side stop.
- With the spacer between the door and the stop, fasten the strip to the head jamb as you did the latch-jamb stop. Hold the strip flat against the head jamb as you go (#4).

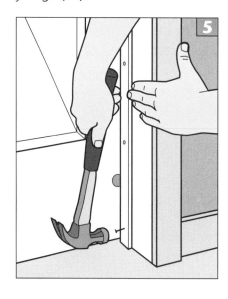

3. Attaching the latch-side stop

- With the door latched closed, position the latch-side stop against the jamb so the beveled end is at the top.
- Place a $1/16$-inch-thick spacer—a 25 cent coin will do—between the door and the stop. The spacer will enable the door to latch properly without rattling when it is closed.
- At the top of the stop, drive a $1\frac{1}{2}$-inch finishing nail partway through the stop into the jamb (#3). Leave the nail head protruding—you will sink it later (Step 6)—and work carefully to avoid hitting the door with the hammer. Wear safety goggles to protect your eyes.
- Drive a nail every 12 inches along the doorstop until you reach the floor, repositioning the spacer as you go.

6. Setting the nails

- Open the door, then hold the tip of a nail set on the head of one of the finishing nails.
- Wearing safety goggles, tap the nail set with a hammer until the nail head is $1/16$ inch below the surface of the wood (#6).
- Sink the other nail heads the same way.

A DEADBOLT LOCK FOR AN EXTERIOR DOOR

Installing a deadbolt lock on an exterior door in addition to a regular key-in-knob lock offers an extra measure of security. Deadbolts are opened from the outside with a key and from the inside with a thumbturn (single-cylinder mechanism) or a key (double-cylinder mechanism). For a door with large glass panes, a lock with a key on the inside is the best choice. Both types are installed in a similar way. When you purchase the lock, make sure it is suitable for the thickness of your door.

Metal doors and some wooden doors are predrilled to accommodate both a key-in-knob lock and an accompanying deadbolt; in this case, the only drilling required is for the strike plate in the doorjamb.

HOW LONG WILL IT TAKE?	TOOLS	MATERIALS
Two to four hours	• Tape measure • Awl • Cordless drill • Drill guide • Hole saw • Spade bit • Screwdriver • Chisel • Wooden mallet • Safety goggles	• Deadbolt lock assembly • Chalk • Masking tape

1. Marking the holes

SAFETY TIP *While drilling, protect your eyes from flying wood chips with safety goggles.*

• Tape the paper template supplied with the lock assembly to the edge and face of the door, 6 to 8 inches above the doorknob.
• Most deadbolts allow two possible positions for the cylinder on the face of the door—known as the lock's backset. On the template, choose the position that best aligns with the center of the doorknob. With an awl or nail, mark the center point of the cylinder on the face of the door (#1) and the position of the latch bolt on the edge of the door.
• Remove the template.

2. Drilling the cylinder hole

In cutting the lock cylinder and latch bolt holes, it is important to keep the drill perpendicular to the

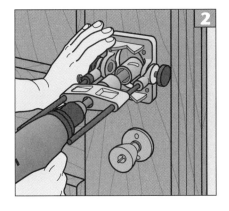

face of the door. Attaching a guide to the drill will help you to drill the holes accurately.
• Fit the drill with a hole saw of the diameter indicated in the manufacturer's specifications. Close the door and line up the pilot bit of the hole saw with the awl point marking the center of the hole. Resting the base of the guide firmly against the face of door, begin drilling the hole (#2).

DOORS & WINDOWS

• To avoid splintering the opposite surface, stop drilling when the pilot bit reaches the other side. Complete the hole from that side.

3. Drilling the bolt hole

• Fit the drill with a spade bit of the size indicated in the manufacturer's specifications.
• Attach lock pins to the guide, then position the guide so it is flat against the edge of the door and the pins are tight against each face of the door.
• Line up the tip of the spade bit with the awl mark on the edge of the door and drill through the door as far as the cylinder hole (#3); if recommended by the manufacturer, continue to drill $\frac{1}{2}$ inch past the cylinder hole.

4. Test-fitting the latch bolt assembly

Before installing the latch bolt assembly, a mortise must be cut in the edge of the door to allow the faceplate to sit flush with the surface.
• Insert the latch bolt assembly in the bolt hole and position the faceplate vertically against the edge of the door.
• Trace around the edge of the faceplate with a pencil (#4), then remove the assembly.

5. Chiseling the mortise

• Select a chisel of the same width as the faceplate. Holding the chisel so the blade is bevel-side in along the pencil mark, lightly tap with a wooden mallet. Score the edge of the mortise in

this way to a depth equal to the thickness of the faceplate.
• With the chisel held at a 45-degree angle to the door edge, bevel-side down, make a series of horizontal cuts across the mortise to the depth of the faceplate $\frac{1}{8}$ to $\frac{1}{4}$ inch apart (#5).

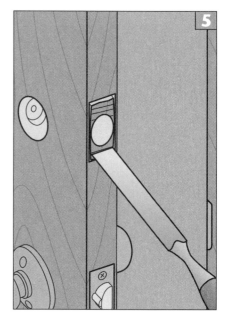

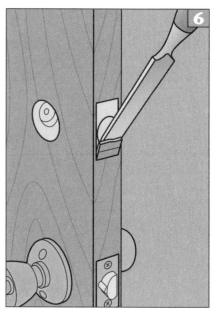

6. Completing the mortise

• Pry out the scored wood pieces with the chisel, holding it at an angle close to the surface and keeping the bevel-side facing the work. Start from the middle of the mortise and work upward, then finish the job by turning and working toward the bottom (#6).

• Rotate the bolt to the desired backset position, then slide the assembly into position through the bolt hole. Fasten the faceplate with the wood screws provided.

7. Installing the lock cylinder

• Pass the tailpiece of the lock mechanism through the hole in the latch bolt mechanism from the outside of the door (#7).

• From the inside of the door, position the thumbturn retaining plate so the tailpiece passes through the central hole in the retaining plate.

• Fasten the retaining plate to the lock mechanism with the large machine screws provided.

8. Fastening the thumbturn

• Fit the thumbturn on the retaining plate, fitting the tailpiece into the thumbscrew mechanism (#8).

• With the small wood screws provided, fasten the thumbscrew through the retaining plate into the door surface.

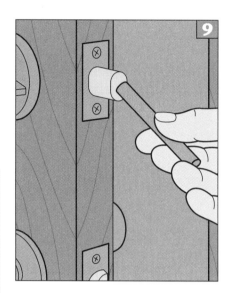

11. Installing the strike plate

For added security, many deadbolt strike plates are fastened with a combination of regular wood screws and 3-inch screws that penetrate the rough framing behind the doorjamb.

- Center the strike plate over the strike box hole and trace the edge with a pencil mark (#11).
- Chisel out a mortise in the same way as you did for the latch bolt faceplate.
- Reposition the plate and mark the screw holes.
- Drill pilot holes and fasten the strike plate to the doorjamb.

9. Marking the strike box location

The best way to mark the location of the strike box on the doorjamb is with the end of the bolt. Many bolts have extending points or dimples that, when the bolt is forced against the frame, leave an indentation in the wood surface. Alternatively, the bolt end can be marked with chalk (#9) or lipstick, then transferred onto the door-jamb in the same way.

10. Drilling for the strike box

- Fit the drill with a spade bit of the same size as the one used to drill the bolt hole in the edge of the door. To determine the depth of the strike box, measure the length of the bolt extending from the door. Mark the spade bit with a piece of masking tape at this depth as a guide.

- Drill the strike box hole at the marked spot on the doorjamb (#10), stopping at the marked depth.

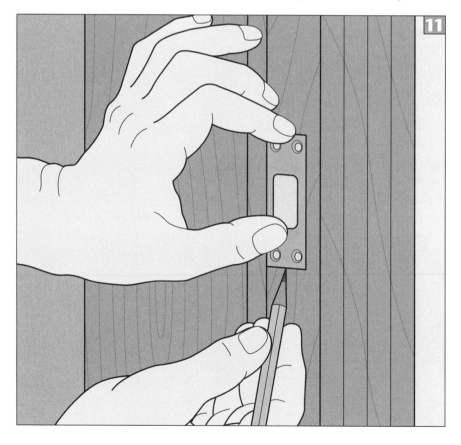

DOORS & WINDOWS

INSTALLING A WINDOW

Window sashes and jambs can be made of a variety of materials. Vinyl-clad wood is an economical and long-lasting choice. Windows that insulate well are double- or even triple-glazed and may have argon gas between the panes. A low-E coating can further increase the insulation value.

To remove your old window, carefully pry off the interior molding, slice through the caulk on the exterior, and unscrew the jambs from the rough framing. Before buying your new window, make sure it fits the opening in the siding and allows room for shims between the jambs and the rough framing. For a renovation project, avoid windows with an exterior nailing flange since these require the removing of a section of siding.

If your old window was installed without exterior trim, you can install the new one in the same way—as shown in this project. Otherwise, buy new trim at least as wide as the old and, if necessary, trim the siding to accommodate it.

HOW LONG WILL IT TAKE?
Two to four hours

TOOLS
• Utility knife • Carpenter's level • Tape measure • Cordless drill • Staple gun • Hammer • Nail set • Hacksaw • Backsaw and miter box • Combination square • Caulking gun • Safety goggles • Work gloves

MATERIALS
• Prehung window • Cedar shims • Wood screws • Finishing nails • Drip edge • Building paper • Staples • Silicone caulk • Fiberglass insulation • Trim stock

1. Preparing the opening

Building paper placed between your new window and the rough framing provides an added layer of moisture protection. In removing your old window, existing building paper may be damaged and will have to be replaced.

• With a utility knife, cut 8-inch-wide strips of building paper to fit the top, bottom, and sides of the window opening.

• Lay each strip of building paper flush against the edge of the inside wall and make a fold mark along the edge of the sheathing.

• Fold back the building paper and slide it between the sheathing and the siding. Fasten the building paper with staples (#1).

• Cover all sides of the window opening.

2. Installing a drip edge

An exterior wall of brick provides an automatic setback for the window. With other types of siding, a drip edge is required at the top of the window to deflect moisture.

• With a hacksaw, trim the drip edge to the width of the window opening.

• Insert the flange of the drip edge between the siding and the

building paper at the top of the opening (#2).

3. Lifting the window into place

Because there will be little space on the exterior between the siding and the jambs, place and adjust the window from indoors.

• Tack a 1x4 a few inches longer than the width of the window to the top of the jambs. This safety brace will prevent the window from falling outside.
• Lift and place the base of the jambs onto the rough sill (#3). Push the window into place so the jambs are flush with the interior wall.
• Have a helper check the position of the window from outside. The edges should sit between $\frac{1}{8}$ and $\frac{1}{4}$ inch beyond the surface of the siding to provide a ledge for a bead of caulk to be applied later.

4. Leveling the window

• As added support for the window's sill, place a block of wood under the center of it flush with or set back from the wall.
• Slide a single shim between the bottom of each side jamb and the rough sill.
• Place a level on the sill and tap in the shims with a hammer until you get a level reading (#4).

5. Shimming the jambs

• Insert pairs of shims near the top and bottom corners and at every 12 inches along the top and sides of the jambs. Slide in one shim wide-end first, following it with one thin-end first.
• With a carpenter's level, check for plumb on both faces of the jamb (#5). Make adjustments as needed by gently tapping shim pairs at different locations. Be careful not to drive in the shims so far that the jambs bow.

Note: *Leave the window a little out of plumb rather than too offset from the wall. Otherwise, you'll have difficulty in fitting the trim.*

6. Fastening the jambs

Countersink screws so you can cover the heads, making for an installation neat in appearance.

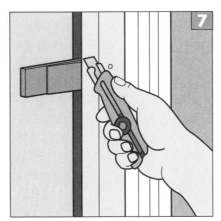

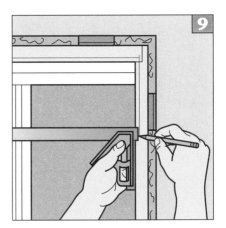

• Once plumb is established, countersink holes at the shim locations near the top of each side jamb. Drive screws through the holes into the rough framing. Fastening these two points first will stabilize the window.

• Check that the window opens and closes properly. If you have difficulty sliding the sash, the fit is too tight. Loosen some shims and check again for plumb.

• Remove the safety brace.

• Countersink and drive screws through the jambs at each shim location (#6).

7. Trimming the shims

• With a utility knife, score the shims on both sides (#7), then snap them off. If a cut is not quite clean, trim off the excess.

• Fill the space between the jambs and the rough framing with strips of fiberglass insulation.

8. Caulking the exterior

On the exterior, the seam between the window frame and the siding should be sealed.

• Lay a bead of paintable silicone caulk around the entire window assembly (#8).

9. Marking for trim

Trim covers the gaps between the window assembly and the surfaces of the interior wall.

• With a combination square, mark each jamb and the sill $\frac{1}{8}$ inch from its inner edge (#9).

10. Installing trim

• Align trim pieces at the marked lines and mark the inside corners.

• With a miter box and a back-saw, trim the pieces at 45-degree angles.

• Nail the trim pieces both to the window assembly and through the wallboard into the rough framing (#10). Drive the nails until the heads are just above the surface of the pieces.

• Sink the nails with a nail set. Fill the holes with wood filler and apply a clear finish or paint.

FREEING A BINDING WINDOW SASH

Trying to open a jammed window is frustrating. Wood-framed windows, in particular, are prone to sticking. Usually the problem is easily solved, such as when the cause of the binding is paint buildup or swelling due to humidity.

Run a double-hung sash tool—also called a window zipper—along the joint between the sash and the stops indoors and outdoors. The tool not only slices through any paint seal, but will often separate the sash from the stops enough for the window to move freely.

If the problem persists, remove the side stops and take out the window, then scrape, sand, and lubricate the sash channels. Don't plane the sash—a loose-fitting window that rattles may be the result. Never scrape or sand sash channels of plastic or metal. Leave enough space for the sash to move freely when reinstalling the stops.

HOW LONG WILL IT TAKE?
Less than two hours

TOOLS
• Double-hung sash tool • Pry bar • Putty knives • Cold chisel • Ball-peen hammer • Utility knife • Screwdriver • Locking-grip pliers • Spokeshave (or cabinet scraper) • Sanding block • Hammer • Paintbrush

MATERIALS
• Masking tape • Wood pads • Furniture polish (or paraffin wax) • Finishing nails • Paint • Spacers

1. Separating the sash and the stops

• Apply masking tape along the edges of the panes and in an "X" across them. If you accidentally break the glass, the tape will keep shards from falling out as fast.

• Run a double-hung sash tool along the joint between the stop (A) and the sash (B) on one side of the window. Repeat along the bottom (#1) and the other side.

• Do the same on the exterior. If the window continues to stick, move on to the following steps.

2. Removing the stops

To free the window from the frame, pry off the side stops. In order to reach the stops, you may need to remove the trim at the sides and bottom of the window.

• Pry trim off the window frame with a pry bar, placing a wood pad under it to protect the wall.

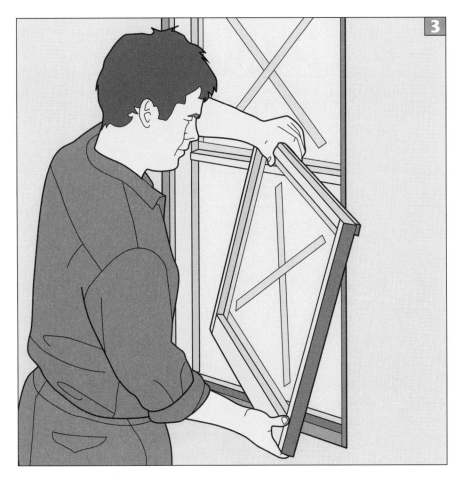

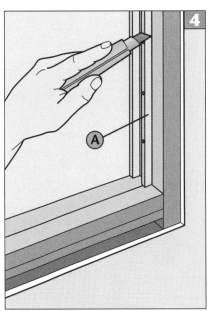

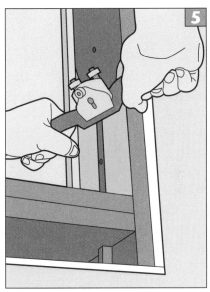

• To remove each stop, push two putty knives into the joint between the sash and the stop, then insert a cold chisel and tap with a ball-peen hammer (#2). Repeat at 18-inch intervals along the stop until it comes off.

3. Removing the window

• Pull the window out of the frame (#3).
• If the window is held by sash cords, take them off the window and knot them to keep them from being pulled through the pulleys.

4. Removing the parting strips

Remove one parting strip (A) at a time to more easily scrape, sand, and lubricate the sash channel.
• Break the paint seal between the parting strip and the frame with a utility knife (#4).
• Remove any screws holding the parting strip in place.
• Clamp locking-grip pliers to the bottom of the parting strip, cushioning the jaws with wood pads, and pull out the strip. Repeat at 18-inch intervals along the parting strip until it comes off.

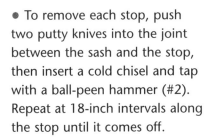

5. Scraping the sash channels

• Scrape paint and debris from the sash channel with a spokeshave (#5) or a cabinet scraper.
• Lightly sand the channel with sandpaper wrapped around a sanding block.

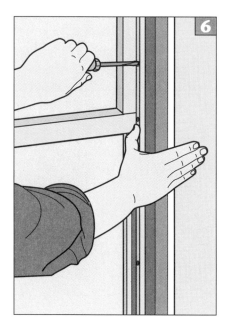

6. Replacing the parting strips

- Reposition the parting strip and secure it with finishing nails or reinstall the screws (#6).
- Remove the other parting strip to scrape and sand the other sash channel, then reinstall it.
- Touch up scraped and sanded surfaces with paint as needed and let them dry.
- Lubricate the channels and parting strips with furniture polish or by rubbing them with a block of paraffin wax.

7. Reinstalling the window

The side stops of some windows are face-nailed to the frame, as shown here; with other windows, the stops are nailed to the inside edges of the frame.
- Put the window back into place.
- Position one side stop and secure it at 6-inch intervals with finishing nails (#7).
- Reinstall the other side stop the same way.
- Put back any trim you removed from around the window, then peel the masking tape off the panes of glass.

Note: *Use cardboard spacers to position the side stops at a uniform distance from the sash.*

REPLACING WINDOW SCREENS

A single broken window screen is often all it takes to put an end to a bug-free summer. Fortunately, replacing a screen is a quick and easy project. The most common screening materials available are vinyl-coated fiberglass and aluminum. Although aluminum is less likely to tear or sag, it dents easily and may corrode—problems that have led to the popularity of fiberglass. Fiberglass has other advantages: It tends to be less expensive and is available in a variety of mesh types (aluminum is available in just one), including a very fine solar-screening mesh that reduces ultraviolet radiation, making it a good choice for sun porches.

Both materials are also easy to patch. Attach vinyl-coated fiberglass patches with acetone-based glue. The acetone partly melts the vinyl coating, bonding the edges of the overlapping patch to the screen. Fasten aluminum patches with very thin wires. However, because patches are unsightly, and take almost as much time and effort to install as a replacement screen, starting fresh is usually the best idea.

HOW LONG WILL IT TAKE?
Less than two hours

TOOLS
· Flat-head screwdriver · Utility knife · Scissors · Shears (or tin snips) · Spline roller

MATERIALS
· Screening material (aluminum or fiberglass) · Spline

1. Freeing the spline

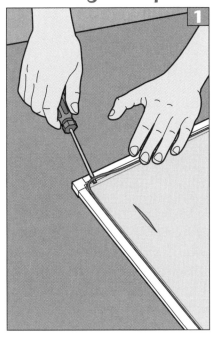

Most screens are held in place with long plastic splines that fit into a groove along the back of the frame.
● Place the screen face down on your work surface.
● Locate the end of the spline in the groove (it is often in a corner).
● With a narrow flat-head screwdriver, dislodge one end of the spline from the groove (#1).

2. Removing the spline

● Hold the edge of the screen to the work surface and carefully pull the spline from the the groove (#2). Do the same on all sides.

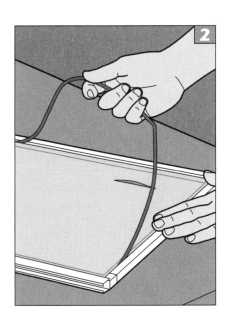

● Avoid stretching the spline if you plan to use it with the new screen.

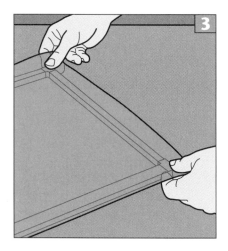

3. Fitting the new screen

● Cut a fiberglass screen with scissors and an aluminum screen with heavy-duty shears or tin snips.
● Measure the frame and and cut the new screen so it overlaps the frame by 1 inch on all sides.
● Lay the new screen over the screen frame (#3).
● Trim $\frac{1}{2}$ inch off the corners of an aluminum screen so they don't bunch up during installation.

4. Installing the spline on one side

Use a spline roller to press the spline and screen back into the groove. If installing aluminum screen, before pressing the spline into place, run the roller over the screen and the groove with a back and forth motion to create a crease.
● Starting in a corner, press the spline into the groove with the edge of the spline-roller blade.

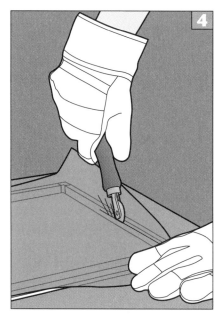

● Continue pressing the spline into place using a gentle back and forth motion (#4).
● Use a flat-head screwdriver to tuck the spline into the corners.
● If necessary, trim the ends of the spline with a utility knife.

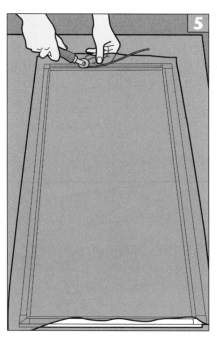

5. Completing the spline

● Once the screen is secured at one end of the frame, work on the opposite end the same way, but use one hand to keep the screen taut against the frame (#5)
● Install the screen and spline in the grooves on the other two sides of the frame.

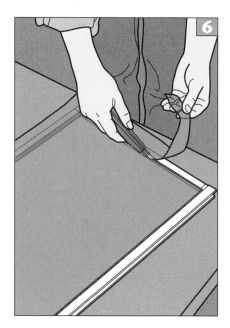

6. Trimming the excess

Use a utility knife to trim either aluminum or fiberglass.
● Starting at a corner of the frame, trim away excess screen by running the blade along the edge of the groove next to the spline (#6). Angle the knife away from the spline to avoid cutting through it. Pull away the excess as you cut.

DOORS & WINDOWS

INSTALLING A SKYLIGHT

Skylights are available with a fixed pane or with a sash that opens. Some fixed skylights have a ventilation flap, handy in a finished attic of a house that isn't air conditioned. Skylights that open can usually be installed without climbing onto the roof because the sash can be removed from the frame.

Choose a skylight that will fit between the rafters or trusses in your attic—cutting roof framing should be left to a professional. If you want to bring light to a room below the attic, you will need to build a light shaft. The shaft can be flared to allow more light into the room below. In selecting a location for your skylight, make sure both the skylight and light shaft will be clear of any plumbing stacks or chimneys.

Before beginning, check the weather forecast to make sure you'll have time to complete the installation of the skylight itself before any risk of rain. The light shaft can then be left for the next weekend. Also check your local building codes for any permits that may be required.

HOW LONG WILL IT TAKE?
More than four hours

TOOLS
• Carpenter's level • Hammer • Circular saw • Pry bar • Chalk line • Cordless drill • Dimpler • Screwdriver • Reciprocating saw • Plumb bob • Carpenter's square • Staple gun • Utility knife • Tape measure • Safety goggles • Work gloves • Dust mask • Hard hat

MATERIALS
• Skylight • Flashing kit • Skylight underlayment • Roofing nails • Framing lumber • Polyethylene sheeting • Wallboard • Finishing nails • Common nails • Staples • Wallboard screws • Joint compound • Joint tape • Corner bead

1. Marking opening dimensions

• Remove any insulation and vapor barrier from the work area.
• With a carpenter's level, mark the rough opening dimensions of the skylight on the roof between rafters. Then, drive a finishing nail in partway at each of the corners.
• Drop a plumb bob from each nail and mark the outline for the light shaft.
• To flare the light shaft, tie a string to one nail. Pull it taut at the desired angle and mark where it touches. Also mark the angle of the string onto the side of the joist (#1) and at the rafter above.
• Measure the distance to the original mark and repeat the procedure for the other side of the shaft, making sure the distance from the original mark to the string is the same.
• Remove the finishing nails.

SAFETY TIP *When working in an attic, wear a dust mask, safety goggles, a long-sleeved shirt and a hard hat. For handling insulation, add work gloves.*

2. Framing the roof opening

The skylight opening is framed with blocking placed between the rafters. You will need to install the

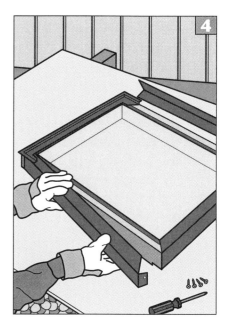

tions to an immovable object on the other side of the house with $\frac{5}{8}$-inch filament nylon rope.

- On the roof, locate the nails at the corners of the opening.
- Remove shingles from around the opening with a pry bar, exposing the building paper. Don't cut any of the shingles.

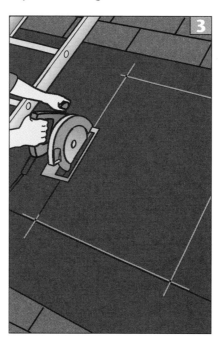

blocking at the same angle as the light shaft and bevel one long edge of each blocking so it will sit flat against the roof sheathing.

- Cut blocking to fit using lumber the same size as the rafters.
- With a T-bevel, measure the angle between the light-shaft marks on the rafters and the roof. Transfer the angle to each piece of blocking and cut the bevel with a circular saw set at the same angle.
- Fasten the blocking to the rafters with 3-inch nails (#2).
- Drive nails through the roof at the four corners of the opening.

3. Cutting the opening

To gain a toehold on a sloping roof, take an extension ladder apart and position a section of the ladder on each side of the skylight opening. Secure the ladder sec-

- Snap a chalk line between the nails, then drive the nails back out with a nail set.
- Set the blade of a circular saw fitted with a carbide-tipped blade to the thickness of the roofing material and cut through the roof following the chalked lines (#3). Stop about $\frac{1}{2}$ inch from the corners to avoid cutting into the blocking and finish the cuts with a reciprocating saw.
- Pull back the building paper from around the opening.

4. Preparing the skylight

- Remove cladding pieces from the skylight frame according to the manufacturer's directions (#4).
- If the skylight opens, remove the sash.
- Attach the mounting brackets to the frame following the manufacturer's directions.

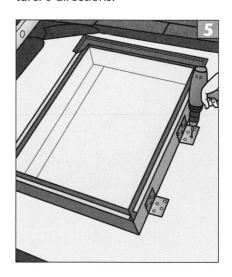

5. Positioning the skylight

- With a helper, center the skylight over the opening and level it.
- Fasten the mounting brackets to the roof using the screws provided (#5)—make sure that the brackets are supported below by rafters.

6. Installing underlayment

- Make sure the area 6 inches around the skylight is clean.
- Cut the underlayment into strips long enough to fit around each side of the skylight with an overlap of 6 inches at the corners.
- Starting at the bottom of the skylight, peel the backing from one of the underlayment pieces and smooth the piece in place from the top of the wooden skylight frame down onto the roof. If your model has a rubber gasket at the bottom of the frame, make sure the underlayment lies under it.
- Apply the underlayment on each side of the skylight (#6), then on the top.

7. Installing sill flashing

- Fit the building paper back in on top of the underlayment and staple it in place.
- Fill in shingles up to the bottom of the skylight.
- Position the bottom flashing (#7) and fasten it to the frame using the nails provided. Don't nail into the roof—the nail holes could cause leaks. For models with a rubber gasket under the bottom sill, make sure that the flashing is placed under it.

8. Installing step flashing

- Starting at the bottom of the skylight, install a shingle, then a piece of step flashing, and then another shingle, interweaving the flashing pieces with the shingles. Overlap each step at least 3½ inches. Nail the flashing to the frame only (#8)—not to the roof.
- At the top of the skylight, cut and fold the step flashing around the top of the frame according to the manufacturer's directions.

9. Installing head flashing

- Reinstall the bottom cladding and then the sides using the original screws. If the top casing was removed, put it back.

- Interlock the head flashing with the top cladding and fasten it (#9).
- Reinstall shingles over the flashing—don't nail through the flashing. Keep the top shingles at the distance from the top flashing recommended by the manufacturer.
- If the skylight sash was removed, reinstall it in the frame.

10. Installing a sister joist

If your roof is framed with joists and rafters rather than prefabricated trusses, one of the joists will interfere with construction of the light shaft. A section of this joist must be removed. Before cutting into it, it must be reinforced with a sister joist.

- Cut a sister joist to fit from the exterior top plate to the nearest load-bearing wall—use the same size lumber as the existing joists.

Cut one end at an angle to fit it in line with the rafter.

- Nail the sister joist to the existing joist with pairs of 3-inch nails spaced every 12 inches (#10). Do not drive in any nails within the area where the light shaft will be installed.

11. Cutting the old joist

- Place a scrap of wood against the joist to be cut and tap with a hammer to loosen the screws in the wallboard.
- With a reciprocating saw, cut the existing joist along the angle marked on the joist (#11).
- Remove the section, working the piece back and forth to pull the screws though the wallboard.

12. Framing the shaft opening

- Cut blocking to fit between the joists using lumber the same size as the rafter. Bevel one edge as you did for the blocking (Step 2).
- Fasten the blocking to the joists with 3-inch nails.

- Cut a trimmer piece to fit between the blocking and fasten it to the joist on the side of the opening opposite the sister joist (#12)—now both sides of the framing line up with rafters.
- Drive finishing nails through the corners of the frame. From below, snap chalk lines between the nails. Remove the nails and cut out the section of ceiling from below with a keyhole saw.
- From the room below, screw the wallboard to the framing.

13. Fastening the studs

- To bring the wallboard in line with the skylight frame, fasten pieces of 1-inch-thick rigid foam insulation to the rafters within the skylight opening using screws and washers. Fasten 1-inch filler boards to the trimmer piece and sister joist within the ceiling opening.

- Holding a 2x4 against the inside corner of the framed openings, mark it where it meets the top of the ceiling framing and the bottom of the roof framing. Cut the piece to length.
- Toe-nail the 2x4 to the ceiling and roof framing so that its inside face is flush with the surface of the foam insulation.
- Install the remaining corner studs in the same way (#13).
- Install additional studs between the corner studs if they are more than 24 inches apart.
- Attach 2x4 nailing strips to the outside edge of each corner stud to provide a surface for attaching wallboard on the narrower walls.

14. Installing a vapor barrier

A polyethylene vapor barrier on the inside of the shaft will prevent warm, moist air from condensing on the insulation or rafters.

- Working on a stepladder inside the shaft, staple the polyethylene sheeting to the studs (#14). Overlap any seams by an amount equal to the space between studs.
- Seal the vapor barrier to the skylight with acoustical sealant.

15. Installing wallboard

If the skylight is in the bathroom or another high-humidity area, cover the walls of the shaft with moisture-resistant wallboard. Note: For illustration clarity, the polyethylene sheeting has been removed from one shaft wall.

- Cut wallboard to fit the walls of the shaft and fasten it to the studs every 12 inches with wallboard screws (#15).
- Fill the screw holes with joint compound and finish the seams with joint tape and compound. Use corner bead at the outside corners at the bottom of the walls.

WEATHERPROOFING DOORS AND WINDOWS

Sealing air leaks in your home not only makes good environmental sense, it will, with only a small investment of time, save you money. In most homes, weatherproofing doors and windows will seal the most significant leaks.

Most new doors and windows have integral weatherstripping. When it wears out, you may be able to get replacement items from the manufacturer. For doors and windows without weatherstripping, a variety of products is available. Most of them can be left in place year-round, while some products used on windows, such as caulking cord and plastic insulating film, are installed only for the winter when the window isn't being opened.

Before applying the weatherstripping make sure that the surface is clean. Repair any bubbling or peeling paint.

HOW LONG WILL IT TAKE?

Less than two hours

TOOLS

• Caulking gun • Hair dryer
• Screwdriver • Cordless drill
• Hacksaw • Scissors • Utility knife • Tape measure

MATERIALS

• Clothes pins and hanger
• Plastic bag • Spring-action weatherstripping • Standard door sweep • U-channel door sweep • Bumper threshold • Vinyl V-strip • Sponge-rubber weatherstripping • Caulking cord • Silicone caulk

Checking for air leakage

The first step in weatherproofing is to find the leaks. A plastic vegetable bag attached to a coat hanger makes a great draft finder. Or, watch for the fluttering flame of a match or the smoke of an incense stick. Detecting leaks is easiest on a windy day.

• Close all the doors and windows in the house.

• Go outside and determine the direction of the wind.

• Open a window on the side of the house opposite to the direction from which the wind is blowing.

• Pass the draft finder in front of all the doors (#1) and other windows, watching closely for any movement or flutter.

• Close and test the last window.

DOORS

Spring-action weatherstripping

On the latch side and top of a door, spring-action weatherstripping fastened to the doorstop will press against the door when it is closed. On the hinge side, weatherstripping with a flexible vinyl edge seals the gap. The two types are generally sold in a single kit.

● On the hinged side, measure the length of the doorstop. Cut the flexible vinyl weatherstripping to this measurement.

● Close the door and position the piece on the doorstop on the hinged side, lightly pressing the flexible edge against the door so the edge compresses by about a third. Mark the screw holes.

● Drill pilot holes and secure the strip with the screws provided.

● Install the spring-action strips on the top and latch sides in the same way (#1). When positioning the strips, place them so the spring-action edge compresses by about two-thirds.

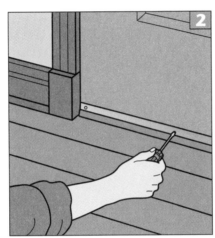

Attaching a standard sweep

Although this type of door sweep is not the most durable, it is inexpensive and easy to install.

● Measure the width of the door and, with a hacksaw, cut the sweep to length.

● Shut the door. Working from inside, position the sweep along the bottom of the door so that it is snug against the threshold. Mark the screw holes.

● Drill pilot holes and attach the sweep with the screws provided (#2).

● Open and close the door a few times. If the sweep binds, loosen the screws and adjust the position of the sweep.

Fastening a U-shaped sweep

A U-shaped vinyl door sweep is sturdier and more effective than a standard door sweep. However, it can only be installed if there is a sufficient gap under the door.

● Measure the width of the door and cut the sweep to length with a hacksaw.

● Slide the sweep over the bottom of the door, with the mounting screw holes oriented toward the inside of the house (#3).

● Close the door with the sweep in place and adjust the position of the sweep so that it rests on the threshold.

● Drill pilot holes at the center of the screw slots and fasten the sweep with the screws provided.

● Open and close the door a few times to check whether it binds. If it does, loosen the screws and adjust the sweep.

DOORS & WINDOWS

DOORS (CONTINUED)

Installing a bumper threshold

This type of threshold is fastened to the existing threshold on the exterior side of the door and makes contact with the face of the door when the door is closed. It's an effective choice when there isn't enough room under the door for a U-shaped sweep. It is easiest to install when the existing threshold is wood.

● Measure the width of the door opening.
● Remove the vinyl strip from the threshold. Cut the bumper threshold to length with a hacksaw. With a utility knife, cut the vinyl strip ¾ inch longer to allow for shrinkage. Reinsert the vinyl strip.
● Close the door and position the bumper threshold snugly against the face of the door. Mark the screw holes.
● Drill pilot holes and fasten the bumper threshold with the screws provided (#4).

WINDOWS

Caulking casings

Silicone caulk can be used to seal fixed gaps of up to ½ inch, such as around window (and door) casings. Paintable caulk can be painted the same color as the trim and walls. Fill gaps larger than ½ inch with foam insulation.

● Apply masking tape on each side of the crack along the edge of the window casing and along the wall, leaving a ¼-inch gap between the two tape strips.

● Holding the caulking gun level, bead caulk along the crack (#1).
● Smooth the caulk with a wet finger.
● Remove the tape and allow the caulk to set for at least two hours before painting.

V-stripping the sides of sashes

Vinyl V-strip seals gaps between two moving surfaces.

● Open the window all the way.
● Measure the channel on the window jamb and add 2 inches. Cut the V-strip to this length and fold it into a V-shape with the adhesive on the outside.
● Insert the strip into the channel on the window jamb, slipping one end behind the window sash. The tip of the V should point toward the interior.
● Starting at the bottom, peel off the backing and press the strip into place (#2).

V-stripping the top of sashes

● Measure and cut two sections of V-strip to the width of the window. Fold the strips into a V-shape with the adhesive on the outside.
● Position one of the strips along the inside surface of the upper sash, the tip of the V pointing up. Peel off the backing and press the strip securely into place.

DOORS & WINDOWS

• Position the second strip along the top of the outside surface of the lower sash with the tip of the V pointing down. Peel off the backing and press the strip into place (#3).

Sponge-rubber weatherstripping

When the window seals fairly tightly at the bottom when closed, V-strip can be installed on the sash to close any small gap. For larger gaps, apply sponge-rubber weatherstripping.

• Measure and cut the weatherstripping to the width of the window sash.

• Press the strip onto the bottom edge of the lower sash flush with

the outside of the window and peel off the backing as you go (#4).

Insulating kit

Designed for indoor use only, this insulating kit is typically installed for the winter and removed in the summer. The kit contains double-sided tape and enough plastic film to cover a fairly large window.

• Apply the tape to the casings around the window.

• Unfold the film and cut it to the dimensions of the window, allowing 2 or 3 inches extra beyond the tape on all sides.

• Remove the top tape liner and apply the film to the window. Remove the other tape liners, stretch the film to remove wrinkles, and press the edges firmly onto the tape.

• Starting at one corner, warm the film with a hair dryer to remove the wrinkles (#5)—do not touch the film with the dryer.

• Trim off the excess film at the edges with scissors.

Chapter 5
PAINTING & HOME DECOR

Although the materials in this chapter—paint, wallpaper, and trim—do not involve the structure of a house, they all have a considerable impact on a home's comfort level and decor. Perhaps because they don't entail structural alterations, the fixes and improvements in the following projects are fairly easy to do.

Professional painters and decorators generally agree that more than half the time devoted to painting or papering a room should be spent on careful surface preparation. That's because no matter how superior the paint quality or how expertly it is applied, defects such as cracks, holes, and old peeling paint will invariably show through and spoil the final result. Dirt and grease can even prevent fresh paint from adhering. You'll find a wide range of preliminary fixes on the following pages, from stripping old paint and repairing cracks and holes to preparing a room for painting and repairing scratches and holes in woodwork.

TOOLS FOR PAINTING & HOME DECOR FIXES AND IMPROVEMENTS

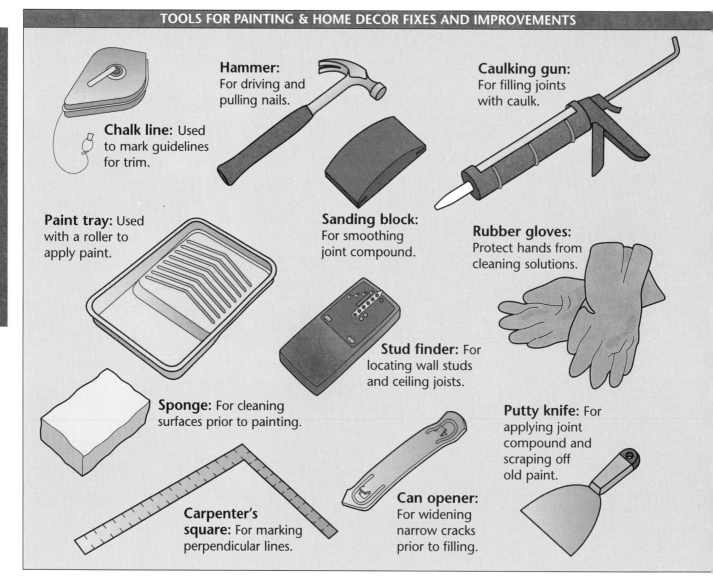

Chalk line: Used to mark guidelines for trim.

Hammer: For driving and pulling nails.

Caulking gun: For filling joints with caulk.

Paint tray: Used with a roller to apply paint.

Sanding block: For smoothing joint compound.

Rubber gloves: Protect hands from cleaning solutions.

Stud finder: For locating wall studs and ceiling joists.

Sponge: For cleaning surfaces prior to painting.

Putty knife: For applying joint compound and scraping off old paint.

Carpenter's square: For marking perpendicular lines.

Can opener: For widening narrow cracks prior to filling.

Paint gives you more bang for your home-improvement buck than just about anything else. Although there's no shame in simply brushing and rolling paint on walls and ceilings, there are a host of other available options that will enable you to create a bold statement or a subdued backdrop. Decorative painting techniques such as stenciling, colorwashing, sponging, ragging, and faux stone are simple to master and don't require specialized skills or tools.

Few elements can change the character of a room as dramatically as wood trim. Baseboard, chair rail, and crown molding are available in a wide range of styles and colors, they are relatively inexpensive, and they are easy to install.

This chapter will also show you how to paint exterior trim. The principles are the same as those that apply to painting indoors: The final result will only be as attractive as the time and effort given to surface preparation.

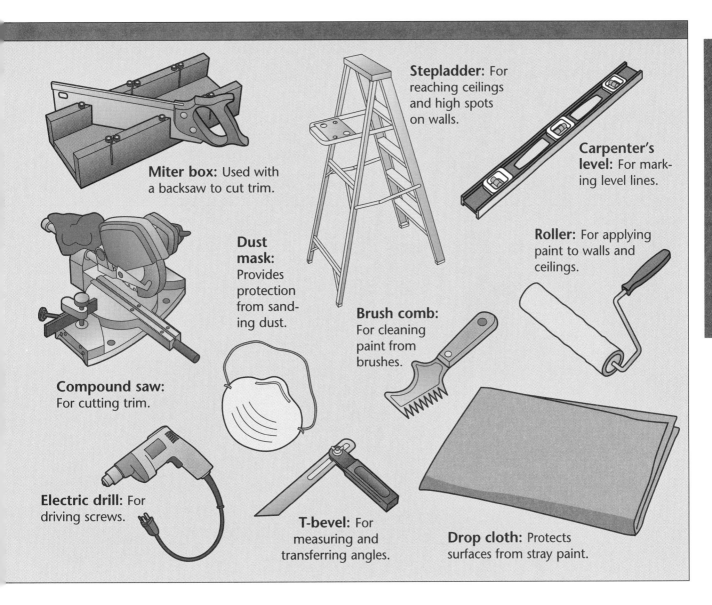

Miter box: Used with a backsaw to cut trim.

Stepladder: For reaching ceilings and high spots on walls.

Carpenter's level: For marking level lines.

Compound saw: For cutting trim.

Dust mask: Provides protection from sanding dust.

Brush comb: For cleaning paint from brushes.

Roller: For applying paint to walls and ceilings.

Electric drill: For driving screws.

T-bevel: For measuring and transferring angles.

Drop cloth: Protects surfaces from stray paint.

STRIPPING OLD PAINT

Stripping paint isn't anybody's idea of a good time. But if surfaces are cracked or peeling, simply painting over them will turn out to be a waste of your time. There are two basic ways to remove paint: with a chemical stripper or with a heat gun. Both methods entail a lot of scraping.

Chemical strippers soften a finish so it can be scraped off the surface; a paste formula will grip better than a liquid on vertical surfaces. Keep in mind that even water-based strippers, although they are more environmentally friendly, are still potentially harmful. Make sure you wear long sleeves, rubber gloves, and safety goggles and work only in a well-ventilated area. If your house was built before 1978 you may have lead-based paint, which requires special precautions. Contact the Environmental Protection Agency (EPA) for more information.

Heat guns work well if you need to remove many layers of paint. Heat the wood until the paint bubbles and then scrape off the residue immediately. Remember to wear the same protective gear you would don for working with chemical strippers.

HOW LONG WILL IT TAKE?
More than four hours

TOOLS
• Paintbrush • Detail brush • Putty knife • Hand scraper • Triangular scraper (or awl) • Contoured scraper • Heat gun • Abrasive pad • Safety goggles • Rubber gloves • Organic vapor respirator

MATERIALS
• Chemical paint stripper • Sawdust • Glass container • Metal container • Steel wool • Cloth • Sandpaper • Denatured alcohol • Mineral spirits • Cardboard • Aluminum foil • Newspaper

USING CHEMICAL STRIPPER

1. Applying stripper

Work on a small area at a time so the stripper-softened paint doesn't harden before you finish scraping.
• Place a glass container of stripper on several sheets of newspaper to protect the area around it from drips.
• Apply a thick layer of stripper to the surface with a paintbrush, brushing in one direction only (#1).
• Let the stripper remain in place according to the manufacturer's instructions.

2. Thickening the stripper

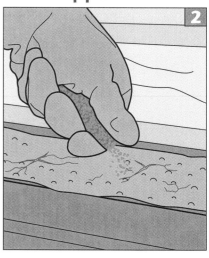

Adding sawdust will thicken a liquid stripper and make it easier to scrape off softened finish.

● Sprinkle a thin coat of sawdust on the blistered and wrinkled paint (#2) just before you begin to scrape.

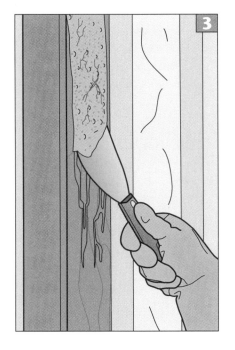

3. Scraping off the paint

● Holding a putty knife at a 30-degree angle, press downward as you scrape off the softened finish (#3). Work carefully to avoid gouging the wood.

● While you work, clean off the blade of the putty knife frequently by scraping the waste into a metal container. (Stripper dissolves plastic.) Consult your local environmental regulations for information on disposing of the waste.

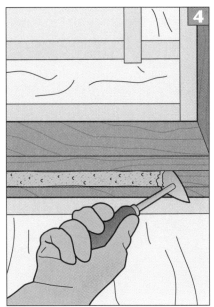

4. Dealing with problem areas

● Reapply stripper to any areas where paint remains.

● Scrape off the softened finish with an appropriate tool such as the corner of a putty knife, a wood chisel, or, for molding, a contoured scraper (#4).

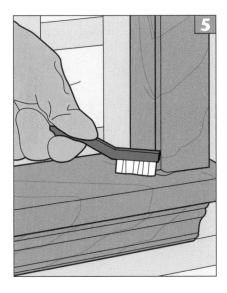

5. Scrubbing the surface

● Remove all traces of the old finish with steel wool or an abrasive pad. Use a detail brush in tight corners (#5).

6. Rinsing the surface

● Check the manufacturer's instructions for rinsing the surface. Typically you will need to rinse off surfaces you have stripped using a cloth dampened with denatured alcohol (#6).

● Once the surfaces are completely dry, sand and apply a new finish.

USING A HEAT GUN

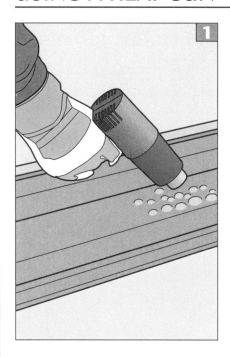

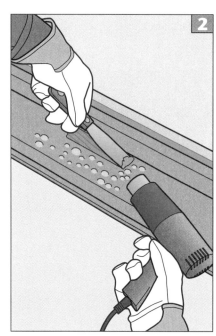

ronmental regulations for information on disposing of the waste.

1. Heating the paint

• Turn on the heat gun and allow it to warm up.
• With the nozzle a couple of inches from the surface, move the gun slowly back and forth over a small area until the paint bubbles (#1). Keep moving the gun or you'll risk burning the paint.

2. Stripping flat surfaces

• Holding a putty knife at a 30-degree angle, press downward as you scrape off the softened finish (#2). Work carefully to avoid gouging the wood.
• While you work, clean off the blade of the putty knife frequently by scraping the waste into a metal container. (Heated paint melts plastic.) Consult your local envi-

3. Shielding surfaces

Areas that you don't want to heat will need to be shielded.
• Wrap aluminum foil around a piece of cardboard and hold or tape it next to the surface you are heating (#3).
• Stop using the heat gun within 2 inches of the surface you don't want to strip. Finish the job with a chemical stripper.

4. Stripping paint from details

• Leave corners and details to the end. Heat these spots carefully and remove the paint with an appropriate tool—a triangular scraper, for instance, works well in tight grooves (#4).
• Finish up with a light sanding and then wipe the surfaces clean using a cloth dampened with mineral spirits.

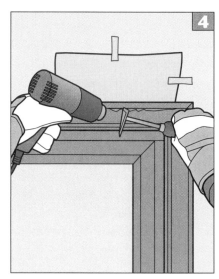

PREPARING A ROOM FOR PAINTING

Preparing a room for painting can sometimes take longer than applying the paint. Furnishings need to be moved into other rooms or placed in the middle of the room and covered. Surfaces to be painted should be washed and damage needs to be repaired. Remove fixtures, cover plates, duct covers, and hardware from the walls and ceiling. Mask off or cover areas that need to be protected from paint splatters.

Experts recommend washing surfaces before painting them—traditionally, with a solution of trisodium phosphate (TSP) (about 2 tablespoons per gallon of warm water); however, less caustic phosphate-free alternatives have become popular in recent years. Whatever type of cleaning agent you use, rinse surfaces thoroughly with fresh water and let them dry so the new finish will adhere properly.

HOW LONG WILL IT TAKE?
Two to four hours

TOOLS
• Plastic buckets • Sponge mop • Putty knife • Paintbrush • Paint scraper • Utility knife • Sanding block • Rubber gloves • Safety goggles

MATERIALS
• Trisodium phosphate (or other cleaning agent) • Drop cloths • Newspaper • Stain remover • Cloths • Shellac • Sandpaper • Spackling compound • Wood filler • Plastic sheeting • Masking tape

CLEANING PAINTED SURFACES

Washing walls and ceilings

• Cover the floor with a drop cloth or newspapers. Fill a plastic bucket with your cleaning solution. Fill another bucket with water for rinsing.
• Wearing rubber gloves and safety goggles, wash the ceiling with a sponge mop soaked in the cleaning solution and wrung out, working out from a corner in 3-foot-square sections.
• Then, wash the walls, again in 3-foot-square sections, starting in a corner at the floor and working up the wall to the ceiling (#1).
• Rinse all surfaces with fresh water and a clean sponge mop or sponge, then let dry.

REMOVING STAINS

1. Applying stain remover

- If a stain doesn't come off with regular cleaning, apply an all-purpose stain remover to a clean, dry cloth (#1) and rub the stain.
- Rinse the spot with a damp sponge.

2. Sealing the stain

Wood knots and stains such as ink or rust need to be sealed with white- or orange-pigmented shellac; otherwise they will bleed through the new paint.

- Remove any resin from wood knots with a putty knife, then sand the surface with medium-grade sandpaper. Also sand any glossy or rough surfaces.
- Paint shellac onto the stain with a paintbrush (#2).
- If the shellac soaks into the surface within an hour, apply another coat.

PATCHING PEELING PAINT

1. Scraping and patching

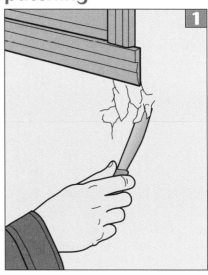

- Remove any flaking paint with a putty knife (#1).
- Spread on a thin layer of spackling compound with a putty knife and allow it to dry.

2. Sanding

- Load up a sanding block with fine-grade sandpaper and sand the patch in a circular motion until it is smooth (#2). Periodically tap the sanding block on a hard surface to remove dust. When the paper wears out, replace it.
- Clean the patched area with a damp cloth.

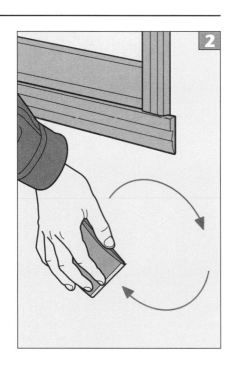

PREPARING WOODWORK

1. Patching holes

- Fill imperfections such as dents or holes with spackling compound using a putty knife (#1). For a surface with a clear finish, apply a stainable wood filler.
- Let the patch dry.

2. Sanding the patches

- Sand the patches with fine-grade sandpaper (#2).
- Clean the dust off the surface with a damp cloth.

MASKING SURFACES

1. Masking windows

Shield windows from spatters with plastic sheeting.
- Cut plastic sheeting a few inches larger than the window frame.
- Secure the plastic sheeting in place with masking tape (#1).

2. Masking baseboards

- Protect baseboards from spatters by taping sheets of newspaper along the top of the baseboards (#2). To prevent any paint from creeping under the masking tape, press firmly to make a tight seal.

REPAIRING CRACKS AND HOLES IN WALLBOARD OR PLASTER

Ridding a wall or ceiling of cracks and holes is often the first—and most important—step of a painting project. Whether small or large, such blemishes will show through your paint job if they aren't repaired first.

The techniques shown here will help you make invisible repairs and prevent problems from recurring. Narrow cracks can simply be covered with joint compound and sanded smooth. But any crack wider than about ¼ inch should also be undercut and reinforced with fiberglass-mesh or paper joint tape. Fixes for holes depend on the size of the opening. Small holes can be filled with compound and taped, but larger ones need to be cut back to the studs on each side of the hole and repaired with a wallboard patch.

Note: *To prevent cracks from recurring, check that the wallboard is securely fastened to the studs. If not, add nails or screws, as needed, before undertaking repairs.*

HOW LONG WILL IT TAKE?	TOOLS	MATERIALS
Two to four hours	• Can opener • Spray bottle • Brush • Putty knife • Taping knives • Sanding block • Stud finder • Carpenter's square • Utility knife • Cordless drill • Dimpler	• Joint compound • Joint tape • Sandpaper • Wallboard • 2x4s • Wood screws • Wallboard screws

FILLING CRACKS

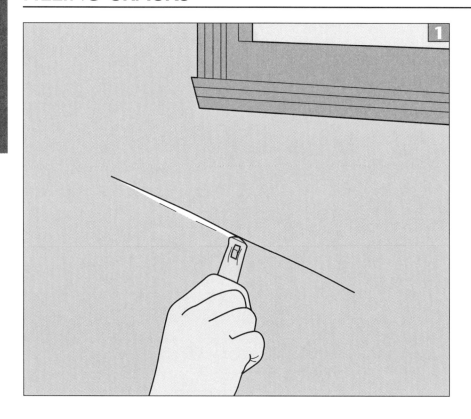

1. Undercutting the crack

This step may appear to worsen the problem, but you need to undercut the edges of the crack—making it wider at the base than at the surface—to give joint compound enough surface area on which to adhere. An ordinary can opener is an ideal tool for undercutting; the tip can hook under the surface and scrape out the interior of the crack.

● Pull the can opener along the crack to widen it (#1).

● Brush loose particles out of the crack.

● Dampen the crack with water from a spray bottle.

2. Filling the crack

- Force joint compound into the crack with a 4-inch taping knife. Pull the blade back and forth across the crack rather than along it (#2).
- Once you have filled the crack, pull the knife along the length of the crack to spread the compound smooth and scrape off excess.

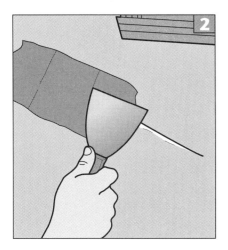

3. Reinforcing the patch

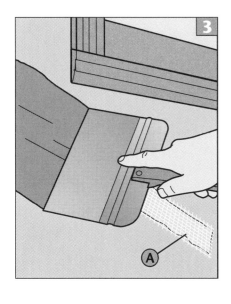

- While the joint compound is still wet, cut a strip of fiberglass-mesh joint tape 2 inches longer than the length of the crack and press it into the compound.
- Apply a layer of joint compound over the tape with an 8-inch taping knife, pulling the knife along the crack to spread the compound smooth (#3).
- Let the patch dry overnight, and apply a second coat of compound. Pull the knife along each side of the patch to blend the repair into the surrounding wall and finish with a single stroke down the middle.

4. Sanding the patch

- After letting the patch dry for 24 hours, fit a sanding block with medium-grade sandpaper and smooth the surface (#4).

PATCHING SMALL HOLES

Repairing the hole

The repair technique for small holes depends on their size and on whether there are cracks radiating from the hole.

- For a small hole with no cracks, simply fill the cavity with joint compound with a 1-inch putty knife so it is flush with the surrounding wall (#1).
- Allow the patch to dry, then sand the area smooth.
- For a hole about 2 inches square in size, cover the hole with fiberglass-mesh tape, then apply compound with a putty knife.
- Scrape off any excess and allow to dry. Sand lightly, apply a second coat, let dry, and sand again.

PATCHING LARGE HOLES

1. Cutting out the damage

- Using a stud finder, locate the studs on each side of the hole.
- With a carpenter's square, outline a 16-inch square around the hole, centering two sides on the marked studs.

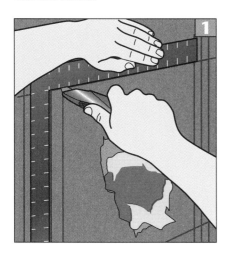

- Cut around the outline with a utility knife, using the carpenter's square as a straightedge (#1).
- Remove the cut wallboard.

2. Installing support blocks

Before cutting and installing a patch the hole, you need to provide reinforcement along the top and bottom of the opening.
- Cut two 2x4 support blocks (A) to fit snugly between the studs. For studs 16 inches apart on center, cut each support block 14½ inches long.

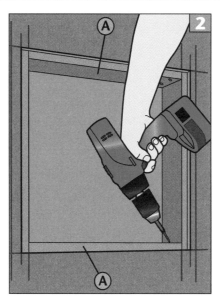

- Place one block between the studs at the top of the opening so the edge of the opening divides the board in half. To secure the block in place, angle two 2½-inch wood screws through each end of it into the stud.
- Fasten the other block to the studs along the bottom edge of the opening the same way (#2).

3. Installing the patch

- Cut a piece of wallboard 16 inches square using a utility knife and a straightedge.
- Position the patch in the opening, shaving its edges as necessary to fit it snugly.
- Secure the patch with two wallboard screws at each corner and one in between. Also fasten the wallboard edges around the

patch, staggering the screws between those in the patch (#3).

4. Finishing the patch

- Cover the seam around the patch with joint compound, then embed joint tape in it (#4).

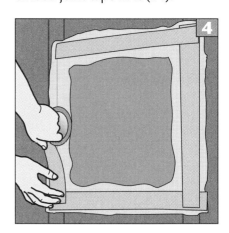

- Apply a layer of joint compound over the tape, then let the patch dry overnight.
- Apply another coat of joint compound and allow it to dry overnight, then smooth the patch with medium-grade sandpaper.

REPAIRING SCRATCHES AND HOLES IN WOODWORK

Nothing may beat woodwork for its warmth and versatility, but it is also susceptible to unsightly scratches and holes. Fortunately, minor damage is easily repaired.

Scratches can be concealed with liquid color (also called furniture dye) or a retouching or felt-tipped pen of a color that matches the wood. Gouges or holes require wood putty, a putty stick, or a wood plug. Unless you're repairing a painted surface, shop carefully for a product that matches the color of the wood. Test color products on an area that is not easily visible or on a matching piece of scrap wood. Finally, gaps in painted window or door trim can be filled with latex caulk—which can be sanded easily. Repairs should be covered with the same paint or varnish used on the rest of the surface.

HOW LONG WILL IT TAKE?
Less than two hours

TOOLS
• Putty knife • Sanding block • Paintbrush • Rubber gloves

MATERIALS
• Liquid color (or wood-tone retouching pen) • Wax-based putty stick • Wood putty • Sandpaper • Cloth • Finish

DISGUISING SCRATCHES WITH LIQUID COLOR

1. Applying the color

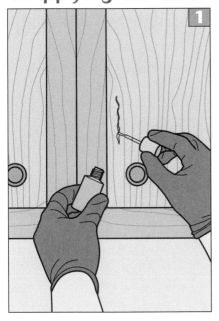

Liquid color is available in many shades, but sometimes it is necessary to mix shades together to match the appearance of certain wood surfaces perfectly. Test the color first on a hidden spot.
● Wearing rubber gloves, apply liquid color to the scratch with the applicator brush supplied (#1).

2. Wiping with a cloth

● Wipe with a soft cloth to remove excess liquid color and blend it into the surrounding surface (#2).
● Let the repair dry thoroughly, then apply a clear finish to match the surrounding surface.

FILLING SMALL HOLES WITH A PUTTY STICK

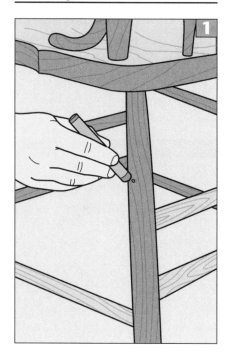

Filling holes

Wax-based putty sticks are sold in a variety of wood tones. They are used to fill deep scratches or holes left by countersunk nails.

● Warm the putty by rolling the tip of the stick between your thumb and forefinger.

● Push the end of the putty stick into the hole and twist it, breaking off just enough putty to fill the hole flush with the surface (#1). Or, scrape a small amount of putty off the stick and press it into the hole with your finger.

● Smooth away excess putty with a soft cloth.

FILLING SMALL HOLES WITH WOOD PUTTY

1. Applying the putty

The trick to filling small holes with wood putty is not to overfill them—which makes for a messy job and difficult sanding. If the hole is deep, you may have to apply several layers, allowing each one to dry before continuing.

● Scoop a small amount of wood putty onto a putty knife.

● Force the putty into the hole (#1) and scrape off the excess flush with the surrounding surface.

● Allow the putty to dry.

● Reapply as needed.

2. Sanding the patch

● Fit a sanding block with medium-grade sandpaper.

● Sand the patch smooth and flush with the surrounding surface (#2).

● Wipe the surface with a soft cloth to remove any residue.

COPING TRIM AND MOLDING

Installing wood trim or molding can add character to a room, whether it is baseboard along the floor, crown molding along the ceiling, or chair rail along the wall in between. The precision with which you cut the wood to fit at corners will have a tremendous impact on the appearance of the job.

A coped joint allows two lengths of contoured molding to meet tightly at a corner, forming an almost invisible seam. The end of the first piece is cut straight and installed flush against the wall (Step 1 to Step 2). The second length is first beveled at a 45-degree angle (Step 3); then, a curved cut is made along the beveled end with a coping saw to mesh exactly with the contoured face of the first piece (Step 4 to Step 7).

Fasten the first piece along the wall opposite the door to the room. This way, the corner joints will be least noticeable when you enter the room.

HOW LONG WILL IT TAKE?

Less than two hours

TOOLS

• Tape measure • Stud finder • Miter box • Backsaw • Coping saw • Hammer • Clamp • Nail set

MATERIALS

• Wood trim (or molding) • Finishing nails • Wood pads • Sandpaper • Dowel • Wood putty

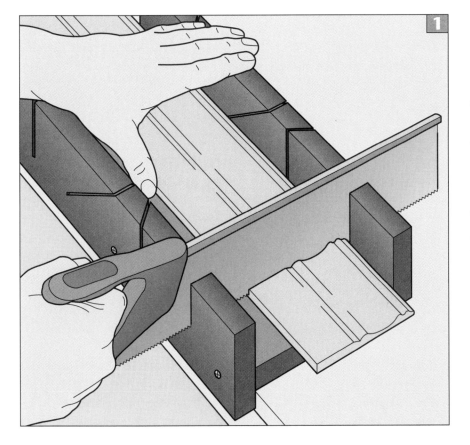

1. Cutting the first piece to length

• Mark the first piece of molding equal to the length of the first wall.
• Place the molding face-up in a miter box so your cutting mark lines up with the 90-degree kerfs in the fence. (The miter box shown has a bottom ledge that overhangs the edge of a worktable and is screwed through the bottom to the table to secure it.)
• Slide the blade of a backsaw into the 90-degree kerfs.
• Holding the molding against the fence with your free hand, draw the blade of the saw back a few times to start the cut.
• Applying uniform pressure, saw through the piece with smooth back-and-forth strokes (#1).

2. Fastening the first piece

- Locate the wall studs with a stud finder and mark their position with a pencil.
- Place the molding against the wall, holding the cut end tightly in the corner.
- Fasten the molding with two 2-inch finishing nails at every stud mark. Drive one nail $\frac{1}{2}$ inch from the bottom of the molding (#2) and the other nail $\frac{1}{2}$ inch from the top.
- Sink the head of each nail below the surface of the wood with a nail set.

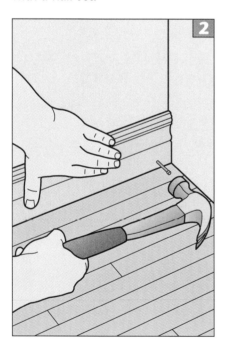

3. Beveling the second piece

- Mark the second piece of molding to length.
- Place the molding in the miter box so the cutting mark is aligned with the 45-degree bevel kerfs in the fence, then saw through the piece (#3).

4. Outlining the contour

To help you guide the saw blade as you cope the beveled end of the second length of molding, it's a good idea to highlight the contour.

- Run the edge of a pencil along the profile at the beveled end of the molding (#4), making the curves stand out.

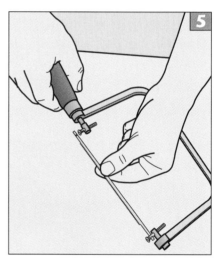

5. Fitting a coping saw with a blade

Coping saws have detachable blades. To cope molding, fit the saw with a narrow blade.

- Follow the instructions of the saw manufacturer to change blades. For the coping saw shown, turn the handle counterclockwise to reduce tension on the spigots. Fit the blade into the spigot slots, the teeth angled toward the handle (#5). Turn the handle clockwise to tighten the blade.

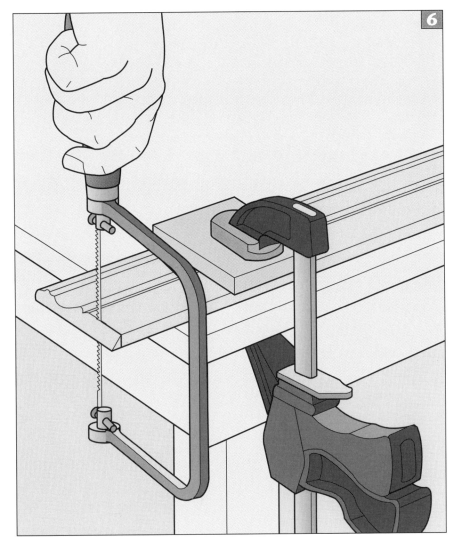

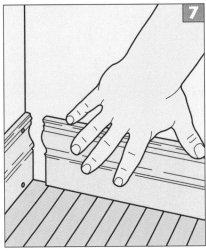

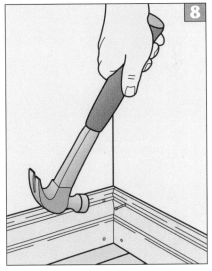

6. Making the coping cut

● Clamp the molding face-up on your worktable, using wood pads to keep the jaws of the clamps from marring the surface of the molding.

● Holding the coping saw vertically, cut along the highlighted contour (#6), biting into the wood on each upstroke.

7. Fitting the coped piece in place

● Slide the coped end of the second length of molding against the first piece (#7). The coped end should fit the contoured face of the first piece perfectly.

● Eliminate small gaps between the pieces by reshaping the coped end of the second molding with a piece of sandpaper wrapped around a dowel.

8. Fastening the coped piece

Fasten the coped molding to the wall as you did the first piece.

● Locate and mark the wall studs.

● Holding the molding flat on the wall, its end flush against the first piece, drive two nails at every stud (#8) and sink the nail heads with a nail set.

● Conceal the nail heads with wood putty.

INSTALLING CROWN MOLDING AND CHAIR RAIL

Crown molding and chair rail are now installed primarily for decorative purposes, but both types of trim originally had practical functions. Crown molding served to hide the joint between walls and ceilings, while chair rail protected walls from being damaged by the backs of chairs.

Crown molding gives a room a formal look. Choose a width that is well proportioned to the height of the ceiling. In a room with 8-foot-high ceilings, for example, molding that is 3¼ inches wide works well. Chair rail is a good choice for dividing two wall treatments. You can paint the portion above the trim and apply paneling or wallpaper below.

If you plan to apply a clear finish to the molding, choose solid wood. If you'll be painting the trim, you can buy it made of medium-density fiberboard (MDF). MDF has advantages over solid wood: It is less expensive and easier to work with and it does not warp, twist, or contain knots.

HOW LONG WILL IT TAKE?
Two to four hours

TOOLS
• Tape measure • Carpenter's square • Chalk line • Stud finder • T-bevel • Protractor • Hammer • Nail set • Putty knife • Sliding compound miter saw • Cordless drill • Utility knife • Stepladder • Safety goggles

MATERIALS
• Crown molding • Chair rail • Finishing nails • Wood glue • Building adhesive • Wood filler

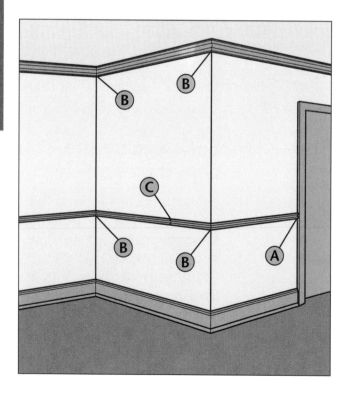

Planning the project

Plan to install the first length of trim along the wall facing the door, then work your way around the room. This way, corner joints will be less conspicuous.
● Where trim meets casing (A), cut it flush to form a butt joint.
● Where trim meets at a corner (B), cut miters (Step 3 to Step 5). (You can also use ready-made corner pieces at corners.)
● Where trim meets along a straight wall (C), cut miters at opposite 45-degree angles to form a scarf joint.

CROWN MOLDING

1. Measuring the crown molding

First determine where the flat part of the crown molding will sit on the walls and the ceiling.

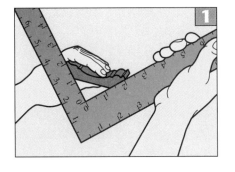

• Cut a short length of molding— 6 inches will do—and hold it against a carpenter's square so one arm represents the wall and the other the ceiling (#1). Make sure the flat portions of the molding are flush against the arms.
• Record how far down the "wall"—vertical projection—and how far out on the "ceiling"— horizontal projection—the trim will sit. For the $3\frac{1}{4}$-inch-wide molding in this example, both measurements are $2\frac{3}{8}$ inches.

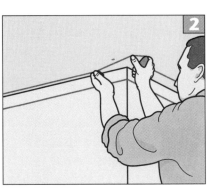

2. Positioning the molding

• At each corner of the room, measure from the ceiling to mark the vertical projection on the walls. Measure from the wall to mark the horizontal projection on the ceiling.
• Snap a chalk line along the ceiling and along the walls between the marked spots (#2).
• With a stud finder, locate and mark where wall studs and ceiling joists cross the guidelines.

3. Determining the miter angle at an outside corner

This step will help you cut tight miter joints at an outside corner, even if it isn't perfectly square.
• If the guidelines stop at the corner, hold a piece of molding so it extends a few inches beyond the corner, aligning the edges with the guidelines.
• Mark a line on the ceiling along the top edge of the trim.

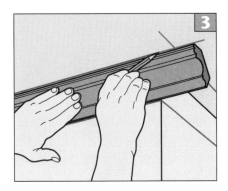

• Repeat on the other wall that shares the corner (#3), extending the mark to intersect the first line.

4. Transferring the angle to the saw

• With a straightedge, mark a line on the ceiling from the corner to the intersection of the two lines.
• Holding the handle of a T-bevel against one wall, adjust the blade so it aligns with the third line (#4).
• Adjust the base and tilt the blade of a sliding compound miter saw to the angle on the T-bevel.

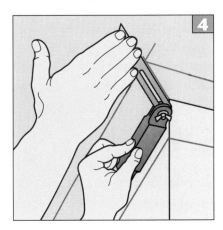

5. Making the cut

Because crown molding is installed at an angle, the miter cuts must angle across the edges as well as through the thickness.
• Set the trim upside down on the saw base, the wall edge against the fence—to the left of the blade if it will be installed to the right of the corner.

CROWN MOLDING (CONTINUED)

• Aligning your cutting mark with the blade, make the cut (#5).

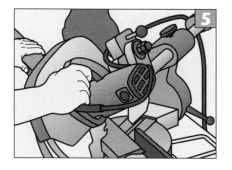

6. Nailing the molding in place

• Fasten the molding with a 2½-inch finishing nail at each stud and joist; for hardwood, drill pilot holes first. If the joists run parallel to the wall, fasten the trim to the ceiling with building adhesive.

• Glue and nail mitered ends at outside corners (#6).
• Sink the nails with a nail set. Fill the holes with wood filler.

7. Mitering an inside corner

• Copy the angle of the corner with a T-bevel, then measure the angle with a protractor. Divide the figure by two and adjust your saw to the result.

• Miter the ends of the mating pieces as you did in Step 5, but with the molding right-side up on the saw base.
• Position the molding (#7) and nail it in place to studs and joists; if the joists run parallel to the wall, fasten it to the ceiling with building adhesive.
• Sink the nails and fill the holes.

CHAIR RAIL

1. Marking guidelines

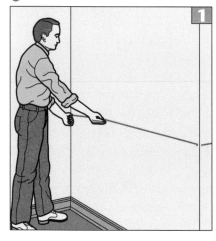

• Mark the walls 36 inches from the floor at each corner.
• Snap a chalk line along the walls between the marks (#1).
• With a stud finder, locate the wall studs and mark where they cross the guidelines.

2. Installing the trim

• Cut the trim to length, making straight cuts at door casing and miters at corners.
• Fasten the trim to studs with 2-inch finishing nails; for hardwood,

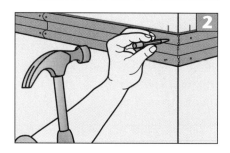

drill pilot holes first. For corners where you cut miter joints, install the first piece of trim, then spread wood glue on the mitered ends and fasten the second piece.
• Sink the nails with a nail set (#2). Fill the holes with wood filler.

INSTALLING A CLOSET ORGANIZER

New shelving systems or closet organizers have made storage in small spaces more versatile and efficient. Although wood or melamine shelving is often more appropriate for storing heavier items, wire kits provide good air circulation, ideal for storing clothing or linens.

Closet organizers are made of wire, metal, and heavy-duty plastic components and are easily assembled with a few standard tools. The wire shelving units can also be cut with a hacksaw to fit any closet width.

Before beginning the project, take a look at the options available and plan your set-up based on space constraints and the types of items to be stored. Although standard kits are available, components are also sold separately, permitting a more customized plan. A combination of different organizer models makes for even greater set-up versatility.

SAFETY TIP *Wear safety goggles when drilling and hammering.*

HOW LONG WILL IT TAKE?
Two to four hours

TOOLS
• Tape measure • Hammer • Carpenter's level • Torpedo level • Cordless drill • Wrench • Screwdriver • Safety goggles

MATERIALS
• Wire shelving kit (including shelves, clips and brackets, vertical pole, and braces) • Basket rack and crossbars • Baskets • Shoe rack supports and clips

Anatomy of a closet organizer

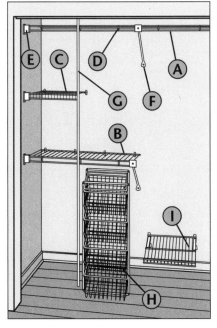

The set-up shown here combines a standard kit with individual components. The top shelf (A) extends in sections the full length of the closet, while the single-section lower shelf (B) extends halfway; both serve as clothes rods, doubling the hanging space. Another smaller shelf (C) is positioned between the two.

The shelves are supported by clips (D) along the back wall and brackets (E) on the end walls. A diagonal brace (F) and joiner plates support the joint in the top shelf sections and another brace supports the end of the lower shelf. A vertical pole (G) supports the front of all three shelves.

A freestanding basket rack (H) fits under the lower shelf, a shoe rack (I) sits just above the floor, and a tie-and-belt rack (not shown) can be placed on an end wall.

1. Marking the layout

The height of each of the shelves, indicated in the manufacturer's directions, is determined by the vertical support pole, predrilled for the shelf brackets.

• Measure and mark the height of each shelf on the back wall and one or both end walls following the manufacturer's layout.

• With a carpenter's level, mark a horizontal line at each mark

along the back wall (#1). Use a torpedo level to mark the narrow end walls.

• Measure and mark the back-clip and wall-bracket hole locations according to the manufacturer's layout. Note that each wall bracket requires two fastener locations.

2. Installing the clips

• Using a cordless drill fitted with a ¼-inch bit, drill holes at each of the back-wall clip locations.

• Insert the drive pins into the clips, then insert the plug section of the clips into the drilled holes.

• Set a screwdriver into the grooved head of the nail, then hammer the drive pin flush with the face of the clip (#2).

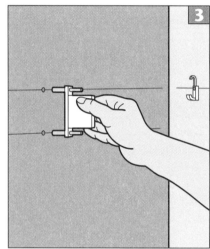

3. Installing the wall brackets

• Drill ¼-inch wall-bracket holes at the marked locations in the end walls.

• Insert the brackets (#3) and secure them in the same way as the back-wall clips.

4. Hanging the shelves

• Snap the back rail of the shelf into the back-clip holders.

• Slide the shelf against the end wall and lower the front edge into the wall bracket (#4).

• To stabilize the shelf, close the flaps on the back-wall clips (inset).

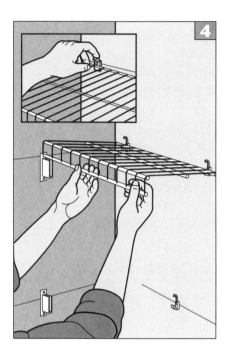

5. Installing the vertical support

• Assemble the vertical support pole.

• Align the pole with the middle of the shelves and fit a metal bracket against the inside of the

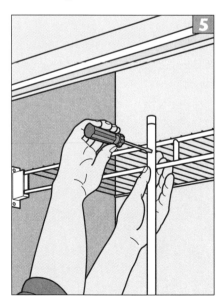

shelf rails. With a screwdriver, fasten the bracket to the pole with the machine screws and hex nuts provided (#5). Tighten the hex nuts with a wrench.
- Secure the pole to the other shelves in the same way.

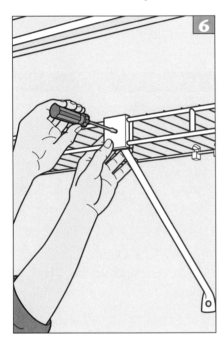

6. Bracing the shelves

Shelving sections are joined together with joiner plates that also connect support braces to the shelves. Braces are also added to the ends of long shelves extending halfway across the closet space.
- Center the front and rear joiner plates over the joint between two shelf sections, sandwiching the upper end of the support brace between the plates.
- Fasten the pieces together with the screw provided (#6).

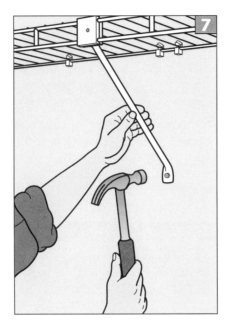

7. Anchoring the braces

- On the wall, mark the position for the screw plug at the base of the brace.
- Hold the brace aside to drill a hole at the marked spot.
- Insert the plug through the hole in the brace into the wall. With a hammer, sink the drive pin provided into the plug (#7).

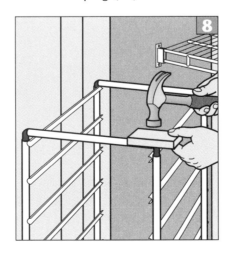

8. Assembling the basket rack

The freestanding basket rack can go anywhere in the closet. It can be fitted with wheels, if desired.
- With the basket rails facing inward, tap the upper and lower crossbars into place with a hammer, protecting the surface with a wood block (#8).
- Slide the baskets into place along the rails.

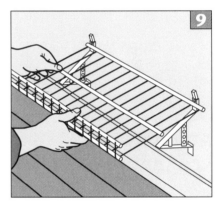

9. Installing a shoe rack

An inverted and angled wire shelf makes an ideal shoe rack.
- Mark the rack's position 12 inches above the floor and mark the location of holes for support brackets 1 inch from each end.
- Drill the holes. Insert the plugs through the brackets, then slide them into the holes. Sink the drive pin provided into the plug.
- Snap the back rail of the inverted shelf into the support clips (#9). Close the clip flaps to lock the shelf in place.

CREATING A COMPUTER CENTER

Making your own computer center allows you to adapt the dimensions to meet your specific needs and requirements. To be comfortable for working, the level of the desktop should position the upper section of the monitor at eye level and the keyboard tray should be positioned at the same level as the elbow. The center should also be designed to accommodate your computer equipment.

The project shown here is built of $\frac{5}{8}$-inch melamine. You could also choose MDF (medium-density fiberboard), which is inexpensive and provides a good surface for paint, or veneered plywood. All these materials are available in 4-by 8-foot sheets. If you adapt dimensions, take care that the desktop doesn't span more than 36 inches without support and that bookshelves don't span more than 20 inches.

HOW LONG WILL IT TAKE?
More than four hours

TOOLS
• Tape measure • Circular saw • Iron • File • Clamps • Cordless drill • Hole saw • Carpenter's square • Screwdriver • Hammer • Safety goggles

MATERIALS
• Melamine sheets • Masonite • Melamine banding • 2x4s • Angle irons • Angle brackets • Melamine screws • Wood screws • Finishing nails • Plastic caps

Anatomy of a computer center

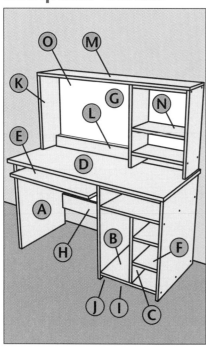

This design includes a cabinet to accommodate the computer, a keyboard tray, and an upper shelving unit. All pieces are cut from $\frac{5}{8}$-inch melamine, except the back pieces which are masonite.

PART		QTY.	DIMENSIONS (inches)
A	Desk and cabinet sides	3	23 x 29$\frac{3}{8}$
B	Cabinet bottom and top		23 x 18$\frac{5}{8}$
	and fixed shelf	3	
C	Cabinet divider	1	23 x 19$\frac{1}{2}$
D	Desk top	1	24 x 53$\frac{1}{2}$
E	Keyboard tray	1	16 x 30
F	Cabinet shelves	2	22$\frac{7}{8}$ x 7$\frac{13}{16}$
G	Desk back (masonite)	1	23$\frac{7}{8}$ x 51$\frac{3}{8}$
H	Support rail	1	6 x 31
I	Kickplate (not visible)	1	2 x 18$\frac{5}{8}$
J	Cleats (not visible)	2	2 x 20$\frac{3}{8}$
K	Shelving unit sides	3	10 x 23$\frac{3}{8}$
L	Shelving unit support	1	33$\frac{5}{8}$ x 4
M	Shelving unit top	1	10 x 51$\frac{1}{2}$
N	Shelving unit shelves	2	9$\frac{7}{8}$ x 15$\frac{13}{16}$
O	Shelving unit back (masonite)	1	23$\frac{15}{16}$ x 51$\frac{3}{8}$

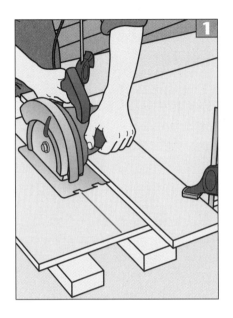

1. Cutting the pieces

Before beginning, plan out your cuts on paper. All the melamine pieces for this project fit on two 4- by 8-foot sheets.

● With a carpenter's square and a tape measure, mark out the cuts.

● Lay the sheet on the floor supported by four 2x4s positioned parallel to the cuts, one at each end of the sheet and the two others a few inches from the cut.

● With quick-action clamps, fasten a straight length of scrap to the sheet as a cutting guide.

● Make the cuts slowly with a circular saw equipped with a carbide-tipped blade (#1). Follow the guide.

● Label the cut pieces with masking tape.

SAFETY TIP *Wear safety goggles when using power tools to protect your eyes from flying particles.*

2. Edge banding

Before assembling the unit, finish cut edges that will be visible with matching banding.

● To hold pieces vertical, make a pair of support blocks from short lengths of 2x4 cut with slots slightly larger than the $\frac{5}{8}$-inch thickness of the material.

● Snap off a length of banding from the roll several inches longer than needed. Center the banding over the edges.

● Pass a heated iron over the banding (#2), then press it in place with a cloth or edge roller.

● With a utility knife, trim the ends. Trim the edges with a medium-cut file, angling it and filing only on the forward stroke.

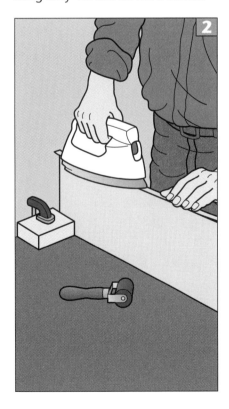

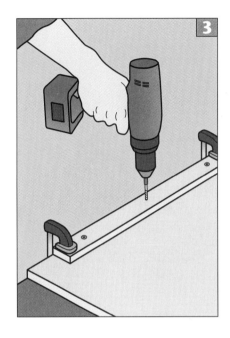

3. Attaching the cleats

Cleats fastened to the bottom edge of the cabinet support the cabinet bottom and kickplate.

● On a tabletop, clamp the pieces in position with the cleats flush with the bottom and back of the cabinet side pieces, leaving a 2-inch gap at the the front.

● Drill pilot holes and fasten the cleat to the side with $1\frac{1}{8}$-inch melamine screws 2 inches in from each end and in the middle. (#3).

4. Assembling the sides and bottom

● Using the support blocks, place the two side pieces on edge, with the front of the unit facing up.

● Slide the bottom piece into place and secure the three pieces with clamps.

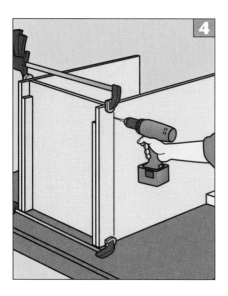

- Mark a line on the outside of the side pieces in line with the edge of the bottom piece.
- Drill pilot holes 2 inches in from the front and back of the unit and two others spaced evenly along the guideline.
- Fasten the pieces with 1¼-inch screws (#4).

5. Drilling the shelf holes

A shop-made jig will ensure that shelf holes are aligned and evenly spaced.

- Cut a straight piece of material 3 inches wide and mark a line down the center. Drill holes 1½ inches apart along the center line using a bit of the same size as the shelf supports.
- Set the jig against the side of the cabinet flush with the front edge. Attach a stop collar to the bit, positioning it to allow the bit to pass through the jig and ¼ inch

into the cabinet. Drill the holes in the cabinet side. Then drill holes near the back of the cabinet.

- In the same way, drill holes in the divider, clamping the divider against the side of the cabinet to keep it vertical (#5).

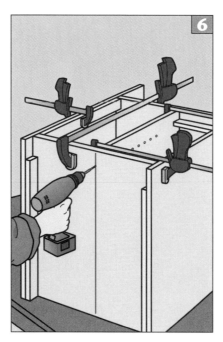

6. Fastening the divider and shelf

- Position the divider and the fixed shelf inside the cabinet. Use two scrap pieces the length of the cabinet divider and two pieces the width of the shelving section to hold the pieces in position. Clamp the assembly together.
- Mark guidelines along the cabinet bottom and fixed shelf, in line with the edge of the divider. Drill pilot holes and fasten the divider with four 1¼-inch screws, keeping them 2 inches in from each edge (#6).
- Fasten the fixed shelf to the cabinet sides in the same way.

7. Installing the kickplate

The kickplate adds support to the bottom of the cabinet.

- Turn the cabinet upside down, and position the kickplate against the cleats. Make sure it is flush with the bottom edge of the cabinet sides, as well as the surface of the cabinet bottom.
- Drill pilot holes and fasten the kickplate to the cleats, driving $5/8$-inch screws through two angle brackets. Add another bracket to secure the kickplate to the cabinet bottom (#7).

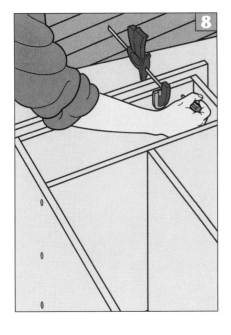

8. Fastening the tops

- Place the cabinet top in position, its surface flush with the top edges of the side pieces. Clamp it in place and fasten it to each side piece with four $1\frac{1}{4}$ screws.
- To attach the desktop, first drill three equally-spaced pilot holes through the front and the back of the cabinet top.

- Clamp the desk top against the top of the cabinet, allowing an overhang of one inch at the front and end. With a stubby screwdriver, drive $1\frac{1}{8}$-inch screws through the cabinet top into the underside of the desktop (#8).

9. Adding the desk side panel

- With the unit on its back, position the side panel against the underside of the desktop. Use the support rail piece as a spacer between it and the shelving cabinet and clamp another spacer of equal length at the top of the pieces. Clamp the panel in place.
- Drill pilot holes and fasten the panel to the desktop with four equally spaced angle irons and $5/8$-inch screws (#9).

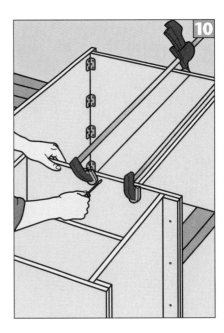

10. Fastening the support rail

The support rail adds stability to the desk, keeping the desk side panel plumb.
- Turn the unit over on its front. Because of the overhang of the desktop, you will have to raise the desk on 2x4s to keep it level.
- Position the support rail $5\frac{7}{8}$ inches from the bottom of the desk and clamp it in position.
- Drill pilot holes and fasten the support rail with two screws at each end (#10).

11. Installing the back panel

As well as covering the back of the unit, the desk back helps ensure that the desk is square.
- Lay the desk back in position, coated side down.

PAINTING & HOME DECOR

• Make sure the two upper corners of the unit line up with those of the panel, then drive nails into each.
• If the edge of the desktop is not flush with the desk back, run a clamp from the top to the bottom of the unit and tighten it to force the desktop into alignment.
• Drive a nail through the desk back near the clamp, then drive nails every 6 to 8 inches along the top edge of the back panel (#11). Also drive nails through the back into the desk and cabinet side panels and the divider.
• Drive $\frac{5}{8}$-inch screws every 6 to 8 inches through the back into the center of the support rail.

12. Fastening the keyboard tray

• Position the unit on its back. Mark guidelines $3\frac{1}{4}$ inches below the desktop on the inside of the cabinet.

• Place the tray glides over the line and mark the screw holes. Drill pilot holes, then fasten the glides to the unit.
• Fasten the hardware to the sides of the keyboard tray following the manufacturer's instructions (#12).

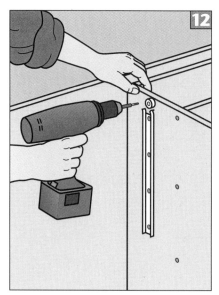

13. Cutting the cable holes

Each computer system may require a different routing of wires. Typically, holes are needed in the desktop and cabinet side to allow wires to pass through from the monitor desktop to the CPU. Plastic grommets cover hole edges and hold cables in place.
• Mark the desired location of the cable holes near the back of the cabinet side and the back of the desktop.
• Bore the holes with a drill fitted with a hole saw the same size as the grommet (#13).

14. Assembling the top shelving unit

The shelving unit is assembled in much the same way as the desk itself.
• Clamp together the top and sides of the shelving unit, then fasten them together with three screws.

- Use spacers to position the permanent shelf inside the unit. Clamp the shelf and fasten it in place.
- Drill holes for the shelf support pegs as for the lower cabinet.
- To fasten the top panel to the shelving unit, drill four pilot holes through the top of the unit 1 inch in from each corner. Clamp the top panel flush against the shelving unit and fasten the screws from the inside of the unit (#14).
- Fasten the side panel with angle irons and a supporting rail as with the desk side panel.
- Nail the masonite back panel in place.

15. Attaching top and bottom sections

- Position the shelving unit on the desktop, lining up the edges of the back panels.
- Fasten the two sections together with a metal strap at each side (#15).

16. Finishing touches

- Cover screws with plastic caps matching the melamine coating.
- Insert the shelf supports at the desired height and drop the adjustable shelves in place (#16).
- If you wish, add adjustable feet to the desk to compensate for an uneven floor.

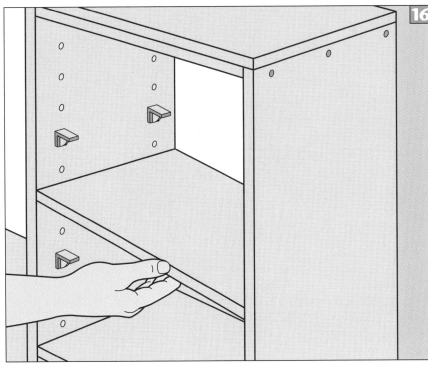

SMOOTHING WOOD BY HAND

Planes and files are indispensible tools in a woodworker's inventory. Even basic projects usually require some kind of smoothing or shaping tool.

Standard hand-planing techniques are the same regardless of the size of plane. Keep your feet apart and your shoulders and hips aligned with the plane. Move your body with each stroke instead of overextending your reach.

Always plane in the direction of the wood grain. To determine the direction of the grain, run your hand up and down the workpiece. The wood will feel smoother when you run your hand with the grain.

The jack plane is a good all-purpose plane for smoothing wide surfaces and edges. Adjust the blade to the right depth by experimenting on a piece of scrap wood. The plane should shave thin layers of wood cleanly away on each stroke. End grain is the most difficult part of a piece of wood to get smooth because it tends to splinter at the corners. Use the smaller block plane on end grain.

HOW LONG WILL IT TAKE?
Less than two hours

TOOLS
• Jack plane • Block plane • Clamps • Straightedge • Vise • File • Work gloves

MATERIALS
• Scrap wood block

PAINTING & HOME DECOR

SMOOTHING A BOARD FACE

1. Leveling the surface

• Place the workpiece face up on a work surface.
• Clamp or screw a piece of scrap wood to the work surface at each end of the workpiece to hold it.
• Plane with firm, smooth strokes, angling the tool slightly to the grain (#1) to remove more wood with each pass.

2. Smoothing the surface

• Hold the plane parallel to the grain and make straight, slightly overlapping passes (#2).
• Adjust the blade if necessary to get a finer cut. Plane until the wood is shiny and smooth.
• Check that the surface is flat by holding a straightedge against the

workpiece in several places and at several angles. The full length of the straightedge should rest flush on the surface. Plane the high spots and check again.

SMOOTHING A BOARD EDGE

1. Choosing the planing direction

Here are typical grain patterns (#1), with arrows to indicate the best direction to plane. The direction may be constant from end to end—A and D—or change—B and C. For very irregular patterns, angle the plane slightly to reduce splintering. If you must plane against the grain, set the blade to cut the thinnest shavings possible.
● Inspect the grain pattern on the workpiece and choose your planing direction accordingly.

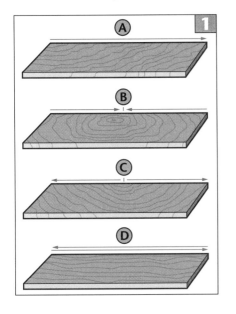

2. Starting the stroke

● Secure the workpiece in a vise.
● Hold the plane with one hand; with the other, position the front, or toe, of the plane on the end of the workpiece.
● As you begin the stroke, move your forward hand to the front knob and apply pressure.

● Guide the plane with a firm steady stroke, distributing pressure evenly over the plane and keeping the base flat (#2).
● Shift the pressure to the rear of the plane as you approach the end of the stroke

THREE METHODS FOR SMOOTHING END GRAIN WITH A BLOCK PLANE

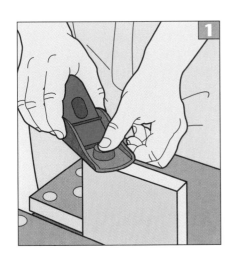

Angling the plane

The trick to smoothing end grain is to avoid splintering the corners. The following are the three best ways to achieve this. Each method calls for a block plane with a very sharp blade. This tool produces small chips instead of the shavings removed by a jack plane.
● Secure the workpiece in a vise.
● Set the blade to remove as little wood as possible on each pass.
● Angle the tool slightly (#1) and guide it from one edge of the workpiece toward the center.
● Lift the plane off as you reach the center and repeat from the other edge.

Cutting a chamfer

A chamfer is a woodworking term for a flattened corner.

THREE METHODS FOR SMOOTHING END GRAIN WITH A BLOCK PLANE (CONTINUED)

and make a pass (#2).

- Plane the entire length of the end grain, holding the plane at a slight angle and ending the stroke at the chamfer.

Using a wood block

The third method for smoothing end grain involves clamping a wood block to one side of the workpiece.

- Secure the workpiece.
- Clamp a wood block to the workpiece on the side where you will end your stroke. The block should be level with the workpiece and the same thickness.
- Hold the block plane at a slight

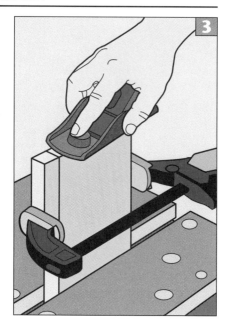

- Secure the workpiece in a vise.
- Hold the block plane at a 45-degree angle against one corner

angle (#3) and plane the full length of the wood grain in a series of single passes.

FILING

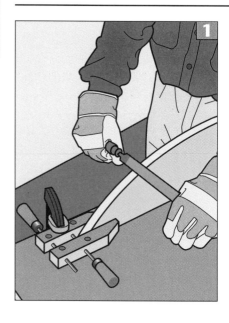

Cross-filing

Cross-filing is a good way to smooth a convex edge. Use a flat file and wear work gloves. Make repeated strokes in one direction; never run the file back and forth across the workpiece.

- Secure the workpiece.
- Hold the toe of the file in one hand and the handle in the other.
- Lay the file perpendicular to the workpiece with the toe flat against the edge.

- Push the file along and across the edge of the workpiece with a long, steady stroke, applying enough pressure to cut into the workpiece.
- As the handle approaches the workpiece (#1), lift the file without stopping and bring it back to repeat the procedure.
- Clean the file of sawdust as it becomes clogged.

PAINTING & HOME DECOR

SMOOTHING WOOD WITH A BELT SANDER

Belt sanders have two principal uses: removing wood from boards and panels, and smoothing rough wood surfaces. Sanding belts come in different grits or grades, ranging from extra-coarse through medium to fine. Depending on the manufacturer, each grit is assigned a number. The lower the number, the coarser the belt. Refer to the chart below as a guide to using the best belt for the job. In many cases, it's best to smooth a workpiece in three stages: Start with a coarse belt, progress to medium, and finish with fine.

GRIT	WHEN TO USE
36, 50	Removing wood quickly from boards and panels.
80	Smoothing wood; leveling scratches and other blemishes.
100,120	Final smoothing of wood.

SAFETY TIP *Belt sanders produce noise and sawdust. Wear ear protection and a dust mask whenever you operate one. Don't wear loose clothing; it could get caught in the sanding belt. Also keep your fingers clear of the belt.*

TOOLS

• Belt sander (and sanding belts) • Ear protection • Dust mask • Clamps • Handscrews

MATERIALS

• Wood stop blocks (scrap)
• Neoprene rubber block

PAINTING & HOME DECOR

SETUP

1. Changing a belt

Sanding belts are looped and fit around two rollers, which are driven by the sander motor.

• With the sander unplugged, set the tool on its side and pull the belt tension lever out as far as it will go (#1). This will release the pressure on the belt.

• Remove the old belt and fit the new one into place, centering it on the rollers. Be sure the directional arrow on the inside of the belt is pointing in the same direction as the arrow on the tool.

• Push down on the belt tension lever to lock the belt into place.

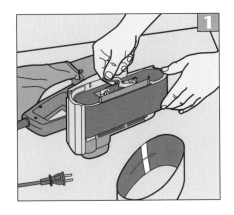

2. Adjusting belt tracking

• Turn the sander upside down and turn it on. If the tool has a button that locks the motor in the on position, activate it.

• Adjust the tracking adjustment knob to center the sanding belt on the front roller (#2). On most models, the knob moves the belt to the right or left depending on which way you turn it.

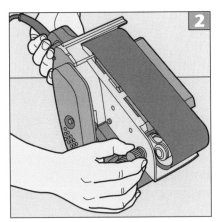

SANDING

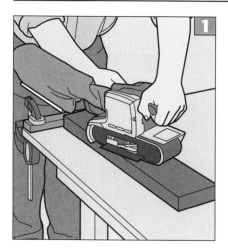

Sanding wood from a board

- Clamp a board as a stop block to one corner of your worktable.
- Set the workpiece on the table with one end flush against the stop block. To prevent gouging the surface of the piece, turn on the sander with the belt clear of the workpiece.
- Gently lower the sander onto the surface at the stopped end, angling the belt at about 30 degrees to the grain of the wood. With the belt flat on the surface, guide the sander steadily forward to the other end (#1). Keep the sander moving at all times to avoid gouges.
- When you reach the end of the stroke, pull the sander back to the stopped end and repeat. Sanding a board at an angle to the grain in this manner will leave scratches on the surface. If the appearance of the workpiece is important, smooth it, as shown in the next step.

Smoothing a board

- Smooth a board the same way you would level its surface, but hold the sander parallel to the grain of the wood (#2). Push the tool forward in long, straight strokes, being careful not to sweep it in a circular pattern. Don't allow more than half the belt to extend over the ends or edges of the workpiece; otherwise, you'll round over the edges.
- Pull the sander back, overlapping the forward stroke by one-half the width of the belt. Continue feeding the sander forward and backward until the workpiece is smooth.

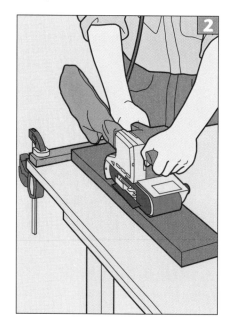

Smoothing a panel

- Set the panel on your worktable and fasten a stop block down at each end. This will keep the panel from moving.
- Holding the sander above the panel at one corner, turn it on. Set the tool flat on the panel parallel to the wood grain and push it forward immediately along the edge of the panel. At the end of the stroke, move the sander over by one-half the width of the belt and pull it back.
- Continue smoothing the panel in this manner, guiding it forward and backward in a "U" pattern (#3).

Gang-sanding edges

In addition to speeding your work, gang-sanding (sanding more than one workpiece of the same width at a time) ensures that you will remove the same amount of wood from each piece.

● Secure the pieces together face to face with handscrews at each end, aligning the edges and ends of the boards. Then, clamp the handscrews to your worktable so the board edges are facing up.

● Smooth the edges of the pieces as you would a single board, being sure to work in the direction of the grain (#4).

Sanding circular workpieces

● To hold your circular workpiece steady as you smooth it, anchor down two stop blocks in an L

shape at one corner of your worktable.

● Place the workpiece against the stop blocks so its wood grain is running at a 45-degree angle to each block.

● Smooth the piece as you would a panel, being careful not to let the belt round over the rim of the piece (#5).

Cleaning sanding belts

● Set the tool on its side and turn it on, locking it in the on position, if possible.

● Remove abrasive material from the sanding belt by holding a block of neoprene rubber against the spinning belt (#6). It takes no more than a few seconds to clean the belt.

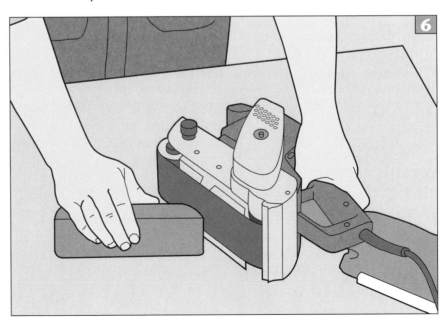

PAINTING TECHNIQUES

For interior painting jobs, select latex rather than alkyd. Modern latex paints are durable; they also dry faster and give off less fumes than alkyds. For ceilings and walls in the living room, dining room, and bedrooms, select a paint with a flat sheen. For the kitchen, bathrooms, and child play areas, use a semi-gloss, which can withstand a good scrubbing. For doors and trim, use semi-gloss or gloss. If the existing paint is in poor condition or if it is darker in color than the new paint, apply a coat of primer before painting.

Mix the paint thoroughly with a wooden stir stick before applying it. If you are using old paint, strain it through cheesecloth to remove any "skin" that has formed. If you will need more than one container of paint the same color, mix them together in a large pail to even out any small variations in color between them.

HOW LONG WILL IT TAKE?
More than four hours

TOOLS
• Work light • Screwdriver • Putty knife • Caulking gun • Sanding sponge • Pole sander • Sponge • Bucket • Drop cloth • Masking tape • Stepladder • Stir stick • Paintbrushes • Paint tray • Roller (with extension) • Brush comb • Roller scraper • Window scraper • Safety goggles • Rubber gloves

MATERIALS
• Patching compound • Wood filler or putty • Gap-and-crack sealer • Trisodium phosphate (TSP) • Primer • Paint

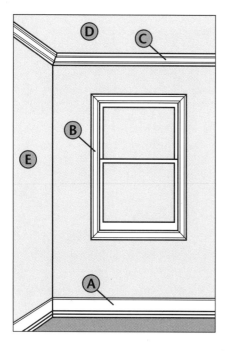

Painting a room in sequence

Painting a room in the proper sequence will help ensure that contrasting colors don't show up on surfaces where they don't belong. Start with the trim: baseboards, window and door moldings, and other woodwork. If crown molding will be a different color than the walls or ceiling, paint it next. Once all the trim is dry, paint the ceiling and finally the walls.

1. Getting the room ready

• Shut off power to the room at the service panel. Run power from an adjacent room to provide necessary lighting.
• Remove cover plates (#1). Tape the screws to the plates so they won't get lost.
• Unscrew light fixtures so they hang from the ceiling or wall.
• Shield fixtures that can't be removed with masking tape.
• Move furniture into the middle of the room and cover it with drop cloths or plastic sheeting.

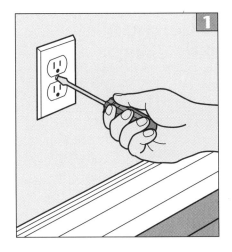

- Turn off any air conditioner or forced-air furnace thermostat.
- Make sure the temperature of the room is within the range recommended on the paint can.

2. Readying woodwork

There is no need to completely strip woodwork before repainting. Just make sure the surfaces are clean and free of loose paint.

- Use a putty knife to remove bubbling, peeling, or flaking paint. Use smooth, even strokes to avoid gouging the wood.
- Fill nail holes, dents, scratches, and other imperfections with wood filler or putty—don't worry if the putty doesn't match the color of the wood.
- Allow the patches to dry, then sand the entire woodwork with a sanding sponge (#2) to provide tooth for the new paint.
- Wearing rubber gloves, thoroughly wash the woodwork with a solution of trisodium phosphate (TSP), then rinse with clean water.

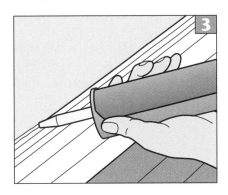

3. Final preparations

- Fill gaps between walls and baseboards with crack-and-gap sealer (#3)—cut the tube close to the tip so it reaches into small crevices. Also seal cracks between walls and door or window casings.
- Wash the walls with a solution of TSP and let them dry. Remove mildew stains with bleach. For ink, water, and smoke stains, use a stain remover, then seal the spots with white pigmented shellac.

- Thoroughly vacuum the floor and window sills.
- Prime all patches.

Note: *Water stains may indicate a leaky pipe behind the wall; your best bet is to consult a plumber.*

4. The right way to load a brush

- Hold the brush so it feels comfortable in your hand. Gripping it close to the base will help eliminate splatters when painting and won't tire your hand as quickly.
- Dip the bristles only partway into the paint—about one-third of their length (#4).
- Lightly tap the bristles against the edge of the can to remove excess paint. Don't wipe the bristles against the side of the can—this will clean off only one side of the bristles and the brush may still drip. To prevent paint from running down the outside of the paint can, make a few nail holes in the can's U-shaped rim.

PAINTING & HOME DECOR

5. Painting baseboards and trim

• Protect the floor with painter's masking tape. If possible, slip the edge of the tape slightly under the shoe molding.

• With a 2-inch angled brush, paint the baseboards (#5), the window and door casings, and any other trim. Bead a little paint onto the wall; it will be covered over when the walls are painted and will keep the old paint from peeking through the seam where the wall and trim meet.

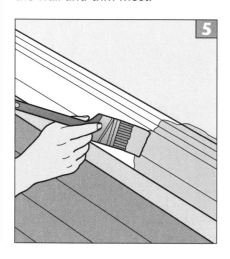

• Check for drips and smooth them with the brush as you go.

• If crown molding will be a different color than the ceiling or the walls, paint it next.

Note: *Tape won't stick to carpeting, so lay down newspaper or kraft paper and paint baseboards and shoe molding using an edge guide. Wipe paint off the guide each time you reposition it.*

6. Painting window frames

You will have to open the windows to paint the frames. Get this part of the job done in the morning so the windows will be dry by evening and can be closed.

• For double-hung windows—those that move up and down—slide the inside sash down 6 inches from the top. Slide the outside sash up 6 inches from the sill. Open casement-style windows out about 6 inches.

• Remove or mask all hardware.

• Paint all exposed surfaces, except for the sides and bottom of the sashes—this can stop the window from opening and closing properly.

• Reverse the position of the sashes on double-hung windows and paint the remaining surfaces.

• Once the paint has dried, use a window scraper to scrape paint off the glass (#6).

7. Cutting in the ceiling

Before rolling, you need to "cut in" around the perimeter of the ceiling. However, if you cut in all the way around the ceiling before you begin to work with the roller, some of the paint around the perimeter will have already dried, leaving a visible seam. Instead, work in sections, alternating between cutting in and rolling.

• Starting in a corner, cut in the ceiling along the shortest wall with a 2-inch angled brush (#7). Bead about $\frac{1}{4}$ inch of paint on the walls.

• Cut in partway along the two adjoining walls—about three roller widths.

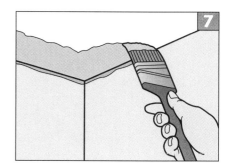

8. Rolling the ceiling

• Load a roller with paint and roll off excess on the ramp of the paint tray. The roller should be evenly coated with paint, but not dripping.

• Roll the paint onto the ceiling along the shortest wall. Maintain even pressure on the roller, reloading it as needed.

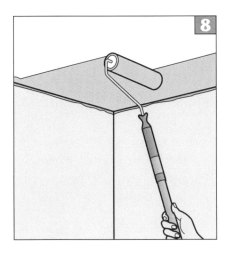

• Roll a second line, overlapping the first by about 3 inches (#8). Keep as parallel to the first line as possible.

• Once three lines are rolled, go back and lightly draw an almost dry roller over each line. At the end of each pass, lift the roller off the ceiling and start again from the same wall. This will ensure that the paint is evenly textured.

• Continue to cut in and roll in sections until the ceiling is painted completely.

9. Cutting in the walls

Wait until the ceiling is dry before starting to paint the walls. As with the ceiling, alternate between cutting in and rolling.

• Starting in a corner with a 2-inch brush, cut in the wall on one side of the corner. Bead about a $\frac{1}{4}$ inch of paint on the adjacent wall.

• On the same wall, cut in along the ceiling. To keep paint from getting onto the ceiling, make 4-inch-

long overlapping vertical strokes (#9), keeping the bristles about $\frac{1}{8}$ inch away from the ceiling. Start in the corner and cut in about three or four roller widths. Then, smooth over the brush strokes with one long finishing stroke.

• Cut in along the baseboard using the same technique. Work very slowly, checking for drips.

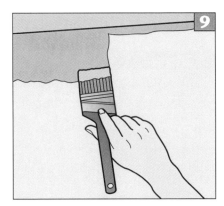

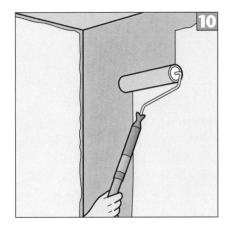

10. Rolling walls

• Load the roller with paint. Starting as close to the corner as possible, roll a first line from the top of the wall to the bottom, staying as vertical as possible. Reload the roller as needed. Roll

a second line that overlaps the first by about 3 inches (#10).

• Once three or four lines are rolled, go back and lightly draw an almost dry roller over them vertically from the top to the bottom of the wall to ensure an even texture. Lift the roller at the end of each stroke and return to the top of the wall for the next finishing pass.

• Continue to alternate between cutting in and rolling.

11. Cleaning brushes

If you are storing the brushes only overnight, wrap them in a wet cloth and seal them inside a plastic bag. For long-term storage, the brushes need to be cleaned.

• Use a brush comb to scrape the bulk of the paint from the bristles (#11).

• Rinse the brush repeatedly in water until the water runs clear.

• Inside a bucket, twirl the brush between your hands to remove excess water.

STRIPPING WOOD FURNITURE

Stripping and refinishing a painted piece of furniture can restore it to its original beauty. Stained furniture can also benefit from refinishing, but is harder to strip because stain penetrates more deeply into the wood. Strippers can contain a variety of different chemicals and most give off harmful fumes—safer strippers are available, but take longer to act. Strippers are available as liquid or paste—paste clings better to vertical surfaces. Avoid strippers that require rinsing with water as this can raise the wood grain.

Wood stains are either oil- or water-base. In addition, some penetrate the wood, while others simply form a surface layer of color. Penetrating oil stain gives the most even results; however, it gives off more toxic fumes than water-base stains.

A clear finish will protect and enhance the surface—polyurethane is a popular choice, providing a tough and durable finish. For antiques, however, a traditional oil or shellac finish may be more appropriate.

HOW LONG WILL IT TAKE?
More than four hours

TOOLS
• Natural-bristle brush • Metal scraper • Wooden scraper • Corner scraper • Nut pick • Cuticle stick • Stripping pad • Putty knife • Sanding block • Angled sanding sponge • Sanding strips • Tack cloth • Rubber gloves • Safety goggles

MATERIALS
• Stripper • Newspaper • Wood screws • Sandpaper • Steel wool • Wood filler

1. Applying the stripper

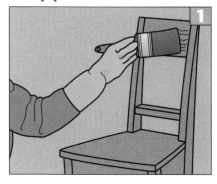

Strong strippers act within minutes, while safer ones may need to be left on for several hours.

• Drive screws into the bottom of the furniture piece's legs to lift it off your work surface. Set the piece on newspaper or cardboard to absorb excess stripper.

• With a thick natural-bristle brush, apply a generous coating of stripper to a section of the piece (#1). Allow the product to work for the time indicated by the manufacturer. The effectiveness of slow-acting products can be improved by covering the piece with plastic wrap.

SAFETY TIP *Wear long sleeves, rubber gloves, and safety goggles to protect hands and eyes during both stripping and finishing. Work in a well-ventilated area.*

2. Scraping off the finish

Once the stripper has worked for the recommended time and the paint has bubbled, you can begin removing the finish. As you work on scraping one section, let another soak with stripper.

• For very thick layers of paint, make only an initial pass with a metal scraper, drawing the tool across the surface in the direction of the grain. Then, switch to a wooden scraper, which is less likely to damage the surface.

• With a wooden scraper, remove a layer of finish in one complete stroke, running the tool parallel to the direction of the grain (#2). After each stroke, wipe the tool clean into a can or onto a section of cardboard.

● If necessary, apply one or two additional coats of stripper.

3. Stripping details and corners

A special corner tool is effective for removing finish from joints and crevices (#3)—apply extra stripper to these areas and try to avoid scratching the face of the piece. The concave side is ideal for table

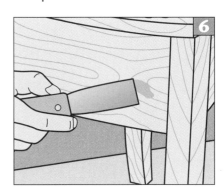

and chair legs, posts, and spindles. A pointed tool such as a nut pick or cuticle stick is useful for removing finish from carved areas.

4. Completing the stripping

To remove traces of the finish left after stripping, apply another coat of stripper and let it work. Then, following the grain, rub the area with fine steel wool (#4) or a nylon stripping pad until all the finish has been removed. If you plan to use a water-base stain, do not use steel wool because the stain can cause particles of steel to rust and leave marks.

5. Sanding

● To remove scratches from flat surfaces, begin with medium-grade paper in a sanding block, passed at a slight angle to the grain. Then, smooth the surface with fine-grade paper passed parallel to the grain (#5).

● Sand joints and other tight spots with an angled sanding sponge; round legs and spindles with sanding strips drawn back

and forth around the part.

● Remove the dust with a soft brush or a tack cloth.

6. Repairing the surface

Wood filler is available in a variety of colors named for the type of wood it best matches. Choose a wood filler that is stainable.

● Fill gouges and dents with wood filler, then pass a putty knife over the area parallel to the grain (#6). To fill cracks and scratches over a larger area, lay a bead of filler at one side of the area and spread it with a wider knife.

● Let the filler dry for the time recommended by the manufacturer. Sand away excess with fine-grade paper in a sanding block.

● Wipe off dust with a tack cloth.

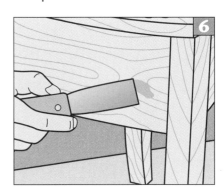

FINISHING FURNITURE

The technique you choose for finishing furniture depends on the product you'll be applying and the number of pieces you'll be covering. For example, a drying oil, such as tung oil or linseed oil, is best wiped on with a cloth. Apply most other finishes, such as varnish, polyurethane, or lacquer, with a brush—or, if you have several pieces to finish, with a spray system, which will speed up the work.

Whichever product or technique you select, it usually takes several coats of finish to get the desired effect. Check the manufacturer's instructions for details. Allow each coat to dry before applying the next one. Depending on the product, you may need to sand lightly with fine or extra-fine sandpaper between coats.

SAFETY TIP *Many types of finish produce dangerous fumes. Only apply a finish in a well-ventilated room, and wear rubber gloves and safety goggles while you work. If you'll be spraying a finish, wear a respirator as well.*

HOW LONG WILL IT TAKE?
Two to four hours

TOOLS
• Paintbrush • Spray system • Hammer • Safety goggles • Rubber gloves • Respirator

MATERIALS
• Wood blocks • Finishing nails • Cloths • Finish

PRELIMINARIES

Reading product labels

The label on a finish container (#1) provides important product information, ranging from application and clean-up techniques to safety precautions and first-aid information. Read the label carefully to learn how to use the product safely and effectively.

Making drying supports

By placing the furniture piece on small wooden blocks, you can more easily apply finish to the base of the legs.
● Cut four blocks of wood about 2 inches square.
● Drive a finishing nail through the center of each block (#2).
● Use the blocks on a level surface with the nail tips pointing up so they support the legs or corners of the piece.

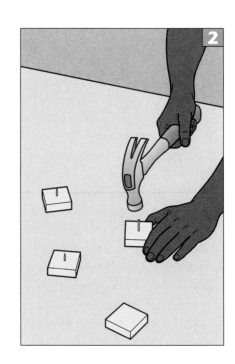

FINISHING BY HAND

- Apply the first coat of a heavy, slow-drying finish against the grain, then smooth it by brushing with the grain. Apply all other finishes with the grain.
- Apply a fast-drying finish—such as shellac or lacquer—to successive small areas without overlapping them.
- Work out from the center of a larger piece, starting from the bottom (#2).

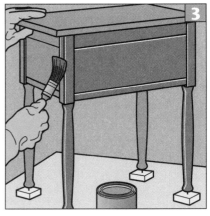

Wiping on a finish

- Set the piece of furniture on support blocks.
- Dip a soft cloth in the finish and squeeze out the excess, then wipe a thin, even layer of finish over the surface (#1).
- Let the finish soak in for a few minutes, then wipe away the excess with a clean, dry cloth.
- Allow the finish to dry according to the manufacturer's instructions before wiping on additional coats.

Brushing techniques

Brushing techniques vary according to finish type, drying time, and size of the piece. Use a good quality brush—it will hold more finish without dripping.

Brushing overview

- Dip about one-third of the brush's bristle length into the finish.
- Apply a thin coat of finish, making as few strokes as possible to avoid air bubbles and lap marks (#3).
- Allow the finish to dry before applying additional coats.
- Depending on the finish, clean brushes with alcohol, mineral spirits, turpentine, or lacquer thinner. Hang brushes on a hook; never store them resting on their bristles.

SPRAYING FINISHES

PAINTING & HOME DECOR

1. Adjusting the spray pattern

Many sprayer systems have three spray-pattern settings: vertical, horizontal, and circular. Use the vertical setting for wide horizontal surfaces, the horizontal setting for vertical surfaces, and the circular setting to create a wide, multi-purpose spray.

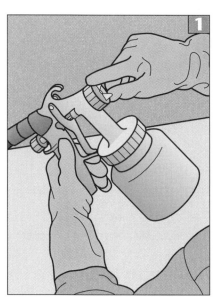

- Fill the sprayer container with finish and screw on the nozzle.
- Set the spray pattern by adjusting the air cap on the nozzle (#1).

2. Adjusting the flow

Test the sprayer on a large piece of scrap wood. As you pass the nozzle over the surface, it should apply a thin, even coat without dripping or leaving bare spots.

- Hold the sprayer 8 to 10 inches from the piece of scrap wood and pull the nozzle trigger to release the spray. As necessary, decrease the flow by turning the flow adjustment knob counterclockwise or increase the flow by turning the knob the other way (#2).
- Experiment with the various spray patterns.

3. Spraying flat surfaces

- Keeping the sprayer 8 to 10 inches away from the surface, start spraying at the bottom of the piece, making straight, overlapping passes back and forth across the grain. Aim the center of the spray at the outside edge of the previous pass (#3). Keep your wrist straight as you work.
- After the first coat dries, apply the next coat by moving up and down across the piece, spraying with the grain.

4. Spraying corners

Spraying corners can be tricky. Experiment with a piece of scrap wood of the same dimension.
- Finish a corner by spraying directly at the corner's edge, applying finish to the adjacent surfaces equally (#4).

STENCILING

Decorating with stencils creates a unique, handcrafted look; they often are used to create borders on walls, ceilings, or other surfaces. Stencils are available in a wide variety of designs at hobby shops and hardware stores; most types are made of acetate—a durable, transparent material that is washable. Patterns either are repeated at intervals or are part of a continuous, linked design. For a first project, choose a simple, self-contained design applied at intervals that requires just one color.

Making your own stencil can bring added satisfaction and a personal touch to the job. Look to sources such as fabrics, wallpapers, and illustrations for design ideas. You can also repeat an existing design element in your home. Making a stencil involves tracing a pattern onto acetate and cutting along the outline with a craft knife. You may need to draw in "bridges"—connecting strips of acetate that hold together long, narrow sections of a design, such as the tail of the sea horse in the example here. The gaps left by bridges after stenciling can be touched up later.

Clean stencils made of acetate with water. Scrape off thick paint buildup with a craft knife. Store stencils flat.

MAKING A STENCIL

1. Tracing the design

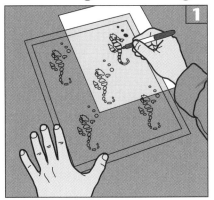

The stencil acetate must be large enough for a series of two or three of the chosen images set apart at the desired distance. Make sure the corners of the acetate sheet are perfectly square.

• With a felt marker and a straightedge, draw a reference frame onto the acetate sheet 1 inch from the edges.
• Place the acetate sheet over the design, aligning the design with a corner of the frame. Trace the design onto the acetate (#1).
• Trace the design at the other three corners; if desired, trace a fifth image at the center, positioning it by eye.

2. Cutting out the design

• Place the acetate on a cutting board and cut out the shapes with a craft knife (#2). For cutting circles and curved shapes, use a swivel-headed craft knife.
• If you accidentally cut through the edge of the design, reinforce the edge with masking tape.

CREATING A BORDER WITH STENCILS

1. Snapping a chalk line

To keep your border design level, snap a chalk line on each wall as a reference. The height of the line should correspond to the lower edge of the stencil.

• With a tape measure and a pencil, mark an X at the desired height of the line at each end of the wall.

• Drive a small nail into the wall at one of the marks and tie the chalk line to it—alternatively, have a helper hold the end of the chalk line at the mark. Run the chalk line to the other mark, stretching it taut against the wall. Pluck the string (#1) so it snaps against the wall and leaves a chalk line.

• Repeat the procedure on the other walls.

2. Taping the stencil in place

Most commercial stencils have a reference line that can be aligned with the chalk line on the wall. You can also line up the bottom of the stencil itself with the chalk line.

• Starting in a corner of the room, lay the stencil flat against the wall and tape it loosely in place.

• Line up your reference line on the stencil with the chalk line on the wall, then secure the upper edge of the stencil with additional pieces of masking tape (#2).

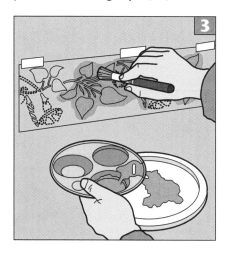

3. Dabbing on paint

To avoid painting under the edges of the stencil cutouts, keep the brush perpendicular to the wall as you paint.

• Pour a little paint into a plastic container or a paint palette.

• Lightly dip the brush into the paint, then dab it against a tray or a plate to remove excess.

• Lightly dabbing with the brush, fill in all the stencil cutouts (#3). For a sense of depth, allow some of the wall's base color to show through slightly in some spots.

Note: *For extra precision when painting narrow cutouts, wrap masking tape around the brush just above the joint between the bristles and the handle.*

4. Overlapping the stencil

Most commercial stencils repeat a design twice so that one set of cutouts can be aligned with the last design painted to ensure perfect sequencing of the pattern.

• Carefully remove the stencil from the wall.

• Align the stencil so that one set of cutouts aligns with the last design painted on the wall, making sure it also lines up with the chalk line (#4).

• Tape the stencil in place and continue painting.

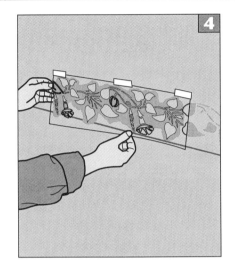

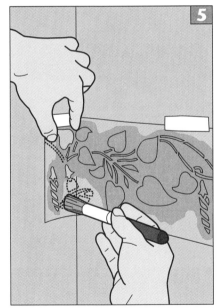

- Lightly fill in two or three cutouts on the other wall as reference points (#5).
- Remove the stencil and place it on the other wall, lining up the painted references points with the cutouts. Tape the stencil in place and continue applying paint.

5. Dealing with corners

It's important not to crease the stencil when painting at corners or it will become difficult to use.
- Gently press the stencil into the corner with your free hand and finish painting the first wall.

6. Filling in gaps and touching up

- Fill in unwanted gaps left by bridges in the stencil with an artist's brush (#6). To match the texture created by the stencil brush, don't overload the bristles with paint; dab them on a tray or plate to squeeze out excess.
- Touch up corners, if necessary, the same way.
- Let the paint dry, then touch up smeared stencil edges using an artist's brush dipped in paint of the wall's base color.

7. Applying the second color

Most two-color stencil designs require a second acetate sheet unless the different colors are far apart in the design. Along with its own sequence of cutouts, this second stencil usually includes the first stencil's cutouts for reference.
- Beginning at the same start point in the room, line up the reference cutouts with the design painted and tape the stencil in place.
- Apply the second color to the second set of cutouts in the same way as you did the first (#7).
- Touch up the second color as needed.
- Follow the same directions to add a third or more colors.

COLORWASHING

PAINTING & HOME DECOR

Colorwashing involves painting with a mixture of water-based paint and transparent glaze. Instead of working with standard brush strokes, other techniques are used that highlight the rustic, time-worn appearance associated with colorwashing. Each application technique offers a slightly different variation on the same basic effect.

Regardless of technique, the right colorwashing proportions are roughly one part glaze to two parts paint. Mix the paint and the glaze together in a plastic bucket.

Two of the three colorwashing techniques explained here call for moistening the wall before painting. This allows colors to bleed slightly and softens the end appearance. Consider experimenting with your technique on a piece of wood or on section of wall that will be hidden from view (such as behind the refrigerator).

Protect floor surfaces from paint with a drop cloth; wear rubber gloves to protect your hands. Line hardware and surfaces next to those being painted with anchor tape—avoid using masking tape.

HOW LONG WILL IT TAKE?

More than four hours

TOOLS

- Plastic bucket • Paintbrushes
- Sea sponges • Paint (or car-waxing) mittens • Rubber gloves

MATERIALS

- Latex paint • Transparent glaze
- Drop cloth • Anchor tape

Choosing colors

Colorwashing looks best when a darker shade is added to a lighter base. When adding more than one color, each color should be darker than the last one applied. Choose different shades from a sequence of colors on a paint sample at a hardware store. Or, add a higher proportion of glaze to the same paint to create a lighter second color. Here, two shades of orange will be applied to a yellow wall.

BRUSH-WASHING

1. Applying the first coat

Brush-washing damages the bristles, so use inexpensive brushes.

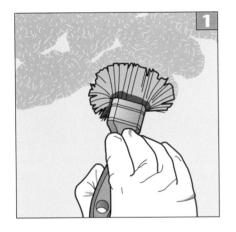

Work on successive 3-foot-square sections.
- Dip a soft-bristled brush into the paint-and-glaze mixture.
- Push the brush against the wall, splaying the bristles (#1); do not make sweeping strokes. Let the base coat show through in places to create contrast.

2. Applying a second color

- Dip a clean brush into the darker second color and use the same application technique described in Step 1 (#2). However, apply this

coat a little more sparingly than the last one. The base coat should still show through in places.

SPONGE-WASHING

1. Applying the glaze

- Moisten a 3-foot-square section of the wall with cold water.
- Dip a soft-bristled paintbrush into the paint-and-glaze mixture and apply it to the dampened area with sweeping, irregular strokes, leaving streaks of the base

color showing through (#1). If the section dries before you finish applying the mixture, moisten it again. Don't worry; it's supposed to look like a mess at this point.

2. Sponging off the surface

Going over the painted area with a sea sponge tones down streaks and removes excess glaze, creating a more uniform appearance.
- Soak a sea sponge in cold water and wring it nearly dry. Dab the sponge against the painted area (#2), paying particular attention to the hard edges of brush strokes.

- Wash the sponge often in cold water and wring it out. Change the water several times for each painted wall.
- To soften the overall effect, wait until the surface is nearly dry, then go over it with a clean, dry brush, making figure-eight motions. Wipe the brush clean on a wet cloth after every few passes.

MITTEN-WASHING

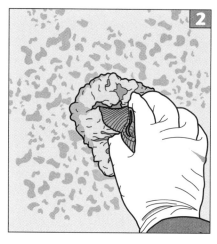

will show through. If the section dries before you finish, moisten it again with a cloth.

3. Applying a second coat

● Wait for the first coat to dry. (Alternatively, for a softer appearance, moisten the first coat with a damp sponge—just as you did the base coat—working in successive 3-square-foot sections.)

● Apply a second, darker color by repeating the same procedure with a new mitten (#3). However, be more sparing with the second color by tamping very lightly. Some of the base coat should still show through in places.

1. Preparing the mitten

Colorwashing with a paint or car-waxing mitten creates an interesting appearance.

● Moisten a 3-foot-square area of the wall.

● Apply paint-and-glaze mixture to one side of the mitten with a paintbrush (#1).

2. Applying the first coat

● Bunch up the mitten, then pat the wall with it, creating a roughly consistent pattern and allowing some of the base coat to show through (#2). Don't wear the mitten to apply the paint-and-glaze mixture—the shape of your hand

PAINTING & HOME DECOR

SPONGING

Sponging is a fast and easy technique that can be used for a variety of effects, depending on how you handle the sponge and the colors you chose. There are two basic sponging techniques: sponging on and sponging off. With the first technique, thinned paint is applied with a sponge; with the second, it is applied with a brush and distressed using a clean sponge.

Use latex paint thinned with either water or glaze, depending on the technique you plan to use. Paint that has been thinned with glaze dries more slowly, providing the time needed to complete the longer sponging-off process. Paint thinned with water is fine for sponging on. In either case, mix roughly equal measures of thinner and paint in a plastic bucket.

The trick to attractive sponging is to create a relatively consistent look without allowing it to become too repetitive. To do this, move the sponge in your hand while you work and alternate between two different-shaped sponges.

Protect floor surfaces from paint with a drop cloth; wear rubber gloves to protect your hands. Line hardware and surfaces next to those being painted with anchor tape—avoid using masking tape.

Choosing colors

There are no rules about colors for a sponging project. But if you get too adventurous, you're more likely to be disappointed with the result, especially if you don't have much decorating experience. For a foolproof project, decorators recommend working with colors from the same paint-sample card. When sponging a single color, choose a base color that is two shades lighter on the card. For a two-color job, choose the base color and first color the same way, then select another color two shades lighter than the base color. Apply the darker shade to the base coat and the lighter color last.

SPONGING ON

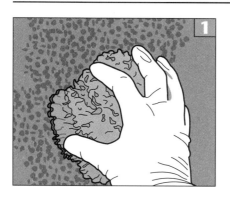

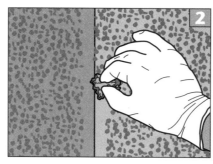

1. Applying the first color

● Lightly dab the wall with the sponge (#1). Work in roughly 2-foot-square areas, applying paint from top to bottom so you can catch drips that form.
● Move the sponge around in your hand as you proceed to slightly vary the effect. Alternate occasionally with a different-shaped sponge.
● Cover about 50 percent of the base color.
● Avoid overlapping the edges of areas as much as possible.

2. Dealing with corners

Cramming a large sponge into a corner creates an unattractive dark line that will detract from the desired effect.
● Tear off a piece of sponge small enough to fit into the narrow unpainted strips on each wall.
● Load the piece of sponge and dab off the excess.

● Carefully finish sponging one wall (#2), then go on to the other.
● Touch up spots the sponge can't reach with an artist's brush—but avoid making brush strokes.

3. Adding a second color

A second, lighter color creates a sense of depth. Thin the paint the same way you did the first color. Use clean sponges or thoroughly clean the first set of sponges and allow them to dry for at least several hours.
● Working as you did for the first color, sponge on the second color (#3), this time applying the paint a little more sparingly.

SPONGING OFF

1. Brushing on glaze

Make sure that the base coat is dry before you begin. Apply the glaze mixture in a 2-foot-square area at a time and work from top to bottom to catch any drips that form.

● Thin the paint in a plastic bucket.

● Brush on the glaze mixture with a 3-inch paintbrush, making criss-cross strokes (#1). Make lighter strokes as you get to the edges of the section to avoid noticeably thick overlaps.

Note: *Thinned paint can also be applied with a sponge roller. This method takes less time, but it creates a more uniform final result.*

2. Sponging off

After covering a 2-foot-square area with the brush, go over it immediately with a damp sponge. This tones down streaks, removes excess glaze, and creates a more uniform appearance. Rinse and wring out the sponge and change the water several times for each wall painted.

● Dab the sponge lightly over the wet surface (#2).

● Move the sponge around in your hand as you work to slightly vary the texture. Alternate occasionally between two differently-shaped sponges.

RAGGING

Ragging is an easy painting technique that involves pressing a soft cotton cloth against a surface to create a textured impression. There are two basic ragging techniques: ragging on and ragging off. With the first technique, thinned paint is applied with a cloth; with the second technique, thinned paint is applied with a brush and distressed with a cloth.

Use latex paint thinned with either water or glaze, depending on the technique you plan to use. Paint that has been thinned with glaze stays wet longer, providing the extra time needed for ragging off. Paint thinned with water is fine for ragging on. In either case, mix roughly equal measures of paint and thinner in a plastic bucket. Cloths should be roughly 2-foot-square and free of frayed edges and lint.

The effect you get depends on how you handle the cloth and on the type of cloth. The softer the cloth, the softer the texture. Several variations on the technique are shown here. Consider practicing on a piece of wood painted the same base color or on a section of wall that will be hidden, such as behind a chest of drawers.

Before beginning, mask hardware and adjacent surfaces with anchor tape—avoid masking tape. To make clean up easier, put down drop cloths and wear rubber gloves.

HOW LONG WILL IT TAKE?
More than four hours

TOOLS
• Plastic bucket (or paint tray) • Paintbrush • Rubber gloves

MATERIALS
• Latex paint • Glaze • Drop cloth • Anchor tape • Cloths

Choosing colors

It can be fun to experiment with colors, but unless you're really sure of the effect you'll end up with it's a good idea to play it safe. For colors that are certain to work well together, choose different shades from the same paint-sample card. When ragging a single color, make it two shades darker than your base color. A second color should be two shades lighter than the base coat. This creates a greater sense of depth.

RAGGING ON

1. Loading the cloth

Make sure your base coat is dry before you start.
- Thin the paint in a bucket.
- Soak a clean, dry cloth in the mixture (#1).

2. Wringing out the cloth

- Wring out enough excess paint (#2) to avoid drips while you work. You'll quickly get a sense for just how much paint to keep in the cloth.

3. Ragging on

- Lightly dab the cloth against the wall (#3). To create a more varied pattern, change the position of the cloth in your hand while you work. Cover successive

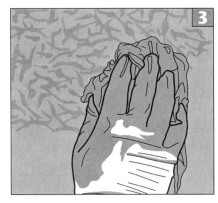

3-foot-square areas, working from top to bottom to catch drips.
- Work carefully in corners to avoid overlapping coats.

4. Applying a second color

Allow the first color to dry, then thin the paint of the second color.
- Soak a clean, dry cloth in the mixture and wring it out.
- Dab the cloth against the wall (#4) as you did for the first color, but work with a lighter touch to allow plenty of open spaces for the base coat and first color to show through.

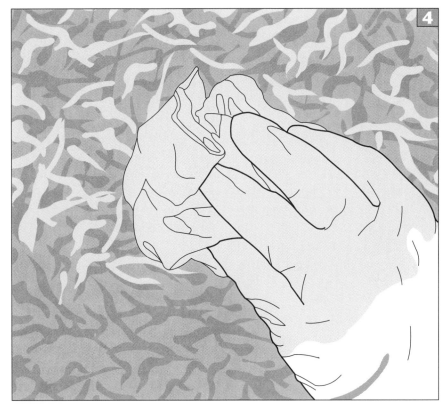

RAGGING OFF

1. Applying glaze

Make sure your base coat is dry before you begin.

- Thin the paint in a bucket.
- Apply the mixture with a 4-inch paintbrush (#1), working in successive 2-foot-square areas. Don't smooth out the brush marks.

2. Ragging off

Going over each 2-foot-square area while it is still wet reveals some the base coat, creating a softer-edged pattern than that produced by ragging on.

- Soak a clean cloth in water and wring it out.

- Lightly press the cloth into the wet glaze (#2) and remove it quickly. Rinse and ring out the cloth as needed.

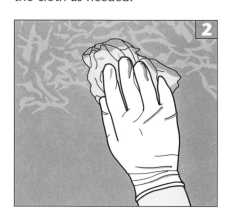

TECHNIQUE VARIATIONS

Rag rolling

Creating the wrinkled effect shown at left is a little trickier than basic ragging, but the end result

can be striking. You can use this technique for both ragging on and ragging off. When ragging on, load the cloth with paint by brushing it on lightly with a paintbrush. When ragging off, apply thinned paint to the wall with a paintbrush.

- Twist a thick cloth into a long ropelike shape.
- Holding the cloth horizontally, rag on or off by rolling the cloth down the wall (#1). Work in successive vertical strips.

Soft texturing

As the term suggests, soft texturing softens the appearance of a ragged surface.

- Dab a soft cloth against the wet

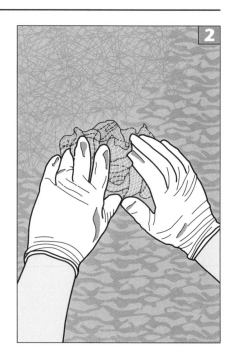

pattern (#2), pressing very lightly.
- Rinse and wring out the cloth periodically as you work.

PAINTING & HOME DECOR

FAUX STONE

Creating a granite or marble finish is more difficult than other decorative painting techniques, such as ragging and sponging, but with a little practice and the right tools you'll soon get the hang of it. And besides, if you don't create the effect you want on your first try, you can always apply another coat of base paint and start again.

If you take a close look at a real marble surface, you'll notice that some of the characteristic veins appear sharper-looking and darker, while others are blurred and faint. This coloration gives marble a feeling of depth—an effect that can be reproduced with a few simple tricks in a faux marble finish.

Granite is characterized by flecks of various colors. These flecks are reproduced in a faux granite finish by sponging and splattering techniques.

Faux stone finishes applied to baseboards or other features that get a lot of wear and tear should be protected with a few coats of glossy varnish. The varnish will also give these finishes the look of polished stone.

Before beginning, mask hardware and adjacent surfaces with anchor tape—avoid masking tape. Wear rubber gloves and protect floors with drop cloths.

HOW LONG WILL IT TAKE?

More than four hours

TOOLS

- Plastic bucket • Sea sponges
- Plastic tray (or plate) • Feather
- Paintbrush • Artist's brush
- Toothbrush • Paint stick
- Rubber gloves

MATERIALS

- Latex paint • Glaze • Glossy varnish • Anchor tape • Drop cloth • Newspaper

Choosing colors

Natural marble comes in many colors, but the most realistic faux finishes are created by mimicking the look of white marble streaked with dark blue or black. Because white marble is, in fact, off-white, the base coat in the following first example is a pale gray that has a hint of brown for added warmth. The dark veins are created with midnight blue.

The colors used to create the granite finish in the second example come from the same paint-sample card, with the exception of the red color applied near the end of the procedure. The base color is a mid-tone gray. The next color applied is a darker, charcoal gray and the second color is a pale gray four shades lighter. The red is used for highlight flecks.

MARBLING

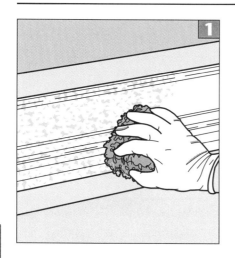

1. Sponging over the first color

After applying the base coat and letting it dry, mix some base paint with a small quantity of the darker gray paint in a plastic bucket. Add just enough gray to make a slight difference in color. Applying this mixture with a sponge will create a cloudy effect typical of marble.

● With a paintbrush, coat one side of a sea sponge with the mixture.
● Dab the sponge against a tray or plate to remove excess paint.
● Lightly dab the surface with the sponge (#1). Rotate the sponge in your hand as you work to vary the pattern.

2. Dealing with corners

A successful faux marble effect requires a consistent base pattern over the entire surface. This can be difficult to achieve in tight spots, such as at corners, where a large sponge is unwieldy.

● Pull off a piece of sponge small enough to use in these tight spots.
● Apply paint to the sponge and dab off excess.
● Carefully sponge corners and other tight spots with small pieces of sponge (#2), working carefully to keep the pattern consistent.

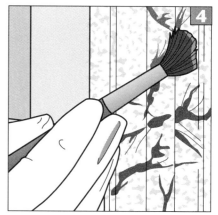

3. Painting the veins

Apply the veins with a with large supple feather—available at art-supply stores. Have a container of water on hand. In another container, mix two parts glaze to one part midnight-blue paint.

● Dip the end of the feather into the water, then into the paint-and-glaze mixture.
● Pull the feather at an angle across the work surface with a light, shaky touch (#3). Allow some veins to cross each other.
● Paint a few veins without dipping the feather in water to create darker lines.

4. Softening the veins

Softening the look of some of the veins adds to the sense of depth. This must be done before the veins are dry.

● Lightly brush some of the still-wet veins with a clean artist's brush (#4). Rotate the brush as you work to more effectively blend edges of lines into the background colors.

PAINTING & HOME DECOR

FAUX GRANITE

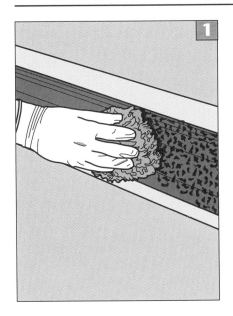

1. Sponging on the first color

- Apply the mid-tone gray base coat with a paintbrush and let it dry. Don't worry about visible brush strokes; they will add to the stone effect.
- Thin two parts charcoal-gray paint with one part water in a plastic bucket.
- Apply the mixture to one side of a sea sponge using a paintbrush.
- Dab the sponge against a tray or plate to remove excess paint.
- Lightly dab the work surface with the sponge (#1). Allow 20 to 30 percent of the base color to show through.
- Rip off pieces of sponge to work in corners and other tight spots. Carefully sponge with these small pieces, keeping the pattern as consistent as possible.

2. Adding the second color

The next step involves splattering paint to create the distinctive speckled look of granite. This can get messy, so be sure to protect adjacent surfaces with newspaper or cardboard.

- Thin two parts pale-gray paint to one part water.
- Dip a 2-inch paintbrush in the mixture and dab off the excess on a paint tray or plate.
- Brace a paint stick at an angle over the work surface and knock the loaded brush against it (#2) so the impact spatters tiny droplets onto the work surface.
- Repeat the action along the length of the work surface.

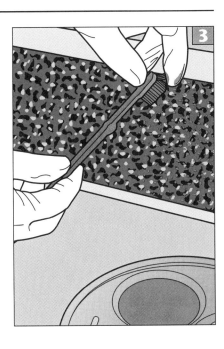

3. Applying an accent color

Spraying, or stippling, an accent color adds drama and completes the color scheme.

- Load a toothbrush and tap off excess on a paint tray or plate.
- Holding the toothbrush several inches from the surface, run your finger over the bristles (#3), bending them so they spray droplets as they snap back into place. The farther you hold the brush from the surface, the smaller the droplets. Repeat along the entire surface, reloading the brush as necessary.
- Complete the desired effect by selectively adding splatters of pale- and charcoal-gray paint.
- Apply a coat of varnish when the surface is dry. Apply a second coat once the first coat is dry.

REMOVING OLD WALLPAPER

Remove old wallpaper before papering again or painting. Although you can get away with papering over some types of wallpaper, you risk loosening the adhesive below the old paper with water or paste, causing the new and old papers to peel off together. Applying paint over wallpaper produces results that are usually unsightly.

Some types of wallpaper, such as vinyl-coated papers, are classified as strippable. In most cases, this means they peel off with little trouble; but not all strippable papers live up to the name—stubborn sections often need to be scraped off.

Vinyl-film wallpaper comes off in two layers. The first layer peels off fairly easily to reveal a layer that can be soaked with wallpaper stripper and scraped off. This method is the best way to deal with most types of wallpaper that put up a fight. However, stripper isn't effective with some types of non-strippable papers that use water-proof adhesives; with these papers, it is necessary to dry-scrape.

HOW LONG WILL IT TAKE?
More than four hours

TOOLS
• Utility knife • Putty knife • Spray bottle • Scoring tool • Sponge • Garden sprayer (or wallpaper steamer) • Scraper

MATERIALS
• Water • Wallpaper stripper • Stain sealer

DRY STRIPPING

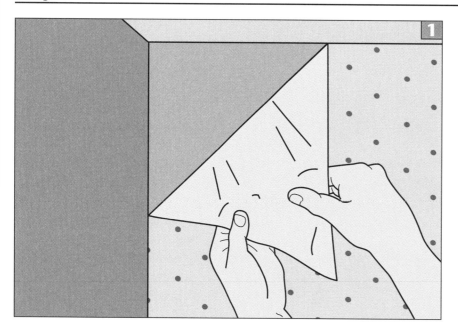

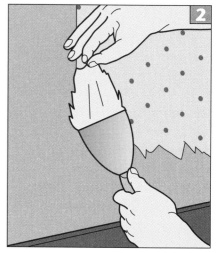

1. Peeling off strips

• Peel back a corner at the top of a strip of wallpaper with your fingernail or a utility knife.

• Continue peeling, keeping the paper flat against itself to avoid tearing it (#1).

2. Removing stubborn pieces

• Hold a putty knife at an angle and push it under the wallpaper, taking care not to gouge the wall. Peel off the loosened paper with your free hand as you work (#2).

STRIPPER SOAKING

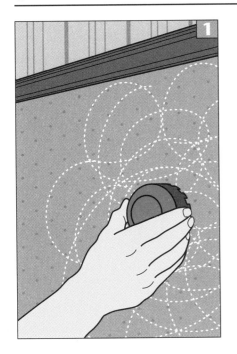

1. Scoring the wallpaper

Vinyl-coated and other papers need to be scored so that stripper can penetrate. If your paper does not peel off easily, test it by spraying it with a little water; if the water penetrates, the paper does not need to be scored.
● Score the paper by passing a wallpaper scoring tool over it (#1) to make small holes or by cutting horizontal slits in it with a utility knife. Take care not to press too hard so the wallboard under the paper isn't damaged.

2. Applying wallpaper stripper

Wear rubber gloves to mix and apply wallpaper stripper.
● Prepare a solution of wallpaper stripper and water according to the manufacturer's instructions, then apply it to the paper with a sponge (#2).
● Wait the recommended time, then wet the paper again and begin scraping.

Note: *You can also apply wallpaper stripper with a garden sprayer—a useful option for big jobs. Wear safety goggles, lay down drop cloths, and set the nozzle for a fine stream, not a mist. Another time-saving option is to rent a wallpaper steamer.*

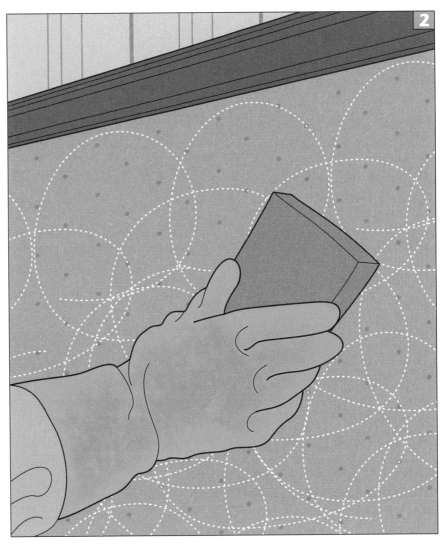

PAINTING & HOME DECOR

STRIPPER SOAKING (CONTINUED)

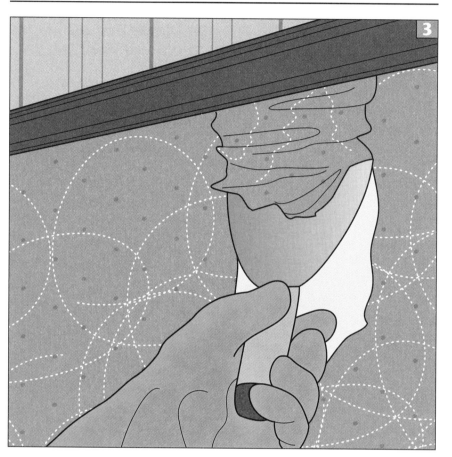

3. Loosening the paper

• Hold a putty knife at an angle to the wall and push it under the wet paper (#3), taking care not to damage the wallboard under it. If the paper does not come off easily, soak it again.

4. Stripping the paper

• Peel the loosened paper upward with your hand, keeping it flat against itself to avoid tearing (#4).

Continue loosening the paper with a putty knife and peeling it off with your hand until the wall is completed.

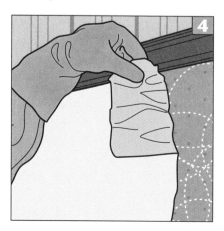

DRY SCRAPING

Scraping off paper

Non-strippable wallpaper with waterproof adhesive that cannot be loosened with wallpaper stripper must be dry-scraped with a wall scraper.

• Make horizontal slits in the paper with the scraper, taking care not to damage the wallboard by pressing too hard.

• Holding the blade of the scraper at an angle to the wall, insert it into a slit and push upward to loosen a strip of paper (#1), then peel it back with your fingers.

• Work on successive strips of paper the same way until the wall is completed.

WALLPAPERING A ROOM

Not all wallpaper is actually plain paper—both vinyl and vinyl-coated papers are also common. These are better choices for kitchens and bathrooms because they are more washable and withstand humidity better than paper.

When making your choice of wallpaper, think ahead to a time when you may want to remove it. Strippable papers can be pulled right off the wall, while only the top layer of peelable papers can be easily removed. Removing non-strippable papers can be a major undertaking.

Wallpaper of the type shown in this project is prepasted and must be soaked in water to activate the paste. To hang unpasted wallpaper, you will have to apply paste to the backing with a roller. Before you start hanging the wallpaper, be sure to read all of the specific instructions given by the manufacturer.

HOW LONG WILL IT TAKE?
More than four hours

TOOLS
• Tape measure • Scissors • Wallpaper trough • Carpenter's level • Plastic smoother (or smoothing brush) • Wallpaper knife • Taping knife • Trimming tool • Sponge • Seam Roller

MATERIALS
• Wallpaper • Drop cloth

1. Measuring and cutting

Until you've gained some experience, it's best to cut and soak no more than a couple sheets of paper before hanging them.

• Set up a worktable and cover it with a drop cloth.

• Measure the height of the wall from ceiling to baseboard.

• To cut the first sheet, unroll the paper onto your table. Measure and mark the wall height plus 3 inches to allow for some excess at the top and bottom. Mark a straight line and cut the paper with heavy scissors.

• For the second sheet, line up the pattern at the top with that of the first sheet (#1) and note the distance by which the two sheets are offset—referred to as the pattern repeat. Mark the spot, fold the paper back, and trim off the excess along the fold line. Cut the second sheet to the same length as the first.

• Number the back of each sheet in pencil and add an arrow indicating the end that will go along the ceiling.

• Before cutting additional sheets, double check the distance from the ceiling to the baseboard.

PAINTING & HOME DECOR

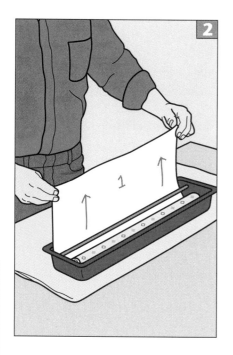

2. Soaking

● Fill a wallpaper trough about two-thirds full with water at room temperature.

● Roll your first cut sheet with the backing facing inward, starting at the bottom edge.

● Set the roll in the trough and gently press down to remove any air bubbles. Let the paper soak for the time recommended by the manufacturer.

● Holding the top corners of the paper, pull it straight up approximately 18 inches, feeding it along the divider to unroll it (#2).

Note: *Place a folded cotton sheet under your trough to absorb water.*

3. Booking

After the paper is soaked, it needs to sit for a short time to give the wet paste a chance to soak in. Before setting the sheet aside, book it to keep it from drying out.

● Once you have pulled about 18 inches of paper from the trough, fold the paper back on itself, pasted surfaces together. (Avoid creasing the paper.) Pull the paper out further and fold it back in the other direction.

● Continue folding the paper back and forth like an accordion (#3). When you reach the bottom edge, fold the paper back in the opposite direction to the other folds, creating a hem.

● Arrange two or three booked sheets in order of hanging on a clean section of the drop cloth and let them sit for the time specified by the manufacturer.

4. Hanging the first sheet

The first and last sheets you hang won't match perfectly. To keep this mismatch hidden, start in the middle of a wall and work around the room in each direction, ending at an inconspicuous corner.

● With a level and a pencil, draw a very light plumb line where you want the right edge of the paper to fall.

● Unfold the top part of the booked sheet, aligning the pattern along the ceiling.

● Open up the rest of the sheet, aligning it with the plumb line and smoothing it with a plastic smoother (#4).

● With the smoother, crease the paper where the wall and ceiling meet, allowing about $1\frac{1}{2}$ inches of excess to overlap the ceiling.

Note: *Use a smoothing brush for very delicate papers.*

5. Unfolding the bottom

The hem you made when you booked the sheet keeps it from adhering to the bottom of the wall, allowing you to adjust the position of the sheet as you work your way down.

● Once you've smoothed the sheet down to the bottom section of the wall, unfold the hem (#5).

● With the plastic smoother, push the paper down against the top of the baseboard.

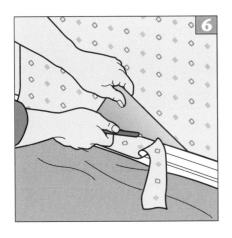

6. Trimming

After you've hung and smoothed the sheet, trim the excess at the baseboard and the ceiling.

● Press a triangular trimming tool into the crease at the baseboard and trim the excess with a wallpaper knife (#6). Trim along the ceiling in the same way.

● Sponge the wallpaper surface with clear water, then pat it dry with a towel.

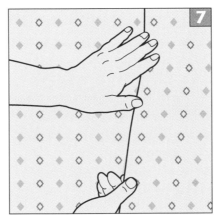

7. The second sheet

Each sheet must be aligned with the previous one so that it is vertical and the pattern matches.

● Hang the second sheet from the top of the wall and gently butt it to the first sheet, matching the pattern (#7).

● With the smoothing tool, crease the paper along the ceiling, then smooth downward, adjusting the paper position with your hand.

● Gently roll the edges with a seam roller—for a delicate or embossed paper, use a sponge.

Note: *You may find that certain patterns won't match along the entire length of the sheet—in such cases, make the match at eye level.*

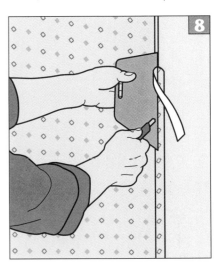

8. Dealing with corners

A slight overlap in a corner will keep a gap from opening up.

● When you reach the corner, hang the last sheet so it overlaps the adjacent wall, folding the paper over at the ceiling.

● To crease the sheet into the corner, make diagonal cuts in it where it overlaps the ceiling and the baseboard. Smooth the paper into the corner along its length.

● Trim the excess at the ceiling and the baseboard. Then, trim down along the corner, switching from the trimming tool to the smoothing tool for a guide (#8). The thickness of the smoothing tool will leave $\frac{1}{8}$ inch of paper on the adjacent wall.

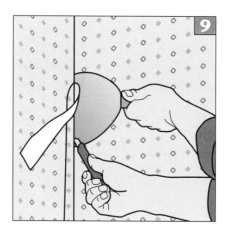

9. Continuing on the next wall

Corners are rarely perfectly vertical. Each time you turn a corner, readjust for plumb.

• Measure from the corner onto the unpapered wall surface the width of a sheet minus 2 inches. Mark a plumb line at this point.

• Hang the new sheet at the ceiling, lining up the right side with your plumb line and wrapping the paper onto the previous wall. Fold the paper at the ceiling line.

• Move the new sheet back and forth to align the pattern at its edge with the sheet underneath it, making sure the new sheet is still vertical. (If the corner isn't straight, you won't be able to match the pattern perfectly.)

• Slice a diagonal in the corners, top and bottom, and trim at the ceiling and the baseboard.

• Trim the new sheet exactly along the corner using a taping knife as a cutting guide (#9), trying not to cut through the sheet underneath.

10. Fitting around windows

Don't try to cut your sheets in advance to fit around windows; instead, hang the paper over the window and trim it in place.

• Hang the first sheet that reaches the window, allowing it to cover the window frame. Smooth it toward the window, creasing it against the frame.

• Pressing the paper against the frame, find the corner of the window with the tip of the knife blade and make a diagonal cut downward (#10). Make another cut at the bottom of the window.

• With a taping knife as a cutting guide, trim off the excess along the top, side, and bottom of the window frame.

• Hang short sheets above and below the window, matching the pattern, then repeat the procedure to paper the wall on the other side of the window.

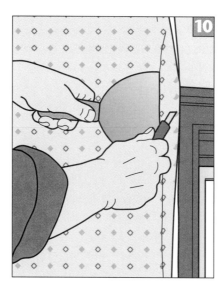

11. Cutting around electrical boxes

• Turn off the power to the room and remove the face plate.

• Wallpaper right over the electrical box.

• As you smooth the sheet over the opening, mark the corners with the tip of the knife blade. Finish smoothing the sheet down to the baseboard.

• Make diagonal cuts between the marked corners, then cut away just enough paper to expose the electrical box and the ears of the outlet or switch (#11).

SAFETY TIP *Make sure the power to the room is shut off at the service panel before cutting around outlets or switches.*

PREPARING AND PAINTING EXTERIOR TRIM

Preparation and painting the trim is often the most time-consuming part of an exterior paint job. Preparations typically include scraping off peeling paint, cleaning out and patching rotten wood, removing rust from wrought-iron railings, and replacing missing or damaged caulk along the frames of windows and doors. Painting trim can be slow work because these areas are often narrow and hard to reach. Have a cloth on hand to wipe up drips or streaks as they occur. On wrought-iron and aluminum surfaces, apply a rust-inhibiting primer first. A general-purpose latex primer is a good option for other surfaces. Talk to your paint dealer about your paint and primer selection and the type of exterior caulk that best suits your needs.

HOW LONG WILL IT TAKE?
Two to four hours

TOOLS

- Putty knife (or paint scraper)
- Awl • Wood chisel • Rasp
- Sanding block • Caulking gun • Wire brush • Power drill (with wire-brush attachment)
- Paintbrushes • Paint mitten
- Paint tray • Safety goggles

MATERIALS

- Cloth • Rust-inhibiting metal primer • Wood primer • Exterior caulk • Sandpaper • Liquid wood hardener • Epoxy wood filler • Aluminum cleaner • Paint
- Masking tape • Drop cloth (or newspaper)

PREPARING SURFACES

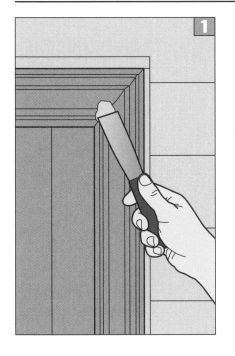

Preparing wood trim

- Scrape peeling paint off wood trim with a putty knife or paint scraper, then sand down the edges of the paint chips with medium-grade sandpaper.
- Check for signs of rotting wood by probing weathered or stained areas with an awl or a nail. Rotting wood is usually gray and spongy.
- Chip out rotten wood with a wood chisel.
- Apply a liquid wood hardener to the cavities with a brush, then let the hardener dry.
- Fill each cavity with an epoxy wood filler (#1) following the manufacturer's instructions.
- Allow the filler to dry, then smooth the patches flush with a rasp before smoothing with medium-grade sandpaper.

Sealing joints

- Chip away loose or damaged caulk around the frames of windows and doors with a putty knife or old screwdriver.
- Seal open joints with caulk using a caulking gun. Set the tip of the caulk tube into the joint at

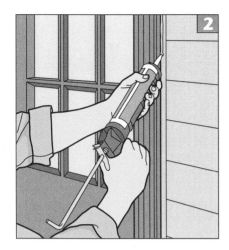

PAINTING & HOME DECOR

Wear safety goggles to remove paint with a wire brush or wire-brush attachment.

Using a wire-brush attachment

Loose paint can also be removed from aluminum and wrought iron using a circular wire-brush attachment fitted into a power drill. Make sure the drill is unplugged when you install the brush attachment in the chuck.

● Holding the brush just clear of the surface, activate the drill and begin passing the brush over the peeling sections (#4).

an angle and move the gun slowly along the joint (#2).

● Run a wet finger along the caulk to push it into the joint and create a concave surface.

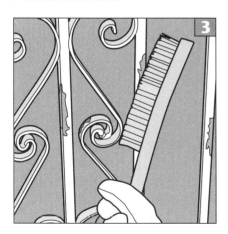

Preparing metal trim for painting

● Clean unpainted aluminum trim with aluminum cleaner.

● Remove peeling paint from a wrought-iron railing with a wire brush (#3).

● Wipe loose paint chips and dust off the railing with a dry cloth and apply primer immediately.

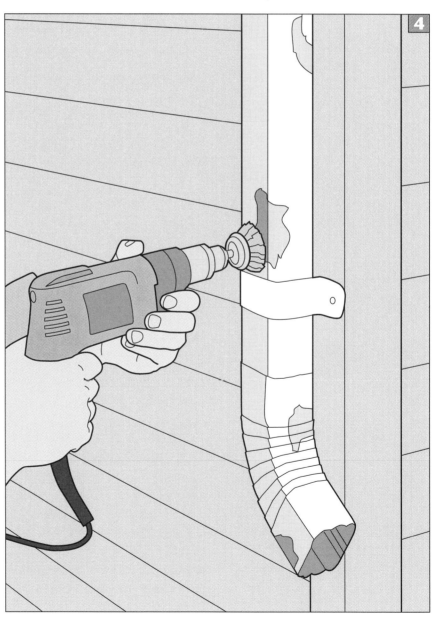

PRIMING AND PAINTING

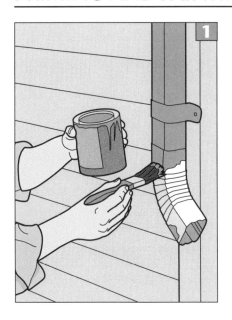

Priming metal trim

All surfaces must be clean and dry before applying primer and paint.
● Use a paintbrush to apply rust-inhibiting primer to downspouts and other metal trim (#1).
● Let the primer dry, then paint.

Painting soffits, eaves, and fascias

After priming and painting the gutters and downspouts, move on to the soffits, eaves, and fascia, in that order. Use a sash brush and start with edges and corners.
● Paint against the bristles of the brush in tight spots and corners (#2). (Corner rollers are another useful option here.)

Painting wood trim faces

Before painting window and door trim, protect adjacent surfaces with masking tape.
● Use a trim brush and paint in the direction of the trim face (#3). Work from top to bottom.

Painting railings

A paint mitten can make short work of painting railings.
● With the mitten on your hand, dip the palm side of it into a paint tray and allow paint to soak into the thick material.
● Grasp the railing and slowly slide the mitten along the surface (#4). Dab the mitten against the railing to eliminate streaks.

Note: *Paint mittens are messy—protect the ground from drips with a drop cloth or newspapers.*

REFINISHING A DECK

Pressure-treated decking is protected from rot and insect damage. Water penetration, though, can still make the wood crack and warp. To keep the wood looking new and to increase its life, finish your deck with a water sealer. For a second-floor deck, you may want to finish its underside, too.

Water sealers are either oil- or latex-base. Since both types are equally durable, choose a latex-base product—there will be fewer noxious fumes and you can clean up simply with water. Make sure the sealer contains a mildewcide, and if you want to prevent the wood from graying, choose one with ultraviolet (UV) protection. Water sealers are available clear or slightly tinted.

Water sealers last from one to four years. Every May or October, test the condition of the finish by pouring a glass of water on the decking boards. If the water discolors the wood, it has penetrated the finish and you should refinish. Clean the deck with a deck cleaner to remove dirt and brighten the color, then apply a new coat of finish. If your deck has been stained, test the deck cleaner in an inconspicuous corner to make sure that the cleaner will not strip the stain.

HOW LONG WILL IT TAKE?

Two to four hours

TOOLS

• Putty knife • Push broom • Nail set • Hammer • Cordless drill (with screwdriver attachment) • Bucket • Scrub brush • Garden hose • Paint tray • Roller (with extension pole) • Small roller • Paintbrush • Rubber gloves • Safety goggles

MATERIALS

• Deck cleaner • Water sealer • Deck screws

1. Removing debris

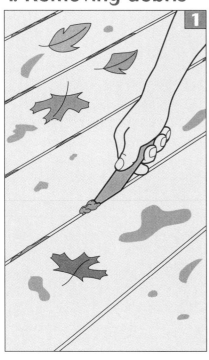

• With a plastic putty knife, remove the dead leaves, dirt, and other debris between the decking boards (#1). You can also use an old screwdriver or a long nail.
• Sweep the entire deck with a push broom, brushing parallel to the direction of the boards to avoid working the debris back into the spaces.

2. Setting popped nails

Movement of the decking boards can cause nails to pop. The nails should be driven back into place—removing a nail will leave a hole, allowing water to penetrate the wood and promote rot.

• Drive popped nails back under the surface of the decking board with a nail set and a hammer.

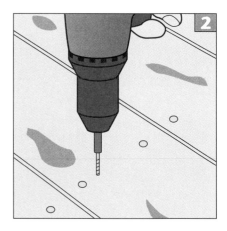

• To ensure that a nail will not work its way out again, drive a deck screw into the board next to the nail with a drill (#2).

3. Applying the cleaner

• Pour deck cleaner into a square-cornered plastic bucket, then dip a push broom into the solution and apply it to the deck.

• Scrub four boards at a time lengthwise, starting at one end of the deck and working back to the opposite end (#3).

• If the handrail and balusters appear stained or dirty, apply cleaner to them with the broom or a scrub brush.

SAFETY TIP *Deck cleaners contain bleach. Wear old clothes, safety goggles, and heavy rubber gloves when working with the cleaner—and don't stand directly over the bucket when pouring it. Don't pour the cleaner into a metal container and never mix it with a product containing ammonia—the combination will create poisonous fumes.*

4. Scrubbing the deck

• Scrub the entire deck lengthwise with the push brush.

• Areas of the deck may need more intense cleaning. Scrub especially dirty or stained areas, such as under the barbecue or a planter, with a scrub brush (#4).

5. Rinsing with water

• Thoroughly rinse the surface of the deck, the handrails, and the balusters with water from a garden hose (#5). Keep rinsing until no more bubbles appear.

• Allow the deck to dry for the time recommended by the cleaner manufacturer—generally a minimum of two days.

Note: *Shrubs and plants surrounding the deck can be harmed by contact with the cleaner. Before rinsing the deck, soak the plants and the surrounding soil with water to dilute any cleaner that falls on them. Hose them off again after rinsing the deck.*

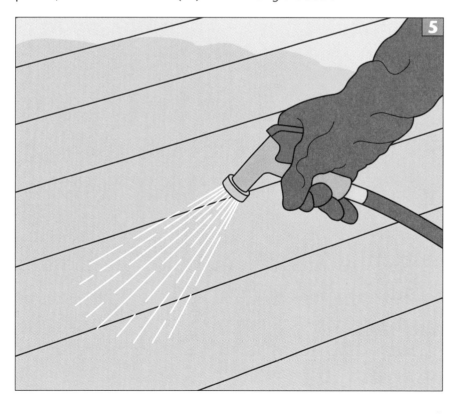

6. Applying finish to decking

Before applying the finish, be sure the deck is fully dry.

● Pour some water sealer into a paint tray and apply the finish with a roller or paint pad. If you're using a roller, roll it back and forth on the ramp of the paint tray a few times to remove excess finish. To avoid drying lines, apply the finish lengthwise along sections of four boards at a time (#6).

● Let the water sealer dry for the time recommended by the manufacturer—usually 24 hours, but can be up to 2 or 3 days in humid weather.

● If the deck has not been refinished in more than a year, apply a second coat.

7. Finishing railings

● Roll finish onto the handrails and balusters using a 3-inch short-nap roller (#7). Smooth any drips with a paintbrush. Allow the finish to dry.

● If the railing assembly appears to be gray and dry, apply a second coat.

8. Dealing with end grain and tight spots

● With a paintbrush, coat the end grain of boards with finish and allow them to dry. Since end grain tends to soak up moisture, apply a second coat.

● Work finish into the joints and spaces where wood parts meet, such as between handrail posts and decking boards (#8). Allow the finish to dry, then apply a second coat.

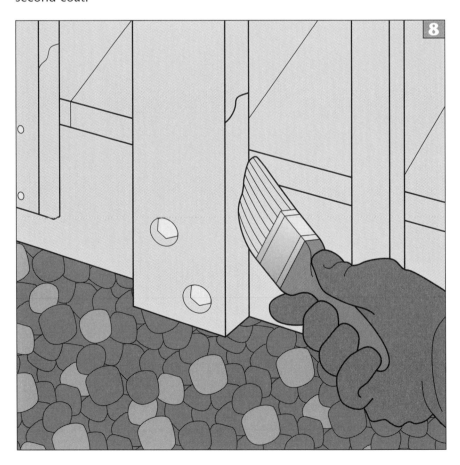

PAINTING & HOME DECOR

PATCHING DAMAGED ROOFING

Annual or biannual roofing checks will help prevent major problems—and major expenditures. Begin your inspection in the attic. Water marks on the interior indicate areas to check on the exterior.

Asphalt shingles can be patched with roofing cement without much difficulty. Blisters in tar-and-gravel roofing, usually caused by moisture buildup below the membrane, can be easily repaired. Extensive damage, however, requires a professional consultation.

Work safety on your roof begins by determining its pitch. This can be done by measuring attic rafters with a pitch gauge or using a carpenter's level and a tape measure. The highest roof pitch for work safety is 6-in-12—that is, a 6-inch vertical rise over a 12-inch horizontal distance. If the roof pitch is steeper than 4-in-12, wear a safety belt or harness fastened to a fall-arrest rope.

HOW LONG WILL IT TAKE?

Two to four hours

TOOLS

- Extension ladder • Putty knife
- Push broom • Utility knife
- Mason's trowel • Heavy-duty scissors • Work gloves

MATERIALS

- 2x2 • Eye screws • Nylon rope
- Roofing cement • Fiberglass screening (or building paper)
- Gravel • Cloth

WORKING SAFELY AT HEIGHTS

1. Setting up an extension ladder

An extension ladder should be placed out from the wall by one-quarter its extended length—the distance from the ground to the roof edge plus 3 feet.

- Have a helper stand against the wall and brace the shoes of the ladder with his feet. Lift the other end of the ladder and walk toward the wall, moving your hands along the siderails. Continue until the ladder is upright.
- With your helper holding the lower siderails of the ladder, pull the rope to raise the extension to the desired height.
- If the ground under the ladder is uneven or soft, level it and place a flat board under the shoes.
- Drive a 2x2 stake into the ground between the ladder and the wall, then tie the siderails to it with a good-quality nylon rope using slip-proof knots (#1).

2. Securing the top of the ladder

- If the ladder rests against a gutter, reinforce the gutter by placing a 2x4 inside it.
- Drive eye screws into the fascia near the ladder siderails. Loop a good-quality nylon rope through each eye screw and tie it around a siderail with a slip-proof knot (#2).

REPAIRING ASPHALT SHINGLES

1. Sealing cracks

Roofing cement is specially formulated to bond with asphalt roofing material. It is used to fasten shingles and is ideal for filling cracks. Wear work gloves when working with shingles and roofing cement.
● Lift up the tab of the shingle,

exposing the damaged area. If the tab is stuck, loosen the seal with a putty knife.
● With the putty knife, apply roofing cement to the damaged area on the underside of the tab (#1).
● Seal the tab by applying roofing cement on the underside 2 inches from the bottom corners, then press the tab firmly into place.

2. Patching shingles

The top of damaged shingles also should be patched.
● With a putty knife, apply roofing cement to the damaged area (#2), filling any cracks or gouges.
● Smooth the edges of the roofing cement and scrape away any excess with the knife.

PATCHING TAR-AND-GRAVEL ROOFING

1. Clearing away the gravel

Blisters are possible signs of water trapped between the layers of the roofing membrane. To repair a blister, the gravel must be cleared away from the area. Because the gravel will tend to adhere to the surface when it is hot, work during cool weather. Protect your hands from contact with roofing material by wearing work gloves.
● With a stiff push broom, brush the gravel away from the blister, clearing a circle about 2 feet in diameter (#1).

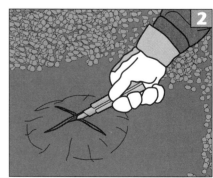

2. Cutting the blister

Blisters are repaired by cutting into the roofing membrane and drying the surface underneath, then patching with fiberglass screening or building paper and roofing cement.

• Cut into the roofing membrane with a utility knife, making an X through the blister (#2). Force air out of the blister by pressing down on the cut membrane.

• Lift up each flap of roofing membrane and wipe away any moisture with a clean dry cloth. Let surfaces air-dry for an hour.

3. Sealing the blister

• With a mason's trowel, apply roofing cement to the underside of each flap and the surface under them (#3). Force the cement as far under the uncut edges as possible.

• Fold the flaps of roofing membrane down flat and press them firmly into the roofing cement.

4. Cutting patches

In addition to roofing cement, the sealed blister needs to be patched with two layers of membrane—fiberglass screening, as shown here, or 15-pound building paper.

• Using heavy-duty scissors, cut two square patches of fiberglass screening (#4). Make the first patch about 6 inches longer and wider than the damaged area, the second patch about 12 inches longer and wider.

5. Installing the first patch

• Apply a layer of roofing cement to the repair and an area 3 to 4 inches larger than the small patch.

• Lay the small patch on the roofing cement, centering it over the repair. Press the patch down into the cement so it bonds firmly.

• Apply another layer of roofing cement over the patch, covering an area 3 to 4 inches larger than the second patch (#5).

6. Installing the second patch

• Center the second patch over the roofing cement and press it down firmly in place (#6).

• Trowel on a final layer of roofing cement, extending the edges a few inches beyond the patch. Be sure to embed corners completely.

• Brush the gravel back evenly onto the repair before the roofing cement dries. Add more gravel as needed for full coverage.

Chapter 6
LAWN & GARDEN

For many homeowners, the lawn and garden are integral parts of home, natural extensions of indoor living space. As a result, improving the outdoor portion of your property and keeping it in good repair are goals as important as indoor fixes and renovations.

A healthy, weed-free lawn does not develop by chance. With regular mowing, watering, and fertilizing, a lawn will remain attractive and in good shape all summer long.

Whether your landscaping plan involves planting a single tree or a full row of shrubs, adding trees and shrubs to your lawn and garden has a panoply of benefits. Apart from being visually attractive, these plants earn their keep by providing shade or privacy, serving as a border, or shielding a lawn, deck, or patio from the wind. Trees and shrubs will increase the value of your property. Best of all, planting trees and shrubs is simple and straightforward, and with a regimen

LAWN & GARDEN

TOOLS FOR LAWN & GARDEN FIXES AND IMPROVEMENTS

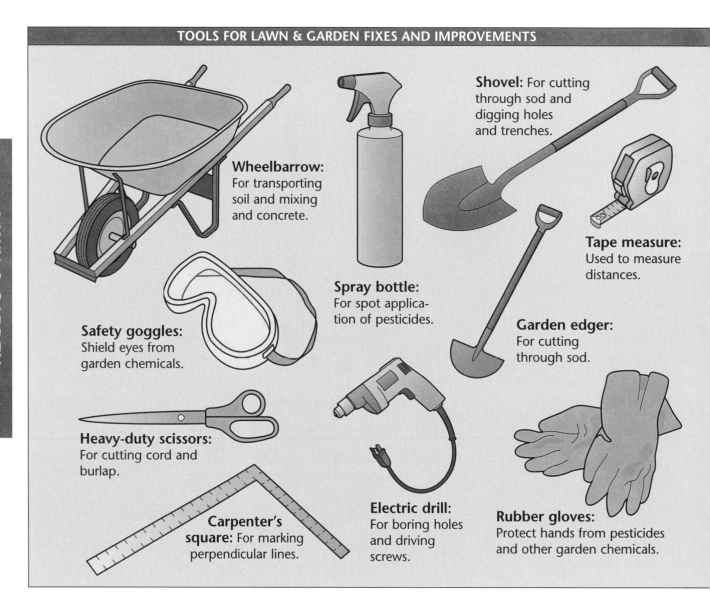

Wheelbarrow: For transporting soil and mixing and concrete.

Spray bottle: For spot application of pesticides.

Shovel: For cutting through sod and digging holes and trenches.

Tape measure: Used to measure distances.

Safety goggles: Shield eyes from garden chemicals.

Garden edger: For cutting through sod.

Heavy-duty scissors: For cutting cord and burlap.

Carpenter's square: For marking perpendicular lines.

Electric drill: For boring holes and driving screws.

Rubber gloves: Protect hands from pesticides and other garden chemicals.

of care and maintenance that includes pruning, pest control, and winterizing, they can easily provide generations of pleasure. You'll find all of these gardening skills explained in detail on the following pages.

Mother Nature provides virtually everything you need for an attractive lawn and garden. However, there are plenty of backyard projects you can undertake to enhance the appearance and value of your property as well as solve specific landscaping problems. This chapter includes a number of useful and easy projects, including creating a water garden, installing landscape edging, and building and hanging a trellis. There are also step-by-step instructions for erecting a vinyl or wood fence, laying a patio with precast slabs, or paving a walkway with stone. Installing gutters and downspouts will help your home shed rainwater and spring runoff away from its foundation.

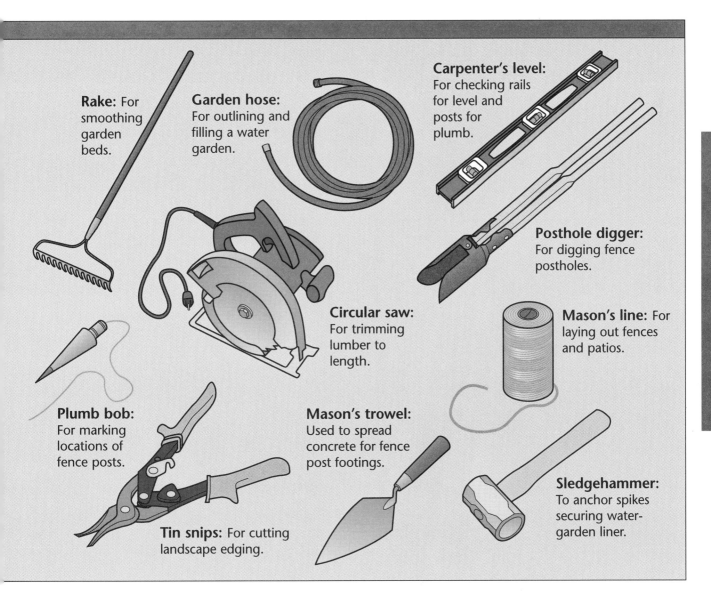

Rake: For smoothing garden beds.

Garden hose: For outlining and filling a water garden.

Carpenter's level: For checking rails for level and posts for plumb.

Posthole digger: For digging fence postholes.

Circular saw: For trimming lumber to length.

Mason's line: For laying out fences and patios.

Plumb bob: For marking locations of fence posts.

Mason's trowel: Used to spread concrete for fence post footings.

Sledgehammer: To anchor spikes securing water-garden liner.

Tin snips: For cutting landscape edging.

SPREADING LAWN FERTILIZER

The quest for the perfect lawn has preoccupied homeowners since time immemorial. One way to help out nature is to apply a fertilizer to your yard and garden. Lawn fertilizers come in several different forms and grades. Liquid fertilizer is easy to apply in spray form, but it tends to leach into the soil quickly, requiring frequent reapplication. The most popular choice is dry, granular fertilizer; it is quick-acting, relatively inexpensive, and simple to apply.

The three primary ingredients in fertilizer are nitrogen, phosphorous, and potassium. The proportion of each ingredient in a given product is given as a three-digit code on the bag, indicating the percentages of nitrogen, phosphorous, and potassium in that order (most of the rest is filler). In most cases, you can use a standard 21-3-7 formulation in spring and a fertilizer with half as much nitrogen and a little more phosphorus in fall. You can also test samples of your soil (Step 2 to Step 3) to determine more precisely what nutrients your lawn is lacking. This way, you can feed your lawn a customized fertilizer formulation.

HOW LONG WILL IT TAKE?
Less than four hours

TOOLS
• Shovel or garden edger • Bucket • Garden trowel • Soil-testing kit • Spreader (trough or broadcast) • Work gloves • Dust mask

MATERIALS
• Fertilizer (liquid or granular) • Paper towels

1. Timing fertilization

A lawn should be fertilized during peak growth periods, the timing

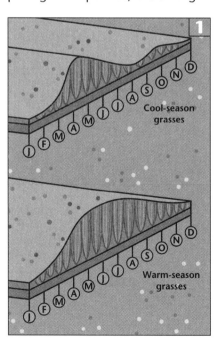

of which depends on where you live (#1).

• In the northern U.S., where cool-season grasses such as bluegrass, fescue, and ryegrass flourish, lawns have a peak growing period in the spring, decline in the summer, and have a small growth spike in the fall. In the southern U.S., warm-season grasses such as bermuda grass and St. Augustine peak in midsummer, then decline steadily in the fall.

• Depending on the species of grass, you can apply from 1½ to 3 pounds of nitrogen per 1,000 square feet of lawn per year. But you should never spread more than 1 pound of fertilizer per month for 1,000 square feet of lawn. Excessive amounts of nitrogen at one time can burn grasses.

2. Collecting soil samples

For an accurate soil analysis, plan on gathering samples from several different spots of the lawn. Wear work gloves so you don't mix any impurities into the samples.

LAWN & GARDEN

- With a shovel or a garden edger, make a semicircular cut through the sod.
- Lifting the sod with one hand, use a garden trowel to slice a wedge of soil about 6 inches deep and wide from under the sod.
- Deposit the sample in a clean, dry bucket and press the sod back down.
- Once you have collected a few samples, remove any debris, such as stones, grass, or roots, from the soil, and mix the soil thoroughly with a trowel (#2).

3. Analyzing the soil

You can get a soil-testing kit at a garden centers, enabling you to determine if your soil is lacking in nitrogen, phosphorus, or potassium. You can also test the soil's pH level, a measure of its alkalinity or acidity. The tester shown consists of a metal rod with an alkaline and acid indicator.

- With a paper towel, wipe the tester rod clean.
- Insert at least 2 inches of the

rod into the soil sample in the bucket (#3) and let it sit for two minutes. The soil should be packed firmly around the rod. If the soil is dry and crumbly, add some water to moisten it.
- Remove the tester, clean it, and plunge it in the sample again. Let it sit for another minute and take a reading. Like most plants, lawns grow best in slightly acidic soil with a pH level between 6 and 7. You can remedy excessive acidity (below pH 6) by adding dolomitic limestone. Overly alkaline soil (above pH 7) can be corrected with iron sulfate, aluminum sulfate, or ground sulphur.

4. Calculating the quantity of fertilizer needed

If you know the species of grass in your lawn, you can get advice from your garden center on how much nitrogen the lawn requires. The size of the lawn also determines how much fertilizer to apply. Check the packaging for directions on how much fertilizer to spread for a given surface area.
- If your lawn is rectangular, calculating its surface area is simple: Multiply the length by the width.
- If the lawn is irregularly shaped, first divide it into sections that are roughly rectangular. Measure the length and width of each section (#4) to calculate its surface area, then add the results together.

- To ensure that the fertilizer is distributed evenly on the lawn, apply it with a spreader. Both trough spreaders and broadcast spreaders are commonly available.

SAFETY TIP *Many fertilizers contain harmful chemicals; wear long sleeves and work gloves to protect your skin and a dusk mask to avoid inhaling airborne particles.*

TROUGH SPREADER

1. Adjusting a trough spreader

A trough spreader applies fertilizer in rows equal to the width of the spreader body. Because trough spreaders drop their contents onto the lawn through adjustable holes at the bottom of the housing, it is easy to apply too much fertilizer inadvertently. The size of the holes is adjusted with a thumbscrew on the handle. A lever is then used to open and close the holes.
- Making sure the spreader holes

are closed, fill the spreader body about three-quarters full.

● Adjust the hole openings to the setting suggested by the spreader manufacturer (#1).

2. Applying fertilizer with a trough spreader

● With the holes closed, wheel the spreader to a corner of the lawn. The lines and arrows in illustration #2 suggest a route that will ensure full and even coverage. Open the holes and push the spreader at a moderate pace along one end of the lawn.

● At the end of the row, close the holes, turn the spreader around, and move it over by the width of the housing. Open the holes and return to your starting point so the second pass just touches the first without overlapping it.

● Cover two more end rows (A) on the opposite side of the lawn in the same way.

● Cover the area between the end rows with perpendicular passes.

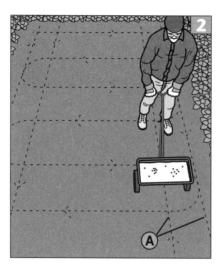

BROADCAST SPREADER

1. Setting up a broadcast spreader

Broadcast spreaders are less likely than trough spreaders to spread too much fertilizer, as the spreading mechanism scatters its contents in a 3- to 4-foot circle.

● Making sure the spreader holes are closed, fill the body about three-quarters full (#1).

● Adjust the size of the holes as suggested by the manufacturer.

2. Applying fertilizer with a broadcast spreader

Because a broadcast spreader lays a lighter load of fertilizer than a trough spreader, two passes are needed to ensure full coverage. The lines and arrows in illustration #2 show an efficient route.

● Starting at a corner of the lawn, open the holes and push the spreader at a steady, moderate pace along the side of the lawn. When you get to the end, turn and come back to your starting point without stopping, overlapping the 3- to 4-foot spread of fertilizer made by the first pass by about 1 foot.

● When you have covered the entire lawn and reached the opposite side, turn 90 degrees and cover the lawn again so that each pass is at a right angle to the first series (#2).

PRUNING A TREE

Pruning trees isn't a frequent part of a regular gardening routine. While fruit trees need annual pruning to produce the best flowers and fruits, prune other trees only when necessary—such as when they have become overgrown, damaged, or diseased.

The right tool for the job depends on the size of the branch. Use pruning shears for water sprouts and small branches, lopping shears or pole shears for branches up to 1½ inches thick, and a pruning saw for branches up to 4 inches thick. Pruning branches that are larger or high up is a job for a professional.

Two features guide the cutting technique, especially on large branches: the collar, a rounded area at the base of the branch; and the bark ridge, a kind of seam in the bark of the trunk or supporting branch. Cut just outside both features without leaving a stub. When pruning diseased branches, clean the cutting blade with rubbing alcohol after each cut to prevent spreading the disease.

SAFETY TIP *Wear work gloves and safety goggles while pruning; when cutting overhead, also wear a hard hat.*

HOW LONG WILL IT TAKE?
Less than two hours

TOOLS
• Pruning knife • Pruning shears • Lopping shears • Pruning saw • Pole shears

PLANNING THE JOB

Assessing pruning needs

The best time to prune a deciduous tree is during its dormant period; in cold climates, prune in the spring before the leaves appear. Before you begin, assess the tree as a whole, taking note of problems as well as characteristics to maintain. Eliminate crossover branches (A), diseased or broken branches (B), and branches growing at a very tight angle to the trunk (C)—these are prone to breaking. Prune water sprouts growing from the branches (D) and suckers sprouting from the roots (E). Lightly prune other selected branches on a mature tree to reduce crowding, making sure to conserve the tree's natural form.

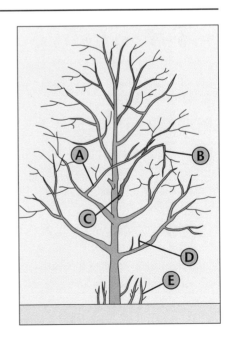

PRUNING SMALL BRANCHES

Cutting with pruning shears

Use pruning shears to cut water sprouts and branches less than ¾ inch thick.

● Hold the pruning shears as close as possible to the trunk or supporting branch without damaging the bark (#1) and make a single, clean cut. Avoid twisting the shears or the bark may tear, damaging the tree.

Pruning with lopping shears

Use lopping shears to cut lower branches ¾ inch to 1½ inches thick. The long handles provide extra leverage.

● Holding the upper blade against the trunk or supporting branch and the lower blade outside the bark ridge and collar (A), make a single, clean cut (#2). Avoid twisting the shears so the bark doesn't rip.

Cutting with a pruning saw

Use a pruning saw to cut branches 1 to 2 inches thick.

● Rest the blade of the pruning saw on the branch just outside the bark ridge (#3).

● Angle the blade outward to avoid cutting into the collar (A) and make the cut.

Cutting with pole shears

Cut high branches between ¾ inch and 1½ inches thick with pole shears.

● Standing away from the branch, place the hook of the pole shears over the branch and rest the side of it against the trunk or branch.

● Pull the cord on the pole shears to cut the branch (#4).

LAWN & GARDEN

PRUNING LARGE BRANCHES

1. Making the first cut

Cut a branch 2 to 4 inches thick with a large pruning saw in two stages so it does not snap off, damaging the tree. First, cut the branch about 10 inches from the trunk, beginning from below and finishing from above. Then, trim the stump close to the trunk.

• Trim the branch of secondary branches and clear the area below.

• Position the pruning saw under the branch (#1) and cut upward until you are almost halfway through it.

2. Completing the cut

• Position the blade of the saw about 1 inch outside the first cut and steady the branch with your free hand, then begin cutting (#2). The branch will snap off when you have cut about halfway through it.

3. Trimming the stub

Working from above, position the saw outside the bark ridge (A) and cut at an outward angle (#3) to avoid the collar (B).

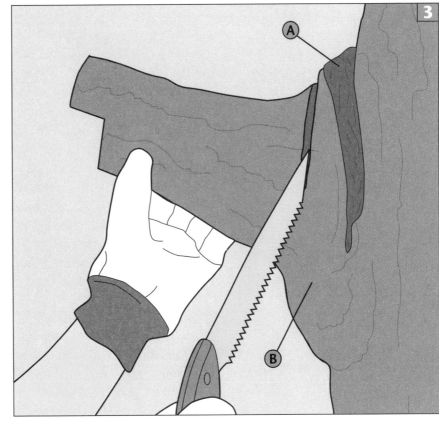

SPRAYING LIQUID PESTICIDES

When it comes to getting rid of garden pests, start simple. You can often control pests by handpicking them off plants, or knocking them off with a water spray. In some cases, insecticidal soaps or sticky traps will do the trick. But when all else fails, you may have to resort to chemical pesticides.

A successful and safe pesticide treatment depends on using the right chemical for the job and applying it at the right time. Contact your local garden center or Cooperative Extension Service, and describe the symptoms of the pest infestation to get advice on appropriate products, application equipment, and spraying times.

The type of applicator you choose depends largely on the type of plants and the size of the area to be treated. Step 2 through Step 8 show how to use a wide variety of applicators.

SAFETY TIP *Before using a pesticide, read the product label for health and safety instructions. Only spray on a calm, windless day. Wear appropriate safety gear: rubber gloves to protect your hands, safety goggles to shield your eyes, and a respirator to prevent inhaling toxic dust and airborne spray. A wide-brimmed hat will protect your head and all-purpose polypropylene overalls will shield clothing.*

HOW LONG WILL IT TAKE?
Less than two hours

TOOLS
• Measuring cup • Spray bottle • Hand-pump sprayer • Garden-hose sprayer • Garden hose • Backpack sprayer • Heavy-duty plastic container • Funnel • Rubber gloves • Respirator • Polypropylene overalls • Wide-brimmed hat

MATERIALS
• Pesticide • Dishwashing liquid • Light machine oil

1. Mixing pesticides

Many pesticides come ready-to-use in their own applicators. If you buy a pesticide in liquid concen-

trate form, however, you will need to dilute it in water according to the manufacturer's instructions.
• Put on your safety gear before preparing the pesticide and work with containers and utensils that you will only use for this purpose. Always handle pesticides outdoors or in designated work areas inside, away from children, pets, and food-preparation and eating areas.
• Only prepare as much of the pesticide as you expect to use to minimize what has to be disposed of after you are finished (Step 9).
• Fill the applicator canister—here, a hand-pump sprayer—with the required amount of water before adding the concentrate.

• Pour the concentrate into a measuring cup (#1), add it to the canister, then close the applicator tightly and shake it.

2. Making spot applications

Ideal for treating individual plants and small shrubs, a spray bottle with an adjustable nozzle makes close-range applications easy and prevents over-application.

● Adjust the nozzle to a fine mist and spray 4 to 6 inches from the affected area (#2).

● Shake the container occasionally to ensure the concentrate remains well mixed in the water.

3. Preparing a hand-pump sprayer

Hand-pump sprayers are ideal for applying a pesticide to a medium-sized area such as a small tree.

● Prepare the pesticide solution as described in Step 1.

● Slide the pump-and-handle assembly into the canister and screw it on tightly.

● Pressurize the canister close by where you will be working. For the model shown, rotate the handle one-quarter turn, then pump it fully up and down (#3) until it can no longer be pumped or air releases from the valve.

4. Using a hand-pump sprayer

● To adjust the intensity and spread of the spray, turn the nozzle (A): clockwise for a coarse, narrow spray; counterclockwise for a fine, wide spray.

● Holding the canister in one hand and the wand in the other, press the trigger (B) to start spraying. Aim at the underside of leaves where many pests feed (#4).

● When the spray pressure begins to fall off, pump the handle as described in Step 3.

● When refilling or emptying the canister, remove the pump-and-handle assembly slowly to release pressure.

5. Filling a garden-hose sprayer

A garden-hose sprayer employs the water pressure from a garden hose to both mix a pesticide concentrate with water and spray the solution over a wide area in a short time. A dial on the sprayer cap (A) enables you to adjust the concentrate-to-water mixture. This type of applicator is ideal for treating lawns, plant beds, and trees.

● Unscrew the sprayer cap from the canister and fill the canister with the pesticide concentrate (#5).

SAFETY TIP *Fill the sprayer canister near your work area, well away from children, pets, and food-preparation and eating areas.*

6. Using a garden-hose sprayer

• Connect the end of your garden hose to the water supply valve on the sprayer cap, then screw the cap back onto the canister tightly.

• For the model shown, adjust the deflector (A) for a fine, wide spray, or a narrow, concentrated spray.

• Set the dial on the cap to "On," opening the water supply valve. Turn on the water at the faucet.

• Turn the dial to the setting specified in the manufacturer's instructions. The pesticide-water mixture will start to spray.

• To treat a tree, aim the spray at the underside of the leaves (#6).

7. Preparing a backpack sprayer

A backpack sprayer is a good alternative when a garden hose is unavailable or impractical. Despite its large capacity, this sprayer is easily portable, making it well suited for spraying a large area.

• Prepare the pesticide mixture in a separate container, unscrew the backpack canister cap, then add the solution to the canister, filtering it through the strainer (#7).

• Screw the cap on tightly.

8. Using a backpack sprayer

• Put the backpack sprayer on, adjusting the shoulder straps so the canister fits snugly against the middle of your back.

• When you're ready to apply the pesticide, pressurize the sprayer by pumping the operating lever (A) at the side of the backpack. Pump the lever up and down until it resists further pumping.

• Adjust the intensity and spread of the spray by turning the nozzle (B): clockwise for a coarse, narrow spray; counterclockwise for a fine, wide spray.

• To treat a tree, aim the spray at the underside of the leaves (#8).

• When refilling or emptying the canister, remove the cap slowly to release pressure.

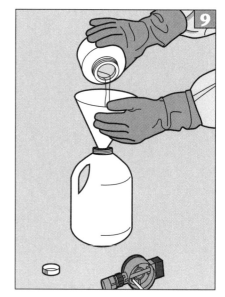

9. Disposing of unused pesticides

Disposal of pesticides is strictly regulated in most communities. Contact your local toxic waste facility for information on local disposal methods. Many municipalities have annual or biannual pickup services for household toxic wastes.

- Still wearing your safety gear, pour leftover pesticide from the sprayer canister into a heavy-duty plastic container. Use a funnel to prevent spills (#9). Immediately clean up any pesticide you do spill and dilute remnants with water.

- Label the container clearly and store it in a safe place (Step 12) until you dispose of it.

SAFETY TIP *Dispose of a pesticide at your work site, well away from children, pets, and food-preparation and eating areas.*

10. Cleaning spray equipment

- As soon as you have emptied the sprayer canister, fill it with clean water, then pour the water into a plastic bucket (#10). Soak loose sprayer parts in the bucket.

- Rinse the canister again, this time adding a little dishwashing liquid to the water. Screw on the applicator cap and shake. Pour the soapy water into the bucket and rinse it again.

- Clean all loose and detachable parts of the sprayer in the rinse water. For the hand-pump sprayer shown, this would include the pump-and-handle assembly and the nozzle and wand connections. Also clean any containers or utensils used to prepare or dispose of the pesticide.

11. Rinsing sprayer parts

- Fill the canister with more water and dishwashing liquid. Reassemble the applicator wand and nozzle, then screw them back onto the canister. Screw on the pump-and-handle assembly.

- Spray the canister's contents into the plastic bucket (#11).

- Rinse the canister with fresh water, then fill it and spray the water into the bucket until the water runs free of soap.

- Dispose of the rinse water as described in Step 9.

12. Storing pesticides and sprayers

- Dry the sprayer thoroughly and lubricate all its moving parts with light machine oil.

- Clearly label all pesticide containers and dispose of any product by its expiry date.

- Store applicators and pesticides in a cool, dry cupboard out of reach of children. Lock the storage area for additional safety (#12).

PLANTING TREES AND SHRUBS

When you select a tree or shrub, make sure the species is hardy enough to withstand your local climate. Also check that the site you've chosen provides the sunlight and drainage required by the species. Poorly placed plants are doomed from the beginning, no matter how well they are planted. In a freezing climate, the best time of year to plant trees and shrubs is in the spring. However, they can be planted at any time throughout the summer.

Trees and shrubs are most commonly sold in plastic containers, although they also may be held in fiber pots or in wire baskets, be bare-rooted, or be balled and burlapped. The techniques for planting them are similar.

Be patient. Depending on the species, it could be a year after transplanting before you see signs of new growth. It may take several years for trees and woody shrubs to become well established.

HOW LONG WILL IT TAKE?
Two to four hours

TOOLS
• Tape measure • Shovel • Bucket • Wheelbarrow • Utility knife • Work gloves • Rubber gloves • Safety goggles

MATERIALS
• Landscape fabric • Gravel • Peat moss • Potting soil (or topsoil) • Manure (or compost) • Fertilizer • Mulch

1. Digging the planting hole

Trees and shrubs planted too deep will not thrive, so it is important to calculate the proper hole depth. The roots of the tree or shrub will penetrate the surrounding soil more easily if they are supported by a backfilled layer of worked soil. In poorly draining areas, an extra 6 inches of soil must be removed to accommodate a layer of gravel.

• Measure the width of the container and double it to determine the required diameter of the hole.

• To determine the depth of the hole, measure the height of the container. Subtract 2 inches to allow for some settling of the soil and to ensure that the root collar of the tree or shrub will sit above the surface. Add 6 inches to allow for backfilled soil at the bottom of the hole under the root ball.

• With a shovel, dig the planting hole to these dimensions (#1).

2. Providing proper drainage

Proper drainage must be provided so water is carried away and does not pool around the root system.

LAWN & GARDEN

Excess water will drown the roots and eventually kill the tree or shrub. In areas of poor drainage, a layer of gravel at the bottom of the planting hole will do the trick.

- Dig the planting hole an additional 6 inches deeper to accommodate the gravel.
- Line the inside of the hole with landscape fabric. Use enough fabric so that it can be folded over the top of the gravel.
- Fill the hole with a 6-inch layer of ¾-inch gravel (#2).
- Fold the edges of the landscape fabric over the gravel, covering it completely, and cut off the excess.

3. Backfilling with existing soil

On top of the gravel and the landscape fabric, shovel a 6-inch layer of soil into the hole (#3). Use the soil that you removed from the hole. If the soil is heavy and compacted, break it up slightly with the shovel before adding it.

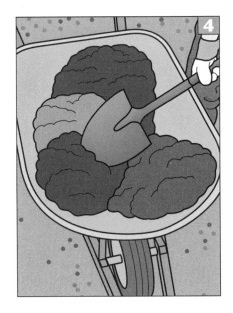

4. Mixing new backfill

- In a wheelbarrow, prepare an enriched backfill mixture (#4). Measure the ingredients by the shovelful according to the following recipe: two parts existing soil; two parts new soil (potting soil or quality topsoil); one part peat moss; one part manure or compost. Prepare a bit more mixture than is needed to fill the hole.
- Gradually add water to the new backfill, pouring in small amounts until the backfill is fully saturated. Squeeze a small amount of the backfill in your hand—it should be moist, but not dripping.

5. Positioning the tree or shrub

- Holding the tree or shrub at the root collar and supporting the root ball, gently position it in

the center of the hole (#5). Place it so that its best side faces the direction in which it will be most often viewed.

- If the roots are contained in a wire basket, cut and fold down the top half of the basket. For burlap, remove the strings and fold the burlap back to uncover about half of the root ball. Remove a fiber pot entirely. Take off any plastic liner, tag, or label.
- Check that the root collar sits above ground level.

Note: *If the root ball is encircled by a tangle of roots, the tree or shrub is "root-bound." With a utility knife, make a few crisscross cuts into the root ball to stimulate new root growth.*

6. Backfilling

- Add a small amount of the new enriched backfill around the tree or shrub to hold it upright.
- Back up a few feet and walk around the tree or shrub to make sure it stands straight. If straightening is necessary, handle the tree or shrub by the root ball rather than the trunk or stem.
- Fill the hole completely with new backfill to the level of the surrounding soil (#6), making sure no wire or burlap is exposed.
- Tamp the soil firmly around the base of the tree or shrub with the balls of your feet. Avoid using your heels—they can damage the roots.
- Add more soil until it is level with the surrounding ground.
- Just beyond the area where water will flow off the foliage, create a soil dam 4 to 6 inches high around the tree or shrub to help retain water.

7. Watering and fertilizing

Ask for assistance in choosing the appropriate fertilizer for your species and make sure that it is intended to promote growth of roots—not foliage. Do not fertilize in very hot or very dry conditions.
- Water the tree or shrub thoroughly to moisten the entire root system. Let the water soak into the soil completely.
- Water again, this time with fertilizer (#7). Avoid splashing any fertilizer onto the foliage.
- Water again in a week—sooner if it is hot, later if it is rainy.
- During the first growing season, water often enough to prevent the soil from drying out. Add fertilizer to the water once a month, but stop fertilizing by early autumn.

SAFETY TIP *Wear long sleeves, rubber gloves, and safety goggles when mixing fertilizer.*

8. Adding mulch

Finely ground cedar or hemlock mulch is the best choice for newly planted trees and shrubs. Chips or bark should only be added once the tree or shrub is well established. Commercial mulch is preferable because it is sterilized.
- Distribute a layer of mulch inside the protective ridge to a maximum thickness of 3 inches (#8). To prevent diseases from being transferred to the tree or shrub, keep the mulch away from the trunk or stem.
- Add new mulch every two years. During the growing season, break up the mulch every month with a shovel so it does not compact into a hard layer.

PREPARING TREES AND SHRUBS FOR WINTER

In cold climates, protecting small trees and shrubs for winter is an important part of maintaining a healthy and attractive garden. Evergreens laden with snow may look beautiful, but accumulations of snow and ice can cause branches to sag or break, permanently disfiguring them. Deciduous trees, too, are vulnerable; young birches and silver maples, in particular, should be wrapped to protect the bark from the cold.

A number of preparatory techniques exist, each with its own advantages. For example, binding evergreens with cord or wrapping them with burlap to reduce their branch span is a simple way of protecting them from accumulations of snow. Or, building a sloped-canopy structure offers more complete protection from falling ice and snow for shrubs and bushes alongside the house. Few of these strategies take very long to accomplish; plan ahead, though, so you have the necessary materials on hand before winter strikes.

HOW LONG WILL IT TAKE?

Two to four hours

TOOLS

- Sledgehammer • Hammer
- Tape measure • Carpenter's square • Heavy-duty scissors
- Staple gun • Hand-pump sprayer • Work gloves • Rubber gloves • Safety goggles

MATERIALS

- Adhesive tree wrap • Burlap
- Nylon cord • Plastic tree netting • Antidesiccant liquid
- 2x2s • 1x3s • Galvanized nails

DECIDUOUS TREES

Protecting with adhesive wrap

The bark of young trees—especially birch and silver maple—is prone to cracking in cold temperatures. Protect the lower trunks of trees with adhesive tree wrap.
● Beginning at ground level, wind adhesive tree wrap around the trunk of the tree, overlapping it by about 1 inch each turn (#1).

● Continue wrapping the trunk until you reach the lowest branch, then trim off the excess with heavy-duty scissors.

Note: *Discourage rodents from nibbling bark by wrapping the trunk with perforated plastic wrap up to about 12 inches higher than the expected snowfall.*

LAWN & GARDEN

EVERGREENS

Binding with cord

Binding the limbs of narrow ever-greens helps protect them from the weight of accumulating snow and ice.

- Using good-quality nylon cord, tie a tight loop around the base of the evergreen.
- Unwind the cord from its spool and wrap it around the evergreen, moving higher with each turn (#1). Tighten the cord as you go so the limbs of the tree are pulled upward and the spaces between them are reduced—but make sure that the cord doesn't cut into the branches.
- When you reach the top of the evergreen, tie a knot in the cord and cut off the surplus.
- Be sure to remove the cord early in the spring before new shoots begin to grow.

SHRUBS AND BUSHES

1. Spreading mulch

Moisture loss during the winter is especially damaging for plants such as holly and rhododendrons. To help plants retain ground mois-ture, cover the root area of shrubs and bushes with a blanket of mulch. Organic mulch not only makes a good protective covering, but provides valuable nutrients to the soil during the spring melt, reducing the need for fertilizer.

- Spread a ring of mulch around the base of shrubs and bushes to a depth of about 3 inches (#1). Make sure the mulch is aged—new chips or bark can leach nitrogen from the soil. A mixture of pine needles and oak leaves is ideal.

2. Applying an antidesiccant

An antidesiccant is an excellent product for helping to retard moisture loss in broad-leafed shrubs and bushes.

- Dilute the antidesiccant liquid with water according to the manufacturer's instructions. Fill the canister of a hand-pump sprayer with the mixture.
- Spray each shrub and bush thoroughly, making sure to coat the underside of leaves where the stomata—the pores that transpire moisture—are located (#2).
- Check shrubs and bushes midway through the winter. If the waxy coating has rubbed off, make another application.

SAFETY TIP *Antidesiccant is nontoxic, but leaves a sticky, waxy residue. Protect your hands with rubber gloves.*

3. Building a shelter

Tepee-type structures of 1x3s and burlap make sturdy and reliable winter shelters for vulnerable shrubs and bushes.

- Cut four 1x3 stakes about 6 inches longer than the height of the shrub or bush.
- Position the stakes at equal distances around the shrub or bush, angling them so they just touch the outer limits of the branches. With a small sledgehammer, drive the stakes into the ground so that they meet at a central point above the shrub or bush (#3).
- Bind the top of the stakes together with nylon cord.

4. Covering the shelter

- With heavy-duty scissors, cut a piece of burlap large enough to fit around the stakes with an overlap of several inches, trimming it narrower at the top than at the bottom.
- Staple one edge of the burlap to a stake every 4 to 6 inches (#4), then wrap the burlap around the stakes and staple the other edge.

Note: *For shrubs and bushes that need insulated protection, use plastic foam sheeting instead of burlap.*

LAWN & GARDEN

SHRUBS AND BUSHES BORDERING THE HOUSE

1. Framing the structure

Shrubs and bushes bordering the house are best protected with a sturdy sloped-canopy structure.

- Cut two pairs of 2x2 stakes longer than the height of the shrubs or bushes: one pair about 1 foot longer; the other pair about 2 feet longer.

- With a small sledgehammer, drive the stakes into the ground: the tall ones behind the shrubs or bushes, close to the house; the short ones in front of the shrubs or bushes, in line with the tall ones. Use a tape measure and a carpenter's square as necessary to square the corners.

- Nail a 2x2 crosspiece to the top of each pair of stakes so it sits as level as possible (#1).

SAFETY TIP *Wear safety goggles when hammering.*

2. Building the canopy roof

The canopy roof of the structure consists of a grid of 1x3 slats spaced at $2\frac{1}{2}$-inch intervals.

- Measure the length and the width of the structure, then cut 1x3 slats to size, planning on a gap of $2\frac{1}{2}$ inches between them.
- On a flat work surface, use a carpenter's square to lay out the grid of slats. Maintaining a $2\frac{1}{2}$-inch space between the slats, fasten the short ones to the long ones with $1\frac{1}{4}$-inch galvanized nails (#2).

Note: *To maintain a uniform $2\frac{1}{2}$-inch space between the slats, use one of the slats as a spacer.*

3. Fastening the canopy roof

- Lay the completed canopy roof on the structure.
- Fasten the canopy roof to the structure by driving nails through the end of slats into the cross-pieces (#3).
- Alternatively, fasten the canopy roof with galvanized screws—which can be easily removed to disassemble the structure intact in the spring.

CREATING A WATER GARDEN

Ground level and exposure to sun are two main considerations in choosing where to place a water garden. Find a level spot, avoiding low-lying areas that will tend to flood in rainy weather. Also avoid placing a water garden in an area of prolonged direct sunlight—too much heat and light promote uncontrolled algae growth. A shade site directly under a tree, however, should also be avoided since fallen leaves can contaminate the water.

A water garden can be created using a fiberglass shell or a flexible liner. Fiberglass shells are available in a limited number of shapes and sizes, but are easy to install. Flexible liners, though, can be adapted to any shape you want and allow you to create natural-looking pond edges. Synthetic elastomer (EPDM) is fast becoming the standard material for liners, replacing more expensive polyvinyl chloride (PVC).

If your water garden also will be stocked with fish, the water needs to be aerated and should be cleaned with a filter powered by a pump. Check the manufacturer's specifications for the model best suited to the size of your pond.

HOW LONG WILL IT TAKE?

More than four hours

TOOLS

- Garden hose • Sledgehammer
- Mason's line • Tape measure
- Shovel • Pick • Spade • Line level • Utility knife • Bucket
- Wooden ruler

MATERIALS

- Pond liner • Landscape fabric
- 1x1s • Rocks and pebbles
- Metal spikes (with washers)

Anatomy of a water garden

Every type of aquatic plant requires a different ideal depth of water. To be able to support a variety of species, the water garden shown in this project has three levels: (1) the perimeter margins, (2) a shelf, and (3) the floor. The pond liner (A), laid between two layers of landscape fabric (B), follows the contours of these levels and extends 2 feet beyond the perimeter.

Determine the width and the length of the pond as described in Step 1, then apply the following

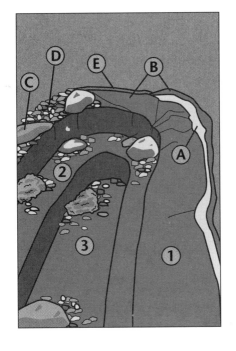

formulas to calculate the required dimensions of the liner and the landscape fabric:

- Liner and fabric length = (2 x depth) + pool length + 4 feet
- Liner and fabric width = (2 x depth) + pool width + 4 feet

The edges of your pond can combine three types of borders: large rocks (C), pebbles (D), and a "key" (E), where spikes anchor the liner and fabric in a shallow trench at the perimeter.

LAWN & GARDEN

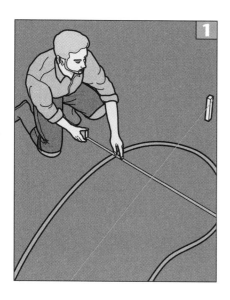

1. Marking the perimeter

Purchase your pond liner and landscape fabric after you lay out and measure the perimeter of the water garden.

● Make a sketch of your water garden on paper. Then, outline the pond perimeter in the desired shape with a garden hose. Study your layout from several vantage points and smooth out any sharp angles.

● Drive a 1x1 stake into the ground at each end of the greatest distance across the pond—the length. Run a mason's line tautly between the stakes, then measure the line between the points where it crosses the hose.

● Measure the width of the pond at the widest section, laying a tape measure at a right angle to the line (#1).

● Untie the line from the stakes and set it aside.

2. Starting the excavation

● Break the ground at the perimeter of the pond, then remove the garden hose. Beyond the perimeter, dig a 2-foot margin area to a depth of 2 inches.

● Dig the entire area of the pond to slightly less than the final depth of the shelf—here, 10 to 12 inches (#2). Use a pick to remove rocks and break up compacted soil.

● Tie the mason's line back onto the stakes and level it as close to ground level as possible with a line level.

● Check your depth by measuring at different points along the line. Move one of the stakes and level the line again to make checks at additional locations.

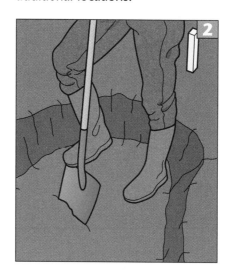

SAFETY TIP *Bend your knees when lifting so you don't hurt your back. Wear knee pads for protection against sharp stones and ground dampness.*

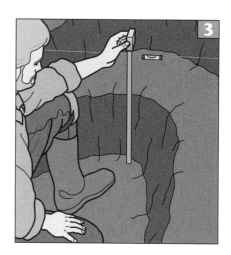

3. Completing the excavation

● Remove the line and dig out the central area of the pond, leaving a shelf about 12 inches wide at the perimeter.

● Before reaching the finished depth of 24 inches, replace the line, level it again, and check your digging depth at several locations (#3).

● Complete the pond bottom and sides with a spade.

Note: *Avoid digging too deep. Backfilling with loose soil will make a less sturdy base for your liner and shelf walls could collapse.*

4. Laying the first layer of fabric

Choose thick landscape fabric that resembles felt. As you cut it to size, plan ahead to keep the largest pieces for the top layer and make use of any small pieces for the bottom one.

- Unfold the landscape fabric over the pond. Smooth the fabric against the walls, the shelf, and the floor. Make sure the fabric extends at least 2 feet beyond the pond edges.
- If you need to use more than one piece of fabric, overlap the side pieces with the bottom pieces by 6 inches (#4).
- With a utility knife, trim the surplus fabric to 2 feet beyond the pond edges.

5. Installing the liner

- Unfold and spread the liner over the pond, smoothing it against the landscape fabric. Leave at least 2 feet of liner extending beyond the pond edges.
- Working inside the pond, smooth the folds along the walls. Work all the wrinkles into one location, then make one large fold with the excess created (#5).

- Trim back the edges to 1 inch inside the landscape fabric.

Note: *Before installing the liner, check for holes. Have helpers unfold the liner and hold it up to the light.*

6. Adding another layer of fabric

The upper layer of landscape fabric protects the liner from rocks and stones and draws up moisture for plants along the edges of the water garden.

- Lay fabric along the length of the pond. When using more than one piece, overlap the edges by 12 inches.
- Trim back the edges of the fabric to 1 inch inside the liner.
- Place several large rocks at the bottom of the pond and along the shelf close to the walls (#6) to keep the landscape fabric from "floating" as water is added.

7. Filling the pool

Water pressure from a garden hose tends to stir up loose soil on the landscape fabric and rocks, causing the water to seem cloudy for several days. Avoid this problem by running water into a bucket weighed down at the bottom of the pond (#7). Fill the pond up to several inches from the top.

LAWN & GARDEN

8. Adjusting the edges

● With a long wooden ruler, check the depth of the water at the central section of the pond (#8). Make sure the stick is vertical and rests on the pond floor—not on a submerged rock. Determine how many inches of water need to be added to reach the full depth of 24 inches.

● Around the edges of the pond, take a look at how much room there is between the water surface and ground level.

Note: *As you construct your pond border, you will need to dig out or build up the edges so rocks and pebbles are partially submerged, but trench areas remain 3 inches above the water.*

9. Placing border rocks

Rocks and pebbles absorb heat and too many can encourage algae growth. Limit rocks and pebbles at the edges of the pond to half the perimeter margins.

● Place the rocks on the top layer of landscape fabric, tipping them slightly away from the pond. Add or dig out soil under the fabric and liner so that the inner face of each rock will be submerged 2 or 3 inches once the rest of the water is added.

● Fold back a section of fabric against the outer face of each rock and, with a utility knife, trim it just below the top of the rock.

● To keep the fabric from "wicking"—drawing water from the pond—fold the liner back over the top layer of fabric (#9). Trim back the liner, if necessary.

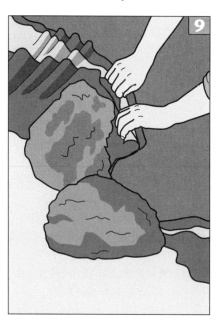

● Trim back the bottom layer of fabric and fold it up over the liner, making sure it doesn't touch the top layer of fabric. Pack soil up against the layers so they are held snugly in place against the rock.

10. Making a pebble beach

To help keep the small stones in place, create your pebble beach between two larger rocks.

● Lift the layers of liner and fabric and create a 2- to 3-inch-high retaining ridge along the inner edge of the pond where pebbles will be placed. Be sure the ridge is low enough to be submerged once remaining water is added.

● Slip a spade under the layers of liner and fabric, then scrape soil back from the ridge, creating a gradual upward incline over a distance of about 18 inches.

- Reposition the layers of liner and fabric, then trim each layer back to 18 inches—so the bottom fabric exceeds the liner by 1 inch and the liner exceeds the top fabric by 1 inch.
- Lay pebbles behind the ridge, covering the top fabric (#10).

11. Digging the trench

Where there are no rocks or pebbles to hold the layers of liner and fabric in place, spikes anchor them in a shallow trench.

- Dig out or build up the edge where the key will be located so the soil is 3 inches above the final water level.
- Lay a long 2x4 over the water along the bank of the pond where the key will be dug. Fold the layers of liner and fabric back over it.
- Dig a trench 6 inches deep along the edge of the pond 2 to 3 inches from the water (#11). Take care not to disturb the edges of the pond. Keep the soil nearby for backfill.

12. Anchoring the liner and fabric

- Fold back the layers of liner and fabric, then lay them against the bottom and walls of the key.
- Trim back the top layer to the edge of the key.
- Drive spikes with washers every 24 inches along the bottom of the key through the layers of liner and fabric (#12). If the key follows a curve, drive spikes every 12 inches.

13. Filling the key

Once the layers of liner and fabric are fastened, the trench is hidden with soil and plants.

- Trim back the liner, leaving enough to fold over the top layer of fabric to prevent wicking (#13).
- Fold the lower layer of fabric to

the lip of the liner and trim it.
- Pack soil behind the layers of liner and fabric, holding them up against the pond-side edge of the trench.
- Finish filling the pond up to 3 inches from the rim.

INSTALLING LANDSCAPE EDGING

Plastic edging is inexpensive and easy to work with, and is the edging material of choice for creating garden beds with curved borders. Other edging materials, such as brick and aluminum, are much better suited to garden beds with sharp-angled corners.

Laying out your garden bed with a hose is a good way to get a feel for what you want. And while you can dig out a trench for the edging using the hose as a guide, you may damage it while digging. Instead, trace the outline of the hose onto the ground with powdered chalk and dig along the chalk line.

Always purchase a few extra feet of edging—it's a lot easier to trim off excess than to add extra pieces after the rest has been put in place.

HOW LONG WILL IT TAKE?
Two to four hours

TOOLS
• Garden hose • Powdered chalk • Spade • Pick (or sod lifter) • Tin snips (or pruning shears) • Sledgehammer • Knee pads • Work gloves

MATERIALS
• Edging • Couplers • Anchoring stakes • Masking tape

1. Outlining the bed

Before beginning, lay the hose and the edging in the sun for a few hours so they become more pliable and easier to manipulate.
• Lay out the hose, trying several different shapes until you get a result you like.
• Squeeze powdered chalk along the outside edge of the hose (#1), then remove the hose.

2. Digging the trench

The trench you dig should be a uniform depth and deep enough that about $\frac{1}{2}$ inch of edging sits above ground.
• With a spade, dig a trench along the chalk line, making sure

the outside edge of the trench is vertical to support the edging properly (#2).
• Strip off the sod inside the bed with a pick or a sod lifter.

3. Placing the edging

For the least noticeable joints, avoid joining edging at corners.
● Place the edging in the trench (#3), adding or removing soil as necessary to keep it level.

Note: *Prevent soil from falling back into the trench by working as much as possible along the outside edge of the garden bed.*

4. Cutting edging pieces to length

● Mark the point where the ends of edging pieces overlap with masking tape.
● Cut the edging with tin snips or pruning shears at the mark (#4). A straight cut will make the joint least noticeable.

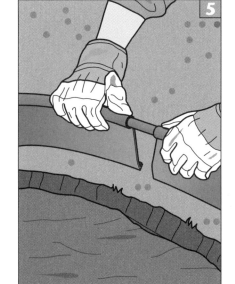

5. Making a joint

The ends of edging pieces are joined by a coupler, a length of rolled edging material that slides into a channel along the top of the edging.

● Slide a coupler halfway into the channel at the end of one piece of edging.
● Holding the end of the first piece of edging tightly to keep the coupler in place, slide the end of the second piece of edging onto the coupler (#5).

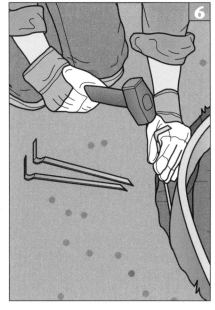

6. Anchoring the edging

Unless plastic edging is anchored, it will eventually work itself out of the ground. Some types of edging are anchored with stakes hidden below grade; others, like the type shown here, have stakes that hook over the top of the edging.
● With a small sledgehammer, drive a stake into the ground along the outside of the edging every 3 to 4 feet (#6).
● Backfill the trench and pack down the soil.

DIGGING POSTHOLES AND SETTING POSTS

It is said that good fences make good neighbors. But what makes a good fence? A large part of the answer is posts—well laid out, properly installed ones. A good fence also requires careful planning and the right materials.

Depending on the height of the fence and the weight of the fencing material, set posts at 6- to 8-foot intervals. Corner, end, and gate posts, in particular, need to be well anchored in the ground. The most common post material is pressure-treated 4x4 or larger wood stock; naturally rot-resistant species, such as redwood and cedar, are also popular.

Draw your fence layout on paper to get an idea of how many posts you will require. You'll also need gravel to line the bottom of each posthole. Plan to backfill around corner, end, and gate posts with concrete; tamped soil may be used to backfill around intermediate posts.

Postholes should be dug at least 6 inches deeper than the frost line and at least one-third the height of the posts should be below ground. Check local building codes for restrictions such as required setbacks from property lines and limitations on fence heights and materials.

HOW LONG WILL IT TAKE?

More than four hours

TOOLS

- Tape measure • Mason's line
- Powdered chalk • Water level
- Post level or (carpenter's level)
- Plumb bob • Sledgehammer
- Spade • Posthole digger (or power auger) • Wheelbarrow (or mixing tub) • Mason's hoe
- Mason's trowel • Work gloves
- Safety goggles

MATERIALS

- 4x4s • 2x2s • 1x3s • 2x4
- Masking tape • Gravel
- Premixed concrete

1. Laying out posts

Plot your fence layout and posthole locations with pairs of batterboards and mason's line.

- To make a batterboard, nail a 2x2 crosspiece to two 2-foot-long 2x2 uprights.
- Drive batterboards into the ground 18 inches past the endpoints of each fence run.
- Run a mason's line tautly between pairs of batterboards, tying it to the crosspieces (#1).

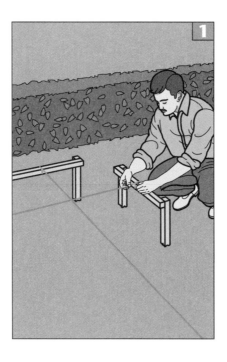

2. Adjusting batterboards

Level the mason's line marking each fence run with a water level—which consists of two clear-plastic graduated tubes that screw onto the ends of a hose.

- Attach the graduated tubes to the hose following the instructions of the water-level manufacturer.
- Working with a helper, lay out the hose between a pair of batterboards and hold the tubes so the water level in one of them aligns with the top of one crosspiece (#2). Adjust the height of the

LAWN & GARDEN

other crosspiece until the top of it aligns with the same water level in the other tube.

● Level the mason's line between each pair of batterboards the same way.

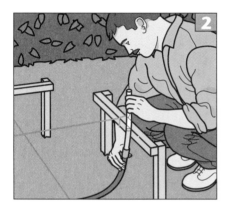

3. Laying out square corners

● To check that lines cross at 90 degrees, measure 3 feet from the intersection on one line and mark the point with masking tape. Mark the point 4 feet from the intersection on the other line.

● Measure the distance between the marked points (#3). If the distance is 5 feet, the corner is square. Reposition the lines on the crosspieces as necessary until they cross at 90 degrees.

4. Marking post locations

Start at a corner or an endpoint of the fence to mark the location of each post.

● Place a piece of masking tape on the mason's line at each post location.

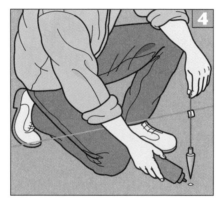

● Transfer each taped point on the mason's line to the ground with a plumb bob and mark the spot with powdered chalk (#4).

● Mark the position of each mason's line on the crosspieces, then untie it and set it aside to use later as reference.

5. Digging postholes

Postholes must be at least 6 inches deeper than the frost line and deep enough for one-third the height of the posts to be set below ground. Postholes that will be backfilled with concrete should be three times the thickness of the posts in diameter; postholes that will be backfilled with soil may be a little narrower.

● Using the chalk marks on the ground as a guide to the inside edge of the posts, dig out a circle of sod with a spade.

● With a posthole digger, dig the holes (#5) to the required depth, angling the tool to make each hole a little wider at the bottom than at the top.

● Shovel a 4-inch layer of gravel into each posthole and tamp it with the end of a 2x4.

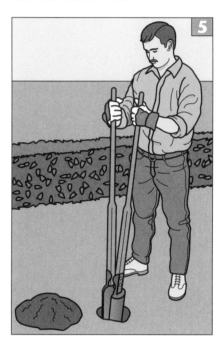

Note: *For a big project, rent a power auger. You will need a helper on hand to operate the tool, but it will get the job done more quickly, especially in hard-packed soil.*

6. Bracing posts

Secure each post in its hole with three 1x3 braces, each fastened to a 2x2 stake with a single screw.
● After all the holes are dug, tie the mason's lines onto the cross-pieces at the marked locations.
● Using the mason's line to align the posts, set each post in its hole, plumb it with a post level or a carpenter's level, and secure it in position with braces (#6).

SAFETY TIP *Wear safety goggles when operating a drill.*

7. Backfilling with concrete

Prepare enough premixed concrete to backfill one or two post-holes at a time.
● In a wheelbarrow or a mixing tub, use a mason's hoe to mix a quantity of premixed concrete according to the manufacturer's instructions (#7).

● Backfill around each corner, end, and gate post with concrete, working a 2x4 up and down in it to eliminate pockets of air.

SAFETY TIP *Concrete can burn the skin, so protect yourself from contact with it by wearing a long-sleeved shirt, long pants, work gloves, and safety goggles.*

8. Sloping concrete footings

● Backfill a posthole with concrete until the footing rises about 2 inches above grade.
● With a mason's trowel, smooth the surface of the footing, sloping it away from the post and toward the ground (#8) to direct water away.
● Let the concrete harden for at least 24 hours before removing the braces from the posts.

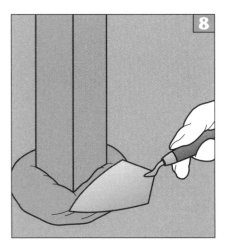

9. Backfilling with soil

● Backfill around intermediate posts with soil, shoveling it into the holes (#9) and tamping with the end of a 2x4 after every 6-inch layer.
● Fill the holes to about 2 inches above grade, then slope the soil away from the posts so water drains away.

CHECKING A GAS BARBECUE FOR LEAKS

A large part of the appeal of a gas barbecue is its convenience. You can fire up the burners one minute and have your meal on the grill the next. But it is important to take the time periodically to check the appliance for leaks.

Gas barbecues are perfectly safe when they work properly: A controlled amount of propane gas passes from the metal tank through fittings and a hose to the burners, where the gas is slowly consumed. However, any leak along the gas-delivery route can have disastrous consequences. The escaping gas could ignite and cause the entire contents of the tank to explode.

Testing a gas barbecue for leaks takes only a few minutes. Perform the test at the start of the grilling season and each time you refill and reconnect the tank or move the appliance. If you discover a leak, don't use the barbecue until the leak is corrected. If you cannot stop the leak by tightening the tank connection, close the tank valve and call your propane dealer or your local gas utility.

SAFETY TIP *Only transport a propane gas tank upright with the valve completely closed and the safety plug screwed in tightly. Don't let the tank tip over.*

HOW LONG WILL IT TAKE?	TOOLS	MATERIALS
Less than two hours	• Wrench • Container • Paintbrush	• Dishwashing liquid

1. Installing the tank

• Position the propane tank following the manufacturer's instructions. For the model shown, place the tank in its supports on the barbecue cart.
• Insert the regulator fitting (A) at the end of the hose into the opening of the tank valve (B).
• Tighten the connection by turning the spring handle (C) counterclockwise as far as it will go (#1). On models without a spring handle, start tightening the regulator fitting by hand and finish tightening with a wrench.

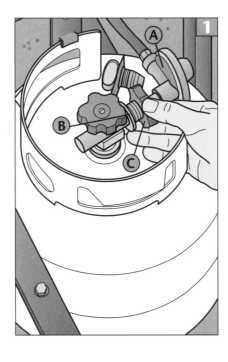

2. Preparing the test solution

• Mix equal parts of dishwashing liquid and water in a small container (#2).

3. Adjusting the grill controls

● Turn the grill control knobs on the front of the barbecue to the "Off" position (#3).

● If your model has side controls, turn them off as well.

4. Opening the tank valve

● Turn the propane tank valve counterclockwise as far as it will go (#4). This will release gas from the tank into the hose.

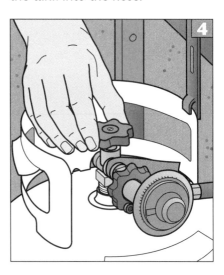

5. Testing the tank valve

● Dip a small paintbrush into the test solution and apply solution liberally to the connection point between the regulator fitting and the tank valve (#5).

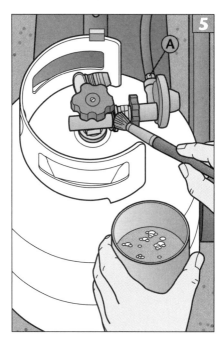

● Apply solution to the valve handle and threads, the length of the hose, and the connection point (A) between the hose and the regulator. If bubbles appear at any test point, there is a gas leak. Close the tank valve and tighten the tank connections (Step 1), then test again. If you still see bubbles at any of the test points, close the tank valve and replace the leaking component. Test again. If the problem persists, call your propane dealer or your local gas utility.

6. Testing the hose fittings

● With the tank valve still open, brush some test solution on the fitting at the other end of the hose, just under the control knobs (#6).

● Turn the right control knob to "High" and test the hose and fittings leading from the control knob to the grill. Turn the right control knob to "Off." Repeat for the left control knob. If you see bubbles during any of these tests, close the tank valve and call your propane dealer or your local gas utility. Do not use the barbecue until the leak is corrected.

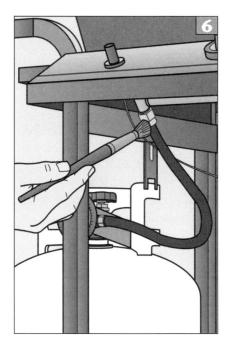

LAWN & GARDEN

BUILDING AND MOUNTING A FAN TRELLIS

You can buy a ready-made fan trellis—typically available in white- or green-colored plastic in limited sizes—but there are certain advantages to making your own trellis. You can size the trellis to best suit your garden design and you will save a little money.

There is a limit to how wide you can fan out a trellis before the wood splits. As a rule, the taller the trellis, the wider you will be able to fan it out.

Also, the thicker the wood, the less you will be able to bend it. The trellis shown here stands 6 feet high and fans out 4 feet at the top; it is made of $\frac{3}{8}$- x 1-inch lumber.

For a sturdy trellis that withstands the elements, use pressure-treated wood or a naturally rot-resistant wood—such as cedar or redwood. Assemble the trellis with galvanized carriage bolts and mount it at least a few inches off the ground.

HOW LONG WILL IT TAKE?
Two to four hours

TOOLS
• Tape measure • Combination square • Carpenter's square • Carpenter's level • Quick-action clamps • Circular saw • Hammer • Combination wrench • Electric drill • Safety goggles

MATERIALS
• Wood (rot-resistant)   • Galvanized carriage bolts   • Galvanized finishing nails   • Masonry screws

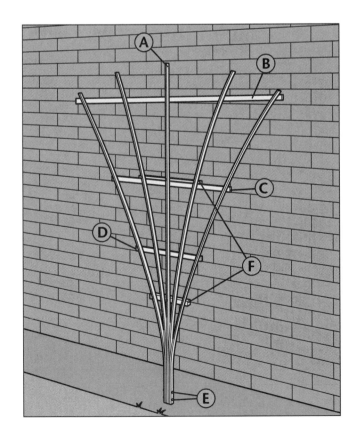

Anatomy of a fan trellis

The fan trellis that is the focus of this project is made of five $\frac{3}{8}$- x 1-inch uprights (A) 6 feet in length. Three $\frac{3}{8}$- x 1-inch crosspieces hold the uprights together in a fanned-out position. The top crosspiece (B) is 48 inches long, the middle crosspiece (C) measures 30 inches, and the bottom crosspiece (D) is 17 inches long. Two $\frac{1}{4}$- x 2-inch carriage bolts (E) join the uprights at the bottom. Two 2x2 furring strips (F)—one 18 inches long, the other 8 inches long—hold the fan trellis in place on the wall.

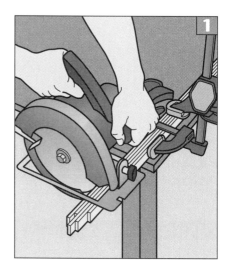

1. Cutting the pieces

- Clamp the five uprights together, all of them aligned at one end.
- Measure and make a cutting mark on one upright. Extend the mark across all the uprights with a combination square.
- Clamp the assembly to a worktable so the cutting mark overhangs the edge.
- Cut the uprights to length with a circular saw (#1).
- Saw the three crosspieces to length one at a time.

2. Preparing the uprights for bolts

- Clamp the uprights together again, the ends aligned. Place one clamp at the bottom ends of the uprights, then secure the assembly to your worktable so the clamped bottom ends overhang the edge.
- Mark the center of the uprights 3 and 6 inches from the clamped bottom ends.

- Fit an electric drill with a ¼-inch twist bit and drill a hole through all five uprights at each mark (#2).

SAFETY TIP *Wear safety goggles when drilling.*

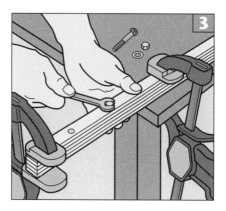

3. Bolting the uprights together

- Insert a 2-inch-long galvanized carriage bolt into each hole drilled in the uprights.
- Add washers and nuts, then tighten the bolts with a combination wrench (#3).
- Remove the clamps.

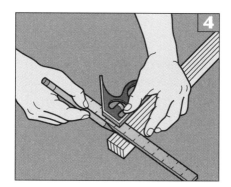

4. Marking crosspiece locations on the uprights

- Holding the unbolted top ends of the uprights together, mark the location of the top crosspiece 1 inch from the top on the two outermost uprights (#4).
- Working the same way, mark the outermost uprights 20 inches and 36 inches from the unbolted top ends for the middle and bottom crosspieces.

5. Marking the crosspieces

You will mark location points for all uprights on the top crosspiece. For the middle and bottom crosspieces, mark location points only for the middle and outer uprights.

- Mark the top crosspiece 1 inch from each end, at the center, and midway between the center and each end—in this case, 12 inches from each end. Use a tape measure to make the marks, then extend lines across the piece with a combination square.

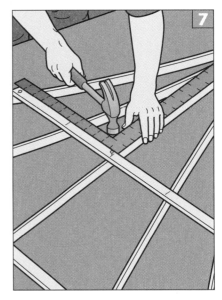

• Mark the middle and bottom crosspieces 1 inch from each end and at the center (#5). Extend lines across the pieces at the marks with a combination square.

6. Fastening the top crosspiece

• Set the uprights on edge on your worktable and clamp the bolted bottom ends in place.
• Lay the top crosspiece on the uprights so the location mark at the center aligns with the middle upright. Fasten the crosspiece to the upright with a 1-inch galvanized nail.
• Gently pull one outer upright until it is aligned with its mark on the crosspiece and nail it in place.
• Fasten the other outer upright to the crosspiece the same way (#6), then nail the other two

uprights to the crosspiece at their location marks.

Note: *To keep the nails from splitting the wood, flatten the tips with a hammer before driving them.*

7. Attaching the middle crosspiece

• Lay the middle crosspiece across the uprights so the location marks near the ends align with the outer uprights.
• Nail the crosspiece to the outer uprights.
• Holding a carpenter's square against the crosspiece and the middle upright, nudge the upright to one side or the other, if necessary, so the two pieces are perpendicular to each other. Fasten the crosspiece to the upright (#7).
• Nail the crosspiece to the other two uprights.

8. Adding the bottom crosspiece

Fasten the bottom crosspiece to the uprights in the same way as you did the middle one.
• Position the bottom crosspiece across the uprights and nail it to the outermost uprights. Then, nail the crosspiece to the middle upright, making sure they form a right angle (#8).
• Fasten the bottom crosspiece to the other two uprights.

9. Locating the furring strips

You can fasten your fan trellis to a wall, as shown here; or, for a more open, freestanding design, fasten it to a post.

● Position the trellis against the wall at the desired location, making sure the bottom is at least a few inches off the ground to prevent rot. Holding the trellis plumb and level, run a pencil along the top edge of the middle crosspiece to mark a location line on the wall for the upper furring strip (#9).

● Put the trellis aside and mark a second line 2 feet below the first for the lower furring strip.

10. Preparing the strips for mounting

To mount the furring strips on a brick wall, as shown here, use masonry screws; most manufacturers provide a drill bit with the screws so you can drill pilot holes of the correct diameter. If you are fastening the trellis to wood, aluminum, or vinyl siding, drive wood screws or lag bolts through the siding into the sheathing, preferably at studs.

● Cut the furring strips from rot-resistant 2x2, the upper one 18 inches long and the lower one 8 inches long.

● Place the upper furring strip at its location line on the wall. Shift the strip, if necessary, to offset it from mortar joints, then drill a pilot hole for a 2½-inch masonry screw near each end of it into the wall (#10). (Drill into the bricks rather than the mortar for the strongest hold.)

● Drill pilot holes for the lower furring strip in the same way.

11. Mounting the furring strips

● Fit the drill with a screwdriver bit, then reposition the upper furring strip on the wall and fasten it in place with two 2½-inch masonry screws (#11).

● Mount the lower furring strip in the same way.

12. Fastening the trellis

● Position the trellis on the wall, the middle and lower crosspieces flat against the furring strips so that the trellis stands out from the wall.

● Holding the trellis plumb with a level against the middle upright, fasten the middle crosspiece to the upper furring strip with three 2-inch galvanized finishing nails (#12). Have a helper hold the trellis steady, if necessary.

● Nail the bottom crosspiece to the lower furring strip.

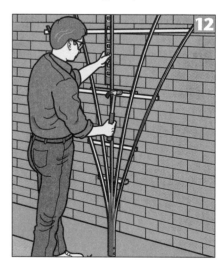

LAWN & GARDEN

ERECTING A VINYL FENCE

Vinyl fences are popular because they are relatively simple to install and they need virtually no maintenance. Proper planning at the outset will help avoid potential problems. Start by checking your local building codes for restrictions; you may, for example, be required to set the fence back from your property line. Also check with local utility companies to determine the location of underground lines before digging postholes. It's also a good idea to discuss your plans with the neighbors adjoining your property—you will want to sort out any complications before you start the project. Lay out the fence on paper before breaking ground; this will help you plan the location of posts and gates, and make it easier to estimate materials you need.

For the fence shown in this project, the posts are installed first (see pages 270 to 272), followed by the rails and the panel sections. After installing post caps, the gate is hung. Refer to the manufacturer's instructions if your fence comes with different installation procedures.

(see pages 270 to 272)

Anatomy of a vinyl fence

Each 4x4 post (A)—pressure-treated pine or a naturally rot-resistant species such as cedar— is anchored in concrete. A vinyl post sleeve (B) is slipped on each post and covered with a post cap (C). Each fencing panel (D) fits between a top rail (E) and a bottom rail (F). The rails are fastened at each end to a post with a bracket (G). A gate (H) is attached to one post at the top and the bottom with a hinge (I) and secured to another post by a latch assembly (J). A tensioner (K) keeps the gate rigid.

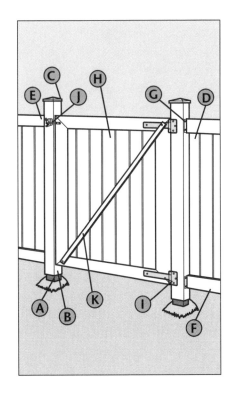

1. Slipping on the post sleeves

• Lay out the fence, mark the post locations, and anchor the posts (see pages 270-272).
• Prepare premixed concrete in a wheelbarrow or mixing tub and backfill around the posts with it. Slope the top of the concrete footings away from the posts with a trowel so that water won't pool around them.
• Wait 24 hours for the concrete to harden, then mark each post 52 inches above the ground.
• Extend the mark across all four sides of the post with a combination square.

(see pages 270-272)

LAWN & GARDEN

- Cut the post at the mark with a circular saw, cutting on two opposite sides. (The cutting depth of a circular saw is insufficient to cut through a post in one pass.)
- Drive a nail into each post 2¼ inches above the ground, leaving about an inch of the nail head protruding.

- Slide a vinyl sleeve over each post (#1). The nail will hold the sleeve ¼ inch higher than the top of the post.

2. Installing the bottom rails

- Once you have put up all the posts, install the rails and panels for one fence section at a time. Start by sliding a bracket (A) onto each end of the bottom rail.
- Attach one bracket to a post

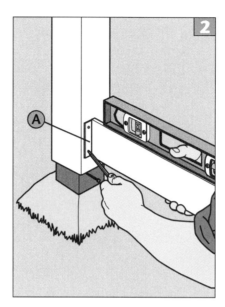

4 inches above the ground with 2-inch wood screws and the plastic washers supplied. Position the bracket so the rail is centered on the post.
- To fasten the bracket at the other end of the rail, position the rail against the post, then level it and mark the bracket screw holes onto the post (#2). Remove the level, line up the screw holes with the marks, and drive the screws.
- Pull out the nails you drove into the posts to hold up the post sleeves.

3. Attaching end panels

- So that each end panel will fit flush against the post, use a utility knife to cut notches along the top and bottom edges of it to accommodate the rail bracket. Make each notch ⅛ inch wide and 1 inch long.

- Slide the end panel into the bottom rail so the notch fits over the bracket. With the panel centered on the post, fasten it in place with three ¾-inch wood screws and the plastic washers supplied (#3).

SAFETY TIP *Wear safety goggles when driving screws with an electric drill.*

4. Filling in between posts

- Starting at the installed end panel, hook and slide one panel edge into the end panel and seat the bottom in the bottom rail.
- Repeat for the length of the fence section, interlocking each remaining panel the same way (#4) and sliding it into the bottom rail.
- Fasten the other end panel to the post at the end of the fence section.

6. Attaching the rails to panels

- Near the middle of the fence section at a point where two panels interlock, fasten the top rail to the two panels with a ¾-inch screw and a plastic washer (#6).
- Attach the bottom rail to the two panels in the same way.

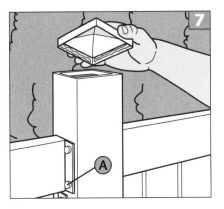

7. Adding the post caps

- As a finishing touch, cover the screws and washers with the plastic caps (A) supplied.
- Apply PVC cement along the inside edge of each post cap.
- Fit each post cap on the top of a post sleeve (#7).

5. Installing the top rails

- Once you have installed all the panels in a fence section, insert a bracket into each end of a top rail.
- Fit the top rail in place over the panels (#5).
- Screw the brackets to the posts with 2-inch wood screws and the plastic washers supplied.

8. Attaching the gate hardware

Hang the gate after installing all the rails and panels.

• With the gate flat on the ground, position a hinge on the bottom rail, centering the long, narrow leaf on the rail and aligning the cylinder with the edge of the gate. Fasten the leaf to the rail with 1$\frac{1}{2}$-inch screws.

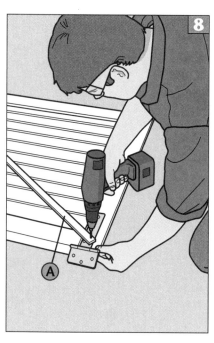

• For the top rail, the tensioner (A) shares one of the screws used to fasten the hinge. Position the tensioner diagonally across the gate. If the tensioner is too long, cut it to length with a hacksaw.
• Fasten the bottom end of the tensioner to the bottom gate rail, then attach the top end of the tensioner and the top hinge to the top gate rail (#8).

9. Attaching the gate to the post

• Position the gate between the posts so the free hinge leaves are

flat against one post. Set the gate on 4x4s and shims, if needed, to hold it level with the fence.
• Place a $\frac{3}{8}$-inch spacer (A) between the gate and each post.
• Secure the free hinge leaves to the gate post with 1$\frac{1}{2}$-inch screws (#9).

10. Installing the latch hardware

• Screw the strike plate to the other gate post at the same height as the top hinge.
• Fit the latch pin into the strike plate and screw the latch pin to the gate (#10).
• Remove the spacers between the gate and the gate posts.

LAWN & GARDEN

LAYING A PRECAST SLAB PATIO

Laying a patio with precast slabs is a great way to add beauty and character to your yard or garden. And the technique shown here, which doesn't rely on a mortar base, is not too difficult to execute. The slabs are embedded in sand over gravel and landscape fabric. In addition to being simpler to install, this kind of patio is also less likely to suffer cracks than one in which the slabs are anchored in mortar.

One of the trickiest parts of the project is sloping the patio—away from the house for a patio built against the house, or from the middle of the patio to the edges for a free-standing patio like the one shown here.

Working with heavy slabs can be a strain; wear a back brace when lifting them and knee pads when kneeling on damp and uneven ground.

HOW LONG WILL IT TAKE?
More than four hours

TOOLS

• Tape measure • Hammer
• Mason's line • Line level
• Plumb bob • Garden edger
• Rake • Shovel • Mattock (or pick) • Wheelbarrow • Tamper
• Scissors • Sledgehammer
• Rubber mallet • Carpenter's level • Push broom • Garden hose • Work gloves • Safety goggles • Back support belt
• Knee pads

MATERIALS

• Precast slabs • Landscape fabric • Gravel • Sand • Mason's sand • 2x2s • 2x4 • Nails

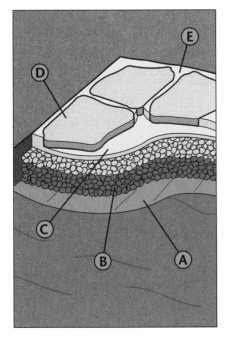

Anatomy of a precast slab patio

The patio sits on a foundation of gravel and sand. Landscape fabric (A), its edges folded up around the border of the patio, prevents grass and weeds from growing through into the patio area. In clay soil, the fabric is laid down first to separate the soil from the gravel; in sandy soil, it is placed over the gravel to keep the sand from sifting down into the gravel. The gravel layer (B) ensures proper drainage by letting water seep through to the ground below. A layer of compacted sand (C) provides a bed for the slabs (D) and is sloped to aid in water drainage. Additional sand (E) fills the joints between slabs and keeps them from shifting.

LAWN & GARDEN

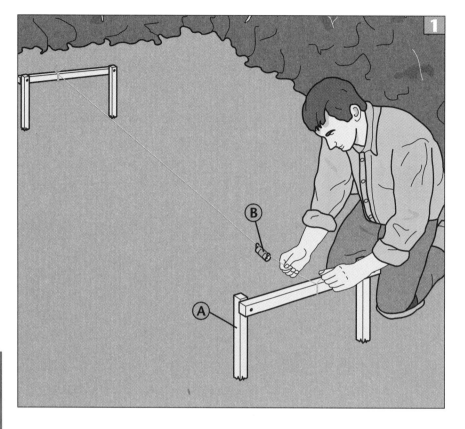

2. Marking the corners

- At each point where the mason's lines cross, hang a plumb bob.
- Mark the spot on the ground just below the tip of the plumb bob with powdered chalk (#2). The marks will indicate the four corners of the patio.

Note: *Double-check the layout for square by measuring diagonally from corner to corner. The two measurements should be equal.*

3. Removing the sod

- With a garden edger, cut through the sod along the sides of the patio layout, using the mason's lines as a guide (#3).
- Use the edger to cut the sod within the layout into sections.
- For easy removal, shovel the pieces of sod into a wheelbarrow as you work.

1. Laying out the patio

Choose a location for the patio that is convenient to the house and well situated relative to sun and shade.

- Roughly mark out the patio, then lay out each side with a pair of batterboards. To make a batterboard (A), cut two 2x2 uprights and one 2x2 crosspiece. Nail the uprights to each end of the crosspiece. Repeat the process to make a second batterboard.
- With a small sledgehammer, drive each batterboard into the ground about a foot beyond the end of the patio.
- Attach a mason's line between each batterboard, knotting the lines on the crosspieces (#1) while checking for level with a line level (B). Repeat for each side.
- Square the corners of the layout (see page 271).

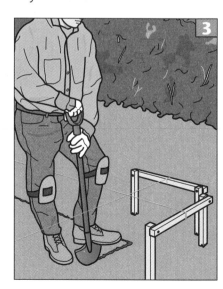

4. Excavating the site

If you have clay soil, you will need to dig to a depth of 9 inches below ground level to accommodate the thickness of the slabs, gravel, and sand. In sandy soil, dig down 7 inches.

- With a mattock or pick, break up the soil within the patio area.
- With a shovel, remove the broken-up soil at the edges of the patio area.
- Periodically check the depth of the excavation by measuring down from the surface of the surrounding lawn.
- Once you have dug to an even depth around the edges of the area, work toward the middle of the site. Use a carpenter's level set on a long 2x4 to level the bottom of the excavation (#4).

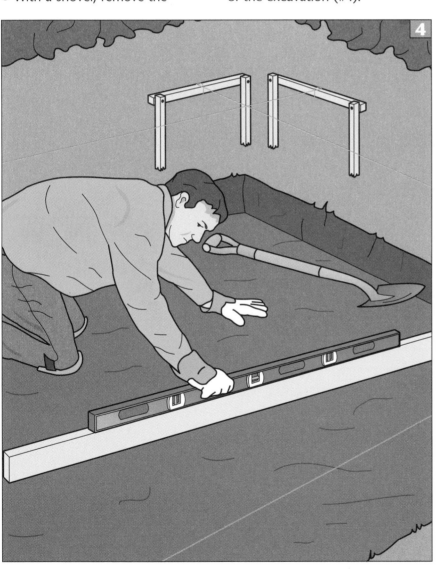

5. Laying the landscape fabric

In clay soil, the landscape fabric separates the soil from the gravel layer. If you have sandy soil, lay down the gravel base (Step 6) before laying the landscape fabric. In either case, spread the fabric on the sides of the excavation as well as over the bottom.

- Beginning in one corner, unroll the landscape fabric, overlapping the lawn by 6 inches (#5).
- Unroll the fabric to complete the first row, then trim the fabric with scissors so it overlaps the lawn by 6 inches.
- Cover the rest of the excavation in the same way, overlapping each row by 6 inches.

6. Compacting the gravel base

- Shovel gravel into the excavation, spreading it out evenly with a garden rake.
- Continue adding and spreading gravel until the excavation is covered with an even layer—about 6 inches thick over clay soil, 4 inches over sandy soil.
- Compact the gravel with a hand tamper until the surface is firm (#6).
- Check the thickness of the gravel base by measuring down from the edges of the excavation. Also check for level. Add more gravel as necessary, tamping as you go.

Note: *A power tamper will take a lot of the effort out of compacting the gravel.*

7. Laying the sand bed

- Shovel several piles of sand onto the excavation.
- Distribute the sand evenly over the bottom of the site with the flat side of a garden rake until the bed is about 1 inch thick.
- Smooth the surface with a long 2x4, check for level, then tamp the sand bed.
- Drive a stake (A) into the ground a few inches beyond each corner and tie two level mason's lines between diagonally opposite corners.
- Measure the distance from the center—where the lines cross—to one of the corners. Create a slope of $\frac{1}{4}$ inch per foot from the center to the edges by adding sand at the center and gradually spreading it outward with the rake. Use a tape measure to check the slope by measuring the distance between the lines and the bed (#7). The measurement should increase progressively from the center to the corners.

8. Arranging the slabs

• To avoid disturbing the sand bed, plan the arrangement of the slabs outside the site, laying out one 4- by 4-foot section at a time.
• Once you have a satisfactory arrangement, transfer the slabs onto the sand bed (#8), starting at one corner and kneeling outside the site. Leave at least $\frac{1}{2}$ inch between slabs and a gap of a few inches between the slabs and the edges of the sand bed.
• Lay out the slabs around the perimeter of the sand bed, then step and kneel on the slabs you have laid to fill out the middle. Avoid stepping on the sand.

9. Bedding the slabs

• Once the slabs in a section are in place, bed them firmly into the sand by tapping with a rubber mallet (#9).

10. Leveling the patio

• Once the slabs in one section are bedded in the sand layer, check for level by laying a long 2x4 over the surface (#10).
• Try setting high slabs with a few taps of the rubber mallet. If this is insufficient, remove some sand beneath the slab and reset it.
• For slabs that are too low, add some sand underneath.

11. Filling the joints

• Once all the slabs are laid, the gaps between them must be filled and the entire surface compacted.
• Shovel several small piles of mason's sand onto the slabs and, with a stiff-bristled broom, sweep the sand into the joints (#11).
• Spray the area with a garden hose to settle the sand. Add more sand and spray again until the joints are full.
• Go over the entire area with a tamper to further compact the sand and settle the slabs.
• With scissors, cut the excess landscape fabric just below the surface along the outer edges of the perimeter slabs.
• Cover the gap between the perimeter of the patio and the edges of the excavation with soil and strips of sod.

HANGING GUTTERS AND DOWNSPOUTS

Gutters and downspouts channel runoff water from the roof to the ground, preventing stains and decay on siding, trim, and masonry. They also divert water away from the house to prevent leakage into the basement and erosion of soil or gravel around the foundation.

Before installing a gutter system, check the condition of your roof-edge components. Make sure that shingles overhang the eaves and that roof edges are lined with a drip edge. The drip edge will direct water into the gutters and prevent it from running back under the shingles.

Most gutter systems are made of vinyl or aluminum. Both materials are durable and light in weight, and require only annual cleaning. Vinyl, however, is easier to install.

HOW LONG WILL IT TAKE?
More than four hours

TOOLS
· Ladder and stabilizer · Tape measure · Line level · Torpedo level · Cordless drill · Chalk line · Hacksaw · Ruler · Hammer · Safety goggles

MATERIALS
· Gutters · Hooks and dovetails · Joiners · End caps · Corner pieces · Drop outlets · Leaf guard · Downspouts · Elbows · Connectors · Clips · Diverters · Wood screws · Self-tapping screws · 2x4 · Nail

Anatomy of a gutter system

This diagram represents the parts of a gutter and downspout system. Gutter lengths (A) are fastened to the fascia with hooks and dovetails (B) and are capped with end caps (C). Gutter lengths are connected with inside and outside joiners (D) and are covered with leaf guards (E). Corners are turned with inside and outside corner sections (F). A drop outlet (G) is installed for every 40 feet of gutter lengths. The drop outlet is attached by a series of elbows (H) to downspout lengths (I), which are fastened to the wall with clips

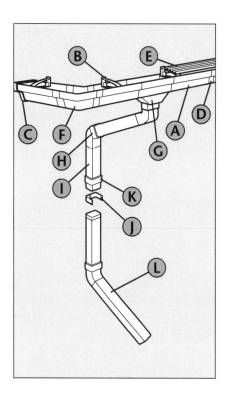

(J) and joined to each other with connectors (K). An extra length of downspout (L) is attached to a lower elbow to channel water away from the foundation.

To determine the lengths and accessories needed for your home, make a sketch of your roof line to scale from actual measurements.

1. Marking a guideline

The gutter must slope slightly so water flows in the direction of the downspout.
● Make a mark $\frac{1}{2}$ inch below the eaves at one end of the fascia.

Tack a nail at the mark and attach a mason's line to the nail. Pull the line tightly to the other end of the fascia and level it with a line level. Mark the line's position.

● Calculate a drop of $\frac{1}{8}$ inch for every 10 feet of fascia and measure down this distance from the mark at the end of the fascia where the drop outlet will be located.

● Remove the mason's line from the nail and replace it with a chalk line. Pull the chalk line across the fascia and snap it at the lower mark (#1).

A ladder stabilizer will not only prevent the ladder from slipping, but will hold it away from the eaves, giving you room to install the gutter.

2. Fastening the dovetails

● Separate the dovetails from the gutter hooks.
● Beginning at the highest point of the guideline, position a dovetail 1 foot from the end of the fascia, the top edge aligned with the guideline. Screw it to the fascia.
● Fasten additional dovetails every $1\frac{1}{2}$ feet along the guideline (#2) until about 3 feet from the other end of the fascia.

3. Attaching the gutter hooks

The gutter hooks should line up roughly with the dovetails that have been installed; however, they can be adjusted as the gutter is hung. Working on the ground, slide the gutter hooks onto the rails along the inside edges of the gutter (#3). Position a hook about 1 foot from the end that will be capped and space the others $1\frac{1}{2}$ feet apart.

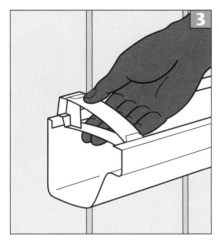

4. Inserting the end cap

Still working on the ground, snap an end cap onto the end of the first gutter section (#4), covering the gutter end with the cap flanges.

Note: *If gutter accessories are difficult to snap into place or do not slide freely, lubricate them with liquid soap and water.*

LAWN & GARDEN

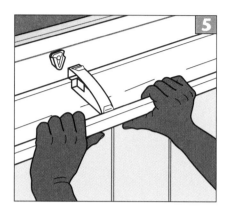

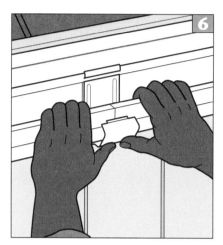

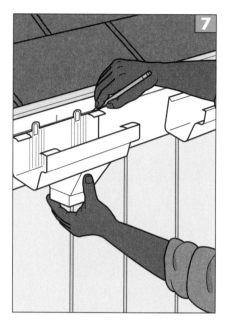

5. Hanging the gutter

• Position the first gutter section so the end is in line with the edge of the shingles at the end of the house.
• Slip the hooks into the dovetails (#5), repositioning the hooks if necessary.
• Hang the remaining sections of gutter, but leave a gap of at least 1 foot between the last section and the desired location of the drop outlet so a final length can be cut to fit.

Note: *Hanging 10-foot sections of gutter can be awkward. Work with a helper or set up an extra ladder to use as support.*

6. Joining the gutter lengths

• Cover the gutter seam with an inner joiner, slipping it under the lip of the gutter closest to the fascia. Snap the joiner into place over the seam, forcing the other edge under the other gutter lip.

• Slide the outer joiner between the fascia and the gutter, lining it up with the installed inner joiner. Snap the lip of the joiner over the inner edge of the gutter, covering the seam. Then, pull the outside lip of the joiner up over the outside of the gutter and snap it into place (#6).

7. Positioning the drop outlet

The downspout commonly follows the corner of the house and is fastened to the corner board of the siding. Since the fascia usually extends beyond the corner, you'll need to measure back to position the drop outlet.
• Mark the desired location of the center of the drop outlet on the fascia.
• Center the drop outlet at this mark. Make two more marks on the fascia in line with the gauges on the drop outlet that correspond to the temperature at the moment (#7).

8. Hanging the last gutter section

Cutting the final section of gutter to align with the correct gauge of the drop outlet allows for expansion and contraction of the vinyl.
• Measure the distance between the edge of the installed gutter and the closest gauge mark (#8).

- With a hacksaw, cut a section of gutter to this length.
- Depending on the length of the section, install the required number of dovetails and hooks.
- Slip the hooks onto the dovetails and add joiner pieces at the seam created between the two gutter sections.

Note: *To keep the gutter rigid as you cut it, place a 2x4 inside it, the end of the 2x4 just to one side of the cutting line.*

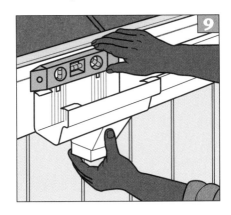

9. Installing the drop outlet

Unlike the gutter, the drop outlet must be installed level.
- Slide the drop outlet over the end of the gutter, repositioning it over its center line.
- With a torpedo level, check that the drop outlet is level (#9).
- Mark the positions for the screws, remove the drop outlet, and drive the supporting screws partway into the fascia.
- Slide the drop outlet back into place, mounting it on the screws.

10. Finishing the run

- Measure the distance between the gauge nearest the end of the roof and the overhang of the shingles beyond the fascia. Cut a section of gutter to this length.
- Fasten a dovetail 1 foot from the end of the fascia, placing the edge slightly above the guideline to ensure a slight slope toward the drop outlet.
- Slide a hook onto the hook rail and install a cap on the end of the gutter section.
- Slide the gutter section into the drop outlet (#10), aligning the end with the edge of the shingles.
- Slip the hook into the dovetail.

11. Inserting the leaf guard

A leaf guard keeps the gutter free of debris and helps direct water into the gutter.

- Position a length of leaf guard over the gutter and drop outlet, its drip edge facing toward the house. Snap the edges of the leaf guard through the ridges on the top of the gutter hooks (#11).
- Make sure the leaf guard's drip edge curves upward to make contact with the drip edge along the eave of the roof.

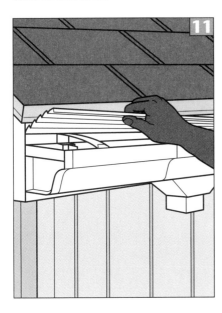

12. Installing the lower downspout

- Mark the center of the corner board a minimum of 6 inches above the ground. Fasten a down-spout clip at the mark (#12); use self-tapping masonry screws for a masonry wall.
- Snap the elbow into the clip, taking note of the directional arrows for water flow.
- Working upward along the corner board, fasten downspout clips every 5 feet until about 2 feet below the drop outlet.
- Insert a 10-foot downspout section into the lower elbow and snap it into the clips.

13. Completing the downspout

- Slip an elbow over the drain of the drop outlet. Position another elbow against the corner board just below the drop outlet. With a long ruler, align the two elbows. Mark the position of the elbow on the corner board.

- Measure the distance between the collars of the two elbows (#13). Also measure the distance between the end of the installed downspout section and the elbow on the corner board.

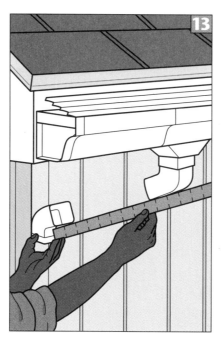

- Cut lengths of downspout for both these sections.
- Fasten a downspout clip just below the mark for the upper elbow. With a connector, attach the length of downspout to the installed section and snap the downspout into the upper clip.
- Insert the upper elbow into the downspout and connect this elbow and the drop-outlet elbow with the other cut section of downspout.
- Secure each elbow with a self-tapping screw, fastening through the elbow into the downspout.

14. Channeling the water flow

An additional length of down-spout attached to the lower elbow will route water away from the foundation. A splash pad placed under the water outlet (#14) will prevent erosion.

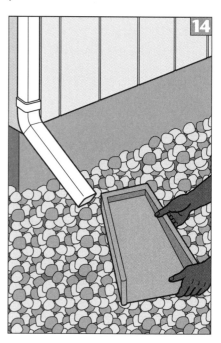

Other accessories include a hinged diverter to lift the extension out of the way for yard work and flexible hoses that can be buried or bent to direct water as desired.

LAWN & GARDEN

PUTTING UP A WOOD FENCE

Before beginning your project, decide on the size and style of fence you would like to build and check local building codes. If you intend to build along your property lines, establish clearly where they are and position your structure 1 or 2 inches inside the lines. Also check with your utility companies for underground lines before starting to dig.

Consider as well the choice of building materials available. Pressure-treated lumber is the most economical and popular choice. Vinyl and polyvinyl chloride (PVC) products, although more expensive, offer a long life and require very little upkeep. Galvanized or stainless-steel fasteners will last and won't cause rust staining.

The fence shown here is built with 4x4 posts and two 2x4 rails, suitable for boards up to 6 feet in height. It is ideal for privacy, as well as for containing children and pets. It qualifies as a "good-neighbor fence" since it looks the same on both sides, with boards spaced uniformly and fastened to opposite sides of the rails.

HOW LONG WILL IT TAKE?
More than four hours

TOOLS
• Tape measure • Carpenter's level • Combination square • Sledgehammer • Mason's line • Posthole digger • Shovel • Mason's trowel • Circular saw • Handsaw • Cordless drill • Hammer • Screwdriver • Safety goggles

MATERIALS
• 4x4s • 2x4s • 1x6s • 1x4s • 1x2s • Masking tape • Gravel • Premixed concrete • Duplex nails • Wood screws

1. Setting the corner and end posts

• Lay out the fence posts, square the corners, and dig the postholes (see pages 270 to 271).
• Lay a 6-inch bed of gravel at the bottom of the holes.
• Retie the layout mason's lines and center the corner post in its hole where the lines intersect.
• Fasten a 1x4 brace to adjacent sides of the post with a single duplex (two-headed) nail.
• Drive 1x2 stakes into the ground and fasten the braces to the stakes with duplex nails.
• Plumb the post on adjacent faces with a level (#1). To adjust

the position of the post, drive one or the other of the stakes further into the ground.

• Set the end posts in the ground.

2. Spacing the intermediate posts

Space the intermediate posts as uniformly as possible up to a maximum of 8 feet apart. Cut a 2x4 fence rail to the same length as the distance you decide on to use as a spacer. The perimeters of your space will play a role, as well as the positioning of your opening for a gate.

• Set the 2x4 spacer rail on the ground flush against the face of a corner or end post, aligned with the mason's line. Mark the ground at the end of the rail.

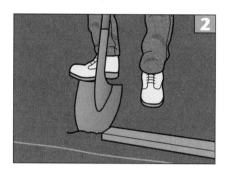

- Untie the mason's line and break the ground at the marked spot with a shovel (#2).

3. Setting intermediate posts

- Dig the posthole and add a bed of gravel.
- Retie the mason's line and put the spacer rail in place, making sure it sits evenly on the ground and flush against the corner or end post.
- Sit a post in the hole flush against the rail and lined up with the mason's line (#3).
- Plumb and brace the post.
- Space and set the remaining posts in the same way.
- For the gate posts, leave a space between them equal to the width of the gate plus $\frac{1}{2}$ inch for clearance—in this project, 42 inches.

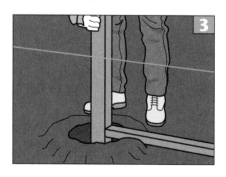

4. Pouring the concrete

Set corner, end, and gate posts in concrete to prevent them from moving. Intermediate posts may be backfilled with tamped soil, but setting them in concrete, too, makes for a sturdier fence.
- Prepare a batch of premixed concrete following the manufacturer's instructions on the bag.
- Shovel the concrete into a hole, working the mixture up and down to remove any air pockets. Add concrete to form a small mound slightly above ground level (#4).
- With a mason's trowel, slope the concrete away from the post so water will drain away from it.
- Fill the other postholes the same way.
- After a week—when the concrete has stopped shrinking—fill gaps at the base of the posts with silicone caulk.

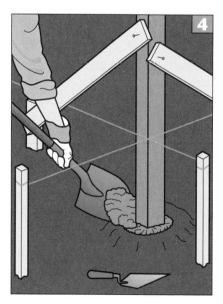

5. Installing the rails

Rails should be positioned no more than 12 inches from the top or bottom of the fence boards.
- On a corner or end post, mark the position of a rail hanger about 6 inches up from where you want the bottom of your fence boards to be placed.
- Align a rail hanger (inset) at the mark and fasten it to the post with screws. Drop in the rail, but don't fasten it to the hanger yet.
- Level the rail against the next post and mark its position (#5), then fasten a rail hanger at the mark. Drop in the rail and fasten it to both hangers.
- Measure up from the bottom rail to mark the position of the top rail, then install it the same way.

Note: *When determining where to position your bottom rail, account for varying ground levels.*

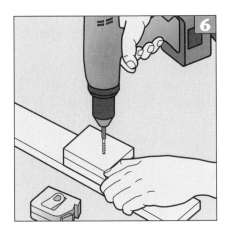

6. Making a spacer

As well as keeping even spacing and alignment, a 1x4 spacer will ensure your 1x6 fence boards overlap uniformly on both sides of the rails.

● Place a fence board against the rails flush against the post at the desired height. Check for plumb, then fasten the board to each rail with two screws.

● Cut a 1x4 spacer the length of the boards. Place the spacer flush against the fastened board, lining up the tops. Mark the top of the top rail on the spacer.

● Make a cleat out of two 1x4 scraps. Line up the bottom of the cleat with the mark on the spacer and fasten it with screws (#6).

7. Fastening the boards

● Butt the spacer against the first board, the cleat resting on the top rail. The board and the spacer should line up.

● Butt the second board against the spacer, aligned with the top, and fasten the board to the rails.

● Space and fasten the subsequent boards the same way (#7), checking for plumb every third or fourth board.

● You may have to adjust the spacing of the final three boards to complete the fence section with a full-width board or a full space.

8. Completing the other side

The boards on the other side are placed alternately to those on the first side, filling in the spaces.

● Position the spacer on the top rail 1 inch from the post. (This will ensure that the first board overlaps the first two boards on the other side equally.)

● Butt the first board against the spacer, aligning the top, and fasten it to the rails (#8).

● Continue the same way.

9. Trimming the posts

● With a combination square, mark the height of the boards on each face of the posts.

● Trim the posts along the marks with a handsaw. (If you decide on a post height 6 inches or so above the fence boards, you can trim the posts with a circular saw—cutting on opposite sides of each post and using a 1x2 guide nailed to the post as a support for the baseplate of the saw.)

● Coat the cut post tops with wood preservative. Let the wood preservative dry.

● Fasten a post cap to the top of each post by driving screws through the predrilled holes (#9).

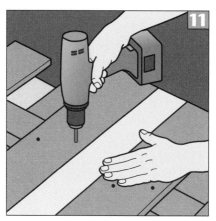

12. Hinging the gate

Because the lower corner of the brace carries most of the gate's weight, the hinges are attached to this side. They are then fastened to the inside face of the post, allowing the gate to open inward.

• Place the hinges on the boards at the edge of the gate, centering them over the rails. Mark and drill pilot holes, then screw the hinges through the boards into the rails.

• Prop the gate in position on blocks, aligning its rails with those of the fence.

• Check for plumb, then fasten the hinges to the post (#12).

11. Cladding the gate

• Position the first board flush against the edge of the frame. Place your spacer next to it, the cleat resting on the top rail. Align the top of the first board with the top of the spacer.

• Fasten the board to the frame, driving two screws into the diagonal brace as well as each rail.

• Space and fasten the rest of the boards, completing one side of the gate. Turn the gate over and fasten boards in the alternating pattern (#11).

10. Framing the gate

Make the width of your gate $\frac{1}{2}$ inch less than the distance between your gate posts to provide enough clearance for the gate hardware.

• Measure and cut a 2x4 gate frame. Cut the horizontal pieces to span the width of the gate to protect the ends of the vertical pieces from moisture.

• Fasten each corner with a single screw drilled at an angle across the butt joint.

• To support the weight of the gate, add a diagonal brace running from the lower corner on the hinge side up to the latch side. To make the brace, place a 2x4 over the frame corners, then mark and cut it to fit. Fasten each end with a single screw drilled at an angle into the frame (#10).

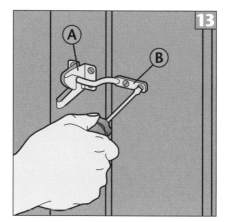

13. Installing the latch and strike

• Position the latch (A) at the desired height on the gate post. Mark and drill pilot holes, then fasten the latch to the post.

• Place the strike (B) into the latch and mark its position on the gate. Drill pilot holes, then screw it into place (#13).

PAVING WITH STONE

Flagstone is made by splitting a stone such as limestone or sandstone into broad, flat pieces. It is available in irregular shapes or cut into rectangles. If you choose irregular stones, try to select ones with straight rather than rounded edges—they will fit together more easily and minimize the amount of cutting. Flagstone is sold by the square foot; calculate the area to be paved and add 10 percent for waste.

Flagstone can be laid on a bed of mortar or sand. Walkways laid in sand require more maintenance, but are much easier to construct. Use concrete sand—it compacts well and inhibits weeds. If your soil is claylike and the paving site drains poorly, add a 4-inch base of ¾-inch gravel before putting in the sand. Flagstone can be laid without a border, giving a rustic, informal look to your walkway or patio.

HOW LONG WILL IT TAKE?
More than four hours

TOOLS
· Tape measure · Mason's line · Spade · Shovel · Pick · Tamper · Scissors · Sledgehammer · Rubber mallet · Stone chisel · Carpenter's level · Push broom · Garden hose · Work gloves · Safety goggles · Back support belt · Knee pads

MATERIALS
· Flagstones · Landscape fabric · Concrete sand · 2x2s · 2x4s

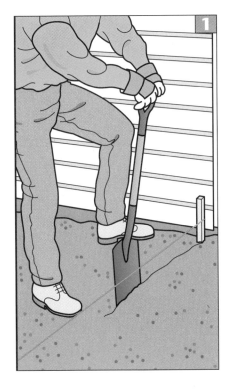

1. Laying out the site

Make sure that the paving site is fairly flat, drains well, and is free of large roots.
● To lay out straight sections, drive 2x2 stakes into the ground and run mason's line between the stakes. For curved sections, outline the paving site with sand.
● Take a final look at the size and shape of the area to be paved before you start to dig and make changes as needed.
● With a spade, cut into the ground along the outline of the paving site (#1).
● Remove the layout stakes and mason's line.

2. Excavating

To determine the required depth of the excavation, measure the thickness of the thickest stone and add 1 inch. With a sand bed of 1½ inches, the stones will sit slightly above the surface, allowing for settling. If the site drains poorly, dig an extra 4 inches for a base of gravel.
● Dig the site to the required depth, using a pick to remove any stones or roots.
● Lay landscape fabric on the excavation (see page 285).
● To check the depth, set a straight 2x4 across the excavation site. Measure from the bottom

edge of the board to the bottom of the excavation. Check every few feet and use sand to mark areas that need to be corrected.

- Once the work area is excavated to a uniform depth, use a hand tamper to compact the soil (#2).

3. Making the sand bed

- Set 2x4s along the edges of the excavation, laying them flat on the bottom.
- Spread a base of sand to reach to the top of the 2x4s.
- Level the sand by dragging a 2x4, cut to the width of the bed, across the surface (#3).
- Compact the sand with a tamper. Add more sand and level it.
- Remove the 2x4s and fill the gaps with sand. Tamp again.
- Curved sections can be leveled without 2x4s at the edges as guides. Check for uniform sand depth by spanning a 2x4 across the sand bed and measuring from the bottom of it to the sand at different points along its length.

- Trim the landscape fabric flush with the top of the sand bed.

4. Laying the stone

- Select a stone with two straight edges that are close to 90 degrees to each other and position it in a corner of the bed.

- Select each stone so it fits together as close as possible with the first one—joints should be at least $3/8$ inch, but no more than 2 inches. Tap the stones into place with a rubber mallet.
- Use a carpenter's level to check that each stone is even with the adjacent ones (#4), then bed the stones (see page 287).

SAFETY TIP *Stones can be very heavy. To reduce the possibility of back injury, work with a helper to lift large ones.*

5. Mark for cutting

When you can't find a stone of the right size or shape, you may have to cut one to fit.

● Place the stone in its approximate position and, with a china marker, trace the desired cut onto its top face (#5).

● Transfer the mark to the edges of the stone, then turn the stone over and join the marks on the other side.

6. Trimming for small cuts

● Position the stone on a flat stable surface—across three 2x4s is ideal.

● Chip off small pieces of the stone at a time using a stone chisel and a small sledgehammer (#6). Work slowly—chipping off larger sections may cause the stone to break unpredictably. If the waste won't break off, turn the stone over and chip at it from the other side.

SAFETY TIP *Wear safety goggles to trim stone.*

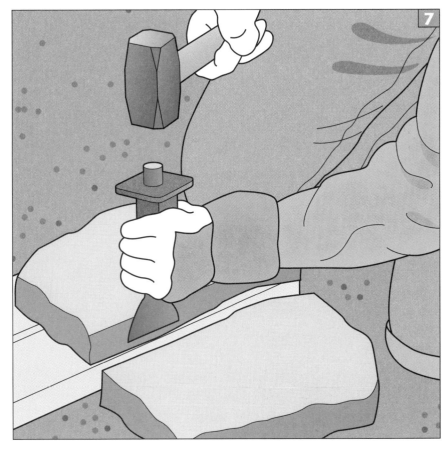

7. Splitting for large cuts

● With a stone chisel and a small sledgehammer, score both sides of the stone along the marked line.

● Rest the stone on the 2x4s with the scored line directly over the outside edge of the last board.

● With the sledgehammer and chisel, tap the stone sharply along the scored line until it breaks (#7).

● Fill the joints as you would for a patio (see page 287).

Note: *A right-angle grinder fitted with a diamond blade is handy for making cuts in stone.*

LAWN & GARDEN

Chapter 7
IN THE WORKSHOP

Tools are the backbone of home repair and improvement. The quality of your tools and how well you care for them will to a large extent determine how quick and easy the projects in this book will be for you.

Always use the prescribed tool for a job and always use it correctly. When you are shopping for a tool, it pays to purchase the highest quality you can afford. A premium-quality tool will last longer and in most cases perform better than a bargain-basement alternative. Consider renting a specialized and relatively expensive tool that you may need to use only once or infrequently at a tool-rental agency.

Tools are much like cars or homes in that they need regular care and maintenance. A blunt and rusty saw, for example, will not cut properly, no matter how good it was when new. A poorly maintained tool can also be dangerous. A tool that requires you to exert more force than you

TOOLS FOR IN THE WORKSHOP FIXES AND IMPROVEMENTS

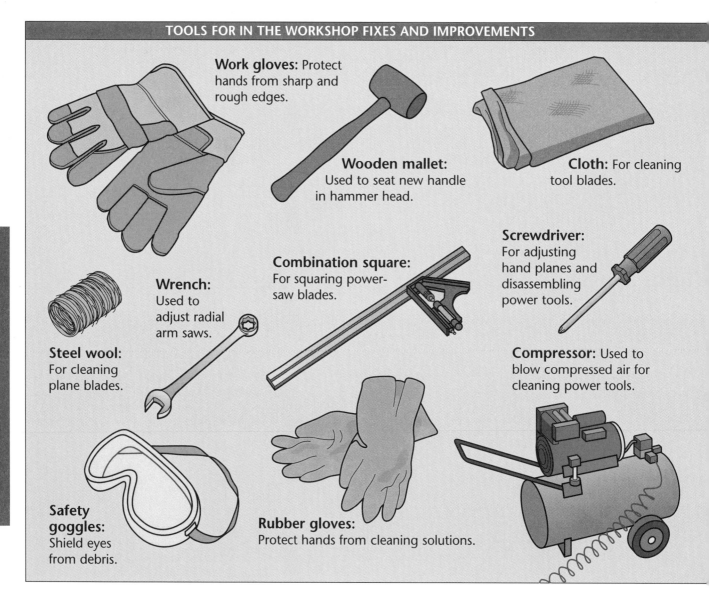

Work gloves: Protect hands from sharp and rough edges.

Wooden mallet: Used to seat new handle in hammer head.

Cloth: For cleaning tool blades.

Steel wool: For cleaning plane blades.

Wrench: Used to adjust radial arm saws.

Combination square: For squaring power-saw blades.

Screwdriver: For adjusting hand planes and disassembling power tools.

Compressor: Used to blow compressed air for cleaning power tools.

Safety goggles: Shield eyes from debris.

Rubber gloves: Protect hands from cleaning solutions.

ordinarily would because it is blunt or out of adjustment is an accident waiting to happen.

There is much you can do to keep your tools in peak working order and this chapter will show you how. Tool care starts with proper storage. More tools are damaged as a result of careless and haphazard storage than they are in use.

Cutting tools such as saws, chisels, drill bits, and hand planes require periodic sharpening. You'll save money and be more prone to do the

sharpening when it needs to be done if you can do it yourself. Sharpening calls for a few specialized tools, but considering the cost of a professional honing, they will pay for themselves in short order.

Given the price of new power tools, it's worthwhile to keep your existing ones in good shape. This chapter will show you how to replace the power tool components that most commonly fail: power cords, plugs, and On/Off switches.

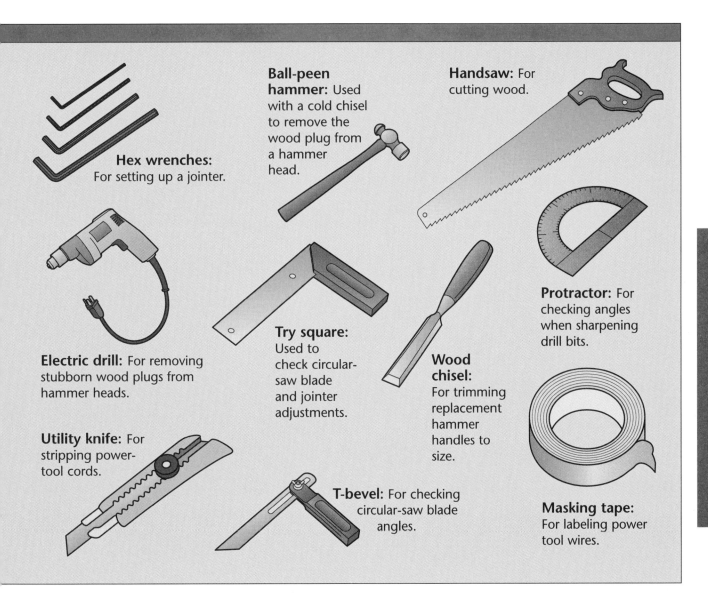

Hex wrenches: For setting up a jointer.

Ball-peen hammer: Used with a cold chisel to remove the wood plug from a hammer head.

Handsaw: For cutting wood.

Electric drill: For removing stubborn wood plugs from hammer heads.

Try square: Used to check circular-saw blade and jointer adjustments.

Protractor: For checking angles when sharpening drill bits.

Wood chisel: For trimming replacement hammer handles to size.

Utility knife: For stripping power-tool cords.

T-bevel: For checking circular-saw blade angles.

Masking tape: For labeling power tool wires.

TOOL MAINTENANCE

Most experts advise that you buy the best-quality tools you can afford. However, no tool works well or lasts long unless it is properly cared for. Tool maintenance isn't just a matter of performance and longevity: A rusty saw blade, a chipped chisel tip, a crooked saber-saw blade, or a dust-caked circular saw also isn't safe to use.

A few basic workshop habits yield big dividends. Storing tools in an organized way keeps them handy, safeguards them from damage, and rids your shop of clutter. Cleaning tools right after a job keeps cutting edges sharp and air vents dust-free. If you attend to tools regularly, cleanup can be quick. And you're unlikely to need more than mild detergent or mineral spirits for cleaning, light machine oil for rust removal and protection.

Some power tools also require periodic adjustments in order to function properly. Refer to your owner's manual for specific instructions.

HOW LONG WILL IT TAKE?
Two to four hours

TOOLS
• Hammer • Wire brush • File • Stiff-bristled brush • Bench grinder • Star-wheel dresser • Combination square • Rubber gloves • Work gloves • Safety goggles

MATERIALS
• Mild detergent • Mineral spirits • Light machine oil • Perforated hardboard panels • U-hooks and racks • Cloths • Steel wool • Chalk • Wire • Compressed air

TOOL STORAGE

Storing hand tools

Store tools in sight and within easy reach by lining your workshop walls with perforated hardboard fitted with special hooks and racks, as shown in #1.
● Nail perforated hardboard panels to the wall of the workshop.
● Fit specially-made U-hooks and racks into place where you want to hang tools.

Note: *Once all your tools are arranged on the wall, outline them on the hardboard panels with a marker as a visual reminder of where they go.*

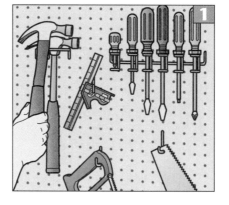

Storing power tools

● Before storing a power tool, remove any bit, blade, or other accessory and wind the power cord snugly around the casing. Place the tool in its storage case.
● Put power tools away in a

closed cupboard fitted with a lock (#2). This will protect the tools from damage—and keep them out of the reach of children.

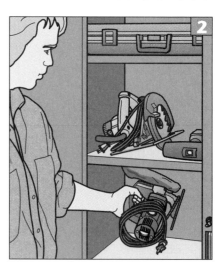

KEEPING TOOLS CLEAN

Cleaning a wood chisel

- Clean the handle of a chisel by wiping it with a soft cloth dampened with a solution of mild detergent and water.
- Wearing rubber gloves, dampen a cloth with mineral spirits and rub the blade with it (#1).
- Remove any rust from the blade by rubbing with steel wool dampened with light machine oil.

Note: *Before storing a wood chisel, wipe a little light machine oil onto the blade.*

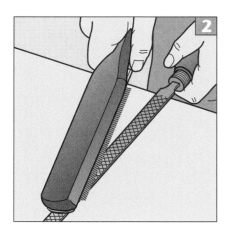

Cleaning a file

Metal filings and dust can build up in a file. It's best to clean a file both before and after using it.
- Remove metal filings by scrubbing the teeth of the file with a wire brush (#2). Use the point of a small nail to dislodge any stubborn particles.
- Rub the teeth with chalk after each use of the file to help keep filings from building up. Never apply oil to a file.
- Store your files in a drawer, separated from each other and wrapped in a cloth.

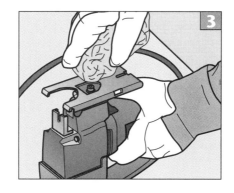

Cleaning a saber saw

- With the saw unplugged, remove the blade following the manufacturer's instructions.
- Wearing safety goggles, blow debris out of vents and crevices with compressed air.
- Use a soft cloth and a solution of mild detergent and water to clean the body of the saw.

- Remove burrs from the baseplate with a file.
- Wearing work gloves, clean pitch, gum, or glue off the saw by rubbing with steel wool dampened in mineral spirits (#3).

Cleaning a circular saw

- Double check that the saw is unplugged.
- Remove caked-on sawdust with a stiff-bristled brush.
- Wearing safety goggles, clean debris from the vents on the motor housing and from the interior of the blade guards with compressed air (#4).
- Clean the saw body using a soft cloth dampened with a solution of mild detergent and water.
- To remove stubborn deposits from the baseplate, wear work gloves and rub with steel wool dampened in mineral spirits.
- Use a file to remove burrs.

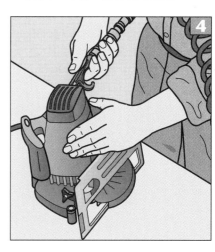

KEEPING TOOLS CLEAN (CONTINUED)

Cleaning an electric drill

- Be sure the drill is unplugged.
- Use a stiff-bristled brush to remove caked-on sawdust.
- Clean grease off the drill housing and handle with a soft cloth dampened with a solution of mild detergent and water. Be careful not to wet any internal parts.
- If you encounter difficulty opening or closing the chuck jaws, rotate the chuck collar back and forth and insert a length of wire into the chuck to dislodge foreign particles (#5). Then, lubricate the chuck with light machine oil.

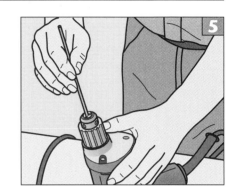

TOOL ADJUSTMENTS

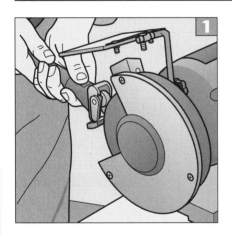

Dressing a grinding wheel

A bench grinder is an indispensable workshop tool, useful for everything from squaring and sharpening blades and bits to smoothing, polishing, and cleaning. Over time, a grinding wheel may become glazed or otherwise develop irregularities that reduce its effectiveness. Rather than throw out a wheel and replace it, you can use a wheel dresser to clean, true, and reshape it.

- Wear safety goggles and keep the eye shield lowered over the grinding wheel at all times. Rest a star-wheel dresser on the tool rest, then switch on the grinding wheel and gently press the wheel of the dresser against the rotating grinder wheel (#1). Work the dresser from side to side until the face of the grinding wheel is clean and smooth.

SAFETY TIP *Work with compressed air in a well-ventilated area and always direct the spray away from your body.*

Squaring a saber-saw blade

Each time you install a new saber-saw blade, you need to square it to the baseplate of the saw.

- Double check that the saw is unplugged.
- For the model shown, set the saw upside down on a worktable.

Loosen the blade clamp setscrew, then fit in a new blade and lock the blade in the clamp.

- Check for square with a combination square, sitting the handle on the saw's baseplate and resting the arm against the blade. The blade and the baseplate should form a 90-degree angle. If not, loosen the setscrew on the baseplate with a hex wrench and swivel the baseplate until it is square to the blade, then tighten the setscrew (#2).

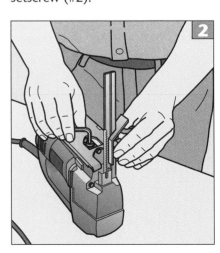

SHARPENING HANDSAW TEETH

A handsaw can only cut cleanly if its teeth are sharp. You can take your saws to a professional for sharpening, but there are benefits to doing the job yourself. You'll be able to sharpen a saw as soon as it's needed and since the tools used are inexpensive, they will start paying for themselves in a short time.

Sharpening a handsaw is a three-step process. Jointing entails filing the tips of the teeth to the same length with a saw-jointing jig. Setting involves bending the teeth to the correct angle with a saw set so the blade doesn't bind. Sharpening involves filing the teeth. Western saws, such as crosscut saws, ripsaws, combination saws, and shortcut saws, require triangular mill files. For Japanese saws, you'll need a diamond-shaped feather file. In all cases, file only on the forward stroke to produce a smooth, sharp edge.

SAFETY TIP *To protect your hands, wear work gloves while sharpening a saw.*

HOW LONG WILL IT TAKE?

Less than two hours

TOOLS

• Saw-jointing jig • Saw set • Flat mill bastard file • Triangular mill file • Diamond-shaped feather file • Sharpening guide • Tape measure • Vise • Work gloves

MATERIALS

• Plywood pads

JOINTING AND SETTING THE TEETH

1. Securing the saw

• To hold the saw securely during sharpening, make wood pads for gripping it in your vise. Cut two straight pieces of ½-inch plywood about 6 inches wide and 18 inches long.

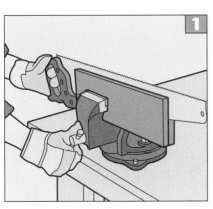

• Sandwich the saw blade between the pads so the teeth extend above the boards by about 1½ inches.
• Secure the saw and pads in a vise with the blade teeth-up and the handle as close as possible to the vise jaws (#1).

2. Jointing the teeth

A commercial saw-jointing jig (A) allows you to slide a file evenly over the tips of the teeth.
• Fit a flat mill bastard file in the jointing jig following the manufacturer's directions, then tighten it in place with the locking nut.
• Place the jig's fence flush

against one side of the saw blade, making sure the file contacts the teeth. Holding the saw handle, pass the jig and file back and forth a few times along the full length of the saw blade (#2).

JOINTING AND SETTING THE TEETH (CONTINUED)

3. Setting the teeth

● The saw set shown here can be adjusted to suit the teeth per inch (TPI) of your saw blade. Measure the saw blade to determine its TPI, then adjust the saw set accordingly.

● Saw teeth are bent alternately to one side and the other of the blade. Starting at one end of the saw, fit the saw set over the first blade tooth that is bent away from you, then squeeze the handle to bend the tooth to the proper angle.

● Set all the other teeth bent in the same direction as the first one (#3), then remove the saw from the vice, turn it in the opposite direction, and set the remaining teeth.

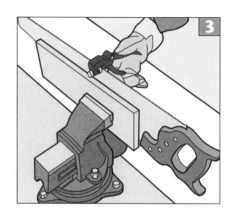

SHARPENING THE TEETH

Crosscut teeth

The teeth of a crosscut saw blade are spaced relatively close together. There are typically 8 to 12 TPI.
● With the saw still in the vise, fit a triangular mill file between the first two teeth at one end of the blade. The edges of crosscut teeth are typically beveled at about 65 degrees. Holding the file flush against the beveled edge of the first tooth that is set toward you and tilted down slightly, slide the file forward stroke along the edge of the tooth.

● File the opposite side of the same tooth the same way, then sharpen all the other teeth that are set toward you (#1).

● Turn the saw around in the vise and file the remaining teeth.

Ripsaw teeth

The teeth of ripsaws are spaced farther apart than those of crosscut saws. There are usually only 5 to 7 TPI. In contrast to crosscut teeth, the edges of ripsaw teeth are not beveled.

● Sharpen ripsaw teeth with a triangular mill file as you would for a crosscut saw, but hold the file flat against the edges of the teeth at a 90-degree angle (#2).

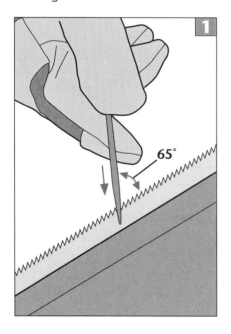

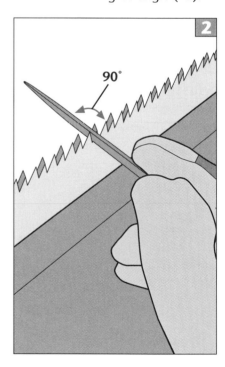

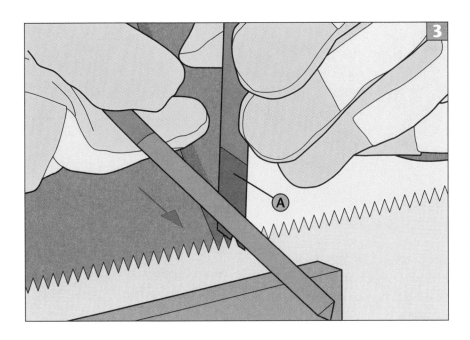

Japanese crosscut teeth

Japanese saw-blade teeth have bevels on both edges as well as a bevel at the top of each tooth. Japanese saws are more supple than Western ones and they bend more easily, so make sure the wood pads that you cut to grip the blade in the vise support it along its full length.

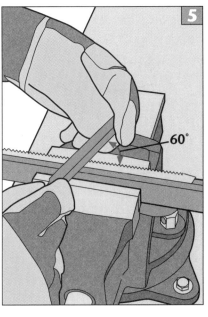

Toolbox saw teeth

Some saws, such as toolbox saws, have an additional beveled edge at the top of the teeth. Specially-made sharpening guides (A) are available for some models to help you sharpen these edges.
• Sharpen the blade teeth as you would for a crosscut saw, then hold a sharpening guide upright so its blade is between the saw blade's first two teeth.
• Rest one side of a triangular file against the guide and the other against the top of the first tooth that is set toward you. Tilting the file handle at about 30 degrees, make two or three forward strokes over the tooth (#3).
• File every second tooth the same way until you reach the end of the blade.
• Turn the saw around in the vise and file the remaining teeth.

Combination teeth

Designed for both crosscutting and ripping, combination saws have teeth that are beveled on both edges.
• File combination teeth as you would for a crosscut saw, holding a triangular mill file at about a 60-degree angle (#4).

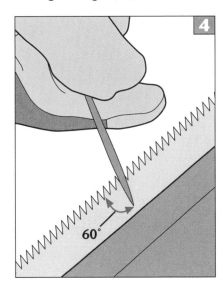

• Sharpen the teeth as you would a Western crosscut saw, but use a feather file angled at 60 degrees and file the teeth set away from you. Push down and to the left to follow the bevel of the tooth and file on only the forward stroke (#5).
• File the top of each tooth following the bevel angle.
• Turn the saw around in the vise to sharpen the remaining teeth.

SHARPENING A CHISEL

Chisels must be sharpened regularly to carve wood cleanly and easily. Two basic steps are involved: honing the bevel, or angled cutting edge; and polishing the resulting burr, or ridge of metal, on the flat side of the blade. A benchstone or a bench grinder may be used.

Benchstones are divided into two categories according to the lubricant used: oilstones and waterstones. They are available in several levels of coarseness, with oilstones generally being coarser than waterstones. Combination stones have a coarse side and a fine side, making them a versatile option. Use light machine oil with an oilstone and wipe it off after every use. Store a waterstone in water.

A bench grinder sharpens much faster than a benchstone, but must be used with care so the blade of the chisel isn't overheated, destroying its temper. A standard grinding wheel is often too coarse, especially for very fine chisels, but a wide range of specialized grinding and buffing wheels is available.

HOW LONG WILL IT TAKE?
Less than two hours

TOOLS

- Benchstone • Bench grinder
- Safety goggles

MATERIALS

- Lapping compound • Honing oil • Glass pane • Scrap wood • Wood screws • Light machine oil • Polishing compound

USING A BENCHSTONE

1. Truing the stone

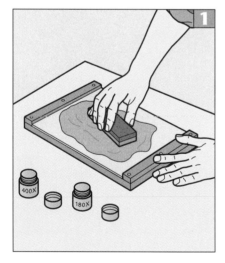

A benchstone eventually develops a hollow in the center. To flatten, or true, the stone, use lapping compound and a glass pane.

- Mount the glass pane between wood cleats screwed to a board.
- Prepare a slurry of coarse lapping compound following the manufacturer's instructions—for an oilstone, mix in honing oil; for a waterstone, mix in water.
- Spread the slurry over the glass, then rub the stone over the surface in a circular motion (#1).
- Clean off the pane of glass and repeat the procedure with a slurry of finer lapping compound, continuing with a slurry of increasingly finer-grit compound until the stone is flat.

Note: *You can also true a waterstone with wet/dry silicone-carbide paper taped to a flat surface.*

2. Setting up for honing

A combination stone can be used to sharpen the blade of all standard chisels.

- Mount the stone coarse-side up between wood cleats screwed to a flat board.

- Saturate the stone with lubricant: light machine oil for an oilstone; water for a waterstone.
- Hold the chisel so the existing bevel of the blade rests flat against the surface of the stone (#2).

3. Honing the blade

- Raise the chisel 5 degrees (#3) and slide the blade along the stone in long, elliptical passes, using moderate pressure. Lift the blade at the end of each stroke.
- Repeat the procedure until a secondary bevel forms on the forward edge of the existing bevel.

- Turn the stone over so the fine side faces up, lubricate it, and make a few final honing passes the same way.

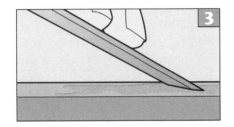

4. Removing the burr

Sharpening the blade creates a ridge of metal, or burr, on the flat side of the cutting edge. Smooth

it away with the benchstone.
- With the fine side of the stone facing up, lay the flat side of the blade flat on the stone and rub it against the surface in a circular motion (#4) until it is smooth.

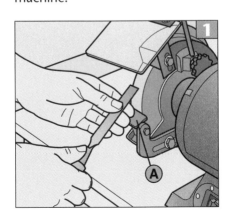

USING A BENCH GRINDER

1. Honing the blade

The key to sharpening a chisel with a bench grinder is to avoid putting too much pressure on the heel or the tip of the bevel.
- Install a grinding wheel on the bench grinder, then adjust the tool rest (A) and turn on the machine.

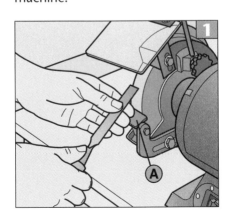

- Holding the blade of the chisel between the fingers and thumb of one hand, rest your hand on the tool rest and place the heel of the bevel against the wheel.
- Draw the blade down the grinding wheel until the tip of the cutting edge touches the wheel (#1).

2. Buffing the chisel

Polish the blade with a buffing wheel and polishing compound to remove the burr on the back of the cutting edge created by honing the bevel.
- Install a buffing wheel on the bench grinder, then turn on the machine and hold a block of polishing compound against the wheel until it is fully coated.

- Hold the flat side of the blade against the wheel (#2), sliding it back and forth until it is smooth.
- Turn the chisel over and polish the bevel the same way.

SAFETY TIP *Wear safety goggles when using a bench grinder.*

SHARPENING A PLANE BLADE

A plane is designed to be a precision instrument, but unless the blade is sharp it will gouge and tear wood instead of shaving it cleanly.

Sharpening a plane blade involves three steps: creating a bevel on the cutting edge; honing a microbevel on the forward edge of the first bevel; and removing the burr, the ridge of metal that results from honing. The first step can be done with a bench grinder or a benchstone; the second and third steps are best done using a benchstone.

Benchstones are divided into two categories according to the lubricant used: oilstones and waterstones. Use light machine oil with an oilstone, water with a waterstone. A combination benchstone, which has one coarse side and one fine side, is your best option.

HOW LONG WILL IT TAKE?
Less than two hours

TOOLS
• Bench grinder • Benchstone • Grinding jig • Angle-setting honing guide • Safety goggles

MATERIALS
• Scrap wood • Wood screws • Light machine oil

1. Creating a bevel

The first step in sharpening the blade is to create a bevel on the cutting edge. This can be done with a bench grinder, as shown here, or using a benchstone.

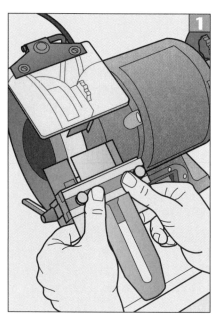

• Secure the blade bevel-side down in a grinding jig with the cutting edge parallel to the front edge of the clamp.
• Adjust the tool rest to make a 30-degree angle, then hold the jig on the tool rest and move it forward until the cutting edge of the blade touches the wheel (#1).
• Applying light pressure, move the blade from side to side across the wheel. Check the cutting edge after every few passes and stop grinding when a bevel is formed.

SAFETY TIP *Wear safety goggles when using a bench grinder.*

2. Setting up for honing

Once a bevel is created on the blade, a secondary bevel—called a microbevel—is honed on the forward edge of it.
• Mount a combination benchstone fine-side up between two wood cleats screwed to a board.
• Soak the benchstone with lubricant: light machine oil for an oilstone; water for a waterstone.
• Clamp the blade in an angle-setting honing guide so the bevel rests flat on the benchstone (#2).

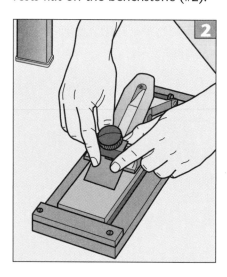

IN THE WORKSHOP

3. Honing the blade

The bevel created on a bench grinder is hollow-ground—that is, slightly concave due to the curved motion of the wheel. If you created the bevel on a benchstone, it will be flat; in this case, raise the angle of the blade about 5 degrees to hone a microbevel.

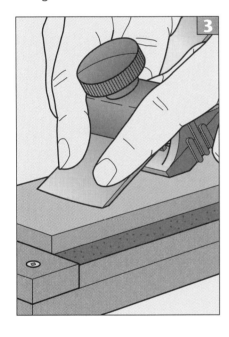

● Applying moderate pressure on the honing guide, slide the blade back and forth from end to end along the benchstone (#3), continuing until a microbevel is formed.

4. Removing the burr

Honing the blade creates a ridge of metal, or burr, on the flat side of the cutting edge that needs to be smoothed.

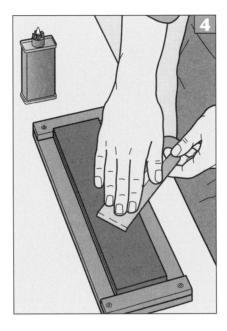

● Soak the fine side of the benchstone with lubricant again.
● Lay the blade bevel-up flat on the benchstone and rub in a circular motion (#4) until it is smooth.

5. Testing for sharpness

● Test the cutting edge for sharpness by pushing the blade into the

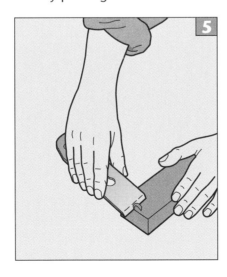

edge of a piece of softwood (#5). A properly sharpened edge will cleanly remove a wood shaving.

6. Honing the cap iron

To properly hold the blade in place, the edge of the plane's cap iron must be perfectly flat. This also keeps wood chips from getting stuck between the cap iron and the blade. If necessary, hone the cap iron.
● Lubricate the fine side of the benchstone again and rub the end of the cap iron in a circular motion over the surface (#6) until it is flat.

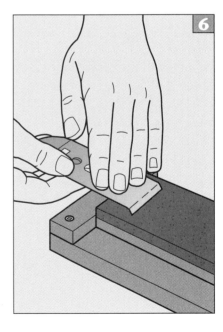

ADJUSTING A HAND PLANE

A hand plane trims and smooths wood prior to sanding, gluing pieces together, or applying a finish. A good-quality plane can be a sizable investment, but it can last a lifetime if it is properly maintained.

If you are shopping for a plane, a 14-inch jack plane is an all-purpose tool for use on board edges and faces. A block plane is a must for use on end grain. You can also get specialty planes—such as a rabbet plane—for joinery work.

You'll have to take apart a plane periodically for sharpening and cleaning. Despite a plane's many parts, disassembly and reassembly isn't too complicated; all you need is a screwdriver.

Note: *To avoid damaging the cutting edge of the blade, rest and store a plane on its side rather than its sole (bottom).*

HOW LONG WILL IT TAKE?

Less than two hours

TOOLS

• Screwdriver • Brass-bristled brush • Rubber gloves

MATERIALS

• Steel wool • Cloth • Mild detergent • Mineral spirits

Anatomy of a hand plane

A handle screws into the toe (front) and the heel (back) of the sole (A). Fastened to the sole with setscrews (B), the frog (C) supports the blade (D), also known as the iron. The blade protrudes bevel-side down from an opening in the sole called the mouth. An adjustment screw slides the frog back and forth on the sole to set the width of the mouth—$\frac{1}{32}$ to $\frac{1}{16}$ inch usually gives best results. The depth-of-cut adjustment knob (E) moves the blade in and out of the mouth—a cutting depth of $\frac{1}{32}$ inch typically is ideal. The lateral adjustment lever (F) angles the blade from side to side in the mouth so it can be centered parallel to the edges. The cap iron (G)

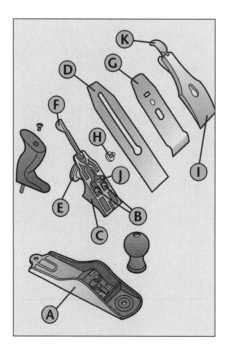

holds the blade in place. The cap iron and the blade are fastened together by the cap-iron screw (H). The lever cap (I) sits on the cap iron and is secured by the

lever-cap screw (J), which threads into the frog. The cap lock (K) holds the cap firmly on the cap iron and blade.

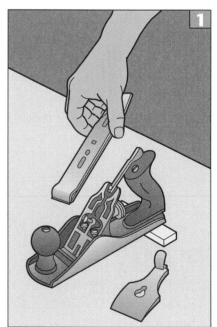

1. Taking off the irons

- Loosen the lever-cap screw and release the cap lock on the lever cap. Slide the lever cap off the plane and set it aside.
- Lift the blade and cap iron off the frog (#1).
- With a screwdriver, loosen the cap-iron screw and separate the cap iron from the blade.

SAFETY TIP *Be careful not to cut yourself on the blade or to knock it against a hard surface and damage it.*

2. Removing the frog and handles

- Turn the two frog setscrews counterclockwise with a screwdriver (#2).
- Lift the frog off the sole of the plane.
- Unscrew the handles at the toe and heel of the sole.

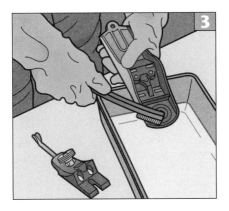

3. Cleaning the parts

A thorough cleaning can make even a well-used plane look like new. With a little extra effort, you can even revitalize an old, rusty tool.

- Rub the parts of the plane with steel wool or a soft cloth dampened with mild detergent.
- Pour a small amount of mineral spirits into a container. Wearing rubber gloves, dip a brass-bristled brush into the mineral spirits and scrub each part individually (#3).
- Wipe the parts dry and, if necessary, sharpen the blade.

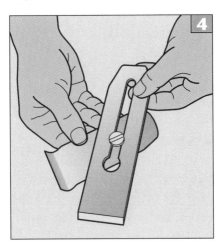

4. Joining the irons

- To reassemble the plane, first thread the cap-iron screw into its hole in the cap iron.
- Slip the head of the cap-iron screw into the hole in the blade so its beveled side faces away from the cap iron.
- Holding the blade steady, rotate the cap iron while sliding the head of the cap-iron screw along the groove of the blade (#4) until the ends of the two irons align.

Note: *Be careful not to scrape or otherwise damage the cutting edge of the blade as you join the irons.*

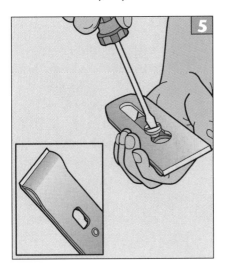

5. Adjusting the irons

- Slide the cap iron back until the end of the blade extends $1/16$ inch beyond it (inset).
- Align the sides of the irons so they are perfectly flush, then tighten the cap-iron screw (#5).

• Set the irons aside, placing them carefully on a wood surface to avoid damaging the blade's cutting edge.

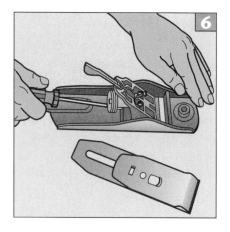

6. Adjusting the mouth

• Turn the frog adjustment screw until it is most of the way in, then set the frog in position on the sole. Tighten the frog setscrews and the lever-cap screw.

• Place the irons in position on the frog so the lever cap screw passes through the irons.

• Check the gap between the cutting edge of the blade and the front edge of the mouth. To plane a softwood such as pine, the gap should be $1/16$ inch. For a hardwood such as oak, the gap should be $1/32$ inch.

• To adjust the gap, remove the irons, loosen the frog setscrews slightly, and loosen or tighten the frog adjustment screw as needed (#6).

• Check the gap again, then tighten the frog setscrews.

7. Installing the irons

• Screw the handles back on and set the plane on your worktable, a wood block under the heel to keep the blade's cutting edge from contacting the surface.

• Position the irons on the frog so the depth adjustment lug (A) is seated in the slot in the cap iron (#7) and the cutting edge of the blade is straight in the mouth.

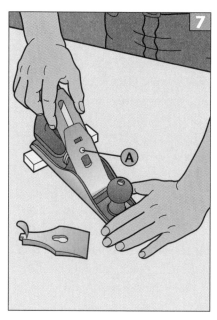

8. Installing the lever cap

• Position the lever cap on the irons so the lever-cap screw passes through the slot in it.

• Depress the locking lever (#8). If it won't close, loosen the lever-cap screw slightly and try again. If the locking lever closes too easily and doesn't apply tension on the irons, tighten the lever-cap screw.

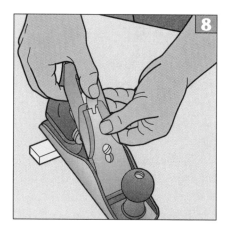

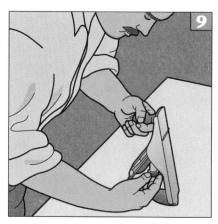

9. Setting the blade depth

• Hold the plane upright on its heel with the sole facing away from you.

• Sighting down the sole at the blade, turn the depth-of-cut adjustment knob so the blade barely protrudes—about $1/32$ inch (#9). Make your last turn of the knob move the blade out rather than in; otherwise, the blade will slip when you next use it.

• Move the lateral adjustment lever from side to side until the cutting edge of the blade is parallel to the mouth edges.

REPLACING A HAMMER HANDLE

The head of a hammer may last forever, but the handle—especially a wooden one—can break or wear out. If your hammer has a well-balanced forged head and a slightly convex face (the best shape for driving nails without marring the surrounding wood surface), it is worthwhile replacing a broken or damaged handle. A wooden hammer handle is easy to remove and good-quality replacements are readily available and simple to install.

The steps that follow show how to replace a wooden hammer handle. A hammer with a damaged fiberglass handle can also be refurbished. Simply cut the old handle flush with the bottom of the head using a hacksaw, then clear out the plug—the part of the handle remaining in the head—with an electric drill. Fasten a replacement fiberglass handle to the head with epoxy glue (usually supplied with the head). Alternatively, you can also use a wooden handle replacement. If you have a damaged one-piece hammer with a metal handle, you're out of luck—you will have to replace the entire tool.

HOW LONG WILL IT TAKE?

Less than two hours

TOOLS

· Hacksaw · Electric drill
· Backsaw (or coping saw or saber saw) · Vise · Cold chisel
· Ball-peen hammer · Wood chisel · Wooden mallet · Metal wedges · Safety goggles

MATERIALS

· Replacement handle (wood or fiberglass) · Wood pads

1. Removing the old handle

Removing a wooden handle is a two-step operation. First, saw off the handle just below the head. Although a coping saw or a saber saw will do the job, a backsaw is easy to control and makes a clean, even cut.

● Secure the head of the hammer face-up in a vise.

● Saw through the handle just below the head (#1).

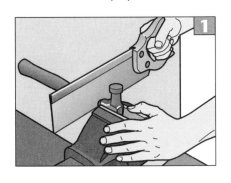

2. Removing the plug

The plug of a wooden handle is held in place with one or more metal wedges. Remove the plug and the wedges together.

● Clamp the hammer head in a vise, the cut end of the handle face-up. Leave a gap between the head and the base of the vise.

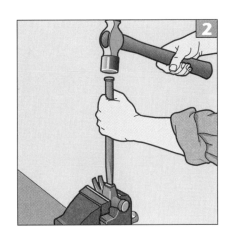

● Holding a cold chisel upright with the tip centered on the plug, tap the handle repeatedly with a ball-peen hammer to drive the plug out of the head (#2).

3. Preparing the new handle

To ensure a tight fit, the top end of a replacement wooden handle is usually made slightly wider than the opening in a hammer head. You will have to trim the top end of the handle to make it fit.

● Hold the top end of the handle against the opening in the bottom of the hammer head to determine approximately how much wood needs to be trimmed.

● Protecting its surface with wood pads, secure the handle in a vise with one side face-up and the top

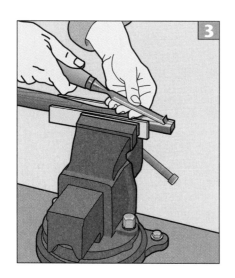

end extending a few inches from the vise jaws.

● Starting about 2 inches from the top of the handle, guide a wood chisel along the surface to shave away waste wood in thin strips (#3). Hold the chisel bevel-side up at an angle to the handle.

● Turn the handle over in the vise and trim the other side by the same amount. Test-fit the handle. Continue trimming both sides of the handle equally—as well as the front and back, if needed—until it fits in the head snugly.

4. Attaching the handle

● Push the handle into the hammer head as far as it will go.
● To seat the handle in the head, grip the handle and hold the hammer upright, then repeatedly rap the bottom end of the handle on a solid work surface (#4). The weight of the head will drive it onto the handle.

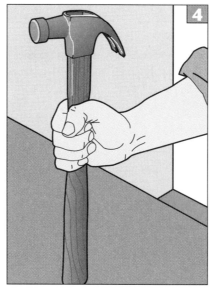

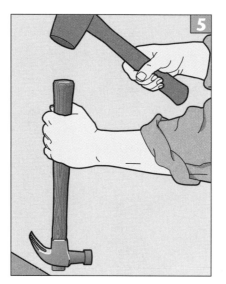

5. Fastening the head

● To seat the handle in the head completely, hold the hammer upside down at waist level and strike the bottom end of the handle with a wooden mallet (#5). The handle will be driven deeper into the head, making the head appear to climb the handle.

● Continue striking until the head stops moving up the handle.
● If the top end of the handle protrudes past the top of the hammer head, secure the hammer in a vise and saw off the protruding bit.

6. Securing the handle

To secure the handle in the hammer head, use two metal wedges to expand the plug (the wood in the head).

● Secure the hammer upright in a vise. With a cold chisel and a ball-peen hammer, cut two parallel $1/16$-inch-deep grooves angled across the top of the handle.
● Holding the hammer upright on your worktable, place a metal wedge in one of the grooves and drive it into the handle with the ball-peen hammer.
● Drive the second wedge in carefully, stopping when it will not go deeper (#6). Forcing the second wedge may split the handle.
● With a hacksaw, trim the wedges flush with the top of the hammer head.

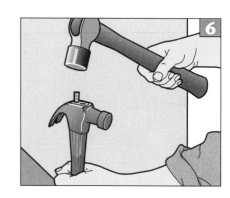

SHARPENING DRILL BITS

To bore holes cleanly and accurately, drill bits must kept sharp. Dull-edged drill bits not only skate off the workpiece instead of cutting into the surface, they also burn the wood and put extra strain on power-drill motors.

You can sharpen most standard drill bits with a small selection of files, a bench grinder, and a rotary grinding attachment for an electric drill. To hold a drill bit steady, clamp it in a bench vise, protecting the base of the bit with wood pads. Sharpening drill bits is delicate work. Take your time and work carefully. If bits are badly damaged, have them serviced professionally.

To keep bits sharp longer, use them at the speed recommended by the manufacturer and feed bits into the workpiece slowly. Wipe them with oil to prevent rust.

TWIST BITS

1. Using a bench grinder

Wear work gloves to sharpen a twist bit with a bench grinder—friction from the grinding wheel will cause the bit to get hot.

• Hold the bit between your thumb and index finger of both hands and rest the tip of the bit against the tool rest (A).

• Angle the bit so that one of the cutting edges is square with the wheel and gently push the bit into the spinning wheel (#1). Rotate the bit clockwise to grind the cutting edge evenly.

• Avoid overheating the bit by working slowly. Stop periodically to check the angle of the cutting edge, as shown in #2.

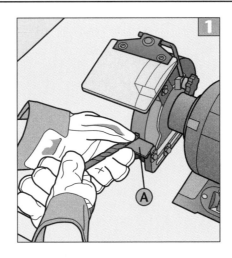

2. Checking the angle of the cutting edges

The cutting edges of a twist bit should be angled at about 60 degrees. To check the angle as you sharpen, use a protractor.

• Butt the cutting edge against the base of the protractor and swivel the arm so it rests against the side of the bit (#2).

• Continue to grind the bit, keeping the angle of the cutting edge at 60 degrees.

• Grind the other cutting edge the same way.

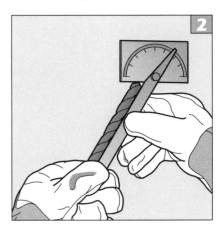

IN THE WORKSHOP

317

SPADE BITS

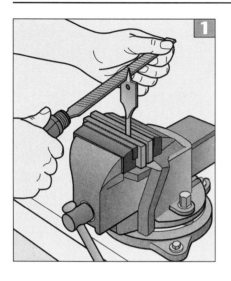

1. Filing the cutting edges

- Use a single-cut mill bastard file to hone a spade bit. File on the push stroke only.
- Hold the file with both hands and file the first cutting edge, angling the tool slightly to match the angle of the cutting edge (#1).
- Repeat the procedure for the other cutting edge.

2. Filing the point

- Sharpen both sides of the point the same way, holding the file at the appropriate angle and filing on the push stroke only (#2).

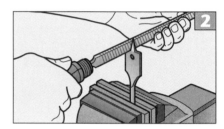

BRAD-POINT BITS

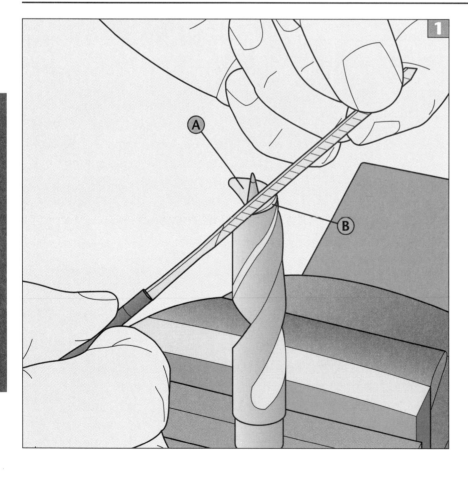

Filing the chip lifters and cutting spurs

Use a triangular needle file to hone a brad-point bit.
- File both chip lifters (A) until they are flat and their edges are sharp.
- Sharpen the edges of the cutting spurs (B) by pushing the file toward the brad point (#1).

REPLACING A TOOL'S POWER CORD

Because tool power cords often undergo a lot of wear and tear, they—along with other working parts—need to be replaced periodically. Constant movement twists the cord, which can eventually crack the jacket—the exterior casing—and damage the interior wires.

Once you have identified the type of cord you need (Step 4), check for a replacement at the service center of the tool's manufacturer before making a purchase from a hardware outlet. Also check the warranty provided by the manufacturer. Any repairs that you make may void the warranty. If this is the case and the warranty is still in force, take your tool to an authorized service center for repair.

SAFETY TIP *Before beginning a repair on a power tool, make sure that it is unplugged.*

HOW LONG WILL IT TAKE?
Less than two hours

TOOLS
• Screwdriver • Utility knife • Wire strippers • Lineman's pliers • Multitester

MATERIALS
• Power cord • Masking tape

1. Accessing the wire terminals

For many power tools, the switch mechanism—which includes the wire terminals—is located in the handle. This is the point of connection between the power cord and the tool.
• Double-check that the tool is unplugged.
• To remove the handle cover, take off the back plate (A), then unscrew the fasteners holding the handle cover in place (#1).
• Lift the handle cover off the tool.

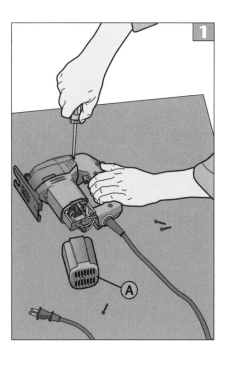

2. Disconnecting the wires

A power cord with a two-prong plug usually has two wires connected to the terminal in the switch. A cord with a three-prong plug will have three wires.
• Before removing the power cord wires from the tool's switch terminal, identify each one with a strip of masking tape. This will help you connect the wires of the new cord to the terminal in the correct order.

IN THE WORKSHOP

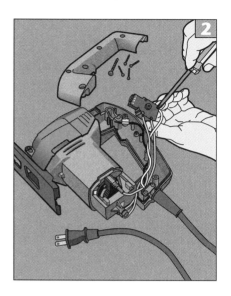

• With a small screwdriver, loosen the terminal screws (#2) and carefully pull the power cord wires out of the terminal. Note the route that the wires follow in the handle. Space in power-tool handles is limited; if the wires are not put back correctly, you may pinch the wires when you replace the handle cover.

3. Removing the old cord

A retaining bracket secures the power cord to the tool housing, preventing the cord from being pulled out from the switch mechanism during use. This bracket must be loosened or removed before the old cord can be taken out.

• Undo the screws holding the retaining bracket in place (#3).

• Remove the power cord, but keep it handy for reference while installing the new cord.

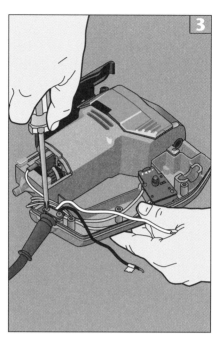

4. Buying a replacement cord

Everything you need to know to buy a new power cord is usually indicated on the nameplate of the tool (#4).

• The model and serial number will be especially helpful if you are buying directly from the tool manufacturer.

• If you are purchasing your cord from a hardware outlet, the voltage and amperage will also help identify the right replacement.

• Depending on the power cord you buy, the wire ends may come ready for connection: stripped and twisted. If not, perform Step 5 and Step 6.

5. Stripping the wires

The jacket—the exterior casing of the cord—usually covers new power cords to the end, and insulation covers each of the wires. In order to connect the wires to the tool switch terminals, a section of each wire must be stripped.

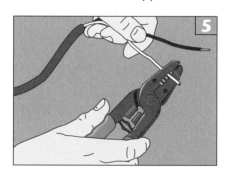

Toolset   JIG SAW
J-60V   DOUBLE INSULATED
120V   AC · 3.5A · 60Hz · 0 ~ 2700 S.P.M
SER NO.   01332 8609
Toolset Limited MADE IN JAPAN
6154 91 847 50
CAUTION: FOR SAFE OPERATION SEE OWNER'S MANUAL
WHEN SERVICING USE ONLY IDENTICAL REPLACEMENT PARTS
UL LISTED 964S

IN THE WORKSHOP

- With a utility knife, make a 6-inch slice along the power-cord jacket, starting from the end of the cord. Be careful not to cut into the individual wires. Peel back the split jacket and, with the knife, trim off the split length of jacket.
- With the wires exposed, use wire strippers to trim away $\frac{1}{2}$ inch of insulation from the end of each wire. Wire strippers are equipped with notches for a variety of gauges, or thicknesses, of wire. Find the one that fits snugly around the wire and squeeze the handle to sever the insulation (#5). Holding the strippers closed, pull the insulation off the wire.

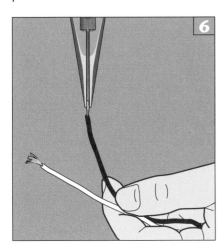

6. Twisting the wires

In order to make a good connection at the terminal screws, the bare wire strands must be twisted together.
- Grasp the wire ends with lineman's pliers and carefully twist them tightly together in a clockwise direction (#6).

- If the wire ends need to be wrapped around terminal screws, grasp each twisted wire end in turn with the pliers, and rotate the pliers clockwise to form the strand into a semicircular hook. (For the tool shown, the wire ends are pushed into slots in the terminal and secured with screws.)

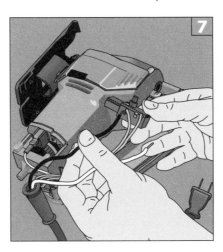

7. Installing the replacement cord

- If necessary, check the old cord and the wires you labeled to help you determine the correct connections. Pass each wire end into the appropriate hole in the terminal (#7) or wrap it around its terminal screw. Tighten the screws.
- Lay the power cord on the tool housing so the section stripped of the exterior jacket is completely inside the body of the tool.
- Reposition the retaining bracket and fasten it to the tool body to secure the power cord to the tool.
- Attach the handle cover and the back plate to the tool.

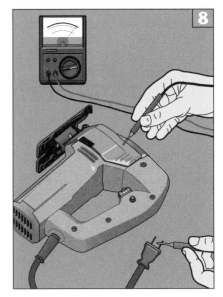

8. Checking for continuity

A bad connection can pass electrical current into the metal housing of the tool—a dangerous electrical hazard. A multitester, an electrical diagnostic tool used to measure resistance and current in electrical circuits, can determine if a circuit is complete.
- Set the multitester selector to RX1. Touch one tester probe to one of the plug prongs and the other to a metal section of the tool housing. The multitester needle should not move. Repeat the test with the other plug prong as well as on other metal sections of the tool housing (#8).
- If the multitester needle moves (that is, registers current) during any test, disassemble the tool and check your switch connections. If the problem persists, take the tool in for professional servicing.

REPLACING A TOOL'S PLUG

Signs that the plug of a power tool needs to be replaced are usually clear-cut. A plug with bent, loose, or otherwise damaged prongs—often due to the plug being pulled from an outlet by the power cord instead of by the plug casing—should be replaced immediately. Plugs that are warm to the touch after a tool is operated, which indicates a voltage leak, should also be replaced.

When buying a replacement plug for a power tool, get a round-cord model. Depending on the original plug supplied with the tool, you will need either a two-prong plug (without ground) or a three-prong plug (with ground). To be sure that the plug you purchase is compatible with the tool, bring the old plug or the make, model number, voltage, and amperage of the tool with you to your supplier.

SAFETY TIP *Before beginning a repair on a power tool, make sure that it is unplugged.*

HOW LONG WILL IT TAKE?
Less than two hours

TOOLS
• Wire strippers • Flat-head screwdriver • Utility knife   • Lineman's pliers

MATERIALS
• Plug

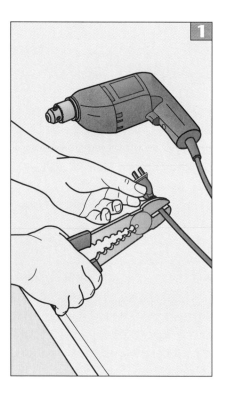

1. Cutting off the old plug

- Unplug the tool.
- With wire strippers, cut through the power cord just below the plug (#1).

2. Preparing the replacement plug

To feed the power cord into the replacement plug, you need to remove the cord clamp (A) and the plug faceplate (B).
- Remove the screws securing the cord clamp to the plug, then take off the clamp and set it aside.

- Unscrew the plug faceplate (#2) and set it aside.
- Pass the end of the power cord through the plug body.

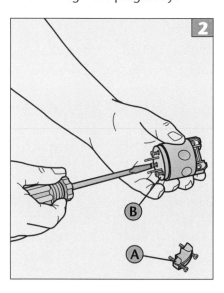

3. Stripping back the cable

To prepare the power cord for connection to the new plug, you need to remove a couple of inches of the insulating sheathing to expose the individual wires inside.

● With a utility knife, carefully make a 2-inch slice up the cable, starting from the cut end of the power cord. Don't nick the individual wires.

● Peel back the split cable and separate the wires from the sheathing (#3).

● With the utility knife, carefully trim off the split length of cable and sheathing.

4. Twisting the wire strands

In order to make a sound connection between the wires of the power cord and the screw terminals of the replacement plug, twist the wire strands together.

● Strip the wires (see page 320), then, holding one wire by its insulation, grasp the strands with lineman's pliers and twist them together clockwise (#4).

● Repeat the procedure for the other wire.

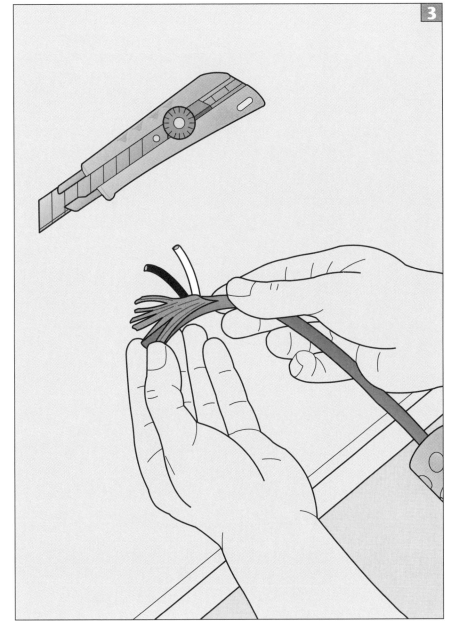

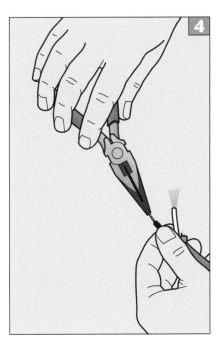

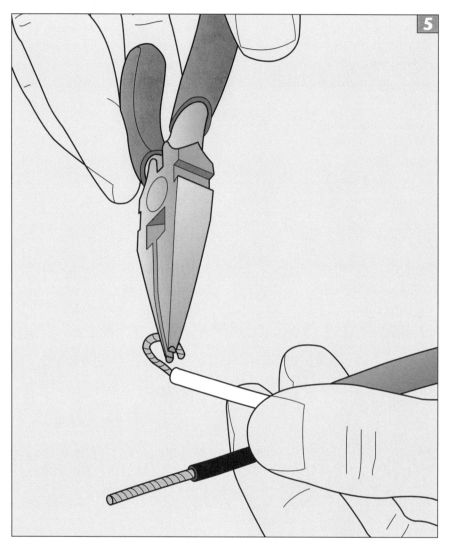

IN THE WORKSHOP

6. Connecting the replacement plug

Check the tool's nameplate for the polarized symbol: a square within a square. If the tool is polarized, connect the white insulated wire to the screw terminal of the plug's wide prong and the black insulated wire to the screw terminal of the plug's narrow prong. If the tool is not polarized, connect the black wire to the brass terminal screw and the white wire to the silver terminal screw.

● Loosen the terminal screws on the plug faceplate with a screwdriver, then wrap the wire hooks clockwise around the shaft of the screws. Tighten each screw terminal until the wires are secure (#6).

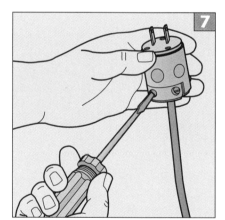

5. Shaping the wires into a hook

To connect the wires of the power cord securely to the terminal screws of the plug, the wire ends need to be shaped into a hook.

● Grasping the twisted strands of one wire with pliers, bend them clockwise into a semicircular hook (#5).

● Repeat the procedure for the other wire end.

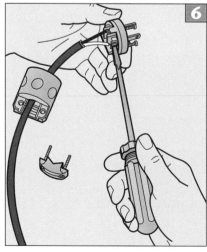

7. Assembling the plug

● To complete the assembly, screw the plug faceplate to the plug body.

● Fasten the cord clamp to the plug body (#7).

REPLACING A TOOL SWITCH

Switches undergo a lot of wear and tear and must be replaced periodically. If you have a power tool that won't function, the switch may be the problem. But before you rush to replace it, check that the cause is not something more basic, such as a blown fuse or frayed power cord.

Replacing a switch is a simple procedure. While the instructions below show a variable-speed switch—the switch most often found in power tools—the steps are the same for all switches.

When shopping for a new switch, check with the service center of the tool's manufacturer before making a purchase from a hardware outlet. Also check the warranty provided by the manufacturer. Any repairs you make may void the warranty. If this is the case and the warranty is still in force, take your tool to an authorized service center for repair.

SAFETY TIP *Before beginning a repair on a power tool, make sure that it is unplugged and that all blades or bits have been removed.*

HOW LONG WILL IT TAKE?
Less than two hours

TOOLS
• Screwdriver • Lineman's pliers • Multitester

MATERIALS
• Switch • Masking tape

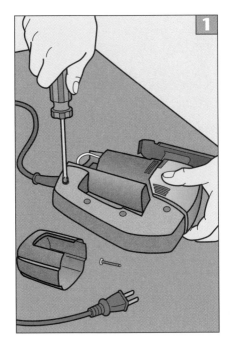

1. Opening the tool housing

Tool designs vary, but in most cases you can gain access to the switch by removing the housing.
• Unplug the tool.
• Unscrew the retaining screws on the housing with the appropriate screwdriver (#1).

2. Exposing the switch mechanism

• Lift off the housing to expose the internal components.
• Carefully lift the switch from the housing (#2).

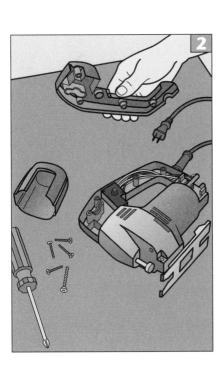

IN THE WORKSHOP

325

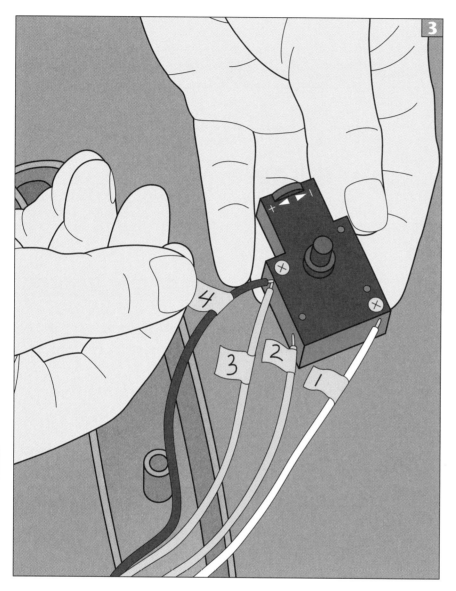

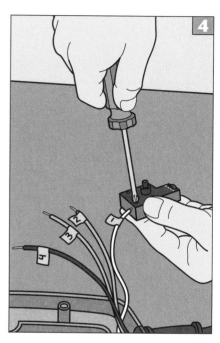

5. Buying a replacement switch

• Check the nameplate on the tool and note the information you need to order a replacement switch. This includes the tool's make, model, and serial number as well as voltage and amperage specifications (#5).

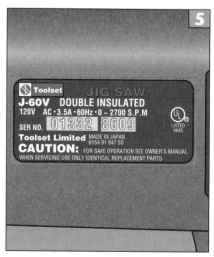

3. Labeling the wires

• Label the wires running from the switch and their corresponding terminal screws with small pieces of masking tape (#3). The labels act as references when connecting the new switch.

4. Disconnecting the switch

• Remove the wires from the terminals by loosening the terminal screws with a screwdriver (#4) or depressing the release buttons with the end of a paper clip. In some cases, you may need to remove wire caps and untwist the wires with lineman's pliers.

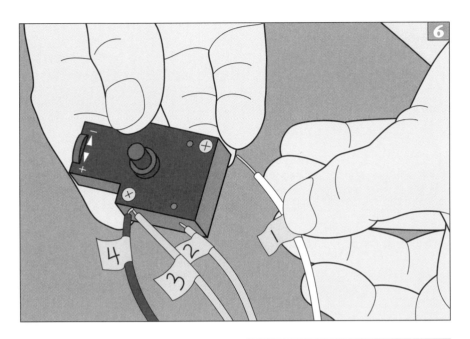

6. Connecting the new switch

- Connect the wires to their terminals on the new switch (#6), using the labels on the wires and on the old switch as references.
- Fit the switch carefully back into the housing.
- Replace the housing and tighten the retaining screws.

7. Adjusting a multitester

A bad connection can pass electrical current into the metal housing of the tool—a dangerous electrical hazard. A multitester, an electrical diagnostic tool used to measure resistance and current in electrical circuits, can determine if a circuit is complete. To ensure an accurate reading, it is a good idea to test the tester itself first.

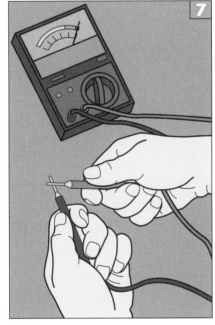

- Set the multitester to RX1000 (or RX1K) and touch the probes together (#7). The needle should sweep across the dial stopping near zero "0". Turn the ohms-adjust dial until the needle is directly over "0".

8. Checking for continuity

- Set the multitester selector to RX1000. Touch one tester probe to one of the plug prongs and the other to a metal section of the tool housing. The multitester needle should not move. Repeat the test with the other plug prong as well as on other metal sections of the tool housing (#8). Only the third prong on a three-pronged plug should trigger movement.
- If the multitester needle moves (that is, registers current) during any test, disassemble the tool and check your switch connections. If the problem persists, take the tool in for professional servicing.

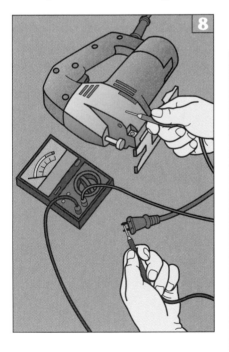

FINE-TUNING A RADIAL ARM SAW

The great appeal of the radial arm saw is the way it can cut at so many angles from so many directions. To make sure that the saw works safely and accurately, fine-tune it often. In addition to cleaning and oiling the tracks and the ball bearings along the arm, check the carriage roller bearings, the column tension, and the clamps, making adjustments as necessary. Finally, check that the blade is properly aligned.

Before you make any tests or adjustments, unplug the saw; except if checking blade alignment, also remove the blade.

HOW LONG WILL IT TAKE?	TOOLS	MATERIALS
Less than two hours	• Socket wrench • Screwdriver • Wrench • Clamp • Work gloves	• Cloth • Ammonia • Light machine oil • Scrap dowel • Scrap wood block

MAINTAINING SLIDING MECHANISMS

1. Cleaning tracks and ball bearings

• Dampen a cloth in a solution of ammonia and water.
• Push the yoke to one end of the

arm and clean the tracks and the ball bearings with the cloth (#1). Move the yoke back and wipe the tracks and the ball bearings at the other end of the arm.
• Apply a thin coat of light machine oil to the tracks and the ball bearings, then wipe away the excess.

2. Adjusting carriage roller bearings

To adjust roller bearings, use a socket wrench with a ratchet extension long enough to access the bearing nuts from above.
• Remove the cover plate from the arm.
• Check bearing tension by pressing your thumb against each bearing, one after the other, and sliding the yoke away from you. The bearings should turn easily.

• If your thumb keeps a bearing from moving, tighten the corresponding bearing nut (#2).
• If the yoke binds on the arm, loosen the bearing nut.

IN THE WORKSHOP

3. Checking column-to-base tension

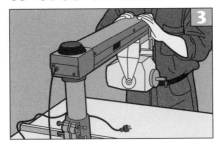

Adjust column tension with the four setscrews or bolts on the base of the column—some saw models have both bolts and setscrews. It may takes several tries to make the right adjustments.

- Hold the end of the arm with both hands and try to push it upward (#3). There should be little or no give to the column.

- Rotate the depth-adjustment handle in both directions. The arm should move up and down smoothly.
- If the column moves or the arm jerks or vibrates as it is raised or lowered, adjust the bolts or the setscrews (or both) on the column base.

ADJUSTING CLAMPS

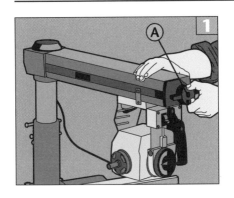

1. Adjusting the miter clamp

- Loosen the miter-clamp lock, swivel the arm to roughly a 30-degree angle, and lock the arm in place (#1).
- Try to push the arm toward the 0-degree position.
- If the arm moves, tighten the miter-clamp adjustment screw (A).

2. Adjusting the yoke clamp

- Rotate the yolk halfway between the positions used for ripping and crosscutting, then clamp it in place.
- Try to push the motor into the crosscutting position.
- If the yolk moves, tighten the yolk-clamp adjustment nut (#2).

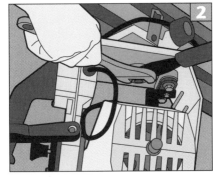

3. Adjusting the bevel clamp

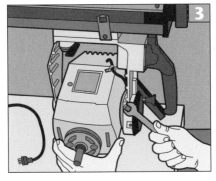

- Tilt the motor to roughly a 30-degree angle and lock the bevel clamp in place.
- Try to push the motor up and down. If the motor moves, tighten the bevel-clamp adjustment nut with a wrench (#3).

4. Adjusting the rip clamp

- Lock the rip clamp (#4) and try to push the yoke along the arm. If it moves, release the clamp and tighten the rip-clamp bolt. Check that the yoke continues to run smoothly along the arm.

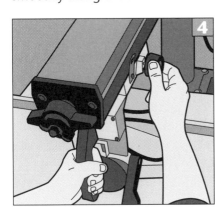

ADJUSTING BLADE ALIGNMENT

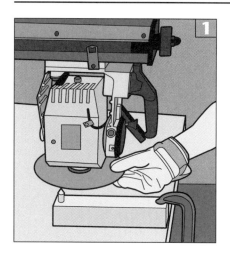

1. Checking horizontal alignment

A blade that is out of alignment will cause the saw to cut poorly. To check blade alignment, make a sounding jig by sharpening a short piece of dowel to a point and inserting it into a hole of the same diameter in a block of wood.

- Double-check that the saw is unplugged.
- Push the yoke to one end of the arm, set the blade parallel to the table, and lock the blade in place.
- With the sounding jig on the table, lower the blade and position the jig so the tip of the dowel touches a saw tooth. Clamp the jig in place.
- Wearing work gloves, rotate the blade backward and listen to the sound of the dowel against it (#1).
- Push the yoke to the other end of the arm and repeat the test. The sound should be the same at both ends.

- If the sounds differ, adjust the blade according to the manufacturer's instructions and repeat the test.

2. Checking vertical alignment

- Double-check that the saw is unplugged.
- With the yolk at one end of the arm, set the blade perpendicular to the table and lock the bevel clamp.

- Turn the sounding jig on its side and lower the blade until a saw tooth touches the tip of the dowel. Clamp the jig in place.
- Wearing work gloves, spin the blade backward and listen to the sound of the dowel against it (#2).
- Push the yoke to the other end of the arm and test. The sound should be the same at both ends.
- If the sounds differ, adjust the blade according to the manufacturer's instructions and repeat the test.

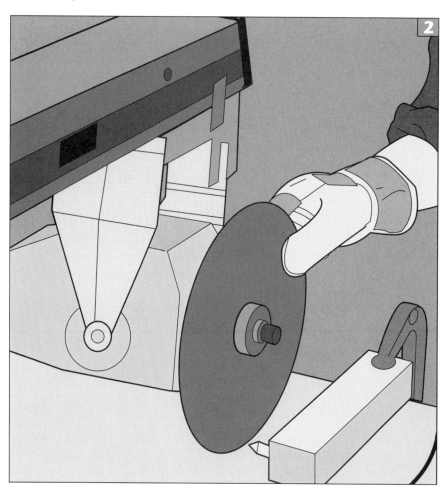

SETTING UP A JOINTER

The jointer is a relatively basic machine tool, but like other cutting tools, it must be carefully checked and adjusted to ensure accurate work. Set the outfeed table to the same height as the knife edges at their highest point and align the height of the outfeed and infeed tables. Setting the table heights correctly may take several adjustments and careful fine-tuning. Adjust the height of the blades by turning the jack screws with a hex wrench.

SAFETY TIP *Make sure that the jointer is unplugged before you conduct any checks or make any adjustments.*

HOW LONG WILL IT TAKE?
Less than two hours

TOOLS
• Clamp • Hex wrench • Wrench • Straightedge • Flat-head screwdriver • Work gloves

MATERIALS
• Wooden wedge • Scrap hardwood board

SETTING OUTFEED TABLE AND KNIFE HEIGHT

1. Checking table height

Accurate work with a jointer depends on perfect alignment between the outfeed table and the top edge of the knives.

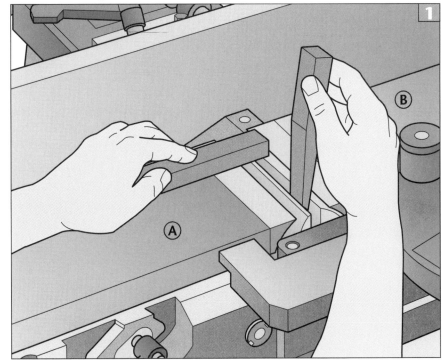

• Push the cutting guard out of the way, clamping it in place if necessary.

• Insert a small wooden wedge between the knives and rotate the cutterhead until one knife is at its highest point.

• Lay a straight hardwood board on the outfeed table (A) so that it extends across the cutterhead, but doesn't touch the infeed table (B). The knife should lightly touch the block.

• Repeat the test along the length of the blade and for the other knives (#1).

• Adjust the height of the knife if it is too high; if it is too low, adjust the height of the table.

SETTING OUTFEED TABLE AND KNIFE HEIGHT (CONTINUED)

2. Adjusting outfeed table height

- Holding the board in place, adjust the outfeed table height (#2) until the edge of the knife just touches the block, then lock the handle in place.
- Check the height of the table in relation to the other knives and make adjustments as necessary.

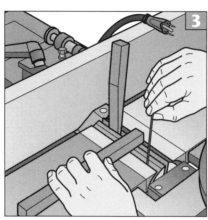

3. Adjusting knife height

- With the wedge holding the edge of the knife at its highest point, adjust the height of the blade by turning the jack screws with a hex wrench (#3).
- When the full length of the blade lightly touches the board, tighten the retaining screws.
- Check and adjust the other knives the same way.

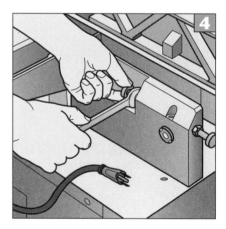

4. Adjusting positive stops

Adjust the positive stops if the outfeed table is still not level with the knives.

- Loosen the lock nuts that hold the stops in position (#4) and pull back the two positive stops.
- Adjust the height of the outfeed table until it aligns with the knife.
- Tighten the table lock, screw the stops back in as far as possible, and retighten the lock nuts.

CIRCULAR SAW ADJUSTMENTS

There's a good chance that you will need to make each of the following adjustments whenever you are getting ready to use your circular saw. Although most saws come with a combination blade—an all-purpose blade that makes both crosscuts and rip cuts—it's a good idea to install a specialty blade for the job at hand, especially when precision cutting is a must. In addition to crosscut and rip blades, you can get plywood blades for sawing plywood and veneered panels, melamine blades for cutting particleboard and other manufactured panels, and hollow-ground planer blades for fine cabinet work.

Store circular saw blades in a dry location and clean them after use. When changing blades, use only the wrench supplied with the saw, and never overtighten nuts, bolts, or adjustment knobs.

SAFETY TIP *Always unplug a circular saw before performing any adjustments on it.*

HOW LONG WILL IT TAKE?
Less than two hours

TOOLS
• Try square • Tape measure
• T-bevel • Protractor • Clamp
• Work gloves

MATERIALS
• Cloth • Light machine oil
• Masking tape

SQUARING THE BLADE

Aligning the blade with the baseplate

Cuts done with a circular saw will only be perfectly straight if the blade is perpendicular to the saw's baseplate. Check whether the blade and the baseplate are square to each other every time you change blades.

• With the saw unplugged, hold it upside down on a worktable and set the blade at its maximum cutting depth.

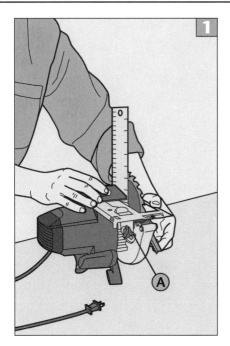

• Retract the lower blade guard, then hold a try square against the baseplate and the saw blade between two teeth (#1).
• If there is a gap between the square and the saw blade, adjust the angle of the baseplate by turning the bevel adjustment knob (A) until the blade is flush against the square.

SETTING THE CUTTING DEPTH

Pivot-foot saw

When it comes to adjusting the blade's cutting depth, there are basically two types of circular saws: pivot-foot and drop-foot models. On a pivot-foot saw, blade depth is adjusted with a depth lever that enables the body and the blade to pivot on the front of the baseplate. As a result, the angle of the handle changes in relation to the baseplate as cutting depth changes.

● Making sure that the saw is unplugged, pull back the lower blade guard, then set the baseplate on the workpiece to be cut. Hold the blade flush against the edge of the piece.

● Release the depth lever, located between the handle and the blade housing on the model shown, then pivot the saw body until the blade reaches the required depth (#1). Tighten the lever. For a cut through a workpiece, set the blade so the bottommost tooth is ¼ inch below the bottom face of the board.

Drop-foot saw

Drop-foot saws have a depth adjustment knob that enables the body and the blade to be raised and lowered straight up or down in relation to the baseplate. As a result, the handle is always at the same angle, whatever the cutting depth.

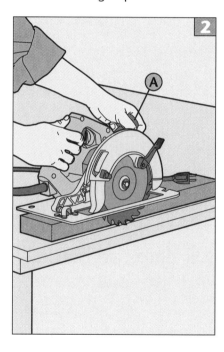

● Place the saw on the workpiece to be cut as you would a pivot-foot model, then loosen the depth adjustment knob (A), located at the front of the saw on the model shown (#2).

● Holding the baseplate steady on the workpiece, lower or raise the body and blade to the required depth.

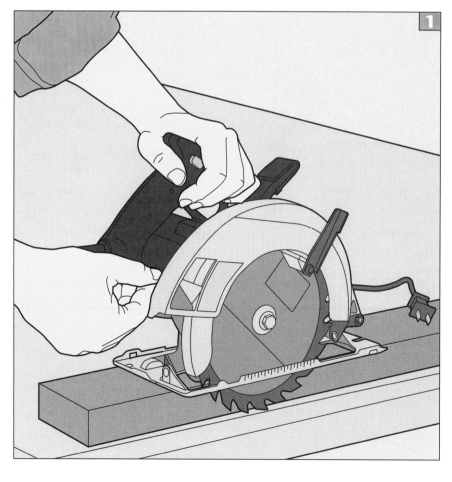

ADJUSTING THE BLADE ANGLE

1. Pivoting the baseplate

You can make bevel cuts by tilting the baseplate.

- Making sure that the saw is unplugged, set the saw on its side on a worktable so you can access the bevel adjustment knob (A).
- Loosen the knob, then pivot the baseplate until it is aligned with the desired cutting angle as indicated on the bevel scale (#1). Tighten the adjustment knob.
- If you are making a precision cut, check the angle, as shown in #2.

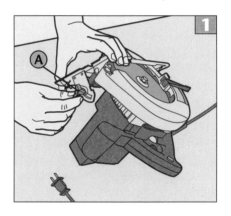

2. Checking the angle

- Adjust a T-bevel to the desired cutting angle using a protractor.
- Set the saw upside down on a worktable and retract the lower blade guard.
- Hold the T-bevel on the saw so the handle is flat against the baseplate and the blade is flush against the saw blade between two teeth. If there are any gaps between the T-bevel and the saw blade, loosen the bevel adjustment knob and tilt the baseplate until the T-bevel is flush against saw blade (#2). Tighten the adjustment knob.

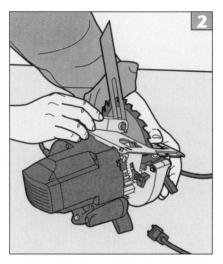

MARKING THE BLADE'S CUTTING PATH ON THE BASEPLATE

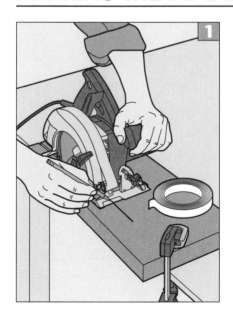

Making a reference mark

When you are setting up to make a circular saw cut, it isn't always easy to accurately line up the front of the baseplate with the cutting mark on the workpiece. And although some saws have a mark on the baseplate that is supposed to align with the cutting path of the blade, the marks aren't always accurate. Make your own reference mark on the baseplate and you'll never have to worry about cuts that are off-line again.

- Cut partway through a scrap board.
- Unplug the saw, then back it up an inch or two, leaving the baseplate flat on the board.
- Apply a strip of masking tape on the baseplate and make a mark on the tape in line with the kerf (#1). Next time you use the saw, line up your mark with the cutting line on the workpiece.

USING HAND TOOLS

Most home-repair and renovation projects involve the use of hand tools. Whether you are marking a straight cutting line across a board, driving a nail, or tightening a bolt, the success of your projects will depend on using these tools correctly.

"Measure twice and cut once" is a common saying among people who make a living working with tools. Many projects begin with a single mark or line made by a tape measure, a square,

or a level. Taking the time to measure and mark accurately will help you get a project off on the right foot, and save you the grief and expense of having to do things twice.

Hammers are the most basic of tools and they are versatile performers in everything from rough carpentry to fine cabinetmaking. Using hammers properly will enhance your projects and help you avoid problems such as dented surfaces, bent nails, and aching thumbs.

MEASURING AND MARKING TOOLS

Using a carpenter's square

Use a carpenter's square to determine if the ends and edges of a board are at 90 degrees to each other. Use the square with a pencil to mark a cutting line that is 90 degrees from an edge. This ensures that a piece will be cut straight. You can also use the square as a ruler or a straightedge.

● To cut a board to length, use a tape measure and a pencil to make a cutting mark, measuring from one end.

● Place the long arm of the square along the edge of the board and the short arm flat across the surface so its outer edge lines up with your cutting mark.

● Holding the square steady, run a sharp pencil along the outer edge of the square's short arm to extend your mark across the surface of the board (#1).

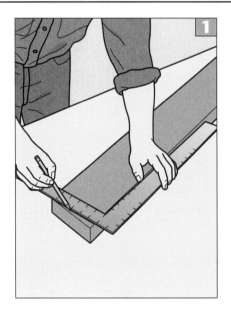

Using a combination square

A combination square has many uses, the most practical being to check and mark 45- and 90-degree angles. This is because one side of the handle is at 90 degrees to the blade and the other is at 45 degrees. The vial bubble in the handle indicates

whether the surface you are holding the handle against is level. As shown in #2, a combination square can also be used to mark a line parallel to an edge.

● Loosen the lock nut on the handle and slide it along the blade so the 90-degree side of the handle indicates the desired measurement. Tighten the lock nut.

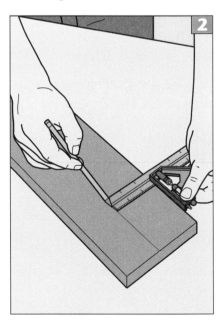

• Set the 90-degree side of the handle flush against the edge of the board. With a pencil against the end of the blade, slide the handle along the edge and pull the pencil with the blade to mark the line (#2). Pointing the handle opposite the direction of travel, as shown, will eliminate binding and chatter while you mark a line.

Using a carpenter's level

A carpenter's level is used to make perfectly horizontal or vertical lines or to check if a surface is perfectly vertical or horizontal.

• To draw a perfectly horizontal (or level) line on a wall, place the carpenter's level flat against the wall. Swivel the ends up or down until the bubble in the horizontally oriented vial is centered between the parallel lines.

• Run a sharp pencil along the top edge of the level to mark the line (#3).

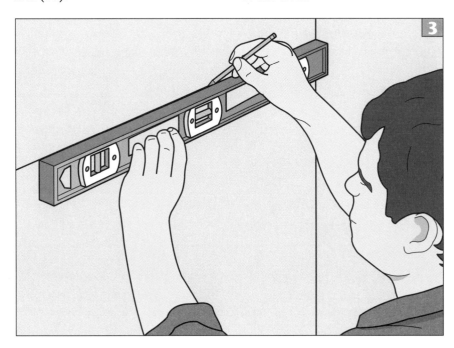

• Mark a perfectly vertical (or plumb) line the same way, except that you should refer to the bubble in the vertically oriented vial of the level.

FASTENING TOOLS

Driving nails

Hammers are used to drive nails in two different types of work: rough carpentry (such as joining a wall stud to a sole plate) and finish carpentry or cabinetmaking (such as attaching baseboard to a wall or assembling furniture). In rough carpentry, nailing speed is more important than appearance. In finish work, it's the other way around. In either case, protect your eyes by wearing safety goggles whenever you are nailing.

In finish work, it is important to avoid damaging the surface of the wood with stray hammer blows. One cabinetmaker's trick involves using a piece of perforated hardboard.

• Place the hardboard on the wood, set the nail in one of the holes, and hold the nail upright with your fingers.

• Lightly tap the nail head until the nail stands on its own, then remove your fingers.

• Continue driving the nail (#1) until the hammer hits the hardboard. Remove the hardboard and complete the job with a nail set.

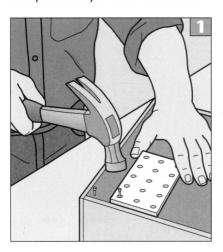

HANDSAWING LIKE A PRO: CROSSCUTTING, RIPPING, AND MITERING

Sawing technique is determined by the type of cut you are making. Crosscuts are done across a board against the wood grain. Rip cuts are made along the length of a board parallel to the wood grain. Miters are cuts at angles—most often 45 or 60 degrees—and usually require a miter box. A typical miter box includes an adjustable backsaw assembly, a pointer indicating the cutting angle, and a support for the workpiece. A miter box is also handy for making perfect 90-degree-angle cuts.

Your ability to make straight, clean cuts with a handsaw depends largely on the condition of the saw and on your work setup. Always use the right tool for the job: a crosscut saw or a backsaw for crosscutting; a ripsaw for ripping; a backsaw with a miter box for miter cuts. Whatever saw you are using, be sure the teeth are sharp. For best results as well as for safety, clamp your workpiece securely to a stable surface—a workbench or sawhorses—and keep your free hand away from the cutting action.

SAFETY TIP *Protect your eyes with safety goggles while cutting. Wear a dust mask to keep from inhaling sawdust particles.*

CROSSCUTTING

1. Marking the cut

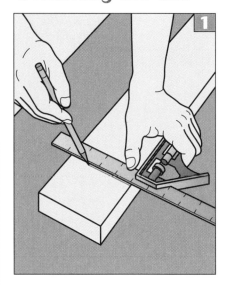

You can mark a rough crosscut with a pencil, but for fine carpentry, score a cutting line with a utility knife—a scored line will help prevent splintering of the wood as you saw.

• Measuring from one end of the board with a tape measure, make a cutting mark on one edge of the board.
• Line up the blade of a combination square with the mark, holding the handle firmly against the edge of the board.
• Keeping the square steady, run the pencil (or utility knife) along the edge of the blade to extend your mark across the surface of the board (#1).
• Extend the line onto the edge of the board the same way.

2. Starting the cut

• Place the board on a worktable, the cutting line overhanging the edge by a few inches. Clamp the board securely.
• Stand in a comfortable position

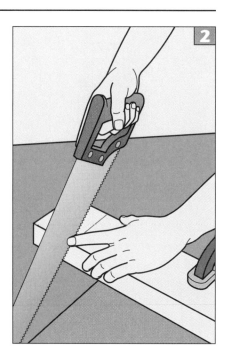

behind the workpiece, holding the saw so the blade is in line with your arm and shoulder and perpendicular to the surface of the board.

- Set the blade just to the waste side of the cutting line at a 20-degree angle to the board.
- Brace the index finger of your free hand against the blade to hold it steady and straight and grip the handle so your other index finger is extended as a guide (#2).
- To start the cut, press lightly on the handle and draw the blade back slowly about half its length. Lift the blade clear of the wood and return it to the start position.
- Keeping the blade aligned with the cutting line and perpendicular to the workpiece, make several strokes the same way until the cut, or kerf, is about $\frac{1}{8}$ inch deep.

3. Continuing the cut

Holding the saw so the blade is at a 90-degree angle to the workpiece provides the quickest cut, but can result in rough, splintered edges.
- After a few upstrokes to establish the kerf, hold the saw so the blade is at about a 45-degree angle to the board (#3). (The handle on some handsaws has angled edges that serve as a guide for keeping the blade at the correct angle.)
- Gradually lengthen your cutting stroke as you saw through the board. Grip the handle firmly and apply uniform back-and-forth pressure on the blade, cutting through the wood on downstrokes.

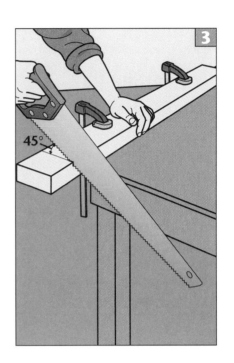

RIPPING

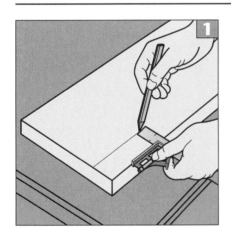

1. Marking the cut

- Adjust a combination square so the blade extends from the handle by the desired width of cut.
- Set the handle flush against the edge of the board.

- Holding a pencil against the end of the blade, slide the handle along the edge of the board and pull the pencil with the blade to mark a cutting line (#1).

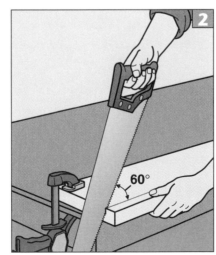

2. Starting the cut

- Place the board on a worktable with the cutting line overhanging the table's edge. Clamp the board in place securely.
- Set the blade just to the waste side of the cutting line at a 20-degree angle to the board.
- Keeping the blade aligned with the cutting line and perpendicular to the workpiece, make several upstrokes to cut a kerf about $\frac{1}{8}$ inch deep.
- Once the kerf is established, gradually raise the handle as you continue sawing until the blade is at about a 60-degree angle to the board (#2).

RIPPING (CONTINUED)

3. Continuing the cut

Ripsaws have fewer teeth per inch (TPI) of blade length than crosscut saws and backsaws, resulting in less cutting resistance. And since rip cuts are made along the wood grain, the blade of the saw can be kept at a higher angle to the board to speed cutting.

● With the angle of the blade at an angle of 45 to 60 degrees to the workpiece, continuing ripping

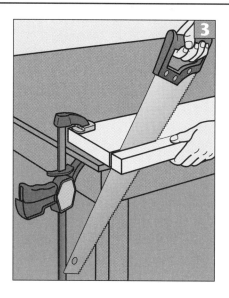

(#3). Make slow, steady up-and-down strokes, cutting with all but 1 inch of blade at the handle and 3 inches at the other end.

● Hold the cutoff with your free hand to keep it from sagging. If you are ripping a long board, clamp the cutoff in place a foot or so into the cut; fit a nail into the kerf so the blade doesn't bind.

● Complete the rip cut with short up-and-down strokes, holding the saw so the blade is almost perpendicular to the workpiece.

MITERING

1. Setting up the workpiece

Before beginning, make sure the miter box is secure. Most miter boxes have a base that can be screwed or clamped to the work surface. If your miter box is different from the one shown here, refer to the manufacturer's directions for setup procedures.

● Make a cutting mark at the edge of the board's surface.

● Raise the backsaw off the base of the miter box and position the board so its edge rests against the fence and your cutting mark aligns with the blade guide.

● Unlock the backsaw assembly and swivel it to the desired angle indicated on the pointer, then lock the assembly (#1).

2. Making the miter cut

● Hold the workpiece steady with your free hand—if the piece is long, clamp it in place—and lower the backsaw onto it.

● Applying gentle downward pressure on the handle, start the cut by drawing the blade slowly back toward you.

● Continue the cut with slow forward and backward strokes, keeping the blade almost horizontal to the board (#2).

● Keep sawing until you cut through the board.

WOOD CHISEL CUTS

Wood chisels warrant a prominent place in your workshop. A chisel is the tool of choice for cutting notches and shallow recesses—such as door-hinge mortises—in wood. It can also make quick work of paring, or smoothing, rough cuts made by other tools. A chisel's sharp edges ensure that cuts will be clean and precise.

Wood chisels come in a range of styles and sizes. Specialty chisels are available for carving or fine cabinetmaking, but you can tackle most jobs with a set of firmer chisels and a set of paring chisels. Firmer chisels are typically intended to be struck with a mallet to remove large amounts of waste. Paring chisels are used with only hand pressure for finer work. Both types come in a variety of widths—typically $\frac{1}{8}$ inch to 2 inches. When using a firmer chisel, choose one with a blade equal in width to the cut you wish to make. For paring operations, use a chisel with a blade that is slightly narrower than the cut.

SAFETY TIP *Always wear safety goggles to protect your eyes when you are using a chisel.*

CUTTING NOTCHES

1. Splitting out the waste

For this job, use a firmer chisel with a blade as wide as the thickness of the board.
● Outline the notch on the board with a pencil, then clamp the board to a worktable with the outline face-up.
● Cut a kerf into the top edge of the board with a backsaw to define the end of the notch. Stop cutting when the blade reaches the bottom of the outline. (This cut will permit the chisel to split the waste without splintering the wood.)
● Holding the chisel horizontally with the blade's beveled side face-up, position the tip of the blade against the end of the board about $\frac{1}{8}$ inch below the top edge.

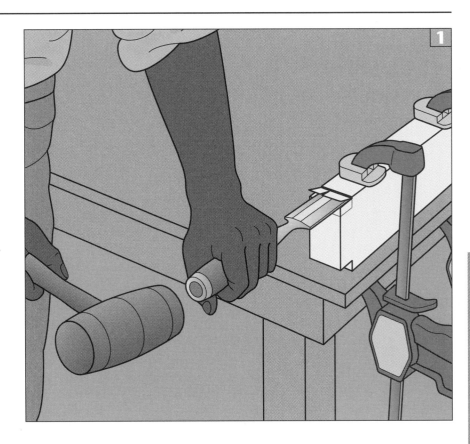

● Strike the handle of the chisel repeatedly with a wooden mallet until the blade reaches the saw cut (#1).

● Continue shearing off waste in $\frac{1}{8}$-inch layers until there is about $\frac{1}{8}$ inch remaining to be removed at the bottom of the notch.

CUTTING NOTCHES (CONTINUED)

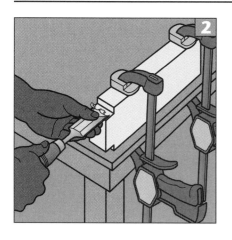

2. Cleaning the notch

- Shave away the last $\frac{1}{8}$-inch layer of waste using only hand pressure on the chisel.
- With one hand holding the chisel handle horizontally, grip the blade beveled-side up between the thumb and fingers of your other hand.

- Gently apply forward pressure on the chisel, moving the blade toward the saw cut (#2). Shave away the remaining waste until you reach the mark for the bottom of the notch.

SAFETY TIP *Bracing your thumb on the bevel and your index finger against the end of the board protects your hand from the blade.*

PARING CUTS

Paring a groove

You can make a groove in a board by cutting the sides with a saw, then clearing out the waste using a paring chisel with a blade slightly narrower than the groove.
- Secure the ends of the board in handscrews and clamp the handscrews to a worktable so the groove is face-up.
- Holding the chisel horizontally and bevel-up, grasp the blade with your thumb on the bevel and your index finger braced against the board and the blade's flat side.

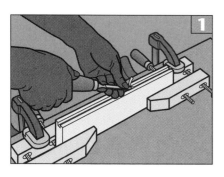

- Cutting in the direction of the wood grain, apply forward pressure to shave away the waste in thin layers (#1). Clean out the slivers of waste as you go.

Paring a curve

Band saws and saber saws are unsurpassed at cutting curves, but they can leave a workpiece a little too rough at the edges for the needs of your project. Use a paring chisel to smooth these cuts.
- Clamp the workpiece to a worktable, using a backup board to protect the worktable from the chisel and a wood pad to protect the workpiece from the clamp jaw.
- Hold the blade of the chisel between the thumb and index finger of one hand, the flat side vertical against the curve. Rest your other fingers on the surface of the workpiece.

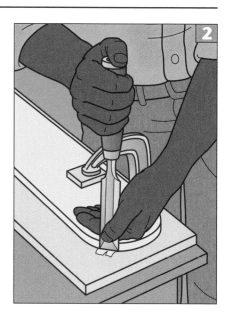

- Grip the handle of the chisel with your other hand and push down on the blade, using the force of your upper body rather than simply the pressure of your hands (#2). Slice away the waste in slivers, moving around the curve with a slight side-to-side rocking motion.

GLUING AND CLAMPING TECHNIQUES

Joining two pieces of wood with glue can create a stronger bond than even the wood fibers that hold a board together. A good bond depends on three things: the glue, the surfaces being joined, and clamping pressure. To join wood to wood, use white glue or yellow carpenter's glue. Make sure the surfaces are even and smooth. Apply the correct amount of clamping pressure.

Here you'll find how to glue edges to edges, corners to corners, and dowels into sockets—techniques that you can apply to virtually any gluing situation you may encounter. Whatever it is you are gluing, wipe away the excess with a damp cloth as soon as you tighten the clamps. If you let the excess dry overnight, you'll need to scrape or sand it off.

Clamps serve as extra hands in the workshop, holding a workpiece upright and steady while you work. You can never have too many clamps. The clamps featured here—pipe and bar clamps, handscrews, corner clamps, C-clamps, and web clamps—are ones that you'll use again and again. Protect the surfaces of your workpiece from uncushioned clamp jaws with wood pads.

Edge gluing

You can assemble a wide panel by gluing boards together edge-to-edge. You'll need one pipe or bar clamp for every 12 to 18 inches of board length.
- Lay enough clamps on your worktable to support the boards at 24- to 36-inch intervals. Set the boards on edge on the clamps. Use a scrap piece as long as the boards to protect them from the jaws of the clamps.

- Apply glue on one board edge per joint, spreading the adhesive evenly with a small brush. Lay the boards flat.
- Tighten the clamps just enough to press the boards together. Don't overtighten or you'll squeeze out too much glue and the boards will buckle.
- Center a clamp across the top of the boards between each pair of clamps below them. Tighten the clamps alternately until a little glue squeezes out of the joints (#1).
- Wipe away the excess glue.

Gluing up a cabinet

Because of the end grain in the corners shown here (ends of the side panels), the glue joints need to be reinforced. In this case, rabbets are cut at the ends of the top and bottom panels and screws, nails, or dowels are driven through the rabbets into the sides.
- Lay two pipe or bar clamps on a worktable, then spread glue on the rabbets in the top and bottom panels as well as on the ends of the side panels.
- Work with a helper, if necessary, to assemble the cabinet, then set it on the clamps.
- Protect the sides of the cabinet with wood pads and tighten the clamps just enough to hold the cabinet together,
- Tighten two more clamps across the top of the cabinet (#2), again using protective wood pads.

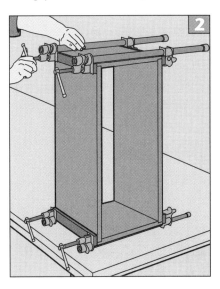

- Tighten all the clamps a little at a time until glue starts to squeeze from the joints.
- Check the corners for square with a carpenter's square or by measuring the opposite diagonals. If necessary, install another clamp across the longer of the two diagonals and tighten it until the cabinet is square.

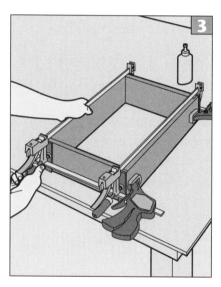

Assembling drawers

Corner joints on drawers can be made a number of ways—from elaborate handcrafted dovetails to simple stapled butt joints. In the example here, the front and back are rabbeted to accept the sides. Since a drawer front is subjected to a great deal of wear and tear, reinforce the front-to-side joints with screws, nails, or dowels.

- Spread glue on the contacting surfaces of the pieces, then assemble the drawer and set it on a worktable.

- Install two short bar clamps across the front and the back, tightening them just enough to hold the drawer together.
- Install two more bar clamps along the sides of the drawer, aligning the bars with the top edges (#3). Use wood pads to protect the drawer from the jaws of the clamps.
- Tighten the clamps until glue squeezes out of the joints. Wipe away the excess, then check the corners for square. Install another clamp across the longer of the two diagonals and tighten it until the drawer is square.

Using web clamps

Web clamps—also called strap clamps—apply uniform pressure in more than one direction and are especially handy for assembling cabinets with beveled corners. Install web clamps following the manufacturer's directions. The type shown comes with a nylon strap, a ratcheting buckle, four corner brackets, and a wrench for tightening.

- Apply glue to the contacting surfaces, then assemble the cabinet and set it on edge.
- Wrap one nylon strap around the cabinet near the bottom and slip a corner bracket under the strap at each corner.
- Slip the strap into the ratcheting buckle and pull it snug.
- Install a second web clamp around the top of the cabinet.

- Tighten the clamps alternately by turning the ratchet bolt on each buckle clockwise with the wrench (#4).

Gluing up mitered corners

If you make and glue up picture frames, corner clamps are a must. The type shown holds the four corners of a frame square with a single assembly. With other models, there may be individual clamps for each corner.

- Apply a generous layer of glue on the mitered ends of the frame pieces (end grain absorbs more glue than edges do).
- Assemble the frame and lay it flat on your worktable.
- Spread the corner brackets of the clamp as far apart as possible and set the clamp over the frame. Push the corner brackets flush with the corners of the frame.
- Tighten the bracket nuts a little at a time (#5) until the joints are

tight and glue begins to extrude. Wipe off the excess glue. Check the corners for square and adjust the nuts as necessary.

Assembling a chair

Another handy application for a web clamp is to hold together chair legs and rails.

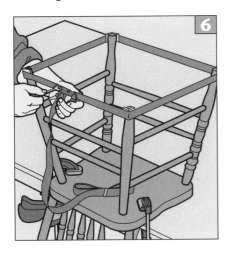

● Clamp the seat of the chair face-down on your worktable with short bar clamps.
● Apply glue to the sockets in the seat and the legs.

● Assemble the chair, fitting the legs into the seat sockets and the rails into the leg sockets.
● Tap the bottom of the legs with a rubber mallet to seat them firmly in their sockets.
● Wrap the strap of a web clamp around the end of the legs and slip a corner bracket between each leg and the strap. Slip the strap into the ratcheting buckle and pull it tight. Continue tightening the clamp by turning the ratchet bolt clockwise with the wrench provided (#6).

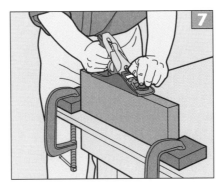

Holding a workpiece steady

With a little imagination, you can make two C-clamps and two short wood blocks serve as a vise. The setup shown anchors a workpiece without getting in your way.
● Place the workpiece near one corner of a worktable and set a block of wood against each end.
● Secure each wood block to the table with a C-clamp. Install the clamps so the handles are under the table and don't interfere with your work (#7).

Holding a workpiece upright

The setup shown transforms two short bar clamps and two handscrews into an extra pair of hands—in this case, to hold a shelf upright while edge banding is applied.
● Secure the bottom corners of the workpiece in handscrews, keeping the outer edges of the clamps and the workpiece flush with each other.
● Set the handscrews on your worktable and anchor them to the top with bar clamps, then get on with your work (#8).

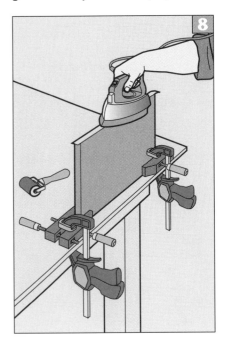

BASIC CIRCULAR SAW CUTS

A circular saw is a versatile cutting tool. It is especially useful for cutting large panels and long boards at the start of a project. But the tool can also be dangerous, so work safely. Run the power cord over your shoulder to avoid cutting it, wear safety goggles to protect your eyes, and avoid wearing loose-fitting clothing. As you prepare to cut, make sure the blade does not touch the edge of the workpiece when you turn on the saw.

There are slightly different procedures for crosscutting (cutting across the grain) and rip cutting (cutting parallel to the grain). Whatever the direction of the wood grain, adjust the cutting depth of the blade to the thickness of the wood. With the workpiece supported by a pair of sawhorses, check the cutting depth by retracting the blade guard and resting the long outside edge of the baseplate on one side of the workpiece. Push the blade flush against the workpiece and adjust it so it extends past the lower face of the workpiece by the length of a saw tooth.

For accuracy, use a cutting guide. Commercial cutting guides are available or you can make your own with a piece of ¾-inch scrap wood. When you clamp the cutting guide to the workpiece, place the clamp heads where they will not get in the way of the body of the saw.

CROSSCUTS

1. Preparing to cut

- Measure and mark the workpiece with a pencil or utility knife.

- Clamp the workpiece to a pair of sawhorses.
- With the baseplate (A) resting on the workpiece, align the blade with the cutting line (#1).
- Butt the cutting guide against the baseplate and clamp it to the workpiece.

SAFETY TIP *Keep the saw unplugged as you prepare to cut.*

2. Making the cut

- With the edge of the baseplate butted against the cutting guide and the blade clear of the workpiece, turn on the saw.
- Hold the saw firmly and guide the blade gently into the cutting line (#2).

Note: *If the blade binds, turn off the saw and back up the blade slightly. Support the waste end of the workpiece with a sawhorse and continue cutting.*

RIP CUTS

1. Making a kerf splitter

A kerf splitter is slotted into a cut, or kerf, just behind the saw to keep the blade from binding on long rip cuts. Commercial kerf splitters are available, but they are also easy to make.

● Cut a 2- by 4-inch piece of ⅛-inch hardboard along with a pair of 2-inch-long ¾-inch pieces of plywood.

● Glue or screw the pieces together so the two plywood pieces sandwich a long side of the hardboard (#1).

Note: To insert a kerf splitter, first turn off the saw and back up the blade slightly. For very long rip cuts, have several kerf splitters on hand and insert them at roughly 2-foot intervals.

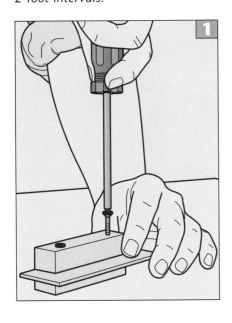

2. Setting up a rip guide

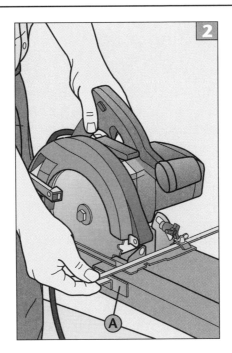

Use a commercial rip guide for ripping long, narrow sections from the edge of a workpiece. Follow the manufacturer's instructions to install the cutting guide.

● Measure and mark the workpiece.

● Clamp the workpiece onto a pair of sawhorses.

● Align the blade with the cutting line and adjust the face of the rip guide (A) so it is flush with the edge of the workpiece (#2).

● Lock the rip guide in position.

SAFETY TIP *Make sure that the saw is unplugged when you set up a rip guide.*

3. Making the cut

● With the rip guide flush against the edge of the workpiece, turn on the saw and gently guide the blade into the wood along the cutting line.

● Keep the rip guide butted against the edge of the workpiece as you cut (#3).

Note: If the blade binds, turn off the saw and back up the blade slightly. Insert a kerf splitter (A) into the cut a few inches behind the saw. Continue cutting, inserting additional kerf splitters as needed.

APPENDIX

CUTTING THICK STOCK

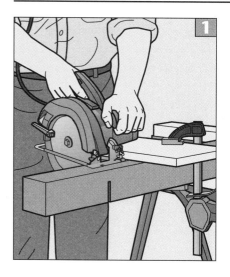

Cutting a post

To crosscut stock such as a post that is thicker than the maximum cutting depth of the blade, make passes on opposite sides of the workpiece.

● Mark a cutting line on one face of the workpiece and extend the line around it with a combination square.

● Clamp the workpiece to two sawhorses.

● Set the blade to its maximum cutting depth.

● Clamp a straightedge cutting guide to the workpiece and guide the saw along the cutting line.

● Turn the workpiece over so that the kerf faces the floor and clamp the cutting guide in place.

● Cut the workpiece a second time (#1).

SAWING PLYWOOD

1. Building a panel support

To rip a piece off a large plywood panel, set it on a pair of 2x4s supported by sawhorses. The 2x4s should be the same length as the workpiece and overhang each sawhorse by 1 foot. (To cut across a plywood panel, go to Step 5.)

● Set two sawhorses opposite each other. Place a 2x4 across the sawhorses.

● Wearing safety goggles, nail the 2x4 to the sawhorses with 3-inch common nails.

● Set a second 2x4 across the sawhorses and nail it in place (#1).

● Place the plywood panel on the 2x4s.

2. Reinforcing the cutting line

To avoid splintering the edges of the plywood, cut through a piece of masking tape.

● Measure and mark the cutting line with a chalk line.

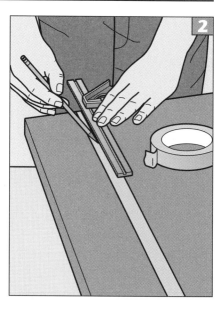

● Cover the chalk line with masking tape and draw the beginning of a cutting line at each end of the workpiece with a combination square and pencil (#2). Use these marks to align the cutting guide in Step 3.

3. Setting up a cutting guide

For a long cutting guide, use the factory-cut edge of a piece of ¾-inch particleboard. The cutting guide should be about 10 inches wide and at least as long as the panel.

● Set the cutting guide on the panel.

● Rest the baseplate of the saw on the workpiece and align the blade with the cutting line.

● Butt the cutting guide against the baseplate of the saw (#3) and clamp that end of the cutting guide in place.

● Before clamping the other end of the cutting guide, measure to make sure it is the same distance from the cutting line.

4. Ripping

● With the baseplate butting against the cutting guide and the blade just short of the workpiece, turn on the saw.

● Keep the baseplate against the cutting guide as you make the cut (#4).

Note: *If the blade binds, turn off the saw, back up the blade slightly, and insert a kerf splitter a few inches behind the saw. Continue cutting, inserting other kerf splitters as needed.*

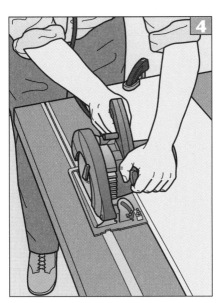

5. Cutting across a panel

To cut across a plywood panel, place it across several long 2x4s on the floor.

● Lay a sufficient number of 2x4s on the floor to support the panel at 12-inch intervals.

● Draw a cutting line.

● Shift two 2x4s so they are about 3 inches on each side of the cutting line.

● Place a piece of masking tape over the cutting line and draw the line again on the tape.

● Clamp a straightedge cutting guide to the workpiece.

● Begin cutting, kneeling on the panel with most of your weight over the 2x4 next to the cutting line (#5).

Note: *Before repositioning yourself on the panel, turn off the saw and back the blade up slightly.*

ROUTER BASICS

The router is often called the universal tool because there is so much that it can do. The router can shape wood edges, plow grooves, and even cut circles.

A router is almost never used freehand. If you are using a piloted bit, a bearing on the cutter guides the router through the cut. With non-piloted bits, you need to set up an edge guide or use a jig to guide the router.

Two types of routers are available: standard and plunge models. They work pretty much the same way, except for starting interior cuts. A standard router must be tilted on its baseplate to drive the bit into the workpiece, whereas a plunge router can sit flat on the workpiece and the bit plunged into the wood.

Although there are dozens of bit profiles on the market, all bits fall into one of two categories. Edge-forming bits cut profiles along an edge. Grooving bits plow grooves, circles, and other interior cuts. Carbide-tipped bits are worth the extra expense—they will last virtually forever.

ROUTER ADJUSTMENTS

Removing the baseplate

On most routers, you need to remove the baseplate (A) before changing bits.

• Making sure the router is unplugged, set the tool upside down on a work surface and loosen the depth adjustment clamp screw (B).

• Holding the clamp screw with one hand, turn the depth adjustment knob (C) counterclockwise as far as it will go with the other (#1). Then, lift off the baseplate.

Changing a bit

Use the two wrenches supplied by the manufacturer to remove a bit.

• With the router unplugged, fit one wrench around the router shaft to hold it steady and fit the other wrench around the collet nut. Loosen the nut by bracing the wrenches in the palm of your hands, interlocking your fingers, and squeezing your hands together (#2).

• Lift out the bit by hand. Do not use pliers to extract the bit.

• Blow or brush any sawdust out of the collet and insert a new bit all the way in. Hold the bit $\frac{1}{16}$ inch above the bottom of the collet as you tighten the collet nut.

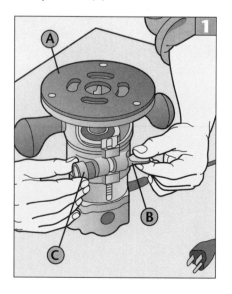

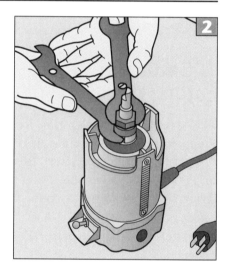

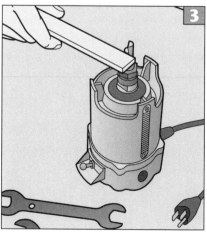

Freeing a stuck bit

If after loosening the collet nut, a bit remains stuck in the collet, do not use pliers or any other metal object to pry it loose—an almost sure way to damage it. Instead, try the following technique.

• Tap the bit sharply with a wood scrap (#3) until you are able to remove it.

• Clean out the collet and insert a new bit.

Setting the cutting depth on a plunge router

• Set the router on the workpiece as for a standard router, then loosen the depth scale stop clamp (A) all the way to release the depth scale bar (B).

• Push the router body down until the bit is aligned with the depth mark.

• Tighten the plunge lock knob (C) to lock the bit at the required depth (#4).

• Tighten the depth scale stop clamp.

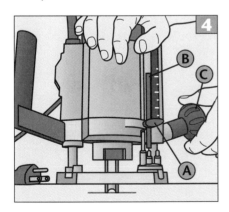

• Loosen the plunge lock knob to let the router spring back up to its starting position. Once you turn the router on, you will be able to plunge the bit to the required depth.

Setting the cutting depth on a standard router

The depth of cut is the amount of the bit that extends beyond the baseplate. For deep cuts, it's best to reach your final depth in two or three passes rather than in a single cut.

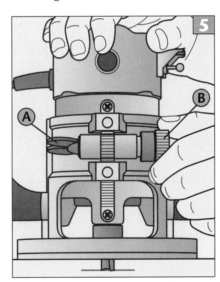

• Mark the cutting depth on an edge of the workpiece, then, with the router unplugged, set the tool flat on the piece so the bit overhangs the marked edge.

• Loosen the depth adjustment clamp screw (A) and turn the depth adjustment knob (B) to raise or lower the bit so the tip

of the cutting edge aligns with the depth mark (#5).

• Tighten the clamp screw to lock the bit at the required depth. If you want to cut to a specific depth ($\frac{1}{2}$ inch, for example) rather than to a marked line, the procedure is similar. Simply set the router upside down on a worktable and measure up from the baseplate to the tip of the cutting edge to adjust the depth.

BASIC CUTS

Feed direction

Despite the wide array of cuts you can perform with a router, all of them are guided by the same basic principles.

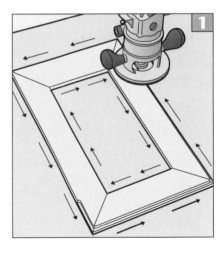

• Always move the router against the direction of the bit's rotation (#1). This means moving the router counterclockwise when you are shaping an outside edge and clockwise for an interior cut. This

BASIC CUTS (CONTINUED)

will help you maintain control over the router.

• Pull the tool through the wood toward you, instead of pushing it.

• Always apply steady pressure. If you move the router too slowly, you will leave burn marks on the wood. And moving it too fast will cause tearout.

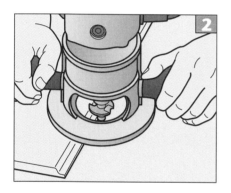

Edge-forming with a piloted bit

• Clamp the workpiece to your worktable with the edge you want to shape extending off the table by a few inches.

• Set the router on the workpiece at one end with the bit clear of the wood. Turn on the router.

• Keeping the baseplate flat on the surface, slowly ease the bit into the edge of the workpiece until the bit's pilot bearing contacts the edge. Use both hands to hold the router.

• Pull the tool carefully and steadily toward you (#2), keeping the bit's pilot bearing pressed firmly against the edge of the

wood at all times, until the cut is finished.

• Turn the router off once the bit is clear of the workpiece.

Edge-forming with a non-piloted bit

A non-piloted edge-forming bit requires a commercial jig or a shop-made edge guide to guide it through the cut.

• Secure the workpiece on your worktable, then outline the cut at one end of the piece.

• Hold the router over the workpiece so the bit is aligned with the mark and set the bit's cutting depth. Then, with the bit still aligned with the outline, clamp a long board with perfectly straight sides as an edge guide on top of the workpiece against the router's baseplate.

• Shape the edge as with a piloted bit, but with the baseplate pressed firmly against the edge guide throughout the cut (#3).

Plowing a groove

When routing a groove, you need an edge guide to keep the router in a straight line. You can set up a straight board as a shop-made guide or use a commercial jig sold as an accessory by the router manufacturer, as shown here.

• Outline the groove on the workpiece and clamp the piece to your worktable. Set the router on the piece so the bit is aligned with the outline. Set the cutting depth.

• For the jig shown, insert the bars of the edge guide through the machined holes in the baseplate. With the bit aligned with the groove outline, press the guide fence flat against the edge of the workpiece and lock it.

• For the plunge router shown, set the tool flat on the workpiece at one end, with the guide fence tight against its edge. Turn on the router and push it down until the bit penetrates the wood.

• Pull the router along the surface, the guide fence flush against the edge of the workpiece (#4).

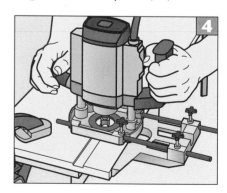